THE

# COURSE OF CREATION:

BY

JOHN ANDERSON, D.D.

WITH A GLOSSARY OF SCIENTIFIC TERMS.

---

"In these morning-days of existence, Nature at once stamped, with her plastic hand, her lineaments of beauty and adaptation on everything she made. There is nothing omitted to be afterward supplied—nothing formed defective in a single part or organ that required to be corrected. The first discoveries in Geology at once speak conclusively of a plan or Course of Creation devised from the beginning—a power, not delegated, but linked forever with the first intelligent Cause—a world, through all its changes, continually presided over and ruled by Him who made it."

---

CINCINNATI:
WM. H. MOORE & CO., PUBLISHERS,
118 MAIN STREET.
1851.

E. MORGAN & CO.,
STEREOTYPERS, PRINTERS AND BINDERS,
111 Main Street.

# PREFACE.

It is no mitigation of an author's temerity in publishing, that he can say for himself he had no intention, when collecting and arranging his materials, of ever submitting them to the eye of the public, or of provoking criticism by his speculations. Certain it is, however, I have often, and with severity at times, questioned myself as to the propriety of my geological pursuits, my ardent love of them, and their compatibility with the strict discharge of professional duty. My answer generally was, I sought not these things of themselves; they were hung up and displayed before me, wherever I went on pleasure, on business, or on duty. I simply inquired after their names; and of all the geological phenomena that have passed under my review, I can safely affirm of them, in their darkest, deepest places, they have uniformly led me "from nature up to nature's God," and have inscribed upon them in brightest characters—Benedictum sit nomen Dei.

How often, I have argued, in the leisure hours of life do we find men idling away their time, wasting it in vain talk, or consuming it in the most trifling pursuits, when a most interesting branch of science can be learned by wandering over the green fields, the rocky dell, the mountain side, or by the walk at even-tide, and there to hold converse with the Creator's works and the records of his will? I have recalled the list of great and good men, whose names are imperishably connected with the science of geology, who have given much of their time to these researches, and who have reaped laurels from their discoveries. Can Buckland, Conybeare, Sedgwick, Sumner, Smith, Fleming, and Chalmers — all either explorers or expositors — and other eminent divines, have been engaged in improper pursuits, or have given the sanction of their authority to tenets and views connected with the scheme of nature that do not accord with the religious principle? Often on such occasions have I dwelt upon, and compared with my own humble pursuits, the lofty and impassioned descriptions of the Psalmist, where, sometimes in a single piece, he takes a magnificent sweep of the great master-keys of creation — the foundations of the steadfast earth — the course of the fluid waters — the revolutions of the sun and moon — the vicissitude of the seasons — the habits and instincts of the lower animals — the earthquake and volcano — and all recited as demonstrations of Divine wisdom and goodness, and all calculated to awaken and to sustain the devotional feelings of the heart.

Having, under the influence of such impressions, gathered, and now put together in this form, the notes of my researches, I do not mean to aver that I have visited every locality referred to, or personally observed everything noticed in the publication. Where so much has been done by others I have carefully examined their works. Where the field is so boundless, and the course of illustration necessarily so discursive, I have freely made use of their collected materials. Still, I have been chiefly induced to adopt the line of description from the Grampians to the Alps, because, at sundry though often distant periods, I have examined the various suites of rocks comprised betwixt these mountain boundaries. If there be any novelty in the volume, it will be found, not in the subject-matter itself nor in the mode of treating it, but by following the geographical sequence in the descriptions of the several geological formations, and their relations to each other in the countries passed over.

I have to express my acknowledgments to Messrs. W. and R. Chambers for a considerable number of the figures contained in the volume, and which have already appeared in one or other of their numerous publications. To Mr. David Page, than whom I do not know a better practical geologist, I am indebted for much valuable information, gleaned by him in an extensive acquaintance with most of the ground passed under review. The errors of the volume are my own, and these, I doubt not, in a science subject to such daily mutations and receiving daily such additions as the science of geology, will be found neither few nor venial.

Newburgh Manse, May, 1850.

# CONTENTS

## PART I.

## GEOLOGY OF SCOTLAND.

## CHAPTER VII.



## CHAPTER VIII.



## CHAPTER IX.



## CHAPTER X.



## CHAPTER XI.



# PART II.

# GEOLOGY OF ENGLAND.

## CHAPTER I.



## CHAPTER II.

### CHAPTER III.



### CHAPTER IV.



### CHAPTER V.



### CHAPTER VI.



### CHAPTER VII.



## PART III.

## FRANCE AND SWITZERLAND.

### CHAPTER I.



### CHAPTER II.



### CHAPTER III.

## PART IV.

## GENERAL PRINCIPLES.

### CHAPTER I.



### CHAPTER II.



### CHAPTER III.



### CHAPTER IV.



### CHAPTER V.



### CHAPTER VI.



## CONCLUSION.

THE

# COURSE OF CREATION.

# GEOLOGY OF SCOTLAND.

## PART I.

### CHAPTER I.

#### INTRODUCTORY.

Geology is that branch of science which comprehends the knowledge of all that relates to the form, structure, mineral and fossil constituents, of the earth. The Scottish Grampians, it is generally admitted, form part of the lowest sections of its crust, to which the researches of geologists extend. We must go to other countries for any coeval, and to North America for any older, competing land: and still, there, the rocks are of the same mineral qualities and arrangement. The Ben-Mac-Dhui group form the highest and most prominent masses in the whole range of these crystalline mountains.

When I first stood on the broad flat top of Ben-Mac-Dhui, I had no thought or purpose of ever recording its geological history. The excursion was undertaken simply for recreation, and a delightful one it proved. I longed to plunge into the deep recesses of the old forest, and to see the trees which nature had strewed with careless hand, ere, perhaps, Caledonia was tenanted by the human family. I looked down from its rugged sides, as I ascended, with awe and wonder—snatched a little alpine as I drew breath for the next spring—chipped a piece of granite as I obtained a footing over a yawning chasm, or breasted along by jagged precipitous defile,—and when, having fairly scaled the summit, I gazed out upon the world beneath, the feeling which for a moment flitted across my mind was one of no merely vain complacency, that I was then the most elevated subject of all the twenty-six or twenty-seven millions inhabiting the British Islands—and the lowest, too, in their stony regions! The mountains of the earth serve to inspire some of the loftiest sentiments that can fill the breast of its intelligent inhabitants. Imbosomed in their deep solitudes, man feels his own littleness, and is forced to inquire who made these wonders, and who sustains them? We are all the better, morally speaking, for leaving occasionally our daily-trodden haunts, where we see only human things, and hear only of the triumphs of human craft, the excitement of human passions, the littleness and vanity of even the noblest human daring. There is an image of Jehovah's greatness impressed upon the outward face of nature, which for a time will awaken and sustain the most salutary reflections, breathing, as it were, a new life into the soul of the wayfarer. A man escapes from himself, forgetting the burden of a thousand petty cares, and rising above his sensual condition, when he looks upon the physical world in these its grander features and secluded scenes, which irresistibly speak to the inner sense of divinity, wisdom, and omnipotence.

The philosophy of the mountains, in the classic ages of Greece and Rome, inclined but little to any analysis of their grosser materials of earth and stone. The poetic and ideal were exclusively associated with their structures and form. The dii majores dwelt upon, and thundered from, their lofty summits. The clouds hovered in peaceful majesty over their council of sage or fierce debate. The elements were the ready ministers of their will; and Oreads, Dryads, and Naiads, peopling all the hills, forests, and streams, were the creations of that principle of the inner man, which has always searched for the spiritual behind and beyond the tangible attributes of Nature. Hence, too, the gnomes of the caverns, the spirits of the mists, the fairies of the glens, the kelpies of the torrents, were all the embodiment of forms, which fancy, in her later superstitions, has cast around the mountain landscape, with the witchery at once of the terrible and beautiful. The charm that spell-bound the human mind for ages, is not dissolved when, with ruder intent, we traverse these rocky solitudes, listening to the echo of our obedient hammer, learning the secrets of the universe amidst the voices of the everlasting hills, and seeing the wonders of the material world throwing light on the wonders of the spiritual.

We are reminded, among the mountains, of one of the first and loveliest of all material things, the creation of light. Loving them for their own sakes, as well as for the legends of the old world with which they are everywhere inscribed, the geologist takes to the hills with the first faint fresh streak of dawn. Emerging with earliest day from the somber shades of the forest which, like night, invests the prospects with its own sadness and gloom, speedily a scene of joy and activity bursts upon the sight. The light comes upon you like a real tangible thing. You see it glinting and breaking on the lofty ridge, then nearing down along the brown slope of the mountain, here projecting in long bright lines through the trees, and there—delicious, golden morn! first-born of Nature's children, harbinger of life and gladness. How beautiful are thy first footsteps upon the heath-clad mountains! What a brood of gloomy thoughts thou dispellest, chasing them before thee, like yonder envious mists rising lazily from the plains, valleys, and streams, which they would fain hide from the eyes that now revel amid their exuberant loveliness. These lofty peaks are worthy altars for the beacon-fires of the orb of day, after he has finished his journey through the nations; and comes back to us, over the floating splendor of the sea, in the eastern heavens. And see! he hath lit a hundred on these splintered summits, which blaze now as they blazed centuries ago, and diminish not!

The view from this remarkable group of mountains—the most remarkable by far in the island—differs much from any other with which I am acquainted. The impressions at first are all very confused, and some time is required to resolve into distinct pictures the wondrous panorama before you. We have stood upon Skiddaw, where everything is clear, distinct, and palpable in distance and form; on Ben Lomond, where the far-stretch of perspective over lakes, rivers, and plains, is like a first lesson in painting; on Ben Lawers, where the eye sweeps rapidly over well known, familiar objects, spots of wood, glen, and mansion; on Ben Nevis, where you fancy yourself in mid-air, every object is so separate and apart, and so disposed the whole you are looking on, that the view is all *downward* upon the picture. But here, these dark giant masses crowd as it were against you. There is a struggle for the post of elevation. You are highest, no doubt of that; but so jealous all are these proud somber peaks, that every one seems to overlook, though yet actually beneath, the broad ample table-head of the center of the group. Sometimes one is tempted to leap across the narrow dells of separation, and at once master the geology of the district, so near seems every hill-top as almost to be touched. But as you approach their several positions, expanding valleys, deep fathomless chasms, and the channels of noble rivers, bar farther approach, and attest the wide, independent domains of each. They are monarchs every one of them—Brae-Riach, Cairn-Toul, Cairn-Gorm, Ben-Avon, Ben-y-Bourd—each holds his own regal court, over tarn, lake, and stream; torrents, cataracts, and all the appurtenances of the boldest mountain scenery.

After one has time to gather up his thoughts and perceptions, the scene resolves itself, still indeed as of one whole, but of distinct component parts. In the far distance you attempt in vain to number the peaks that everywhere rise against the sky line; but more closely around, five or six summits are seen to spring from a single root; a common circumference marks out the limits of the group; and, by no unreasonable liberty with the imagination, you easily replace the old materials into the vacant interstices, before the water had begun its work of abrasion, or the earthquake coming to its assistance shivered their solid rounded forms into these hideous, precipitous gorges and chasms. The great hills here stand, every one of them, upward of four thousand feet above the level of the sea; and when entire, one aggregated whole, as possibly they originally were, the center mass may have towered thousands more into the overhanging firmament. The scene is utterly unmatched, as it cannot be described, by any other in Great Britain: and make your ascent when you may, there are sights and objects to be met with at every step, in every salient dell, that will cause you evermore to rejoice you commenced your travels among the Aiguilles of Ben-Muich-Dhui.

It is in the great mountain groups that the true key is to be found to the science of geology, as well as all those collateral circumstances which impart so much charm to it as a healthful and invigorating exercise to mind and body. Here, amidst these piled-up masses, we are furnished with the lowest ascertained sections of the earth's crust, from which we can at once study the nature of its rocky divisions, and the laws which prevail in the order of their superposition. When the world was in its primeval state of chaos, without form and void, we are warranted to assume that the mountains as yet had no place on its surface, but subsequently arose out of the bosom of the deep; and lifted up, as they emerged above the waters, the rocky strata already enveloping the globe. These strata are still to be seen folded round the central masses, disrupted and torn like a garment too tight for the body, and displaying through innumerable cracks and fissures the inclosed rocks. This fact lies at the foundation of all geological inquiries, gives to the subject all its pretensions as a science, and before proceeding on our "Course" a word of explanation will be in place.

The first condition of the earth, of which we have any historical notice, is that which is represented in Genesis, where, after the initial declaration that God was creator of all things, we are told of a period when the whole of its materials were as yet unarranged, "and darkness was upon the face of the deep." The Divine Spirit moved upon the surface of the shapeless mass, when the various elements of air, earth, and water gradually assumed their respective positions. The form which the earth had impressed upon it, as philosophy has demonstrated, was that of a spherical body, flattened at the poles, a figure resembling as nearly as possible that of an orange. There is reason to believe, therefore, that every part of the solid mass of earth is symmetrically arranged, and that every individual particle occupies the position which Divine wisdom has assigned it.

Rocks, let the reader be assured, have not been indiscriminately heaped together. Everything here, amidst all the apparent confusion which surrounds us, is in the most perfect order, following one uniform law of superposition. When God fixed the foundations of the earth, stretched his compass "upon the face of the deep," and laid "the beams of his chambers in the waters," he completed the mighty edifice agreeably to the plan which he had determined upon "from the beginning:" the different portions of the building rise one above another in regular succession; and the work, so far as we can survey the interior, displays the several *courses* into which the materials have been thrown. These constitute what geologists call the strata of the earth, layers of varying thickness, such as our slates, sandstones, and limestones exhibit, and which nearly envelope the circumference of the globe. The order in which the strata are disposed is uniform from below upward, and this order is never inverted. From the blue slates of the Grampians to the Chalk cliffs at Dover, there is a regular succession of intermediate rocks, piled one upon another like the mason-work of our houses; and while to many there appears nothing but confusion, to the scientific eye every portion of the series, although the same ingredients enter into several classes of rocks, is as well defined and as easily recognized, as the two members at the extreme points are by the common observer.

But beside the stratified rocks, there is another class of rocks equally extensive, and which occupy an important place in the economy of nature. These are the granites and whinstones of which the highest mountain ranges are usually composed. There are many subordinate varieties belonging to both classes, which are characterized by slight shades of texture and composition and distinguished by different names. One thing is common to the members of each group. They are not disposed in layers, and exhibit no lines of stratification, except in the granite rarely, throughout the entire mountain chain. These rocks occupy no fixed place in the order of superposition, but seem to be intruded in the most irregular manner among the stratified rocks, separating one bed from another, filling up fissures and rents, and binding and interlacing the various deposits more closely and firmly together. They are often composed of the fragments of other rocks, agglutinated into a compound mass by a base of clay. Remarkable changes are also produced upon all the strata where they come in contact with granite and whinstone—chalk being converted into crystalline limestone—limestone into chert—clay and sandstone into a substance as hard and compact as flint—and coal is deprived of its bitumen or the quality which renders it so useful as a combustible body.

From these, and other appearances, geologists have been led to the conclusion, that these rocks are of later origin than those which are stratified, that they have been injected among them in a state of fusion; and by the expansive force of internal heat, that they have burst through the stony crust of the earth, and elevated and disrupted the strata which compose it. They are, if we may use the expression, the *levers* which the Almighty has employed in bringing up the lower deposits to the surface, in laying open the interior chambers, and in producing all that infinite variety in our earthly habitation which ministers to the comfort and well-being of man. Much seeming confusion and disturbance mark everywhere the course of these rocks, similar, though upon a more extensive scale, to the disorders attendant upon the irruption of a modern volcano; but throughout the whole there reigns such a harmony of purpose, that the conclusion is irresistible, these operations could only have taken place by Divine permission, and are in accordance with the Divine plan, controlling the most refractory agencies of nature, and causing them to contribute to the general good.

These eruptive rocks have been produced under the sea, at a period, many of them, when the waters and the dry land were not as yet separated from each other. They are therefore termed sub-aqueous products, and are, in consequence of the pressure to which they have been subjected, hard, compact, and heavy. They differ in this respect from the products of modern volcanoes, which are light and porous, as being formed under the simple pressure of atmosphere, and are denominated sub-aerial. The most prevailing ingredient both in ancient and modern lavas is feldspar: this, combined with hornblende, quartz, and augite, characterizes the whole of the two families of the trap and granitic rocks; and completely establishes their claim to be regarded as originating in submarine volcanoes. Geology is thus in its first step, and initial principles, in perfect accordance with the scripture record; and, in walking over the varied fields of creation, we shall tread all the firmer, and enjoy our recreations all the more, that we find the word and works of God illustrative of each other, revelation never contradicted, and science bearing enlightened testimony to the wonderful truth—that the hills melted like wax before the Lord.

Two reasons, therefore, are to be assigned for the starting point of our investigations, and the route fixed upon in following them out. This center group of mountains comprises the first or lowest phenomena connected with the science of geology: here the earliest lessons are inscribed; and here, developed on a great scale, we are presented with the axis of elevation which has given character and outline to the whole surrounding district. Ben-Mac-Dhui is the most prominent type of our primary mountains, and has been mainly instrumental in lifting up a large portion of the Grampian range. Looking abroad from its summit, over all that varied landscape of plain and valley, and further than the eye can reach, summoning in imagination before us the successive strata as they recede in the far distance, a diagram which would faithfully represent the order of the rocks and their relation and proximity to the granite, would be quite correct in making Ben-Mac-Dhui a pyramidal basis, and the other formations as steps to the apex of the pyramid.

This lofty chain of primary rocks on the one hand, and the Alpine region of Switzerland on the other, may likewise be regarded as constituting the barriers or edges of one great basin, within which are inclosed members of almost every rock formation, fossiliferous as well as non-fossiliferous, existing anywhere on the face of the earth. Along the line of tour indicated, you pass over every intermediate deposit, from below upward; and have laid before you, for inspection, specimens of all that is interesting and curious in the science. Betwixt the two points, selected as our termini, lie strata upon strata, organic bed upon bed, not piled up in one colossal mass, but drawn out and slipped over the edges of one another, and so arranged and disposed at successive intervals as most happily to suit the convenience and successive stages of the journey. This is one of the most remarkable facts in descriptive geology, whereby we learn that a depth of nearly ten miles of solid rock can be duly examined, every particle and fossil of it, not by perforation *downward* to the bottom, but by the natural inclination of the beds, and their several outcrops rising to the surface like the inverted tiles on a roof. In consequence of this persistent arrangement, objects, both new and strange, will at every step meet the view. There the whole system of geology, page after page, is spread out before you. Every day opens up a new chapter geographically, as well as mineralogically divided. And when you have gained the summit of Mount Blanc, you can leisurely, in the mind's eye, look back over the whole COURSE OF CREATION.

It is a reproach, I am aware, sometimes cast upon geological researches, that the portion of the earth's surface exposed to view is as nothing compared with the entire mass, and that another portion, by far the largest segment, is concealed by the ocean, and its own debris. In addition to these disadvantages, it may now be objected that the line of description indicated narrows the field of research still farther, and that a few disconnected materials only are all that can therefrom be extracted. It may be answered, —"That the earth is constructed with such a degree of uniformity, that a tract of no very large extent may afford instances, in all the leading facts, that we can ever observe in the mineral kingdom. The variety of geological appearances which a traveler meets with, is not at all in proportion to the extent of country he traverses; and if he take in a portion of land sufficient to include primitive and secondary strata, together with mountains, rivers, and plains, and unstratified bodies, in veins and in masses, though it be not a very large part of the earth's surface, he may find examples of all the most important facts in the history of fossils."* We shall, however, along with our lineal descriptions of the mineral kingdom, notice the occurrence, position, and fossil contents of the strata as represented in other parts of the world.

---

* Playfair.

# CHAPTER II.

## NATURE AND STRUCTURE OF THE GRAMPIANS.

### PRIMARY ROCKS.

In beginning a description of the earth, every one is prepared for the information, that it must have existed in some form or othe- antecedent to the development of life upon its surface. Revelar tion asserts a succession in the objects created, as well as in all the cosmical arrangements connected with the early history of our planet. Things were not perfected at once, and brought simultane-ously into adaptation and form; a preparation and a fitting up, as it were, of the inorganic preceded the introduction of the organic structures of creation; and, accordingly, the solid framework of the globe gives corroborative evidence of this anterior condition of its history. The rocks of the period are, from this circum-stance, denominated Primary, because they not merely denote the absence, but are assumed to have been formed before the exist-ence, of any types of organic matter, vegetable or animal.

Nowhere can this first lesson in geology be more forcibly taught than by an examination of the sterile rocks and rapidly decom-posing precipices of this bleak and hoary region. Once through the glens, and fairly commencing the ascent of the center moun-tain, every symptom of existing life has disappeared; and amid the huge, tabular masses that accompany you in the upward jour-ney, there is no trace of organic forms in these vestiges of the past. The nucleus of the whole group is granite, one dense ag-gregation of crystals; now rent and furrowed by a thousand seams, the heart and penetralia bared and open, a convulsed sea of molten matter still and motionless as the grave! The associated rocks, all of the primary class, are gneiss, mica-slate, quartz-rock, chlorite-slate, and limestone; and these inclose no relic of a living thing. Geology thus ascends the stream of Time; but it gives no farther tidings of a scene like this, save that it arose from the depth beneath at the Creator's bidding.

THE STRUCTURE OF THE DISTRICT.—The mountain of Ben-Mac-Dhui, according to recent measurements, is 4,418 feet in height, and covers a superficial area of nearly forty miles in extent. It occupies a central position in the Grampian range, being about equidistant betwixt Aberdeen on the German Sea and the western coast, so ribbed and indented by the Atlantic. Ranges of granitoid rocks, of the primary class, diverge for nearly forty miles south and north of Ben-Mac-Dhui, thereby giving this mountain a prominence in position possessed by no other within the boundaries of the island.

The valleys by which this monarch is surrounded, open in every direction, and run toward every point of the compass. Two great rivers, the Don and Dee, take their rise in some of the deep gullies of the mountain, while the Spey is fed by the innumerable streams that issue from its sides. These rivers have each an easterly direction, which, by their water-shed, give shape and character to the whole district. A hundred lateral glens, with their tributary streams, and all their tarn-head or loch, debouch upon the three principal straths, whereby their deepest solitudes are reached, and the very foundations of their loftiest peaks bared and laid open. There, remote from human habitation, the geologist sees as it were two conditions of the world,—the one, the shattered framework and fragments of its early convulsions, huge mountains prostrate and crumbling beneath his feet,—and the other, the spring-heads of renewed vitality collecting in countless dripping rills, each to sustain its own little plot of pasturage and flowerets, not the less welcome that they are all so rare and alpine, and looking in their freshness as if they were there purposely to cicatrize and heal up the deep scars in the rugged precipices around.

Loch-na-gar on the south-east, and Ben-y-gloe on the south-west, have also their separate congeries of lofty hills and precipitous defiles, inclosing tarns, lochs, and rivers; likewise their own peculiar grouping of glens and straths, whose inner recesses are all most speedily attained through the velvet pathways of their moss and crow-berry. From the poetic peak the prospect is worthy of its fame. All around is a vast rolling surface of mountains, with steep mural precipices, and separated by deep ravines, while immediately underneath a cliff of 1,300 feet lies the lake, contracted to a span, and rendered even darker in its gloom by the snowy glaciers that sparkle here and there on the overhanging rocks.

From Loch-na-gar eastward to Craigdarroch and the more distant Morven, and through the great forests of Balloch-bowie, Glentanner, and Glenesk, granite is the prevailing rock. Around Balmoral, immediately under "these steep frowning glories," the granite rises into a number of smaller and beautifully dome-shaped hills. Cloch-na-bein and Mount Battock, washed by the Feugh and the Dye, are likewise composed of granite. Gneiss, mica-schist, quartz-rock, and clay-slate hang on the southern slopes, training down into the plains of Kincardine and Forfarshire. To the west of Loch-na-gar, and intermediate betwixt that range and the granitoid masses which cluster round Ben-Mac-Dhui, the same alternating series of stratified rocks occur. From Castleton to the head of Loch Callater, and along by Glen-clunie to the junction with Glen-beg, where the counties of Aberdeen and Perth meet, the strike of these rocks is again passed over in a walk of a few miles; the beds penetrated and tilted up by veins of granite and feldspar. Several dykes of the latter mineral, of an extremely deep-red color and glassy crystalline texture, traverse the district, extending over a vast range of country, penetrating indifferently the granites and schists, and always forming attractive objects in the beds of the rivers.

In the immediate vicinity of Castleton and Invercauld, the geological phenomena of the district are very accessible as well as instructive, in consequence of the comparative smallness of the mountains, and isolated position into which they are thrown. A magnificent amphitheater of hill and plain is spread out before the traveler, through which the Dee, after a course of upward of twenty miles from its wells—mysterious as the fountains of the Nile—rolls its waters, now joined by the Quioch, Clunie, Candlic, and all the tributaries of the surrounding peaks. Some of the hills present bare precipitous cliffs, as Craig Koynach and the Lion's Face, where the granite, schistose, and calcareous rocks are finely exposed to view. Their strike is continued westward, when they are severally crossed in the easy ascent of Morne, half of whose dome-shaped top is covered with quartz-rock, which here, as in most of the neighboring heights, attains to an enormous thickness, and shows in weathering the yellow granular texture of sandstone. So remarkably like are some specimens we picked up by the roadside, that for a time we imagined ourselves to be approaching a region of secondary deposits. Internally, however, the bright crystalline structure is uninvaded by decay. Ben-Beck, Cairn-a-drochel, and Ben-Viach behind Mar Lodge, are chiefly composed of gneiss, passing into a slaty micaceous schist. The same character of rock continues upward through Glen-lui until its junction with Glen-lui-beg and Glen-derry, where the granite maintains its sovereignty over all that primitive lofty region.

The geologist, in penetrating these primeval wilds, has but little choice left him as to the comforts of his pathway. Arrived at the top of Glen-lui, the two diverging passes, right and left, are equally desolate, savage, and grand. He may make his selection as the feeling of the moment prompts, but he will not be able to congratulate himself as the traveler in a different field—

> Hic locus est, partes ubi se via fundit in ambas:
> *Dextera*, quæ ditis magni sub mænia tendit;
> Hâc iter Elysium nobis: ut *læva* malorum
> Exercet pænas, et ad impia Tartara mittit.

No "fiends," indeed, as Dryden renders it, are here, unless the belated traveler may allow his fancy to shape these gnarled withered stumps of the old forest, as it well may, into grisly living forms; or the red deer breaking from their coverts, and gazing in wild amazement from the crags, startle him from his propriety. Still Loch Avon, black as pitch, and imbosomed in horrid rocks, is not an unfitting emblem of the Tartarean lake.

Pursuing his route to Strathspey, either through the desolate openings of Ben-Avon, or by the wild passes of Brae-Riach and

Cairn-gorm, the geologist again drops down among the gneiss, schists, limestone, and quartz. These types of rock line the trough of the Spey, on both sides, as far as the granite district of Ericht and Laggan, presenting the usual phenomena of granitic and feldspathic dykes, and in some places, as at Loch-an-Eilan, remarkable twistings and flexures in the mica-schist around this eagle-haunted lake. Glen Tilt, on the south-west, is distinguished by a singular display of granitic veins, appearing to radiate from a common center—the well-known phenomena which the philosophers of the Hutton and Playfair school pressed so keenly and successfully into the service of their theory. The gneiss is generally to be observed in the form of low ridges, interstratified with quartz-rock, and approaching in mineral qualities to the mica-slate.

The bearing of all these stratified rocks is, on the main, sufficiently indicated by the outline of the Grampian range. The quartz, mica, and chlorite slates, are nearly continuous along the chain, traversing in a S. W. by N. E. direction the breadth of the island, from sea to sea. The line of strike, however, is often interrupted, either by the eruptive veins above mentioned, or by the upheaval of the central axis, which, as it rose with greater violence, or was parted into higher and unequal ridges, would necessarily occasion corresponding changes in the lie and direction of their coverings. This principle in geological dynamics has been satisfactorily established by Mr. Hopkins of Cambridge, who has shown, that in the production of any great line of elevatory disturbance, whether affecting straight, curvilinear, or ellipsoidal masses, the strata would frequently be broken by fissures at various angles to the chief line of strain or elevation. Hence these interminable glens, transverse straths, cul-de-sacs, and countless depressions, forming tarns and lochs, all inosculating into each other, and which give such variety and grandeur to this alpine region. The pent up ebullient matter beneath the crust would thereby force its way to the surface—now in the form of veins—now in long narrow ridges—and in other quarters assuming the contour of broad mountain domes. The dip, in like manner, corresponding to these partial strikes, as well as great axis of the chain, is often various—as at the Linn of Dee, and along the braes of Corry Mulzie, the beds being almost horizontal, while generally they are so highly inclined as to be nearly vertical.

There are also numerous examples where the crystalline strata dip inward toward the granite ridges, and in this manner form an acute angle with the base, instead of being infolded over and welded to them. The only admissible explanation in these instances of the dip is, that the ends of the strata adjacent to the eruptive masses have sunk into depressions occasioned by the evolution of igneous matter, while their upper edges have been tilted backward. Hence the schists often rise into independent elevated crests all along the chain, and even where no granite appears at the surface. The rocks in Glen-Beg and Glen-Clunie afford examples of this kind, where, as in Cairn-na-well, and the other mountains here, they are highly inclined, and plunge in the direction of the principal range. Geology, viewed in this light, becomes an auxiliary to physical geography, explains many anomalous appearances on the earth's surface, and successfully accounts for all the flexures, breaks, undulations, and inequalities, that constitute such marked features in the primary strata.

Until very recently, the doctrine maintained was, that nearly all the inequalities on the earth's surface were produced by the erosive and denuding effects of water; that not merely the small lateral valleys and branches of rivers, but likewise all their main trunks, were caused by the slow and gradual working of the stream, cutting the most solid and massive rocks in the same way and almost with the same instrument by which the lapidary divides a block of marble or granite. Nay, with such a ready agent, acting through incalculably remote and indefinite periods of time, the conclusion was arrived at, that "on our continents there is no spot on which a river may not formerly have run." A sounder philosophy, and one far more accordant with the facts, is now beginning to prevail, namely, that nearly all transverse gorges, by which rivers escape across ridges from one water basin to another, are nothing more than ancient apertures in the crust of the earth, which have resulted from the former disruption and denudation of the rocks: and that rivers, properly so called, have never cut sections through chains, but simply flow in chasms prepared for them.

Nature and Qualities of the Rocks.—The granite is the most prevailing, as well as the most striking in its appearance and texture, in the whole range. Mineralogically considered, every specimen is a gem. Granite is a compound, aggregate rock, here of a lively flesh or rose color, consisting of perfectly formed crystals of quartz, feldspar, mica, and in some instances hornblende, when it merges into what is termed syenite. The sparkling film is mica. It is not metallic; but it shines with metallic luster; and in some places of the chain, as at Rothes on the Spey side, it is found in plates so large as to become a substitute for glass. The component parts of mica are silex, alumine, potash, iron, manganese, and traces of other substances. The colors of the mineral are various, according to the proportions of some of the ingredients. The laminæ are divisible into plates no thicker than $\frac{1}{300,000}$th part of an inch. Entering into the composition of almost every rock from the oldest to the newest, it abounds chiefly in granite and schist, but also occurs in sandstones, and the slaty shales of the coal formation.

I never look at a piece of granite, fragments of which are strewed on every heath, without being reminded of Paley's inaccurate and disparaging comparison betwixt "the stone" and "the watch," in his celebrated argument for the existence of Deity. Take a specimen fresh and living from the rock, or from any bowlder that meets you on the way. There is not a stain in all that composite mass: how bright every ingredient! No workmanship of man can rival it in its closeness of texture, beauty of color, distinctness and delicacy of shading and outline. What chemistry elaborated these particles as they separated and united? What scales weighed their impalpable elements? What hands constructed their nicely harmonizing proportions? Whence derived their principle of cohesion as they cooled and inosculated in the burning crucible? As that fragment of rock, so is the whole interior of the mighty range—the whole basis of the continents of the world—countless myriads of sparkling gems wrought into symmetry and form; the foundations of our earthly habitation literally "garnished with all manner of precious stones."

Paley, forgetful of every law or purpose so conspicuously developed in the whole of these beautiful arrangements, thus commences his great work on Natural Theology:—"In crossing a heath, suppose I pitched my foot against a *stone*, and were asked how the stone came to be there, I might possibly answer, that, for anything I knew to the contrary, it had lain there forever: nor would it perhaps be very easy to show the absurdity of this answer. But, suppose I had found a *watch* upon the ground, and it should be inquired how the watch happened to be in that place, I should hardly think of the answer which I had before given, that for anything I knew, the watch might have always been there."

How many fallacies are there in this statement so far as mention is made of the stone? The science of geognosie, not so far advanced in Paley's time, now clearly establishes the "absurdity" of supposing its having lain from "eternity" in the place where it is found. The relative ages of mountains, and therefore their succession in Time, are now demonstrable and well understood. Then, the component parts of the mineral are as well defined, as accurately proportioned, and arranged in manner and order as precisely, as the several parts of the watch. The mica, the quartz, the feldspar, have each their law or order of structure, as well as their principle of aggregation; and they have taken their respective forms and no other, and have assumed their compound structure and no other, in obedience to chemical affinities and an atomic adjustment, as certain and unalterable as are the conditions and requirements of dynamics.

Nay, more, the parent rock, from which that stone was taken, has its own place in the system; its position, amidst the upheaved disrupted strata around, has been assumed for a purpose; and the very size, form, and outline of the giant mass, are all shaped to an end. Rocks are as easily distinguished as trees or animals, which have not risen up by accident, but have been constructed out of certain materials, and arranged each according to its own class. Their internal characters, and even outward shape, are marked and defined. The gnarled oak in fiber and texture differs not more from the soft, pendulous, graceful willow, than are the differences of rocks and minerals in their normal arrangement of particles; in their diversity of fracture, cleavage, luster, and density. We see at once the mechanism of the watch, the growth and expansion of plants and animals. But so, upon gaining the least knowledge of its frame-work and structure, we cannot open our eyes upon any part of the external world, without being impressed with the conviction, that all which we see and admire, must be the work of a higher power. Design is stamped upon everything. Will, order, and might are everywhere visible.—Geology, discovering harmony amidst apparent confusion, renovation in decay, shows that every rock is fitted to its place; that systems and series of formations are arranged upon a principle of utility; and so thoroughly calculated to exercise their assigned functions have all the parts been formed, that the most elaborate machinery of man's contrivance falls infinitely short of the beauty and perfection everywhere displayed in the material creation. Lain forever! No; such a scene of mountain, valley, river, plain, and ocean—all related to each other—does not exist by chance, is not conserved nor arranged by accident.

Theory of Formation.—When we examine a piece of granite, nothing appears less likely, to a common observer, than that it was once in a molten state through the action of fire, and that its crystalline structure was assumed in process of cooling. Now, the fact of its crystallization, the beautiful and perfect arrangement of its parts, the impress of the one crystal upon the other reciprocally communicating their respective shapes to each other, and the compact, agglutinated state of the whole, is regarded as the strongest proof of the igneous origin of this remarkable rock. Granite is not a mere congeries of parts, which, after being separately formed, was somehow brought together and united; but it is certain that the quartz, at least, was fluid when it was molded on the feldspar. In some granites, the impressions of the substances on one another are observed in a different order, and the quartz gives its form to the feldspar. The ingredients of granite were therefore fluid when mixed; and this fluidity was not the effect of solution in a menstruum, as in that case one kind of crystal does not impress another, but each retains its own peculiar shape; and the conclusion is, that they crystallized from a state of simple fluidity, such as, of all known causes, heat alone is able to produce.

This is the account given in the Huttonian theory, as expressed nearly in the words of Playfair, which, along with the position of veins, the disruption of superincumbent strata, and other phenomena, has resulted in the universally received admission of the Plutonic character of this class of rocks. Dr. Macculloch has extended the principle, and has satisfactorily proved, that granite is but one term in the series of igneous products, the passages from which are distinctly traceable into granitoid syenite, and syenitic greenstone, and thence into greenstone, basalt, and lava. Professor Forchhammer considers granite, when melted, as one simple compound, and which only on cooling becomes separated into the different minerals that compose it.

Granite, wherever it is found, is inferior to every other rock; and as it composes many of the greatest mountain chains, it has the pre-eminence of being elevated the highest into the atmosphere and sunk the deepest under the surface, of all the mineral constituents of the globe to which our researches extend. The associated primary rocks in this upland region overlie the granite, and possess a distinctly stratified structure. They are not now in their original position. They have been tilted up, traversed, and interlaced by the granite while in fusion, and have been altered greatly in their texture and qualities by their contact with the heated mass. Hence they are called METAMORPHIC ROCKS, because of the change to which they have been subjected.

The rocks that immediately overlie the granite are gneiss, mica-slate, quartz-rock, and limestone. They all partake of the crystalline structure, and all, except the last, possess the same ingredients, and assume interchangeably the same aspect. Of gneiss there are three varieties, each composed of feldspar, quartz, and mica, and distinguished by the size and form of the crystals that constitute the mass. This rock, consisting in all cases of thin lenticular plates, has a ribbon-like appearance, and, according to the predominance of one of the parts, becomes glandular, slaty, or aggregate. Mica-slate consists of quartz and mica—the latter predominating—and feldspar frequently entering as an adjunct. Quartz-rock, as the term implies, is formed of the pure siliceous matter, nearly homogeneous in many instances—but scales of mica are often present—and feldspar not always absent. The limestone, again, differs from all the above in the excess of the calcareous element, while, along with talc, steatite, actynolite, asbestus, and other simple minerals, mica, quartz, and feldspar are likewise to be numbered among the imbedded crystals. These rocks, over the entire surface of the globe, are of one family, and generally associated. They are always the lowest of the stratified series, and follow in the order now described. They are essentially one and the same in their constituent mineral qualities—different in the form and proportions in which they are aggregated—and geographically connected with the granite in their distribution. Thus these crystalline rocks not only constitute the floor of our earth, but have in all probability supplied the materials under whose plutonic agency, when fused and molten, the massive pavement was raised above the waters and tempered into its present consistency.

Granite, the derivative rock, is found, accordingly, in every region of the globe—the lowest as well as the most universally distributed—the basis as well as the apex of every great mountain chain. No true Highland scenery is anywhere to be found that does not embrace granite as the most prominent feature in the picture. Not a hill in Scotland, two thousand feet high, but incloses a portion of this rock. The beauties of the English lake country are all derived from this source. The lofty serrated peaks of Wales have been raised upon its crystal foundations. The north-west and central portions of France, the Swiss and Tyrolese Alps, the vast expanse betwixt Dresden and Vienna, the Caucasus, great part of the Himalayan, Uralian, and Altai mountains, and large elevated districts in China, are all less or more of granite formation. Through Northern Russia and Scandinavia the granite may be regarded as merely a continuation of our Scottish range — one great stony girdle, which forms the primary mineral boundary of Northern Europe. America, Africa, Australia, possess not a single ridge of celebrity through which the same fundamental rock is not traceable in every district. How simple, uniform, universal the component elements of the globe! One and the same atmosphere surrounds it, one ocean washes it, one system of massive pillars supports it, one sun enlightens it. How direct and irresistible the inference, that one intelligent, all-powerful Being fashioned and framed it!

The separation of the dry land from the waters was, doubtless, effected through the instrumentality of means. The igneous theory of granite, and other amorphous rocks, is in accordance with this supposition, which thereby imparts a sacred and peculiar interest to all our investigations respecting the origin and elevation of mountains. The range of geological investigation is thus wide as the circumference of the globe—deep as the foundations of the earth—and sublime thoughts are everywhere awakened of Him—

> Whose dwelling is the light of setting suns,
> And the round ocean, and the living air,
> And the blue sky, and in the mind of man:
> A motion and a spirit that impels
> All thinking things, all objects of all thought,
> And rolls through all things!

# CHAPTER III.

## THE SILURIAN SYSTEM. FIRST TRACES OF LIFE.

THE group of rocks on which we next enter are termed fossiliferous, that is, there is contained in their hard stony substance the impressions and actual remains of organic bodies. As we proceed upward through the series in their ascending order, we will find different rocks distinguished by different classes of fossils, and characterized by distinct lithological appearances. They are in consequence divided into different formations, and called by particular names. Hence the origin of SYSTEMS, of which there are five or six recognized by geologists, separable into their respective groups of strata. Descending from the primary, the highest as well as lowest in the series of rocky combinations, the group which first invites attention is the SILURIAN; so denominated because the strata are widely spread over the districts in England and Wales, anciently inhabited by a people called the "Silures." They are found in various quarters of the world, and occupy a large area on the southern frontiers of Scotland.

The rocks of this class consist of a group of argillaceous, calcareous, and arenaceous deposits, varying in color and texture. They are of great thickness and severally impressed with their own written story, the fossil memoranda of the changes and events that occurred betwixt the formation of each. These are the transition rocks of Werner. The newly-adopted term of Silurian implies no peculiar theory as to their origin. It simply expresses the fact that in the district in question a complete succession of fossiliferous strata is interpolated between the oldest slaty crystalline rocks and the old red sandstone. The system is divided by their discoverer and historian, Sir R. I. Murchison, under the ascending series, into the Cambrian System, Llandeilo-flags, Caradoc Sandstone, Wenlock Shales and Limestones, and Lower and Upper Ludlow Rocks.

Do the equivalents of all, or of any, of these groups exist in the Grampian range? Geologists for the most part have been answering these questions in the negative. Hitherto no true silurian deposits have been recognized as existing among the northern Scottish mountains, and no well-authenticated organism of the system has been detected in any of their localities. This, however, will hardly be taken as a conclusive argument after the admission into the family of the Skiddaw slate, in which the faintest traces of organized matter have only very recently been observed, while the over-lying series consisting of chlorite-slate, and alternating beds of porphyry and greenstone, from twenty to thirty thousand feet thick, have not yet been proved to contain a single fossil. "Good fossil groups," Professor Sedgwick argues, "are the foundation of all geology; and are out of all comparison the most remarkable monuments of the past physical history of our globe, so far as it is made out in any separate physical region."

We are convinced that the clayslates and graywackes which repose on the southern flank of the Grampians, as well as abundantly in the interior, will, upon strict examination, have their place assigned among the Silurian class. Mr. Nicol, who has done so much for the Lammermuir deposits, will find ample scope for his investigations, and all his ingenious speculations, in determining the true position of these argillaceous beds, which are of prodigious thickness and vast extent. This is not the place to enter into details, but in support of the view now advanced, the following among other reasons may be given.

First of all, the clayslate of the Grampians resembles in its lithology the slates of Wales and Cumberland, admitted to be silurian. In hand specimens they cannot easily be distinguished from each other: practical men consider the slates of Dunkeld and Glenalmond as softer and less flinty than those of the south. They pass from extremely coarse into the finest grained varieties, when the graywacke character is entirely lost in the homogeneous mass. Their position in reference to the crystalline rocks, in the next place, is very distinct, never alternating with, nor lying conformable to, either the gneiss or mica-schists. They form the outer zone, from east to west, of the Grampian range, where feldspar, porphyries, and trappean rocks are along the whole line mixed up or associated with them. Then overlying the clayslate, precisely as in Cumberland, the old red sandstone is found in immediate succession and resting unconformably. Shall we add that, even in a topographical point of view, these beds will be admitted to vindicate their claim to Silurian origin, constituting, as they do, in extension, a portion of the great primary belt that encompasses the western shores of Great Britain, and beyond the channel, stretches through Brittany and Normandy?

From considerations such as these there are sufficient grounds, we think, for constituting the clayslates and porphyries of the Grampians into a "physical group," existing in a "separate physical region." The absence of organic remains may be accounted for by the fact of the vast disturbance prevailing in the seas at the period, and indicated by the prodigious quantity of igneous matter spread repeatedly over their bottom. These causes would act in so far in preventing the existence and increase of living things, over all these parts, and most certainly in obliterating the traces of their remains, if any were deposited. But as future explorers may yet detect them in abundance we proceed to consider the nature and classes of fossils elsewhere discovered in the Silurian strata.

Animal Remains. Here, in this series of rocks, we are carried back to the beginning of life upon the globe, in which we see the very dawn and commencement of earthly enjoyment, the first forms and races of creatures which were privileged to eat at the banquet of creation. As matter of history, therefore, nothing can be more interesting; as a subject of mere curiosity concerning ancient relics, the most ardent archæologist will be amply gratified; and as showing the manner of the divine actings in replenishing the earth with living things, the word and the works of Deity are again to the devout inquiring mind brought into pleasing harmonious comparison.

We find that the creatures belonging to this first epoch of organic existence are, generally, low in the scale of animated being.

The rocks in which their remains are imbedded are, in some instances almost entirely composed of organic matter, showing that life at first was not bestowed sparingly, or, through some hidden mysterious processes, stealthily introduced upon the stage; it rather appears in an abundance and variety, speaking of a purpose in obedience to a designing creative act. As suitable to the condition of the planet, not at once but by successive arrangements brought into a state of adaptation for sustaining life, the animals now formed appear to have been chiefly of the invertebrate division, that is, animals of comparatively simple structure, destitute of a bony skeleton, suited to live in shallow waters and muddy bottoms, and to be content with such fare as an infant state of things over the young earth could produce. Among these ancient families are graptolites,—many of them zoophytic bodies, allied to the modern sea-pen; crinoids, or lily-shaped animals, of beautifully-developed forms; and trilobites, crustacean creatures divided into three dorsal lobes. There are several species of each. And so accurately has nature adhered to her plan of operations, that we find the corals of that early age doing the same offices, and piling up similar submarine reefs, by which these busy little architects are still distinguished. The mollusca of the period are very numerous, embracing almost every order and form of shell that are found in our present seas, though wholly of different species; conchifera, brachiopoda, gasteropoda, cephalopoda, pteropoda, beside the heteropoda, of which there are no existing analogues. The habits of all these orders must have been nearly the same as those of our modern types. The cephalopoda, embracing the nautilus and orthoceras tribes, were then as they are now, the tyrants of the deep, furnished with eyes and ears, and armed with powers that enabled them to roam and prey at will in the bays and estuaries of the primeval world. There have been named and catalogued of these first forms of the moving creatures of the deep about three hundred and fifty distinct species.

But, beside these, there have been discovered in the silurian rocks six or seven genera, involving a still greater number of species, of fishes of the order of the Placoids, so denominated from the broad scales or plates with which they are covered. The probability is, that more of these higher organisms will yet be brought to light, as all the strata of the system consist of marine deposits, and only the most limited sections have anywhere been explored. They constitute the lowest of the fossiliferous beds; are generally found, except in Russia, in a vertical or highly inclined position, and consequently but little of their superficial area is exposed. Here, however, geologists have named and described an Onchus Murchisoni, a Thelodus parvidens, and other four genera of equally erudite-sounding names. The onchus type is continued, and greatly multiplied in species, in the two succeeding formations, when it dies out, or at least no trace of the genus is found in later times; while the rest appear to come and to depart within their own geological epoch. These organisms are all as yet termed Ichthyolites, that is, simply fossil fragments of fish, as no entire animal has been anywhere detected, while of their true class M. Agassiz affirms with confidence. Teeth, fins, spines, occur so abundantly in a stratum of the Upper Ludlow series in Wales as now to be termed "the bone-bed," giving assurance that the seas were thus early stocked with the finny tribes. The families of most of these fishes have yet to be determined. But nature, though in her operations "simpler than man's wit would make her," was still pretending enough to be shaping out thus early the higher types of life.

The science which introduces to such sights and studies, occupies no mean place among the various branches of human inquiry. To neglect to decipher what is so indelibly recorded on these pages of creation, is willfully to shut oneself out from what has been actually preserved for information—a voice from the past, which speaks in the same distinct articulate language as the present of the fiat of Omnipotence. No object is mean or contemptible which divine wisdom has formed, and no subject is unworthy of investigation which illustrates His ways and works during any period of creation.

The mind, at this starting point of life, is curious to know what amount of information can be obtained as to the organic structure and specific characters of these first denizens of earth, so as to compare them with the forms and species of the analogous families now existing. The information derived from this first chapter in palæontology, we believe is, that the earliest specimens of organization are as perfect as the latest, each after its kind; and that, in these morning-days of existence, nature at once stamped, with her plastic hand, her lineaments of beauty and adaptation on everything she made. There is nothing omitted to be afterward supplied—nothing formed defective in a single part or organ that requires to be corrected. The first discoveries in geology at once speak conclusively of a plan or course of creation derived from the beginning—a power, not delegated, but linked forever with the first intelligent cause—a world, through all its changes, continually presided over and ruled by Him who made it.

Vegetable Remains were long wanting, and sought for in vain, to complete during this period the picture of the ancient world, as described in the pages of revelation. Geology, indeed, had everywhere sternly held back the required evidence, and animals were announced to be the first of living things. This, though contrary to all analogy with regard to the conditions of animal subsistence, was generally received as a well established dogma; and the earliest book of history was laid aside, or its statements in these circumstances regarded as irrelevant. Vegetable remains, however, have been detected in the oldest fossiliferous group of rocks, and this apparent discrepancy has been forevermore disproved. Fucoid plants are found in great abundance in the transition series of Scandinavia as well as in the silurian strata of our own island. That they are not more widely distributed is satisfactorily accounted for by experiments which show that some species of plants entirely disappear in water. A productive flora, therefore, may have existed from the earliest period, but, unable to resist decomposition, all traces thereof have long disappeared from the tablets of the earth.

Nay, so abundant in some quarters of the globe has vegetable matter been at this period, that there are traces of beds, approximating to coal, entirely composed of it, and the rocks inclosing these beds so charged with bitumen and carbon as to be used as fuel. "The silurian strata of the Scandinavian peninsula and the Island of Bornholm, contain," says Professor Forchhammer, "in their oldest parts, large beds of aluminous slate, which is used in a great number of manufactories for making alum; and this aluminous slate has the great advantage over those slates of the carboniferous system of Germany and a part of France, that it contains the sufficient quantity of potash which is required to make alum." It is well known that potash constitutes an ingredient in most vegetable bodies; and that when a plant is burned there remains a skeleton of this substance. Hence, possibly, the origin of the potash in the alum slate. But the argument does not rest upon inference. The same authority relates, that in Bornholm and in Scania, the southernmost part of Sweden, this slate contains a great number of impressions of a fucoidal plant, of which Liebmann has given minute botanical descriptions. Then, pursuing his interesting tale of this first flora of creation, he says,—"According to Professor Keilhau, Professor Boek, and M. Esmark, the same ceramites occurs frequently in the aluminous silurian slate of Southern Norway. Recently M. Hisinger has figured an imperfect specimen of it from Berg, in the province of Ostergothland, in Sweden. Thus this fucus appears to be characteristic of the alum slate of Scandinavia: and I can scarcely doubt that the most characteristic properties of the alum slate, as depending upon its carbon, its sulphur, and its potash, are derived from the great quantity of sea-weed which has been mixed up with the clay, and whose carbonaceous matter so affects the whole rock, that the slate is used as fuel for boiling the aluminous liquor, and burning lime; and in some parts of the province of Westergothland in Sweden, even small courses of true coal occur. There can hardly remain any doubt that this coal is derived from sea-weeds, of which fossil parts have been found, for not the slightest trace of land plants has ever been discovered."

These are instructive facts, yet greatly to be extended, when, we question not, the land will also contribute of its flora to complete our knowledge of the most ancient fossiliferous strata.—But recently, bands of true coal have been discovered completely inclosed in this group of rocks near Oporto, the town of which stands on a ridge of granite, four or five miles wide, with mica-slate and gneiss resting on both sides. To the eastward, these again are overlaid by sedimentary rocks, chiefly clayslate; which, commencing on the coast about thirty miles north of Oporto, run down and cross the Douro, about sixteen miles above that town.—To the south of Vallango, the strata overlie a deposit of anthracite in several beds, some of them from four to six feet thick.—This coal is now worked in several pits, and principally sent to Oporto. Along with it are beds of red sandstone and black carbonaceous slates, with vegetable impressions too indistinct to be determined, but strongly resembling ferns of the coal measures. In the shales above this coal Mr. Sharpe, the discoverer, found many fossils, as orthides, trilobites, and graptolites, most of them new species, but others well known in the lower silurian rocks of Northern Europe. It would thus appear that the coal deposits of Oporto are included in the silurian formation, and are far below the usual level of the coal.

We cannot overvalue the theoretic importance of these discoveries, which do not indeed bring to light any exuberant variety of the vegetable tribes, such as the earth afterward threw out of her affluent bosom. But they mark sufficiently the period when plants, according to the geological reading of the history, first make their appearance on these lithological pages: fucoids and algæ are there in abundance, to give the vegetable portion of the narrative, as trilobites and molluscs form unquestionably the predominating features of the animal department. The coal-beds of Oporto—should their position turn out to be truly defined—show the dawning of a terrestrial flora, not sparingly but luxuriantly developed: and thus the silurian period may be regarded throughout as sufficiently characterized by well-marked types of vegetation, more doubtful in the higher forms, but determinate in the acotyledonous and cryptogamic tribes which prevail indifferently from the lower to the upper beds of the system. Nor do we require to overstrain the statement, by questioning nature or revelation as to the species, genera, orders, and classes of vegetables referred to in their respective pages. They are coincident as to the great truth itself, that PLANTS did exist in the earliest "days" of the earth's history. As a science, nothing is taught in the Sacred Record. None of the technicalities of physical inquiry are employed. But a beautiful progression, and elimination of one thing after another, are intimated. The light is separated from the darkness. A firmament is set in the midst of the waters. The first plant that burst from the soil had thus every element provided which its nature and habits required—the light, to which it turns and ever yearns after—the air, in which to perform its respiratory functions—the water, from which to secrete the juices of circulation—and a dry land, out of which to elaborate materials for its structure. This is a Wisdom which is above all philosophy, instructing in the elements and principles of things, long before botanical arrangements were dreamed of, or "bushy dell" there was, where

> "—————————— hoary-headed frosts
> Fall in the fresh lap of the crimson rose."

The silurian group of rocks is very widely extended, as in Britain, France, Russia, the north-west of Asia; in South Africa, North and South America, the Falkland Islands, and Australia. The most ancient physical features of the Old World can almost be recalled, as we thus trace the outline of the deposit, marking out, by its geographical distribution, the primary islands and mountain peaks of the aboriginal land. How changed the very face of things—continuity between states and kingdoms where seas now roll—and all the great continents occupying the sites over which the waters held unbounded sway!

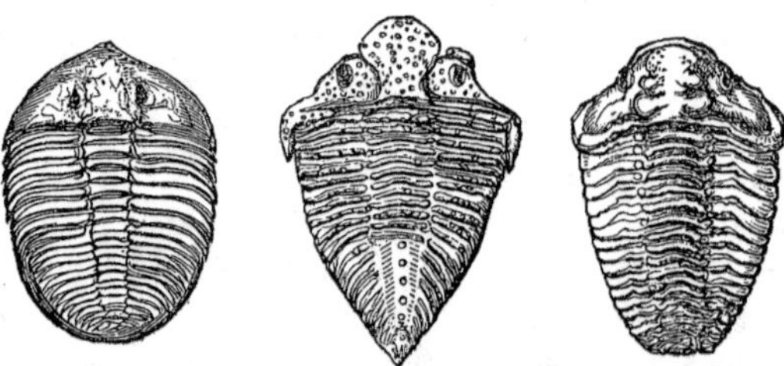

Trilobites of the Silurian System.

## CHAPTER IV.

### THE DEVONIAN SYSTEM, OR OLD RED SANDSTONE.

A GEOLOGIST requires not, like the tourist, to be told of the various conflicting roads that run among the mountains, in what precise course he is to wend his way. He will follow his own pathways, roads of nature's forming, guided by the strike and lie of the rocks rather than by the beaten tracks of every-day life. But come whither he will—through Glentilt, Glenericht, Glenbeg, and the Spittal, Glenisla, and Clova,—or along the Dee, the heights of Glentanner, and penetrating to the sources of the Esks—sure we are, when he reaches by any of those passes the frontiers of the Grampians, he will pause and gaze wistfully, thoughtfully, admiringly, ere he descends, upon the magnificent prospect that stretches before him, unrivaled by any on the terraqueous globe. The GRAN-PEN, *celticè*, the shelvy or precipitous summit, Romanized into Grampius, has its own inner charms, peaceful rock-girt valleys where princes dwell, and happy as Rasselas ever trod.—And escaped from these, what an outer world beneath, fertile, abundant, replete with everything that can charm the eye or interest the student. Looming in the far distance, the Lammermuirs, of silurian origin, can just be descried as a dark-blue line on the verge of the horizon; the Ochils and Lomonds, of carboniferous age, repose like islets on the pendant sky; while, in the foreground of the picture, there is the most charming variety of woodland, meadow, farmstead, town, and mansion, all as I now gaze upon them in their autumn coloring, invested with a Claud-like mellowness that speaks with a moral yet romantic sympathy to the heart. The round tower of Brechin, the moldering walls of Edzell, the frowning battlements of Glammis, the worn-out and now verdant ramparts of Dunsinane, have each their crowds of visitants, and are all within the compass of a single day's journey.

The eye of the geologist is in search of another object as it wanders over that lovely scene: Kinnordie, the birth-place of Sir Charles Lyell, must ever be classic ground in the history of our science. It rests on the old red sandstone, and furnishes some of the most valuable illustrations in Sir Charles's early sketches. What influences, may we here ask, gave being and shape to the ingenious and splendid generalizations of this accomplished geologist? Is it too much to assume that the philosopher, as well as the poet, is all his life-long captive to first impressions, that the scenes of his boyhood claim "a local habitation" for many of his future speculations, and that his most matured trains of thinking have been dependent upon casual circumstances? Born and educated in the shadow of the Grampians, who can doubt that the spirit within was early stirred to lofty views as he gazed upon their elevated forms, and wondered how their peaks rose so high in air, and were thus lifted above the valleys? May it not be presumed, though the philosopher himself may have no recollection of the matter, that his speculations regarding the alternate elevation and depression of land and sea had its germ in some such happy moment of mountain inspiration? Byron owned the influence in all its power, when, in the rocky defiles and dark pine forests of Lochnagar, he had early communings with spiritual beings, the wreathe-forms and kelpies of the streams; and in visions imparted amidst the wilds of the Dee, prepared his mind for the daring flights of the Alps. The geologist had here all the materials of after-thought, which in his various essays and works he has so skillfully expanded—from his explorations of Bakie-loch with its alluvions, peat, marl, shells, and horns, in which he had the type of some of his Alpine tertiaries—the old canoe and ripple-mark here too, the representatives of their far-sundered ages—and onward to his bold speculations on the elevatory hypothesis, of which the Grampians, as well as Sidlaws, supplied him with ample illustrations.

The descent from the mountains upon the series of rocks that occupy the plains, is one not merely of space, but likewise of time. A geological epoch has vanished, and a new order of things has been called into existence. This implies a change in the animal as well as in the mineral kingdom. The change may not have been sudden, but it has been thorough and pervading, accompanied by circumstances that show a general shift in the sea-bottom, and causes that have been nearly uniform in their operation over the surface of the globe. The shift in the sea-bottom is detected in the elevation of the silurian group of rocks, which have been lifted from a horizontal into a highly-inclined position : in some instances they are nearly vertical; and in most cases where the igneous rocks occur, they are bent and twisted, greatly altered and disrupted, by the process of upheaval to which they have been subjected.

Geology notes in this an epoch or age of organic existence. The superjacent series of rocks are seen lying unconformably upon the silurians, that is, the older series had been consolidated and upheaved, and a period of intervening time had elapsed before the deposition of the newer. The fossils imbedded are likewise distinct and peculiar—one and the same over the superficial area of the globe—and thus we learn to mark the great and interesting cosmical changes which had already begun to be effected. We are now among the Old Red Sandstone, or Devonian system of rocks, so denominated from their great development in that district of the sister kingdom.

As contrasted with the former system, the rocks of this period indicate considerable disturbance in the waters of the ocean, currents and agitations widely prevailing, and perhaps also deeper seas. The crust of the earth was still rising, and the mountains becoming higher, and these effects would necessarily follow. A superior order of animals were introduced. The fishes, which begin to appear in the upper beds of the silurian group, are now increased both in numbers and in variety of structures. The invertebrata were the prevailing types of the former age. The old red sandstone is pre-eminently characterized by the vertebrata, when, completely adapted to the element to be inhabited, mailed and plated over with thick horny scales, huge bony heads, fins and tails of corresponding strength and size; the Sauroid family appear upon the stage, capable all of buffeting the waves and fulfilling their destiny amid the greatest commotions. The fish of this early period are generally well preserved, even better than those of the tertiary age, in consequence of their osseous scales being harder than the bones, and which, from their interlocked arrangement, have contributed to preserve the general form of the body when the inner skeleton has disappeared and every other part and organ have been destroyed.

The old red sandstone formation is very extensively distributed in the northern counties, forming a great belt round the coast from Caithness-shire to Aberdeenshire, and consisting of three well-marked divisions, the lower, middle, and upper series of beds. The strata flank the northern walls of the Grampians and their out-liers, traversing the great central or Caledonian valley for a hundred miles, and training round the western coast by Oban, the shores of Mull and Morven. They are of great thickness in many places; and in some of the beds, as at Cromarty, Lethenbar, and Gamrie, contain nearly all the fossils peculiar to the formation.

The order of Ganoid fishes, which afterward fulfill so distinguished a part in the kingdom of nature, is wholly absent from the silurian group, while, in the Devonian, nearly thirty genera, and considerably above sixty species, have been described and named. The scales of these creatures would appear to have been richly ornamented, enameled, and shining, and hence the term Ganoid applied to the order. In the northern districts, beyond Ben Mac-Dhui, the following genera, with several species belonging to each, have been found, namely, coccosteus, cheiracanthus, cheirolepis, dipterus, diplopterus, diplocanthus, glyptolepis, osteolepis, pterichthys. The principal localities of these fossils are—the Dipple on the Spey, Tynet Burn in Banffshire, Seat-Craig near Elgin, Altyre on the Findhorn, Clune, and Lethen-bar in Nairnshire, Gamrie, Cromarty, and various places in Sutherland and Caithness. Shetland is chiefly composed of the old red sandstone, which yields abundantly the fossils peculiar to the deposit. The formation extends through the Orkney islands, inexhaustibly fertile in organic remains, and among which have been found plates and fragments of the Asterolepis, the largest of all the genera belonging to the period: the head and jaws, at least, appear to have been of enormous dimensions, and portions of the inner skeleton must have been bony, contrary to the general cartilaginous structure of the class. The Placoids of the subjacent rocks have many resemblances to the cestracions, centrinæ, and spinaxes of our present seas, their scales being set like plates at irregular distances over the body. The Ganoids, on the other hand, whose scales were continuous, and enveloped the entire animal, have no affinities to any living types.

Specimens of vegetable organisms are very common in some of the flagstones of Orkney, resembling, in some instances, the Lycopodiaceæ, or club-mosses, so abundant in the carboniferous strata: and branching fucoid plants, of which portions have been found from two to three feet in length, and of nearly the same diameter of stem throughout. But in tracing the COURSE of CREATION in this department of her works, the most important fact to relate is, the discovery of a coniferous lignite, imbedded in the old red sandstone of Cromarty. This interesting relic was obtained from these beds, several years ago, by Mr. Miller; and, though still of that remote age an instantia solitaria of its kind, like the foot-print of Robinson Crusoe, it is the sure token of a race that inhabited the island, and harbinger of a luxuriant flora then waving along the shores of the boundless waters. These northern localities, on the mainland, as well as in the islands, are also remarkable for their shell-beds in this deposit, while very few of such organisms have yet been detected in any of the Scottish rocks of the system to the south of the Grampians. The relics are confined to one species of shell, resembling in general appearance the form of the Cyclas, and are found in various quarries in the district.

What a revolution in letters, knowledge, and civilization since the days of the Romans! This, their Ultima Thule! and a science in the very rocks of which they never even dreamed. Proud they were of their fabled origin from the twin boys suckled by the wolves. Here are the spoils of ages long anterior to their myths of remotest genealogy—families of creatures that had fulfilled their destiny—buried in the sand, and upheaved into lofty mountains, while the Seven Hills of their proud city slept beneath the waves.

We now proceed to trace the order of the formation southward of the Grampian chain.

1. The conglomerate, a deep red and well-marked deposit, skirts the base of the mountains, and in some places is of vast thickness, betwixt Stonehaven and Blairgowrie. This rock is composed of fragments of the primary series, gneiss, mica-slate, quartz, and porphyry; the granite constitutes the paste in which these are set and agglutinated together. Excellent sections are to be seen in those localities, where the principal rivers, the North and South Esks, the Wast Water, the Isla, and the Ericht, make their passage in debouching upon the plains. In all these defiles the cliffs are precipitous, and often very picturesque, their variegated and bright flesh-colored sides forming a pleasing contrast with the dark waters as they eddy into pools, or dash headlong over their broken ledges. A momentary inspection of this composite rock leaves not the shadow of a doubt upon the mind as to its derivative origin, while its vicinity to the great chain where its several ingredients are to be found as directly points to the quarry whence it was hewn: not, it may be, slowly accumulating, as generally asserted, during the lapse of indefinite periods of time, but rapidly brought together and consolidated, as so many of the sharp angular edges of the materials most unequivocally attest. The finer beds that occur in the vicinity would seem to have been the talus or outgoing of the coarser conglomerate, formed of the minute particles of the same ingredients which had accumulated in the more tranquil hollows of the sea-bottom. The slaty fissile sandstone of Coventry Quarry near Fettercairn (so remarkably tilted up and welded literally to the igneous dyke), stretching throughout the north-east and south-west parts of the counties of Kincardine and Forfar, and prevailing over the districts of Auchtergaven, Crieff, and Callander, may be mistaken in many places for the clay-slate itself slightly altered in texture and appearance.

These conclusions as to the derivative origin of the conglomerate are fully confirmed and borne out by the fact, that the deposit is everywhere found precisely where such materials would be collected, all around the shores of the Scottish Highlands, overlying or fringing the base of the crystalline rocks, filling up the creeks and bays of the primeval world. After thousands of years the massive blocks of syenite, chiseled and half-dressed, are still lying in the quarries of Upper Syria, while the cities for which they were preparing are heaps of ruins in the desert. Nature, left to her own operations, treasures up the waste occasioned by the elements and other forces, and by thus raising outworks and buttresses protects her crystal foundations against the inroads of consuming time.

2. Forming an outer zone or rampart, and overlapping the conglomerate, a gray fossiliferous sandstone constitutes the next member of the Devonian group. This deposit is widely extended, and consists of several beds. One of these is a fine-grained, compact building stone. Another, the well-known flag-stone, is of a more slaty texture, of a dark-blue color, and abounds in mica. These sandstones occupy a great part of the sea-ward barrier by Montrose, Arbroath, and the high grounds of Carmylie. They fold over the Sidlaws on both acclivities of the range, where they form a well defined example of what geologists term the *anticlinal* and *synclinal* axes, that is, the rock curves and reduplicates, like a soft flexible substance, according to the undulations of the surface. The several beds cross the Tay in the direction of Dundee, and emerge on the opposite banks at Wormit-bay, Parkhill, and Newburgh; ranging eastward along the northern slope of the Ochils by Norman's Law and the high table-land of Balmerino.

3. A limestone rock, termed CORNSTONE, from its practical application to grinding purposes in England, occupies a place among the old red sandstone series. This deposit occurs in thin bands of a dull yellowish or blue-colored stone, containing numerous cherty nodules, and, where compact, is of a sub-crystalline texture. The cornstone generally contains more of silicious than of calcareous matter, and is consequently not much prized for building or agricultural purposes. In Scotland no organisms have been as yet detected in it, but in England it yields abundantly remains of the cephalaspis and various crustaceans. This rock is not coextensive with the other members of the group, nor do we find it continuous in any part of the district which it occupies. It is generally found in small detached patches, as at Glen-Finlay,

Meigle, Cargill, on the north of the Sidlaws; at Ballendean, Rait, Meurie, in the Carse of Gowrie; at Parkhill, Newburgh, Clunie, Kinnaird, on the south bank of the Tay; and at Newton and Craigfoodie, on the southern face of the Ochils. At the Newburgh station of the Edinburgh and Northern Railway the cornstone is inclosed among the eruptive rocks, partaking of their common induration, and, except in its distinct lamination, cannot be distinguished in color or texture from the traps.

4. A rock-marl underlies the cornstone in the form of a reddish, variegated sandstone, and contains about fifteen per cent. of lime. Deep sections of this calcareo-arenaceous deposit are displayed along the basin of the Tay, on both sides, from the confluence of the Isla to Stanley, at Pitcairn Green on the Almond, and occupy the ridge from Methven to Crieff. A remarkable vein of serpentine skirts the base of the Grampians in a south-east and north-west direction, of a beautiful dark olive-green, in some places of a blue and whitish color, and at Cortachie Bridge, where it crosses the Esk, containing crystals of diallage. This dyke widens in some parts to nearly ninety feet, of a hard compact texture, and, as the marble of the district on the lakes of Clunie, it is extensively used for ornamental purposes.

5. The geologist, as he pursues his journey by either of the lines of railway that intersect Forfarshire, has still many interesting localities and objects before him. Traversing "the fertile plains of Gowrie" by the Perth and Dundee Junction, he enters at Inchture upon a higher member of the old red sandstone, a fine-grained yellow-spotted bed. The deposit first appears to the eastward of Inchture, in the den of Balruddery, where its outcrop is seen immediately to overlie the gray fossiliferous beds.—The same variety emerges on the opposite bank of the Tay at Birkhill; at Abernethy, where it abuts at nearly right angles against the trap in a small ravine to the south of the village; whence it skirts the base of the Ochils, and occupies the center of Strathearn at Dumbarnie. The Clash-bennie sandstone, doubly interesting from having furnished the first and best specimen of holoptychius, the type of its age, may be regarded as an extension of the Balruddery and Inchture rock. The beds vary a little in their lithological characters, as well as in the deep flesh-

color predominant in the latter; still the spherical markings are there, and, as their organic remains are identical, their position in the series may be considered as one and the same. The yellow or upper beds of the old red sandstone fall next to be considered; but these, from their geographical limits, are deferred to the subsequent chapter.

6. Approaching Perth by the Midland Junction, the geologist cannot fail to be arrested by the vast accumulations of sand and gravel, which everywhere present themselves, sometimes in the deep cuttings and railway sections; sometimes in the shape of rounded hillocks or long narrow ridges; and at other places as extended plateaux or sea-margins of different elevations. Along the whole western and southern slopes that overhang the city, these objects give a pleasing variety to the landscape, and form interesting subjects of speculation as to their origin, doubtless the gathered wreck of all the rocks we have been contemplating; for after a careful examination of their contents the conclusion cannot be avoided, that with much of the spoil of the primary rocks, we have here the detrital waste of the entire old red sandstone series. The Carpow cutting, in Strathearn near Newburgh, contains large rounded masses of all the varieties, with their peculiar ichthyolites; the gray, red, and yellow deposit that prevails in Fifeshire, and one solitary patch of which still exists *in situ*, near the Kirk of Dron, as if on purpose to mark its ancient and more extended boundaries. Nodules and bowlders of the cornstone are likewise abundant. In the vicinity of Perth, the waste of the yellow sandstone is to be found, unmixed in several spots, consisting of thick beds of fine argillaceous sand.

Similar masses of gravelly debris are spread over the middle-basin of the Earn, from Forteviot to Muthil. The Scottish Central cleaves its way for ten miles through scarcely any other material. The dreary monotony of these endless hillocks, around Auchterarder and Blackford, is relieved in part by the fine undulating grassy braes of the Ochils, and the richly-wooded rising grounds skirting the left bank of the river. The geologist's eye wanders eastward, through the district occupied by the lower basin of the Tay, where the whole was one great estuary or strait, and these the shoals covered by the ancient waters. The eastern shores, from Wormit-bay to Leuchars, are accordingly characterized by vast accumulations of sand and gravel, originating in the same causes and deposited at the same period.

It will excite no surprise, therefore, should we remark that the various beds of old red sandstone now so disjoined, or appearing only as patches, once covered the greater part of the district traced above, extending from the Ochils across the Sidlaws to the Grampians. Nor can there be difficulty in finding an adequate cause for their up-break, especially in the upper members of the group. Consider not merely the constant waste arising from aqueous abrasion and meteroic influences, but also the tearing effects occasioned by the convulsive throes and elevatory movements of the Grampian, Sidlaw, and Ochil ranges, either singly, or, as it may have happened, in combination, when the overlying rocks must have been shattered and broken in every direction, and rendered capable of easy transportation. Although belonging to a posterior geological epoch, these hillocks of gravel and sand are thus the collected records of primeval times, attesting that mighty agencies have been at work in rending the globe, re-adjusting its materials, and preparing them for future combinations.

How speedily, in these first days of creation, does geology make us acquainted with the liability to change and mutation stamped upon all earthly things! The mountains are raised up, and their earliest struggles are to get down again. Nor is it the law of matter, if we may use the expression, to rise. The waters seek the hollows of the earth, because they are material. The rocks, more solid, are subject to the same principle of gravitation, and their course is downward, and their natural place the bottom of the waters. When the rocks were separated from and elevated above the waters, it was not by any virtue or power in themselves to assume these positions. The separation as well as the elevation were the results of direct arrangement; both certainly provided for in the original plan, and yet not the less brought about against their own material tendencies by a special agency. Geology thereby establishes the fact, that the mountains were raised up and the dry land COMMANDED to appear. And now, decomposing and wasting down, we see them seeking back to their old places, to be there re-constructed, and to subserve other purposes.

THE ORGANIC REMAINS, which fall next to be described, are confined to three of the beds, as enumerated above. The first of these, in the order of superposition, is the micaceous flagstone of Carmylie and Arbroath, likewise extending along the south bank of the Tay, and distinguished by the vegetable culmiferous impressions with which it abounds. These, in some places, are so numerous, as to cover the entire surface of the rock. The idea of an ancient marsh is immediately called up in the mind, as one sees stone after stone split up, and all the interstices mottled and streaked over with the stems and leaves of the plants which were fed by its waters. While we write, every pond, and every lake in the neighborhood has crept quietly under its carpeting of ice, a congelation of the living with the dead. How beautiful and distinctly delineated the culms and leaves of the chara locked in its crystal embrace; the flower of the juncus yet lingers on the stalk; and there, how gracefully float the long broad continuous stems of the scirpus lacustris! The pike and perch, both typified in the olden rocks, may be seen motionless as a stone, or softly buoyant as the down, in the clear depths below. Not so brightly, but now as fixedly set, and as minutely preserved, are the fragments of the flora of the Devonian age: if blackened and jetty in their hoary antiquity, these films of mica give light and relief to the darker background of the picture; and shapes, too, were there sporting in the waters, — the seraphim and buckler-headed cephalaspis, — which painter never conceived, nor poet feigned.

These fossils are not in a state of petrifaction, but generally consist in the form of an easily-separated film of carbonaceous matter, or more frequently as a simple coaly marking. Sometimes, but very rarely, the plant is found betwixt the slaty layers, as it were in a dried state, and still perfectly flexible; and the impressions not unfrequently resemble the narrow striated leaves of the alopecurus geniculatus, the floating foxtail-grass, with its knotted culms. There are other specimens, that look like the bark of trees, or the branches of the gnarled oak, ribbed and jointed crosswise. The round dotted patches, varying from the size of a garden pea to an inch in diameter, not unlike, in shape and appearance, the form of a compressed strawberry, are very plentiful. Dr. Fleming, in Cheek's "Edinburgh Journal" for February, 1831, has figured this organism in connection with the stem, which thereby forms a graceful and well-defined flowering plant, while Sir Charles Lyell considers these berry-shaped forms to be the relics of the ova of some gasteropoda of the period. But at Wormit and Parkhill they are so uniformly, and in such numbers, associated with the culmiferous and leaf impressions, as most strongly to vindicate their claim to a vegetable origin. We have in our collection several specimens, with this organism separated certainly from the culm, but still in such closeness and proportionate size, as, with little aid from the imagination, to infer their former connection, and assign to them a place among the phanerogamous and seed-yielding plants. If so, we cannot too highly prize these relics, regarding them, as they undoubtedly are, among the oldest of organic substances—the first of the green herbs that sprung from the earth—the fragile flower, that withers often in a day, there to attest the mandate of primeval creation. How many seasons have returned; how many seed-times and harvests have covered the fields; what revolutions and changes over all these hills and plains, since that flinty rock formed the soil, and these vegetables sprung from its fertility! They are not admitted among the economic order of the gramineæ; nor whether of marine, semi-marine, or lacustrine origin, have geologists been able to determine.

Of the Animal Remains of fishes belonging to the gray sandstone, the Cephalaspis Lyellii was one of the earliest discovered, as it still constitutes one of the most remarkable of these fossil relics. The head of this creature, and hence the name buckler-headed, is large in proportion to the body, forming nearly one-third of its length. The outline is rounded in the form of a crescent, the lateral horns inclining slightly toward each other, while the anterior or central parts project considerably outward; this peculiarity of structure is occasioned by the intimate anchylosis of all the plates which compose the cranium. The body resembles in appearance an elongated spindle, swelling out on the ridge of the back, and narrowing to the extremity of the tail, which terminates in a long slender point. How like, peradventure, the very dagger with which the murderous Thane of Glammis threatened to render—

> "The multitudinous seas incarnadine,
> Making the green one red!"

The sanguineous fluid, in those days, was not indeed very plentiful; but the sharp-horned orthoceræ, and the swift predaceous nautili were cotemporaries; and hence, either for protection or attack, we find that, while the head of the Cephalaspis was one entire plate of enameled bone in the upper division, the body was wrapped in a closely woven net-work of bony scales, of peculiar form, and differing from the scales of every other genus of ganoids. The scales along the center of the sides are so high, that their breadth exceeds their length eight or ten times, occupying more than half the height of the animal. Everywhere meshed in smaller but equally impervious nettings, there are of the larger scales, from twenty-six to thirty covering the sides, thereby completing a mail-clad figure of a singularly warlike aspect, and bidding defiance, like his great anti-type, to all his foes,—"let fall thy blade on vulnerable CRESTS"—but now, like Banquo's ghost, "the bones are marrowless."

These curious fossils were first detected in the quarries at Glammis, by Sir Charles Lyell, and from their striking resemblance to the cephalic shield of certain trilobites, were supposed, for a time, to belong to the class of crustaceans. The beds of Carmylie and Balruddery, yield these organisms in the greatest abundance. One solitary specimen, a fragment of two inches in length, of the smaller scaly net-mesh, has been obtained by me in the gray rock, on the south bank of the Tay. The heads are uniformly in the best state of preservation; indeed hundreds of these lie entire, where no part of the body has left the trace of an impression. M. Agassiz assigns, as the reason of this, the great difference that exists in the structure of these two parts, and especially in the disproportion of their dimensions and forms, which would offer a distinct resistance to the pressure to which the animals must have been exposed. "If, on the other hand," he adds, "the heads usually present their superior surface to us, it is because their inferior surface, the cavity of the mouth, the branchial arch and sinuosities of the inferior bones of the cranium, are points of support comparatively more solid, and more adapted for sustaining the matter which has filtered into them, than a larger surface slightly convex, which would naturally be detached from the rock wherever a separation was found in it."

The Den of Balruddery presents us with a group of very remarkable fossils, comprising, in an area of the gray sandstone of a few square yards, innumerable impressions of the plant-markings already noticed, multitudes of the Cephalaspis, spines, and other ichthyolites, along with two entirely new genera of fishes of the order of Placoids. The sandstone here is of a very slaty character, splitting up into thin layers, betwixt every one of which some organism or other has impressed its form; and the different kinds are often so promiscuously huddled together, as to suggest the idea of some violent commotion in the element which collected and destroyed them. In the "Synoptical Table of British Fossil Fishes," by M. Agassiz, we find inserted a *Parexus recurvus*, and a *Clematius reticulatus*, from this locality; they are represented simply as ichthyodorulites, no complete specimens of the creatures having been presented to him, nor indeed have any been as yet obtained. One of the specimens in the Balruddery collection, when returned by M. Agassiz, was labeled as a *Palæocarcinus alatus:* and in the 14th Livraison of his "Poisson Fossiles," he thus writes:—"Enfin j'en dois aussi plusieurs espèces à M. Webster de Balruddery. Parmi ses échantillons j'en ai trouvé plusieurs d'un grand intérêt, parce qu'ils m'ont fait connaître que le genre Pterygotus que j'avais établi, il y a plusieurs années, sur des fragmens très-imparfaits, n'appartient point à la classe de poissons, mais bien en celle des crustaces. Une pareille erreur semble à peine possible, et cependant elle paraît excusable lorsque je ferai connaître les caractères de ce fossile; des botanistes célèbres n'avaient pas hésité à les ranger parmi les Algues. Les Seraphins fossiles des carrières de Forfarshire, que M. Lyell a soumit à la Section de Geologie de l'Association Britannique réunie à Edinbourg en 1834, sont des ces mêmes crustaces gigantesques du terrain Dévonien. Ils offrent des rapports éloignés avec les Entomestracés gigantesques du terrain houiller, décrits sous les noms d'Edotea et d'Eurypterus." The Lobster, accordingly, of Balruddery is the first discovery of its fossil kind; portions of nearly every organ of the body have been found, so as to make the restoration of the crustacean complete: a creature of at least four feet in length, and as in the fishes of this epoch, the shelly covering is dotted all over with enameled scale-like markings. This magnificent collection remains still undescribed, hundreds of the specimens, from the minute to the gigantic, and of the greatest diversity of character, being only detached fragments of the structures to which they belonged; but enough have we there to testify as to the early prolific abundance of Nature, and that, throughout all ages, her types and forms of life are wonderfully allied.

The interesting locality of Balruddery is succeeded by another in the ascending order of the strata, but lower on the plain of the Carse of Gowrie,—Clashbennie, situated about six miles to the westward. This rock is well entitled to be denominated the Holoptychius Bed, as here the first complete specimen of that remarkable genus was obtained, and of which there are three species in the deposit, namely, H. Giganteus, Noblissimus, and Murchisoni. Three other genera, of the ganoid order of fishes, have left their relics in this bed, some of them in a beautiful state of preservation: these are Glyptosteus reticulatus, Phyllolepis concentricus, and Glyptolepis elegans, all named and described by M. Agassiz.

The Holoptychius ranks among the family of Cœlacanthes, and the term Holoptychius (holos, entire; and ptyche, a wrinkle) is applied to the fossil from the circumstance of the scales being covered with wrinkled dots or markings, the enameled surface of which is indented with deep undulating furrows. Another characteristic feature of this genus consists in the distant position of the ventrical fins, being considerably removed toward the tail, and in the arrangement of the branchial organs, which form two large plates between the branches of the inferior ray, as in the genus Megalichthys. The structure of the "nageoirs," the rounded form of the ventrical fin, and the manner in which the rays of its anterior edge are insensibly prolonged, in connection with their relative thinness, are also marked distinctions. The head of the Holoptychius is remarkably small in comparison with the size of the body, which, in the Clashbennie specimen measures thirty inches in length by twelve in breadth. The scales are still disproportionately larger than either the head or body, some of them being nearly three inches in length by two and a half in breadth, with a corresponding thickness. The structure of the dermal covering is beautiful in the extreme; it is composed of these scale-plates, articulating, and laced together in such a way as to combine the greatest possible strength with the highest degree of flexibility; and, protected by a rich coating of enamel, it must have been capable of the greatest endurance, and of resisting any pressure. Two thickly set rows of teeth; one inner, and extremely minute, the other large and pointed, completed the equipments of a mouth adapted to seize and crush to powder any intruder upon its pasturage. The vertebral column extended to the extremity of the tail, which was forked or divided into two unequal lobes, a contrivance of nature that enabled the animal to turn quickly on its back before striking its prey. This form of the tail is called the HETEROCERCAL; it is characteristic of most of the fishes of the period, and prevailed during the palæozoic age; when it gave way, at the era of the chalk formation, to what is termed the HOMOCERCAL structure, and which still exists in the fishes of the current epoch.

The Phyllolepis is a very striking genus of the same family, and has also been noticed at considerable length by the Swiss naturalist. The scales, or other plates, which covered the body of this fish are of enormous dimensions, being nearly half a foot in diameter, and rounded to an obtuse angle. What distinguishes them from all other scales, and particularly from those of the Holoptychius, with which they have certain external resemblances, is their extreme tenuity, consisting simply of a film of enamel spread over a thin osseous membrane, scarcely so thick as the blade of a knife, and varying from three to five inches in diameter. Their surface is smooth, or slightly marked with concentric wrinkles parallel to the edge of the scale. Two species of this genus have been found, one in the old red, and the other in the coal formation. In the Clashbennie sandstone only a few detached scales have been detected, but sufficiently well preserved to show the superposition, or imbrication, perhaps, in which they stood relatively to each other, the wrinkles serving as grooves by which their adhesion was more firmly effected. One decided characteristic of this organ in the *Phyllolepis concentricus* is, that it is a little raised toward the middle, whence it again declines or sinks on all sides, after the manner of a roof.

The sandstones flanking the hill of Kinnoul, and stretching along the left bank of the Tay, by Scone and Lethendy, appear to be a continuation of the Clashbennie beds, as also those occupying the ridges by Ruthven and Dupplin, where they assume much of the fissile character and micaceous aspect of the Carmylie flagstone, but everywhere destitute of organic remains in the whole western district from Perth to Callander. The absence of fossils from particular beds has been accounted for in various ways. But even in the same series of rocks, and where there is no break in the continuity of the strata, it is a maxim of geology that the range of fossils is not always co-extensive with the mineral deposits. Then, as now, the explanation is, that the slightest physical changes affected the tastes and habits of the animal kingdom; the direction and strength of a current; the depth of water; the character and qualities of the sea-bottom; the force of tidal action; the season of the year, being, it is well known, singly sufficient to produce great differences as to the migrations and favorite haunts of almost every aquatic race. And hence it is laid down as a recognized principle in the science, that a particular bed of rock within certain limits is not to be excluded from its place in a system, and another substituted therein, by the mere presence or absence of a certain class of fossils. Individuals, too, will often outlive the family to which they belong, and be found in certain localities intermixed with the races of a higher group of rocks.—And these remarks are applicable to all the formations, less or more, from the lowest fossiliferous strata to the latest of the tertiaries. Applied to the old red sandstone, they serve to explain the fact that, while the precise relative position of the western beds in the district under review cannot in every instance be determined, large spaces or areas are entirely destitute of organic remains which in the eastern, and not distant, localities are detected in the greatest abundance and variety. The system of rocks is unquestionably the same, but neither cephalaspis, parexus, clematius, holoptychius, glyptosteus, phyllolepis, nor glyptolepis, ever would seem to have frequented these parts; whether for the reasons above assigned, or for any other local cause, or simply that they did not like the region—as the grouse and ptarmigan, even now, will not descend to the plains—is one of the recondite problems of animal life connected with the new as well as the older state of things. These beds may yet, however, be discovered to be fossiliferous, as the smallest space in local distance may reveal their hidden stores, to reward the diligent observer, and add to our knowledge of the aboriginal fauna of the district.

The lesson farther taught by the varied phenomena which have passed under review in this chapter would seem to be, that there is nothing fixed or permanent in such arrangements of nature.—These are the beginnings of creation, and both as respects organic and inorganic matter, change and re-construction have prevailed from the earliest periods to which our researches can penetrate.—The Divine Architect did not complete things as we now see them, in one initial act; nor, as we regard quiescence and stability, were the elements and forces of nature so balanced as not to interfere even in violent collision with one another. A world is called into existence. Storms and commotions rend its frame.—Sea and land contend for mastery. And everything within its bounds, like the flux of time, like day and night, summer and winter, life and death, is observed to have emerged into being and form, to have assumed new arrangements, then to have perished; or gradually, as its nature might be, to have consumed away.

No reason can be assigned for all this, as the law or order of events, except the appointment of Him who made and continues the constitution of nature as it is. No adequate cause of creation can ever be conceived but that of the Divine Goodness; and while we never can expect fully to comprehend the wisdom that planned, and the power that carried into effect, the purposes of that wisdom, still the very effort to attain knowledge concerning them, fulfills one great object for which man is made curious about the works of his Maker. In contemplating the wonders of those days, the variety, adaptation and perfection of everything in itself as then constructed, he will always refer to that Infinite

Intelligence through whose goodness he is permitted to enjoy knowledge. In becoming wiser he will become better. His increasing knowledge will be made subservient to a more exalted faith in that everlasting "Word" who framed the worlds; and in proportion as the vail becomes thinner through which he sees the origin and course of things, he will admire all the more the brightness of Him who was the true light which lighteth every man that cometh into the world.

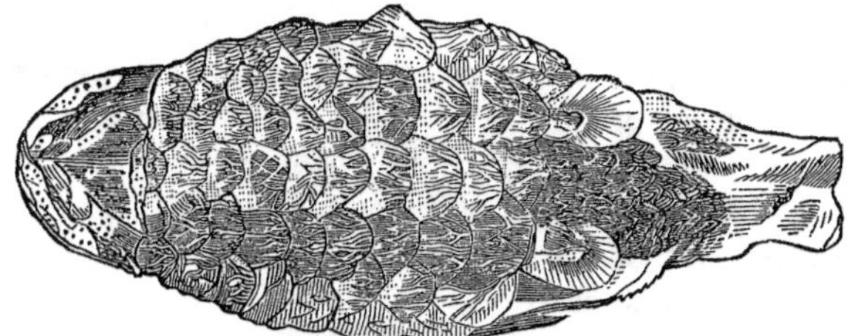

Holoptychius Noblissimus.

# CHAPTER V.

## YELLOW SANDSTONE.

Dura Den, whither the scene of our explorations now shifts, occupies a central position in Fifeshire, and lies equidistant betwixt St. Andrews and Cupar, the county town. This classic field of geology is therefore of the easiest access. The railway traverses the opening to the ravine, a lovely valley of choice archæological as well as fossil remains, where parliaments have assembled and a scepter was contended for, the retreat of learned churchmen, and a refuge in the caverns of its rock for persecuted saints. A day's excursion to such a place cannot fail to be a profitable as well as agreeable one, where the students of geology, or of botany, or of history, will severally meet with objects suitable to their taste; and, if lovers of the tragic, a short detour to the left will furnish a sight of Magus Muir, of cruel memory and most indefensible policy.

The geological structure of Dura Den is more than ordinarily interesting, presenting, as it does within a limited distance, and in close juxtaposition, the two series of the old red sandstone and carboniferous systems, an included mass of overlying trap, a greenstone dyke, and a vein of galena. The whole length of the dell, with its windings, from the ruins of the castle resting on the conglomerate red, to the outgoing on the south into Ceres basin of the coal formation, does not exceed a mile and a half. The rocks overhang the road which passes through the valley, the sandstone in some places rising precipitously into bold mural cliffs of a hundred feet in height, and presenting colored and well-defined sections of the different layers of which it is composed. These constitute the fish beds of the yellow sandstone group, lying toward the northern extremity of the den, and consist of beds of variegated marls, intermixed with friable arenaceous bands, and hard, compact, fine-grained building stone.

The carboniferous series are separated from those of the yellow sandstone by the greenstone dyke referred to, which immediately, and inconveniently for sight of the junction, interposes betwixt the two systems. The lower beds of the independent coal formation are here thrown up to an angle of 26°, the yellow sandstone adjacent being nearly horizontal, and in no place exceeding an inclination of eight or ten degrees. The coal beds have been lifted up by and repose anticlinally upon the trap, where the cutting for the road has exposed the outcrop of the seams; and thus, in a narrow space and lying on the surface, we may mark the outgoing and the incoming of a vast revolutionary epoch, organic and inorganic, in the earth's history. The strata, consisting of alternating bands of coal, shale, ironstone, and sandstone, assume toward the head of the valley a nearly horizontal position, abutting against a mass of trap which separates the lower from the upper workable beds of the bituminous mineral in the Ceres basin.

Dura Den, in addition to the interest arising from lithological structure, presents an excellent example of a valley of erosion. The river which traverses it rises at times into considerable volume, and sweeps with violence through the pass; connected above, at one period, with a lake, and acting continuously on soft friable matter, the abrading powers of the instrument are sufficiently adequate to the production of the effect. The qualities of the rocks penetrated may be easily inferred from the windings of the stream—the harder substances occasioning a divergence from the straight course—the soft and marly scooped out into wider and more extended areas. A section of any one of them is thereby labeled for the fullest inspection, which are arranged, not perpendicularly one upon another, but drawn out in longitudinal succession on the floor and sidewalls of the valley, and exhibiting to the geologist, after so many types and forms of the old red sandstone, the first break and most northern limit of the coal metals in the great central basin of Scotland.

The Yellow Sandstone, as it is termed from its prevailing color, though not uniformly so, belongs to the old red or devonian system of rocks, of which the cornstone and conglomerate beds are in the immediate vicinity, and the position and relation of the three to one another easily determinable. The upper or yellow deposit occupies the valley of Stratheden nearly throughout its entire length and breadth, and ranges along the base of the heights of Nydie, Cults, the Lomonds, Binnarty, and the Cleish hills, dipping under the carboniferous lower group, and generally separated by overlying masses of trap. The sandstones, indeed, of both systems, resemble each other so much in color and texture, that in many instances along the line now indicated the trap must be taken as a guide by which to ascertain the qualities and respective positions of the two series. Glenvale, a beautiful ravine which intersects the Lomond range, presents admirable sections of the whole group, in their regular order of superposition and finely displaying their contrasting mineral characters.

Organic Remains. These are abundantly distributed in scales, teeth, spines, coprolites, and other remains, and are to be found in every opening and quarry throughout the range of the deposit. It is only in Dura Den, however, that any entire animal forms have as yet been obtained, and these all confined to a portion of the rock not exceeding thirty yards by three in breadth, a narrow trough excavated for the purpose of forming a water-shed to the mill, which stands in the center of the valley. The fossils derived from this single spot consist of four new genera, and seven or eight new species, that have been added to our catalogue of extinct animals. These remains were all in a state of beautiful preservation; the scales and fins are brightly enameled, and contrasted with the matrix in which they are set, the colors are as vivid and glistening as when the animals were sporting in their native element. The specimens, I believe, of the various collections made in this rich depository by different parties were all submitted to the examination of M. Agassiz, who has figured several of them in his "Monograph" on the old red sandstone, but without completing, it is much to be regretted, his descriptions of the various fossils. We give the following abridgment of such descriptions as are contained in the work.

There are two new species of Holoptychius represented, namely, *Andersoni* and *Flemingii*, and these are distinguished entirely by the form and tracery of their respective scales. The H. Andersoni is described as a small spindle-shaped (*fusiforme*) fish, thick and short, and narrowing rapidly toward the tail.

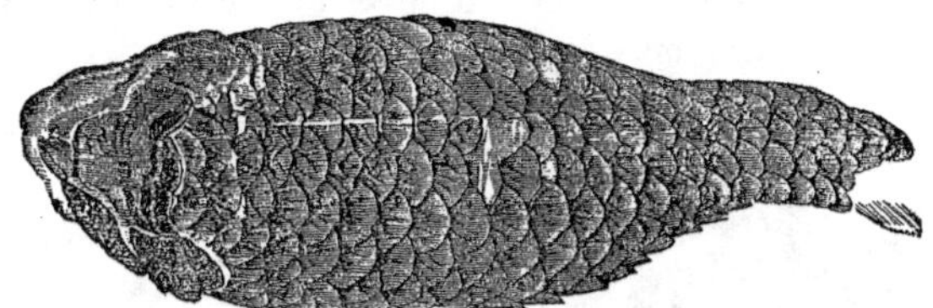

Holoptychius Andersoni.

The scales are much less than those of the other species, as deep as they are broad, and resembling in general form the scales of the H. Murchisoni found in Clashbennie. What peculiarly distinguishes them is the figure of the ornaments (*le dessin des ornemens*) of the surface, which are parallel, horizontal, very marked and distant in the A. and never extending in the striæ to the posterior edge. The scales, again, of H. Flemingii are on the sides of the fish deeper than they are broad, and on the belly they become rounder. Their ornaments are also very distinct in the F., consisting of a system of waving lines, which run horizontally toward the outer edge without any perceptible ramification, while the wrinkles of the scale rise from a series of little hills (*collines*) ranged parallel over the length of the inner edge, undulating and very close. This specimen is represented as very imperfect. The other is nearly entire, the plates of the head and several of the teeth are well preserved, every scale is in its place, and the fins are only wanting to restore the normal outline of the fish. This fossil has been figured and erroneously described in the author's "Geology of the County of Fife" under the name of gyrolepis (holoptychius now) giganteus, from which, says M. Agassiz, it differs specifically.

From the fossils of this locality has been established the new genus of GLYPTOPOMUS, the specimen of which being originally mistaken by Agassiz for a platygnathus, but since found by him to differ from that genus in several material points. The scales of the platygnathus, for example, are round and imbricated, possessing in this respect all the characteristics of the scales of the cœlacanthes, while on the other hand those of the glyptopomus resemble the scales of the sauroids, which are rhomboidal or square (*ou carrées*), closely set and never imbricated, as shown in the subjoined illustration.

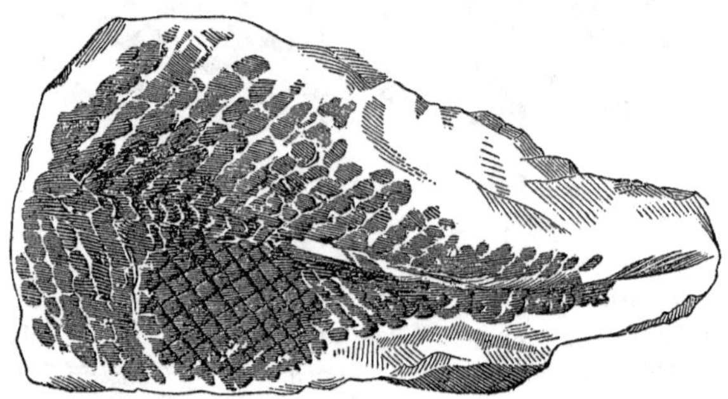

Glyptopomus Minor.

Moreover, the platygnathes are lengthy (*allongés*) in the body, likewise long (*longue*) in the tail, which is furnished with a very strong fin, whereas the body of the glyptopomes is very thick, and the tail short. The ornaments of the scales of G. bear a close affinity to those generally of the cœlacanthes. Only one species as yet has been found, the glytopomus minor, and figured in the tab. 26 of the "Monograph" under the name of platygnathus minor.

The glyptopomus minor, says M. Agassiz, found in Dura Den, and of which there is but one specimen, is possessed of a body broad and thick, approaching in form to that of the holoptychius. The fish is lying on the belly, and turned slightly to the left, so that it is the back and right side which are represented in the plate. The head is proportionally small, covered with bones very irregularly carved, presenting a dense and diversified granular aspect. On the side of the head there is a large enameled plate, which shows that the cheek was covered, as in the polypterus, with one single osseous plate, on the under edge of which was fixed the large masticatory muscle. The scales on the body of the fish are large, high on the sides, and nearly square on the back, where in the middle they form an oblique series converging to an acute angle. The scales are very thick set on the side of each other, and apparently connected only by means of the skin to which they are attached. The enameled surface is not smooth, but rather marked with a fine granulation, which imparts a rich velvet gloss to the scale. Traces only of the fins are preserved, partly of the ventral, partly of the dorsal or caudal, and the rays of which are all apparently short and slender. This specimen forms a part of the author's collection, but inadvertently described as belonging to that of Professor Jameson.

Another genus, established from the fossils of Dura Den by M. Agassiz, is the Pamphractus, of which there are two species, *Hydrophilus* and *Andersoni*. These are both in the collection of the author, and have a special history of their own, from which, when read in all its details, it would appear they have suffered as roughly at the hands of geologists in simply determining their class, order, or genus, as they ever did from the physical revolutions amidst which their lot was originally cast.

Before the type of a new and strange form called *Pterichthys*, had been determined by this learned palæontologist, collectors were everywhere puzzled by the specimens of the animal that, from time to time were casting up. The winged appendages of the sides of the head, as movable fins, had easily given rise to a variety of opinions concerning their true affinities, and which, says M. Agassiz, "have been regarded by the most able naturalists successively as Tortoises, Fishes, Crustacea, and even Coleoptera." The fossils of Dura Den were at first regarded by him as belonging to the type as well as genus Pterichthys, and my specimens were actually returned from Neufchâtel so named—the "broad" and "narrow" species—and the label still remains attached. Meanwhile, five or six species of the genus Pterichthys had been already determined and described by him, from the fossils of Cromarty and Morayshire—these in the collection chiefly of Mr. Hugh Miller; and Mr. Miller being, about the same period, engaged in the preparation of his work, "The Old Red Sandstone," speedily under the new nomenclature, as he was so opportunely furnished with the materials, gave the public the benefit of M. Agassiz's discovery and version of their true and authentic history. What we had hastily, certainly, but still influenced much in the matter by the judgment of others, referred to the order of Coleoptera, he was enabled at once, upon the inspection of a Dura Den specimen, and from its very striking resemblance to his own, to pronounce to be a Pterichthys. A few pages before he had stated that he could make nothing of the creature, although some specimens of the fossil had been in his possession for a period of nearly ten years; but NOW, he was able to record,—"I very lately enjoyed the pleasure of examining the *bona fide* ichthyolite itself,—one of the specimens of Dura Den, and apparently one of the more entire, in the collection of Professor Fleming. Its character as a Pterichthys I found very obvious." But short-lived, indeed, are all mundane enjoyments. The most intellectual, in the revolutions of science, are not exempt from their general character of vanity. While the two northern sages were thus gazing, in all the raptures of a new discovery, "upon the *bona fide* ichthyolite *itself*," the philosopher, under the shelter of the Jura, was doubting, re-examining, and finally correcting, his own first judgment; and, while the virgin pages of "The Old Red Sandstone" had scarcely time to reach their author, the "Monograph" was announcing to the world the determination of a new genus, and that the fossil of Dura Den was a Pamphractus, and no Pterichthys at all.

"I had at first," says Agassiz, "connected with pterichthys the only species known of that genus, by calling it *pterichthys hydrophilus*, but a more profound study and attentive comparison of that species with the genus coccosteus, have proved that it ought to form a distinct genus, intermediate betwixt pterichthys and coccosteus, which I have named *pamphractus*, in consequence of the divided form of the carapace. The pectoral fins of pamphractus resemble very much those of the pterichthys in their form, being slender, elongated, and crooked (courbée). But the plates of the carapace are all differently arranged. The central plate is very large (énorme); it covers two-thirds of the whole carapace, and unites the anterior articulation of the head with the carapace. The lateral plates, which acquire so great a development in the pterichthys, are here reduced to narrow stripes, stretching to the edge of the carapace; while, on the other hand, the posterior plates are of very great size, and form with a small intercalated plate the extremity of the carapace. The disposition of the plates of the head is likewise very different from that of the pterichthys, in which we discern no thoracic cincture as in that genus, but a transverse line, which separates in a striking manner the plates of the head from those of the carapace. *We see not any portion of the tail;* but I presume that it would bear a resemblance to the form of that of pterichthys." Agassiz thus concludes his description of pamphractus, which we have partly abridged :—"The excessive development of the central plate of the carapace which reaches the articulation of the head—the absence of a thoracic cincture making the round of the body—and the distinct separation of the occipital articulation, will always distinguish this genus from that of pterichthys."

Again, however, the ashes of the dead have been disturbed, the history has been recast, and the old genealogy attempted to be restored. Sir P. G. Egerton, in a paper read before the Geological Society of London, on the 19th April, 1848, and a copy of which he did me the honor to transmit, has examined very minutely every organ and portion of the animal as delineated in the "Monograph," and is satisfied that it is, indeed, still to be regarded as a genuine pterichthys. However, Sir Philip very cautiously adds,—"Having never seen a specimen of *pamphractus*, I should not be justified in expressing any positive opinion respecting this genus, but I cannot help thinking that it is founded on a specimen, showing the true dorsal arrangement of the lorication of the Pterichthys." Accordingly, Mr. Miller, who supplies a considerable portion of the paper in question, affirms, with abundant confidence, that he has been able to penetrate the mystery of the error. "I have succeeded," he says, "in tracing to its origin the *Pamphractus* of Agassiz. The specimens which he figures could never have furnished the materials of his restoration.—These materials he evidently derived from the print of a Pterichthys of the upper Old Red (showing the dorsal superficies of the creature), given by the Rev. Dr. Anderson of Newburgh, in his Essay on the Geology of Fifeshire ('Quarterly Journal of Agriculture,' Vol. XI, 1840), as that of a fossil beetle." Now, with all submission, this hypothesis is wide of the fact. While Mr. Miller was inspecting, at Aberdeen, "the bona fide ichthyolite itself," and which, as we shall immediately see, was not a Pterichthys, Agassiz had both the print and the real specimens lying before him. The impressions on the slab are ELEVEN in number, three of the "broad" and eight of the "narrow" species; and, comparing the one with the other, the print with the fossil, he records, "They have been figured VERY FAIRLY by Mr. Anderson, in his interesting Memoir on the Geology of Fifeshire." "But," adds Mr. Miller, "I have ascertained, by the examination of the greater number of specimens of this species yet found, in the general outline of the carapace, which was longer in proportion to its breadth than in the print, and not defined by such regular curves." * * * The print is a perfect transcript of the fossil, as if taken in a mold,—curves, projections, and tubercles all duly and "fairly" preserved, as in the original; and, with all the materials, and so many actual impressions before him, Agassiz hesitated not to change his views, and to feel assured that it was really a Pamphractus, not a Pterichthys, that he was examining. Farther, we have only to add, that in the Essay in the Quarterly Journal of Agriculture, it is not true that the print of a Pterichthys is there "given as that of a fossil beetle; the higher patronymic had, ere the publication of the prize essay, been withdrawn; and the author, along with all others, states, he was waiting the judgment of the highest and most competent authority from the blue lake of Neufchâtel.

And thither also, it would now appear, that other inquiries had been transmitted respecting the organisms of Dura Den, to be famed by modern, as it had already been by ancient, genealogical claims. We suspect, at least, it is of "the bona fide ichthyolite itself" that M. Agassiz, in the "Monograph," speaks in the following extract:—"Dr. Fleming m'a communiqué le dessin d'une pétrifaction recueillie par lui à Dura Den, qui resemble beaucoup, quant à la forme du Pamphractus hydrophilus. La tête est courte, arrondie, large, presque en forme de croissant, le corps est allongé, formant avec la tête un ovale qui se termine en pointe en arrière. Les pectorales sont grêles, courbées et aussi longues que le corps. L'articulation de la tête avec le corps est très-nettement marquée, d'une manière qu'a la forme de la carapace près, qui est beaucoup plus pointue, on croirait voir un Pamphractus. Mais ce qui distingue surtout ce fossile (à en juger du moins d'après le dessin qui n'est, à vrai dire, qu'une esquisse) c'est qu'il n'y a pas de plaques separées, et que toute la surface de sa carapace ne montre qu'une granulation uniforme et continue, si toutefois la délinéation des plaques n'a pas été omise par le dessinateur. Nous aurions donc dans ce fossile un genre nouveau de cephalaspide, caractérisé par la forme de sa tête et par sa carapace uniforme. Quoi qu'il en soit, j'attends de plus amples informations sur ce sujet, avant de préciser davantage les caractères de ce type, et je me borne à reproduire les contours de ce dessin, Tab. 31, fig. 6, afin de fixer d'une manière plus particulière l'attention sur ce fossile."

Now, making every allowance for the imperfection of the sketch of Dr. Fleming, (qu'une esquisse), and which had not the aggravation of being a "print," only see how many marvels have been successively evolved out of "the *bona fide* ichthyolite itself:"—it is not a Pamphractus, though very much resembling it in form—it is not a Pterichthys, of which alliance there is not a hint even dropped by Agassiz, though its character as a *Pterichthys* Mr. Miller "found very obvious;" but "we have in that fossil a new kind (genre) of cephalaspis, characterized by the form of its head, and by its uniform carapace," all which characters have been overlooked in "the pleasure of examining the *bona fide* ichthyolite itself—one of the specimens of Dura Den, and apparently one of the more entire." Has this creature undergone a still further metamorphosis, numerous as those of the Pterichthys itself? Or what specimen is it which now rejoices in the appellation of *Homothorax Flemingii,* also again challenged or suspected at least by Sir P. Egerton, not to be its true designation! But, *quocunque nomine gaudeat,* the cabinet of science is enriched by the addition of a new and remarkable fossil fish.

Repeatedly, since the notice in Mr. Miller's work of the Dura Den fossil, and his fanciful commentary on the truth and accuracy of the plate in the "Geology of Fifeshire," have I examined, compared, and recompared the design and the original, and never have I been able to detect the slightest disagreement, even in the minutest feature. Others, and parties innumerable have examined them freely in my presence, have pronounced as to the fairness of the representation. There are five figures in all upon the plate of the Dura Den fossils; they were all, fossils and figures, under the ocular inspection of M. Agassiz; one of these, *Holoptychius Andersoni*, he has figured in the "Monograph;" the representations are identical, and all are declared to be "figured very fairly." True, the pamphractus had not been able to preserve the tail, nor any trace even of that member. Agassiz did not think himself justified in supplying the deficiency. I added none either, "carefully sinking" the nonentity. But Mr. Miller had a point to establish: the fossil MUST be one and the same with the *bona fide* ichthyolite *itself*, which appears to have retained the caudal appendage. It will not certainly account for the obliteration of this organ in ALL the specimens of Dura Den, that, in common with *Pterichthys* and *Coccosteus*, the *Pamphractus* was not possessed of the *heterocercal* structure, so characteristic of the fishes of the period. But yet it is not there. Then, "the tubercles seen in profile," are exaggerated: Agassiz thought fit, upon examination, to retain the exaggeration, as Nature, he perceived, had designed. And now, Mr. Miller finds it proper to communicate to Sir P. Egerton, that after examining the specimens (presented by me) in the Museum of the Highland and Agricultural Society in Edinburgh, "one of the MOST STRIKING specific distinctions of the creature consists in the length and bulk of the arms, and the comparatively great prominence of those angular projections by which they are studded on the edges—projections which seem to be but exaggerations of those confluent lines of tubercles by which the arms of all the other species are fringed." So, Nature has her "exaggerations," likewise! and the first of the genus which ever rose to the stroke of the hammer, has in no degree been misrepresented in its fair proportions, except that the angular projections referred to are not so prominently developed as in other specimens in the author's collection.

It will readily be inferred from all this that the locality of Dura Den is entitled to much consideration in consequence of the variety of its interesting remains, not to speak of the diversity of views which the remains themselves have occasioned in so many quarters. The Pterichthys, Pamphractus, Homothorax, and Cephalaspis are all of the family *Lépidöides*, and have such a close affinity in outward form as readily, in mutilated specimens at least, to be mistaken for each other. The appendages of the head, having the appearance of wings, suggested the term *pterichthys*, the winged fish: the plates covering the body, according to their number and form, gave rise to the generic distinctions; and the species of each have subsequently been determined by minor differences. The external organs in all were enameled, and discover, like the fish of the period, the tuberculated surface. The Pterichthys of the more northern counties vary in size from nearly a foot to an inch in length, and generally the wings of these, so far as they have been figured in works, are extended horizontally and perpendicularly to the body. The Pamphractus of Dura Den are all nearly of a size—about two inches and a half in length,—the wings in every instance depressed and inclined to the sides, and in no instance of the twenty to thirty specimens exhumed from the rock, has the tail been appended, or a fragment of the caudal organ detected. The cephalaspis has only been found in the lower beds of the system, and highly important would be its discovery in the upper, where, however, we have reason to think the new genus Homothorax has been substituted in its place. Mrs. Dalgliesh of Dura, in whose collection we found a Glyptopomus, and a slab containing several impressions of the Pamphractus, has kindly, and with a commendable love of science, informed us that her quarries are freely open for the researches and explorations of geologists, and that every facility will be afforded them in their interesting task.

In addition to the fossils already referred to, I find in the specimens of my collection returned from Neufchâtel, that two are labeled as Diplopterus, new species; two as Glypticus, new species; and one as Holoptychius, new species. This last is now figured in the "Monograph" as the Platygnathus Jamesoni. None of these are described in the narrative of the work, so that until his return from America, where palæontology will unquestionably reap much from his indomitable perseverence, his almost instinctive skill, and vast learning, we cannot expect that M. Agassiz will have leisure either to supplement the deficiencies of his great work, or confirm his former conclusions against the alterations suggested in his absence—suggested certainly in no small degree upon fanciful organization and mistaken assumption.

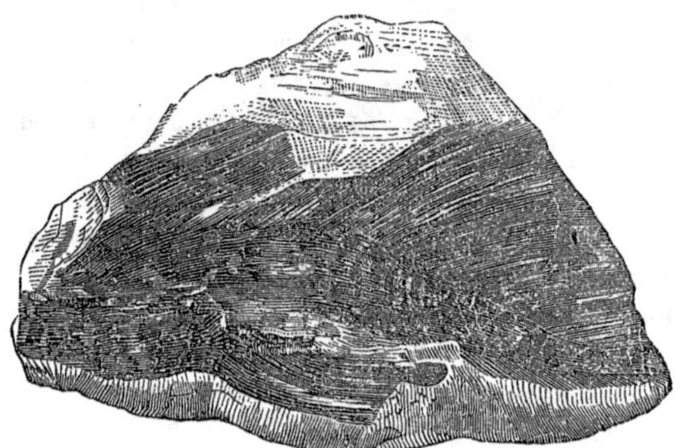

Platygnathus Jamesoni.

In closing our review of the old red sandstone, we shall briefly state the principles of classification of fossil fishes, as determined by M. Agassiz, from which it will be seen by the earliest types of the marine vertebrata, while admirably suited to the perturbed condition of the element in which the strata were formed, differ widely in their structure from all existing races.

The fishes of the present era, it is well known, are divided into two great classes, the cartilaginous and the osseous. In the former are comprehended the sharks, rays, and sturgeons of our present seas; the latter embrace the salmon, cod, herring, and the various kinds possessed of similar forms. The bony structure in all the cartilaginous class is soft, destitute of fibers, and contains scarcely a trace of earthy or calcareous matter. The osseous fishes, on the other hand, are constructed internally of true bone, composed of calcareous matter, like that of birds and quadrupeds, which is possessed of a fibrous arrangement, of great hardness and capable of long endurance. Now, it would appear that the fishes of the old red sandstone belong almost exclusively to the cartilaginous class. The internal frame was composed chiefly of this soft, soluble substance; hence it is that no portion of the inner body of the fish, in any of the fossil specimens, remains.—The teeth and scales, with fragments of the bones of the head, are all that have survived, but so hard and enduring has been the scaly outer coating, that the figure and contour of the animal have been preserved entire. The specimen of Holoptychius Andersoni, from Dura Den, is still enveloped in its original covering, not a scale in the whole body displaced or missing, the head and belly slightly compressed, while the posterior ridge of the back and tail is sharp and angular.

Here, then, in this class of animal life, we find that what is defective in the internal structure—if it be a defect—is completely supplied in the outer appendages, whereby the fishes which have the softest bodies are possessed of hard, horny skins, coated with enamel. Their bones are thus all on the surface, sometimes in the form of scales; sometimes assuming the shape of spines and tubercles; now in small, now in large plates; and often disposed in the most singular and grotesque arrangements, as in the genus coccosteus, or the osteolepis, whose entire skull consisted of shining naked bone, and in the cheiracanthus, a creature possessed of fins scaled and enameled all over.

The Swiss naturalist, accordingly, in adopting a new principle of classification, so essential in the case of the fossils of the old red sandstone, has made the scales and external organs the groundwork of his system. The classification of Cuvier and the older naturalists proceeds mainly upon the character and disposition of the fins. Hence the order of the Acanthopterygii, or thorny-finned; and the Malacopterygii, or the soft finned order.—The classification of M. Agassiz, proceeding upon the characters of the scales and plates, has given rise to the following orders, namely, the Placoid, or broad-plated scale; the Ganoid, or the shining-scale; the Ctenoid, or comb-shaped scale; and the Cycloid, or marginated scale. Upon the simple basis of these four orders, he has constructed his system and composed his "Poissons Fossiles," the standard authority in fossil ichthyology, and elaborate monument of his learning and genius.

The relations, as well as distinguishing peculiarities, of the fishes of the old red, are thus described by Agassiz:—"Of the Placoidian order," he says, "the genera ctenacanthus, onchus, ctenoptychius, and ptychacanthus, are provided with spinous rays to the dorsal fins, resembling the gigantic ichthyodorulites of the carboniferous and jurassic formations, but differing in their less considerable size; they are distinguished among themselves by the forms and ornaments of their rays. In the order of ganoid fishes, the genera acanthodes, diplacanthus, cheiracanthus, and cheirolepis present themselves at first sight as a separate group; for although covered, like the others, with enameled scales, these are so small, that they impart to the skin the appearance of shagreen. The manner in which the fins are sustained by spinous rays, or the absence of these rays, and the position of the fins themselves, have served as characters in the establishing of these genera. The genera pterichthys, coccosteus, and cephalaspis, form a second group exceedingly curious: the considerable development of the head, its size, large plates which cover it, and which likewise extend over the greater portion of the trunk, and the movable appendages in the form of a wing, placed on the side of the head, give to them the most remarkable appearance. It is these peculiarities, indeed, which caused the class to which these genera belong for a long time to be misunderstood. The large bony and granulated plates of coccosteus, led to their being considered as belonging to trionyx: and it will be sufficient excuse for this error to call to recollection, that the greatest anatomist of our age had sanctioned this approximation. The form of the disc of the head of the cephalaspides, which has the appearance of a large crescent, and their more numerous, but very elevated scales, resembling the transverse articulations of the body, explain how it was possible to see in these fishes the trilobites of a particular genus. Lastly, the winged appendages of the sides of the head of pterichthys, as movable as fins, have easily given rise to the variety of opinions concerning the true affinity of these singular creatures, and has caused them to be taken at one time for gigantic coleoptera, at another for crustacea, or small marine tortoises; so little do the types of the classes appear fixed in certain respects at these remote times. Another singularity of these genera is the association to the bony plates of the head of a vertebral appendage, which is far from having acquired the same solidity; but appears, on the contrary, to have remained fibro-cartilaginous during the whole life of the animal—resembling in this respect the skeleton of the sturgeon.

"It would be difficult to find among recent fishes, types presenting any direct analogy with the genera pterichthys, coccosteus, and cephalaspis; it is only from afar that they can be compared to some abnormal genera of our epoch. * * * The analogy which they offer, on the one hand, in form with the dorsal cord of the embryo of fishes, together with the inferior position of their mouth, which is equally met with in the embryos; and on the other hand, the distant resemblance of these fishes to certain types of reptiles, present the most curious assemblage of characters that can possibly be conceived. A third group of fishes belonging to this formation, comprises those genera whose vertical fins are double on the back and under the tail, and which approach very near to the caudal. These are the genera dipterus, osteolepis, diplopterus, and glyptolepis, which differ from one another by the form of their scales and their dentition. And lastly, it seems necessary to regard as a fourth group of this order, the genera which are characterized by large conical teeth, situated on the margin of the jaws, between which are alternately smaller, and indeed very small ones, in the form of a brush. Such are the genera holoptychius and platygnathus, and the genus recently established by Mr. Owen under the name of dendrodus, and respecting which this learned anatomist has given some exceedingly interesting microscopical details."

The philosopher here, in these views as to the primitive diversity of the ichthyoid types in the old red sandstone, adduces such illustrations and others not quoted, as subversive of the theory of the successive transformation of species, and of the descent of organized beings now living, from a small number of primitive forms. He asserts the doctrine that the characteristic fossils of each well-marked geological epoch are the representatives of so many distinct creations, and affirms that he has demonstrated by a vast number of species that the presumed identifications are exaggerated approximations of species, resembling one another, but nevertheless specifically distinct. M. Agassiz introduces the same doctrine in his latest great work, the "Iconographie," wherein he goes the length of saying, that, even when species are, so far as the eye can judge, identical, they may not be so—that there may exist species so nearly allied, as to render it impossible to distinguish them—and reiterates that each geological epoch is characterized by a distinct system of created beings (the results of a new intervention of creative power), including not only different species from those of the preceding system, but also new types. Under his safe guidance we have glanced at the earliest groups and forms of life upon the globe, and have seen the simple structures of the beginning succeeded by higher, if not more perfect or more complex, at least by creatures capable of a wider range of action and enjoyment. The deductions and sweeping inferences of geologists may be often vague and uncertain; but a science, whose direct aim is to decipher the records of the past and compare the successive types of animal life upon the earth, deals with important objects, and leads to salutary trains of thought, keeping continually before the view the Fountain-Head of all being; and adding a new proof to the sublime doctrine, that Man who is privileged so to range through creation and time will himself outlive a term of existence, measurable by a few points of space and a few moments of eternity.

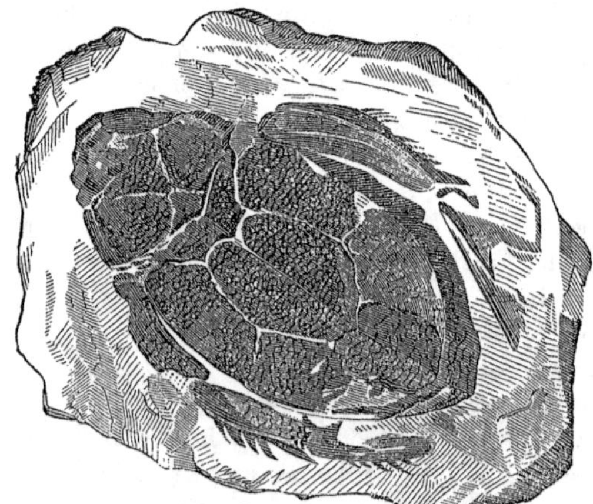

Pamphractus Andersoni.

## CHAPTER VI.

### TRAP ROCKS.

We do not select the rocks which form the title of this chapter from mere arbitrary choice, or because they are geographically connected with the district under review, but because they are immediately the next in the chronological order of our course. The Sidlaws and Ochils have their position as precisely determined in relation to time as to space, for difficult often as it may be to fix the sequence of events within the historical era, there is generally no lack of evidence by which to ascertain, in the far remoter times, *when* the several strata and the igneous masses assumed their respective places on the surface of the globe. The proofs here are of a cumulative character, and irresistibly conclusive. The animate and inanimate things of earth, the living and the dead, are both admissible witnesses in the question, and their testimony is alike unexceptionable. The silurian seas had been disturbed upon the upheaval of their beds; these with their organic contents were elevated by the irruption of plutonic matter, and in their altered position gave a bolder contour and additional bulk to the primitive land. New accumulations were forming during the devonian period in the waters still mightily agitated along the lines of disturbance; new races of scale-enameled creatures occupied their depths, and huge crustaceans anchored among their rocky shallows. The interior regions again let loose their giant forces, and these chains of hills rose above the surface, disrupting and heaving into day the various deposits of the old red sandstone. Hence the formation of the one set of rocks preceded, in the order of time, the elevation of the other: not an islet appeared over all these parts while the sedimentary strata were accumulating beneath: plants and trees covered the flanks of the Grampians, algæ and fuci abounded in the waters, and myriads of fishes sported amid their luxuriance; but as yet there was no basin of the Tay, no fertile Carse of Gowrie, no kingdom of Fife stored to repletion with its precious metals of iron, lime, and coal. The Sidlaws and Ochils, therefore, become invested with even a romantic interest, when we thus view them in their geological relations—their age precisely defined—and themselves, flinty and weather-stained, the memorials of the vast convulsions and changes of nature. They mark the outgoing of a period comparatively barren of vegetable life, and the incoming of the exuberant products of the carboniferous epoch.

I. The structure of the Sidlaw and Ochil ranges, from the amorphous character of the rocks, furnishes little or no room for geological description. These nearly parallel chains of hills, separated only by an interval of from two to five miles, and forming the lower water-shed of the basin of the Tay, consist of the various members of the trap family usually denominated whinstone, and whose structure is very different, upon a glance, from that of the sandstones and other sedimentary deposits we have been considering. This class of rocks have all a tendency, in mineralogical phraseology, to a spathose structure, and discover at least the rudiments of crystallization: there is no lamination in their internal texture, and the lines of stratification which they sometimes exhibit, are assumed, or impressed by the previously consolidated strata among which they have been injected. They are not lavas, which are sub-aërial products, nor are they aqueous formations, whose materials have been deposited in water. These rocks are the results of igneous fusion deep under the crust of the earth, poured over the bottom of the sea, and protruded into the diversified dome-shaped forms which they generally present.

Trap-rock consists of several varieties, as porphyry, clinkstone, compact feldspar, amygdaloid, greenstone, and basalt. These all pass into each other by insensible gradations, often forming one continuous mass, for the most part composed of the same ingredients, and have in consequence been regarded by geologists as belonging to one group, produced under similar circumstances, and elevated at intervals about the same period. The porphyritic structure prevails generally in both chains, and "porphyry has the peculiarity of being rarely found in any but the primary strata: it seems to be the whinstone of the Old World, or at least that which is of highest antiquity in the present." * But not only are both ranges characterized by the same qualities and texture of rocks in hand-specimens, one hill answering to another; they also preserve the same general features of outline, and the same relations to the disrupted sandstones among which they have been injected. The highest point, for instance, in the eastern division of the Ochils, is Norman's Law, attaining an elevation of nearly one thousand feet above the level of the sea: in its uprise the mass has brought along with it the lower beds of the gray sandstone, which flank its northern and eastern sides, within three hundred feet of the summit. To the north and west of Dundee the highest points of the Sidlaws are encompassed in like manner with their analogous beds of the gray rock. And so in every locality, whether along their base lines, or among the numerous ravines and valleys that intersect their cultivated slopes, the strata may be seen cropping out, bearing testimony to the convulsive movements to which they have been exposed, and the altered positions they have in consequence assumed.

A remarkable bed of conglomerate or tufaceous trap intersects the chains at different, but generally corresponding, points of elevation, varying from two to four hundred feet above the sea-level. On the Ochil side this bed crosses the chain of hills from Letham school-house to Lindores Loch, where, along the line of the Edinburgh and Northern Railway, the out-crop may be observed at various places—very interestingly on the western slope of Clatchart—and again appearing at intervals toward Abernethy, whence it is traceable through the glen. In the ravines of the Sidlaws, behind Rossie Priory, in the den of Pitroddy, on the face of Kinnoul and Moncrieffe Hills, and across the ridge intersected by the Perth tunnel, indications of the same tufaceous bed can be traced, consisting, for the most part, of quartz rock, schist, and rounded masses of the different varieties of the trap, mixed not unfrequently with bowlders and smaller pieces of the gray and red sandstones.

---

* Playfair.

This formation has, doubtless, been produced on the bottom of a troubled sea, where the crust has been exposed to violent action—much of it comminuted and broken into fragments, rolled and fashioned into nodules, large portions of it torn up, but retaining their continuity for a space—when the molten flood has poured from below, and diffusing itself through the mass, the whole, after successive eruptions, has been lifted to its present elevation.

II. The amygdaloidal portion of these hills forms an interesting feature, and prevails very widely in both chains. This rock has a conglomerated stratified appearance in some places; but generally the matrix is very compact, rather porphyritic, of a dark brown or greenish hue, and when exposed to weathering, the innumerable small cavities or vesicular tissue by which it is laminated are prominently exposed. These cavities are filled with zeolites, carbonate of lime, chalcedony, prehnite, and various other crystalline silicious deposits. The green hue is derived from the decomposition, on the exposed surfaces, of the imbedded substances. This rock forms the true habitat of the richest and most beautiful specimens of the agate and jasper family, of the purest Scottish pebble, and of large sparkling geodes of amethystine crystals. The agates of Kinnoul and Moncrieffe are prized by lapidaries, as they are admired by amateurs, and no mineralogist should fail to visit the romantic pass of Glen Farg—illustrated by the classic pens of Galt, Lauder, and Scott—adorned and stored, in every niche of its serpentine course, with calc-spars, analcime, chabasie, stilbite, heulandite, konilite, and the entire family of the zeolites, presenting often fasciculi of crystals several inches in length, thin as silken threads, and rivaling frost-work in the transparency and brilliancy of their texture. The mass of rock constituting Bein Hill, and intersected by the turnpike for miles, appears as a simple agglutination of nodules of the size and color of garden peas, and consisting principally of analcime, zeolite, and chalcedonic pebbles.

What account is given of these curious formations—of their color, structure, and qualities—all so different from those of the surrounding matrix? Assuming the igneous origin of the trap family of rocks, and against which there can scarcely exist the possibility of an argument, it is supposed that, when in the act of cooling, cavities would necessarily be produced in the heated molten mass by the expansive power of gases, and that upon their escape silicious and other deposits would be formed in the empty spaces. All the ingredients of the included crystals, of every genus, are plentifully diffused through nature, mixed up with the matter of every kind of rock; air and water are nowhere wanting, and substances sufficiently porous, for their transmission; a lamination or separation of coating, layer upon layer, is discernible in every agate; while the still partially existing hollows in some nodules, and the concentric nature of the bands of earthy matter which lines their surface, clearly demonstrate the deposition of the outer prior to that of the inner layer, and prove that at the very time when the crystallization had commenced, the cavities had assumed the form and shape which they now retain. Sometimes, too, the nodules have a compressed or flattened appearance; and the explanation in such cases is, that the cavities, if formed during the cooling of the beds, must have been altered in their shape by pressure either before the deposition of the silicious matter, or during the successive formation of the layers. Other, and indeed many, theories are broached, among which the most plausible is, that the cavities in which the agates are now found were caused by the "molecular aggregation of the silicious particles compelling the surrounding matter to yield in proportion to the attraction of these homogeneous particles." The former explanation, however, is the most generally adopted, the most obvious in its conditions, and the most accordant with the existing processes of nature, the laws of heat, and the order of crystallization. The porosity and fibrous structure of agates, consisting of a congeries of minute radiating fibers at right angles to the rings or concentric layers, have also been established from microscopical examination, and hence the diversity of their colors, whether from vegetable matter or metallic oxides everywhere so abundant in the soils and crust of the globe.

The same law or mode of formation applies to crystallized minerals generally, and has continued to operate from primitive times to our own in their production. The sparkling topazes of Cairngorm and gigantic crystals of the Alps—the semi-opal of

Iceland and the heliotrope of Kinnoul—the dazzling emeralds of Brazil and Ethiopia—the stupendous garnets of Fahlun—the delicately-colored fluors and calc-spars of Derbyshire and Cumberland—the gorgeous rubies and sapphires of India and Ceylon——the beautiful prismatic idocrase of Vesuvius and Etna—the splendid amethystine geodes of Oberstein, Siberia, and Spain, little grottoes lined with polished geometrical figures, all declare a common birth as they all nestle in rocks of a common origin. The diamond, the richest as it is the rarest of all, belongs to a totally different class of crystallized bodies, and owes its formation to the agency of entirely different causes.

III. THE DYKES OF VEINS form another striking feature among the geological phenomena of these hills, and seem as if nature intended them for lacings or bands to give greater cohesion and stability to its parts. They consist of long narrow strips of rock, which have made their way through the previously consolidated strata, intersecting the planes of their several beds at nearly right angles, and constituting among themselves a system of parallel and vertical partitions in the rock. Once observed in any district, these dykes are of too marked a character not to excite inquiries as to their uses and mode of formation; and occurring, as they do, in every region and among all classes, from the oldest primary to the newest tertiary deposits, they are obviously designed for some great purpose in the plan of Creation.

Veins may be described as tabular masses that penetrate the earth's crust to an unknown depth, and almost invariably consist of different materials from the rocks they traverse. They are supposed to have all been in a state of fusion, and either themselves to have produced rents and fissures in their pressure upward, or to have filled with their molten ingredients such as from other causes were already existing. When detected in sandstone or other stratified formations, they are readily distinguished, and acknowledged to be of foreign origin as well as of posterior date. The matter of them consists generally, among the secondary formations, of basalt or greenstone; more frequently of porphyry and feldspar among the older and crystalline rocks. In their passage through whinstone the sides of the veins are usually smoothed and polished as if by the action of another body rubbing against them; the sandstones and other sedimentary rocks are indurated, or discoloration may be traced for a considerable space inward from the walls of the vein. There is no mixing up of the materials of the dyke, nor any approach to incorporation with those of the including mass. After exposure on the surface to atmospheric influences, the basalt or greenstone splits up into large tabular blocks, which become extremely friable, and scale off in thin layers, leaving a central ball, which exfoliates in like manner, and gradually molders into dust. These dykes are very numerous in the Grampians, occurring everywhere, and diverging in every direction through the primary rocks. They traverse the lower district on the south of the range, five or six crossing the Tay, and running nearly parallel in a north-westerly course. They rise above the sandstone in various places of Strathearn, forming mural ridges, furrowed into broad jointed masses, or piled loosely above each other. The outgoing of some of these remarkable concretions can be traced into the German ocean. From St. Andrews westward, their line of bearing may be detected, both among the trap-hills and the sandstones which flank them, and like well-run stags, after debouching from the Ochills and Sidlaws, converging upon the forest of Glenartney. Doubling, winding, and dragging out and in among the passes from Crieff to Comrie, two of them may be descried on the steep face of Aberuchill, fairly scaling its lofty summits; and driving onward, may others be observed on the south of the Ruchle, to the far heights of Uam-Var.

The etymology of the term *Ochil*, would seem to be connected in some way with these geological phenomena. A tradition exists that, from time immemorial, the earthquakes of Comrie were cotemporaneous with subterranean movements or noises in the *Ochil* range, near Devon. The Gælic word *ochain*, or *ochail*, signifies, according to Armstrong, "moaning, wailing, howling;" and hence it is inferred that the name of the "Moaning Hills" may have been given to the range, from the sounds so frequently heard in the district. There can be no question as to the probability of a subterranean sympathy betwixt the two localities, through the instrumentality of these dykes, or otherwise; and, though the series of events referred to above belong to an anterior age—far remote, indeed, from the human and all its traditions—a plausible origin is thus given to the name, in connection with an analogous series of events that did happen within the human period.

IV. A vast historical interest, therefore, is to be attached to these hills, and their phenomena of veins, connected as they are with the first elevatory movements of the globe, and when form and outline were being given to its massive fullness. The hand of the Creator is clearly seen in raising them up from the depths below. Not a particle of the entire volume is in its original position, or that which it would of itself statically assume. God formed everything for use, while beauty and agreeableness of shape are inseparably combined. When viewed in the light of causation, it is not enough merely to say, and there to stop short, that we see in the outward face of nature the impress of power, wisdom, and goodness—that none of these things made themselves—that the rocks and mountains are an image of Jehovah's greatness—the streams, plains, trees, corns, animals, the effect of His love and care. All this they unquestionably are, but they are more. Their arrangement and disposition, beside their mere existence, evince a continued superintendence—a purpose and a will to maintain an order and construction of elements which would otherwise separate and dissolve—a keeping together, and as one, each after their own kind, the inorganic and organic parts of creation. The philosophy, as well as theology, of these arrangements have been thus beautifully recorded: Thou coveredst the earth with the deep as with a garment, the waters stood above the mountains; at thy rebuke they fled, at the voice of thy thunder they hastened away into the place thou hast prepared for them. Thou hast set a bound that they may not pass over; that they turn not again to cover the earth.—It is demonstrable that, were all the rocks which compose our mountain ranges and dry land to be dissolved and carried into the sea, the waters of the globe are sufficient again to cover and conceal from view their vast and multiform materials, and to replace them in those depths whence they originally arose.

Dr. Chalmers, in his work on natural theology,[*] has not, we think, correctly apprehended the bearings of the argument for the existence of a God drawn from the fact of the existence of a material world. "We do not perceive," he says, "how, on the observation of an unshapen mass, there can from its *being* alone, be drawn any clear or strong inference in favor of its non-eternity: or that simply because it now is, a time must have been when it was not. We cannot thus read in the entity of matter, a prior non-entity, or an original commencement for it: and something more must be affirmed of matter than merely that it is, ere we can discern that either an artist's mind or an artist's hand has at all been concerned with it." Is this either sound reasoning or good philosophy? The fact of the entity of matter does, necessarily and directly, lead to the inference that it had a beginning. It could not originate itself, and just the more as it is viewed in its mere materiality, so much the stronger and irresistible the conclusion that there was no potentiality inherent in itself to cause it to begin to exist. Strip these hills of all their verdure—remove from the mind all consideration of their beauty, variety, and softness of outline—divest that landscape of its ebb and flow of tide—of all that constitutes the scene one of the most charming on the face of the earth, and in its desolation and sterility you would still in idea revert to a period when it was not. These shapeless, inert, barren masses of rock, and soil, and sand, did not place themselves there by any power of their own. Whether on Mount Horeb or Bencleugh, the mind will learn, from its own inner voice, that the traces of Jehovah are there—a Power, beyond and above, that called these rude piles into being—the absence of all form and vitality in themselves the proof and the witness of the Creator's mind and the Creator's hand. Death cannot originate anything into life. Matter, as matter, cannot constitute nor begin of itself to be. A scene like this could not NOW commence its own being, and at no period in the past did it possess a single property of self-existence. The entity and eternity of matter are, therefore, two physically impossible things, as nothing but the one supreme intelligent God

---

* Works, vol. i, page 189.

can be at once self-existent and eternal, and that which is God cannot be material.

But, if the reasoning here is bad, the philosophy is still worse. It is not philosophy at all to speak of anything in nature as *unshapen.* Matter is never presented to us in its simple elements. What we see of the visible, material world, is something in combination with something else, substance united with substance, and the union and combination are not accidental or chancework. There are law, order, and definite proportion in every compound body. Things go together by determinate arrangement. When first summoned into being, the elements of the universe had each separately their own communicated properties; they took their places in the mass, each according to their natures; and now the little and the great, the bowlder on the heath and the orbs on high, the concrete rock and our whole planetary system, are modeled upon a plan, and all subservient to a purpose. In decomposition none of them waste or decay. Resolved into their primary atoms, they unite in new arrangements, and collect into new bodies; and in the putrid corrupting mass, the law of order, symmetry, and beauty, reigns in active operation, eliminating new structures and establishing new harmonies.

Men have long been acquainted with the fact, that in all combinations of two or more substances, there are certain proportions which obtain among the different ingredients, and that the best mixtures are those which are regulated according to a scale. The arts have flourished, and improved in one age above those in another, just in proportion as this principle has been attended to, and the degree in which the properties of compounds have been ascertained. We hence learn to imitate the crystal in its clearness, and to rival the colors of gems and flowers. The metals are thus tempered for the use and benefit of society. The acids are neutralized, and salts are formed, and the health of man is restored or preserved. Dalton discovered the law of combination in definite and multiple proportions to be constant in the thin air we breathe—that water, in all conditions and situations, consists of the two ingredients oxygen and hydrogen, and that these in weight are always as eight of the former to one of the latter—that even the most elastic gases are composed of particles of real, ponderable, definable matter—and that through all substances, palpable or impalpable, gross or ethereal, the principle of aggregation, according to the atomic theory, is universal. Science has not, indeed, as yet determined what is the law of connection between the chemical composition and the crystalline forms of bodies; although Sir David Brewster has clearly established that there is an exact correspondence between their optical properties and their crystalline forms,—the law of the transmission of light through specific substances. Sir Isaac Newton had long before come to the conclusion—and from the heavens brought down a philosophy to explain the theory of the earth—that "All things considered, it seems probable that God, in the beginning, formed matter in solid, massy, hard, impenetrable particles, of such sizes, figures, and with such other properties, and in such proportion to space, as most conduced to the end for which he formed them; and that these primitive particles, being solids, are incomparably harder than any porous bodies compounded of them; even so very hard as never to wear or break to pieces, no ordinary power being able to divide what God made one in the first creation. Philosophy such as this, verified, much of it, by an induction of rigid experiments, discovers a universe of matter worthy of its author, and like him—a God, not of confusion, but of order; things framed, every one of them, according to rule and method, and all stamped with the indelible impress of utility, design and loveliness. The "unshapen" has no place in the physical world.

"It is not," continues Dr. Chalmers, "from some matter being harder than others, that we infer a God; but when we behold the harder placed where it is obviously the most effective for a beneficial end, as in the nails, and claws, and teeth of animals, in this we see evidence of a God."

Now, this is precisely what has been done in the construction and disposition of the several parts of our planet. The hardest matter is placed where it can subserve a beneficial end, on the bottom of the sea, the shores of a continent, the hills that border the valleys of a country. The framework of the globe is in itself of the most durable materials, and these materials have been all so arranged as to render the earth solid, fertile, and beautiful diversity of climate, combined with diversity of soil, moisture, and shelter. These rocks may have been molten in the depths beneath; but no innate powers of nature raised them unto mountains, and separated the hard from the soft, lifting the heavier substance into the highest places, and scooping out the hollows for the lighter. These are acts, all of them, of divine might, directed to a purpose, and what alone could render this world a fitting abode for living things. Wonderfully made are all the creatures of our earth,—every bone, sinew, and muscle in its appropriate place—and so constructed as best to perform their respective functions. But equally wonderful the adjustment and adaptation, through all its parts, of that earth on which they are domiciled, and which ministers so admirably to the various wants and requirements of its diversified tribes of plants and animals. Not more significant of design, nor more effective for a beneficial end, the bony heads and enameled scales of the finny inhabitants of the period, the cephalaspes and holoptychii of the stratified rocks, than the indurated texture of the traps as a solid casement in which their waters were to be retained, and a storehouse of well-assorted materials, whence substance and nutriment were to be extracted for the land. The argument, in short, so far as fitness and utility are concerned, is one and the same in both classes of objects—the house and its inmates alike illustrative of contrivance and skill—equally eloquent in praise of the artist's mind or the artist's hand.

And in this way it is, that the story of our earth should be read, and the course of creation should be traced. In the first ordering of things, we see the interposition of a great First Cause; and the farther back we go in our geological researches, the more closely do we discern the chain that connects our globe, and all that is in it, with the throne of the Eternal. The everlasting hills, we are constantly reminded in Scripture, are the witnesses of his power. They are appealed to as the evidences of his ever-active, ever-sustaining presence. What wonderful manifestations of his might and wisdom have they been called to testify! Mount Ararat, the symbol of his saving interposition—Mount Sinai, for the giving of the law, and surrounded with the thunder and terror of his great name—Horeb, proclaiming his mercy and the gentleness of his love—Gilboa, drenched in the blood of his swift vengeance —Hermon, a token of the minuteness of his care and the sweetness of his grace—Tabor, Olivet, and Calvary! scenes of the mystery of incarnation and awful purity of inflexible justice.—And these very hills and mountains around, standing memorials through all ages and their revolutions, that at his bidding they arose, and by his sustaining agency they are still upheld and preserved on high.

We regard as utterly untenable the doctrine, therefore, that from the "entity" of matter we cannot infer the existence of a God. Matter, as mere matter, we do not see, and know nothing of. All the matter that is brought under our notice, is either organized or elaborated into arrangement and disposition of parts, as nicely harmonized and adjusted as organic shape and form.—The organic and inorganic structure may differ, but the difference is one of degree, as much as of kind. The argument, from the existence and composition of the atmosphere, the salubrious mixture of gases in the formation of water, the capacity and adaptation of soils for the germination of seeds and the growth of plants, is equally pointed as to the proof of design and beneficial end, as that which is derived from the fleece of the sheep, the feathers of the bird, and the silicious coating of the wheat-stalk. The uses of these things are obvious, and seen and appreciated at once.—But so is every molecule of matter and aggregation of rock, in the largest amorphous mass as in the polished crystallized gem, assimilated by law and indurated for use. And when we see the structure of the entire globe so directly conducive to the well being of its numerously diversified families, we have the argument the same in the WHOLE as in the parts, in the lumpish mass as in the order and symmetry of the bones, muscles, and organs of the animal frame. But for these hills the rain would fall perniciously, and the dews distill in vain. Of what use the return of the seasons, with no variety of climate? and while the ocean encompassed the globe, where would be the courses of the rivers, the mists and exhalations of the valleys? We may often mistake the uses of things, the end and purpose of particular arrangements; but the doctrine of FINAL CAUSES we ought never to leave out of our calculations. They pervade all nature. They permeate all bodies.

The world as constituted, the creation which we contemplate and admire, is in all its parts and dispositions a system of means and ends, a combination of instruments and skillfully-balanced agencies, a bright ever-discoursing record of the Eternal Mind, which yet shrouds itself in light inaccessible and utterly unfathomable to the comprehension of all created, finite intelligences, whether human or angelic.

Thus geology takes us up to the beginnings of creation—shows us the ingredients and arrangements of matter—lays bare the foundations of our earthly dwelling, the divisions and conveniences of its apartments—and seeing wisdom in adaptation, design in endurance and suitability, we infer, upon equally irresistible grounds, that the earth is of God, and manifests in everything the perfections of its Author. The SCHEME of creation, in all its parts and relations, we may never know; its course and order we can distinctly trace through many of its arrangements.

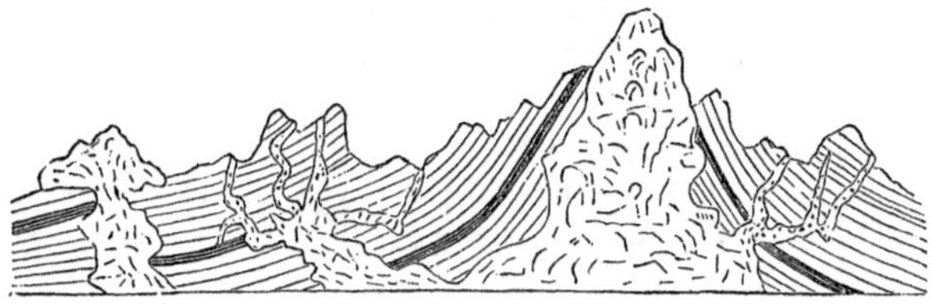

Relative Positions of Trap.

# CHAPTER VII.

## THE CARBONIFEROUS SYSTEM—PERIOD OF GIGANTIC VEGETABLES.

THE system of rocks termed the Carboniferous constitutes the most remarkable, as well as the most valuable, group in the whole range of geological investigation. The strata of which this system is composed, evince design in the clearest and the most unequivocal manner, testifying to the mandate given on the third day of Creation, that the earth was to bring forth grass, the herb yielding seed, and the fruit-tree yielding fruit after its kind; and which, in the prodigious development of vegetable matter that so early and rapidly ensued, demonstrate such productive powers of nature to have been chiefly prospective, and preparatory to the still higher development of life that was to follow.

Milton has finely imagined a tradition in heaven, long subsisting, concerning the creation of a new world, and of man for whose habitation it was intended:

> "Space may produce new worlds, whereof so rife,
> There went a fame in heaven, that He ere long
> Intended to create, and therein plant
> A generation, whom his choice regard
> Should favor equal to the sons of heaven;
> The happy seat
> Of some new race, called Man."

The idea here so beautifully expressed is, that the cosmical arrangements of the earth were, from the beginning, so conducted as to be subservient to man's well-being; and, certainly, nothing could show more the dignity of the new race, or the interest taken in them by their Creator, than this tradition which ran of them in other spheres. But geology, more to be relied on than poetry, furnishes demonstrative evidence of the anterior designs and purposes of Omnipotent Wisdom in actually fitting up "the happy seat," and in storing it beforehand with materials suited to the wants and comfortable subsistence of him who was to be its loftiest inhabitant. The coal-metals, in the discovery of their history and position, alone vindicate the importance of geology as a science. The whole group with which they are associated, in their mineral and vegetable contents, their place in the system, and the means provided at once for protection and excavation, manifest a series of contrivances so expressive of design, as cannot fail, when read aright, to draw forth our gratitude and wonder.

I. The Mineral Ingredients, Position, and Arrangement of the Carboniferous System.—The rocks belonging to this formation, in the order of superposition, succeed the old red sandstone, consisting of a series of deposits of great thickness, of an infinite number of alternations and varieties, and nearly the same in every coal-field all over the earth. They constitute one great group of marked physical characters, formed under similar conditions, and produced during the same epoch or period of time. The out-crop of the beds meets the eye along the ridge of which the Lomonds may be taken as the center, ranging eastward by St. Andrews to Fifeness Point, and extending indefinitely westward by Stirling, Campsie Hills, Port-Glasgow, to the coast of Arran. The southern lip of the great coal basin of Scotland stretches from the German Ocean, near Dunbar, to the Ayrshire coast in the North Channel, flanked by the old red sandstone and Silurian rocks almost continuously throughout. And within the space now indicated are situated all the principal coal-fields of the northern part of the empire.

The lower beds of the formation consist generally of coarse-grained sandstone, termed by the English geologists millstone grit, and inclose a few thin unworkable seams of coal. Bands of ironstone, shale, and sandstone are superimposed in repeated alternations. A thick massive limestone lines the edges, feathering in and out through the area of the basin which contains the coal metals. This is the mountain limestone, the most of which is supposed to have once existed as coral reefs, raised on the bottom of shallow seas, so subdivided as to form suitable compartments for receiving and retaining the matter of the coal. Accordingly, corals, encrinites, and shells everywhere prevail in the rocks of this deposit, and, in some instances, present the appearance of a homogeneous, agglutinated mass of the remains of these marine animals—the first of living creatures which the waters were charged to bring forth, and with which they were now swarming. The bituminous beds, the true coal, generally occupy a central position in the group, firmly caked and inclosed between the arenaceous and shaly strata. The number of seams vary in different basins, ranging in Scotland from eleven to thirty-two or thirty-three, and comprising an average thickness of the useful mineral of a hundred and twenty feet. The varieties of coal—as anthracite or blind-coal, cannel or parrot, and the common house or glance-coal—are occasioned chiefly by the different proportions of the bituminous elements which enter into their composition. Compared with Scotland, the coal-measures of England and Wales are of a greater average thickness, lie far beneath the surface, and contain in general a greater proportion of bitumen.

The basin containing the coals, as defined above, is inclosed within the great chains of primary and secondary mountains of the central district of Scotland, which were upheaved into dry land before the coal-measures were formed. A period of violent disturbance had thus passed away, when the carboniferous formation bears evident tokens of having been begun and completed in tranquil waters. But after being collected, the coal-metals were exposed to the action of disturbing forces: eruptive masses, of igneous origin, have invaded their domain; basalts and greenstone, trap dykes and veins, are everywhere found within their inclosure; and apparently the utmost disorder and irregularity now reign, where order and stillness once prevailed. But look a little closer: examine the length and breadth of any coal-field in any part of the world, and you will discern proofs of a purpose, not only in the quality of their materials, but in the position, arrangement, and grouping of the metals; those very disturbing forces, to which they and all earthly things have been exposed, giving unequivocal testimony of an overruling intelligence continuing, through all ages, to superintend and guide their various operations.

Study any coal-field in your neighborhood, and observe *the place* of the mineral. It does not lie exposed upon the surface, but is placed at a considerable depth in the earth; of which many are apt to complain, thinking that, if a different arrangement had prevailed, much needless labor and expense would have been saved. But the constituent elements of coal are such, that by exposure on the surface the mineral would, in a comparatively short period of time, have run to waste and decay. Even a thick covering of earthy mold would not have been sufficient to protect it; and therefore was the treasure purposely hid in the earth, and so inclosed that the floods could not wash it away. Then consider the *quality* of the rocks by which the coal is protected, and along with which it is invariably associated. These consist of limestone, sandstone, shale, and clay ironstone, which always occupy the same basins, and alternate with the coal sometimes in a series of more than a hundred beds. Such a group of well-characterized rocks not only act as a guide for determining the localities of the valuable mineral, but they serve the double purpose of facilitating the excavation, by affording at once a safe roofing to the mine, and an easy passage for the drainage of the water which accumulates in the pits. No other class of rocks would have been so suitable. The granite and crystalline rocks would have been inconvenient, or wholly unfit: no borings could have been effected through such materials to any extent; the operations underneath would have been equally difficult and unmanageable; and through such hard compact substances the drainage must have been impracticable. But a still more remarkable indication of contrivance arises from *the elevated* and *inclined position* into which the coal strata have been thrown. Had they remained in the position which they originally occupied, and been covered with the vast accumulations which have subsequently taken place, their depth would have been utterly beyond the industry of man to have reached. Hence the waters have disappeared, having accomplished the purpose for which they were, in this instance, spread over the earth, and the rocks formed beneath them have lifted up their heads; not uniformly, or in one continuous unbroken mass, but divided into small sections, and inclined in every possible direction. The wisdom of this appears from two considerations: From their inclined position, the various beds of coal are worked with greater facility than if they had been horizontal, a *level* is produced for the drainage of the water, and the edges of the coal bent upward are brought nearer the surface. But these advantages are, every one of them, increased incalculably by the division of the coal-field into limited sections, whereby less water is allowed to accumulate than if the beds had been indefinitely extended; their lower extremities are prevented from being plunged to a depth that would be inaccessible; and their several portions arranged in a series of tables, like the steps of a stair, rising one behind another, and gradually inclining outward from the lower to the upper seams of the basin. Again, every coal-field is furnished with a system of checks, in the shape of *faults* or *dykes*, against floodings, fire-blaze, and other accidents that occur in the operations of mining. These faults or dykes consist of clay, the detritus of the associated rocks, or of intruded whinstone, with which the fractures produced at the period of the disruption and elevation of the coal-field have been filled up, and the various sections of the metal insulated, and contracted to more workable dimensions. They present the appearance of a vertical wall, cutting the strata at right angles; and, though often occasioning much inconvenience and interruption, yet, as every experienced collier well knows, forming upon the whole his greatest safeguard, and essential every way to his operations. To all which add, as *constants* in every coal-field, the minerals of lime and iron, gifts, both of them, of inestimable value: the former in the amelioration of the soil and construction of every social edifice; the latter ductile and plastic as wax, capable of being welded, and yet, by a slight chemical change, possessed of adamantine hardness; and the coal always there, in juxta-position, to serve as a fuel for the reduction of the limestone and ironstone into their economic properties—properties starting into agency as if by a miracle.

These are a few of the facts connected with the arrangement and distribution of the coal-measures, in whatever quarter of the globe they are found. Is it possible to resist the conclusion, that, in such a disposition of things, there are the clearest indications of contrivance and design? Nay, that the argument derived from the construction and positions of the solid parts of the earth is the same in kind, if not in degree, with that which is so irresistibly demonstrative in the case of the organic structure of the living frame? The dance of atoms imagined by the philosopher of antiquity, could never have terminated in the perfect order and harmony of the heavenly bodies—innumerable systems of worlds maintained,—each hung upon nothing, and duly preserved all of them in their respective spheres. Equally impossible is it to contemplate a disposition of things so adapted, and indeed so indispensable, for availing ourselves of the mineral treasures of the earth—essential to our wants, and ministering so directly to our social comfort and improvement—and yet to refer the whole, or any part, to the blind operation of fortuitous causes. Impossible, indeed, it ever will be, for the human mind to embrace or unravel all the mysteries of creation; but thus admitted to the mighty wonders of the interior, we are almost enabled to trace the history of the moving atoms from their chaotic disorder into their places and arrangement in the visible universe—to see dead matter assuming the forms of life and organization—clothing the earth for a season with luxuriance and beauty—buried for ages under the solid rock—and again, out of coldness and death, affording light, and warmth, and power to the successive generations of men.

II. Origin of the Carboniferous Rocks.—The strata comprised within the coal-measures are variously estimated; being, in some instances, about eleven thousand feet in thickness; in other cases, of much greater depth; and of this mass of matter, the coal itself does not occupy more than a maximum average of one hundred and fifty feet. The shales consist of thin beds of mud, washed down by the rivers from the neighboring heights, and would appear to have formed the soil on which subsisted a rank vegetation; the impressions of plants, roots, and trunks of trees being still found in a standing position. It is from these bands of mudstone that the best specimens of the flora of the period are derived; every thin splitting presenting the most entire and beautifully-preserved figures of fronds and stems. The ironstone is usually mixed up or associated with the shales, and consists, like them, of comparatively thin beds of ferruginous clay. The sandstones, of which the greater proportion of the mass consists, have clearly resulted in the continued action of the same causes that produced the old red deposit of the anterior period. But the two remarkable products of the age are the calcareous and coaly strata, which give character to the system as well as the epoch in which they were formed; the one showing a sudden development of carbonate of lime, and the other an increase of vegetable matter, whose enduring monuments point them out as the most striking cotemporaneous and co-extensive formations on the surface of the globe, or connected with the history of our planet. The bituminous products of the Silurian period, if the anachronism may be pardoned, are but as the gleanings after the full harvest.

The limestone is unquestionably of marine origin, as the countless myriads of testacea inclosed in it testify, and was probably constructed by the primeval families of those island-making architects by which the coral-reefs of our present seas are raised, and whose instincts have found them similar employment in all ages of the world. The limestones of the earlier systems may have been formed in the same manner; and then, as in the subsequent period, we must go to the great original storehouse of Nature for the materials on which they worked. The spoils of the primary rocks could not supply them, as the quantity of the carbonate of lime therein contained bears no proportion to the masses which constitute the mountain limestone group. But the calcareous substance was already, in some elementary form, in combination or otherwise, in existence—the animals capable of secreting and arranging it anew, as the secondary instruments of creation, were abounding in the seas—shallow bottoms over the subjacent sandstones of the devonian system, and within the required conditions of life, were prepared for their operations. The waters had now brought forth abundantly the moving creatures, which, at first more scantily distributed, produced the limestone of the silurian rocks, as the arborial remains of the land, in like stinted measure, are inclosed in the older palæozoic deposits. Their day of increase as it advanced, each after their kind, is recorded in the vast accumulations of animal and vegetable matter which compose the strata of the carboniferous system, both of an order and quality purposely so arranged, and never upon the same scale of magnitude to be repeated in the combustible mineral.

This account, as given by geologists, of the origin of the mountain limestone, is rendered not only probable, but almost certain, by the manner in which we find these little insects, the coral-builders, constructing their piles of masonry at the present day. For example, certain species of polyps, of solitary habits, work alone, each rearing a single stem or stalk, from which others project; then more stems are produced, until, upon the completion of the whole, there results one of those beautiful arborescent structures so much prized as ornaments for cabinets and drawing-rooms. Some, again, attach themselves to the loose stones, upon which they form their little tree or flower-top; others adhere to the solid rock, from which there springs a stony vegetation, rivaling often, in variety, luxuriance, and brilliancy, the most showy vegetable productions of tropical climes. But a certain class are gregarious, and will only work in company. Myriads of these inhabit the Pacific, constructing entire islands, and throwing up mighty barriers of rock, and threading over vast areas of the sea with inosculating lines of coral reef. The calcareous accumulation, known as the Great Barrier Reef, extends for about a thousand miles in length, by about thirty in mean breadth, filling up, with its various reticulations, the whole intermediate space betwixt the coast of Australia and Bristow Island, off the coast of New Guinea. The works of these minute creatures thus occupy an area which may be roughly estimated at thirty thousand square miles; the different branches forming compartments of variable extent, which are divided into linear, outer, and inner reefs, and embracing within their ample folds the entire spoils of ocean living or floating in these parts.

The mountain limestone of our own country, formed in like manner on the sea-bottom of corallines, has a wide geographical range, extending from the bay of St. Andrew's on the north, to the extremity of Wales on the south; passing into Ireland, where it is elevated into long ridges, or occupies the mountain-slopes; and forming outliers or extended barriers in all the southern counties of Scotland, and in the greater portion of the northern, the middle, and the south-western districts of England. These were the coral reefs of an ocean now raised into dry land, divided, too, into outer and inner compartments, or arranged into systems of lines and branches, which diverged from or inosculated with each other. Nor does the resemblance between the recent and the more ancient formations stop here, but extends to the structure of the deposits, lithologically considered, the mechanical, sub-crystalline, and crystalline texture being exhibited in both sets of rocks. Thus, in the examination of Heron Island, the coral beds, one to two feet thick, are found to have a tendency to split into slabs, and joints are observed to cross each other at right angles, parallel to the dip and strike, respectively, giving to the still living coral rock the jointings, cleavage, and stratification of the greater palæozoic deposits. Naturalists divide these polyps into existing and extinct races. But whether extinct and specifically different, or otherwise, they are creatures of a family, possessed of the same habits and performing the same operations, now as of old; and if, as geologists say, millions of ages have elapsed between the actings of the first and last generations, our admiration will be only all the more unbounded by thus witnessing the harmony of creation through indefinite time, and the accuracy of the Book which contains the record of it.

The coal itself, as now universally admitted, is of vegetable origin. Under the microscope, in the most compact specimens, the tissues by which all the coal plants are more or less distinguished can be distinctly traced. Chemically considered, its vegetable origin is equally well established. Carbon constitutes the principal ingredient of the mineral the quality of which enters most abundantly into the composition of vegetables. One theory of its formation is, that vegetable matter, carried to the sea or extensive lakes, has undergone a process of decomposition, by which, while some of its principles may have escaped or been evolved in new combinations, the carbon, with a portion of the hydrogen, has remained; this, mixed with more or less earthy matter, has in its soft state been consolidated by the force of aggregation simply, or by compression from the superincumbent strata, and the action of a higher degree of temperature than now exists. Others are of opinion that coal is the altered residuum of trees and smaller plants that have grown on the spot where we now find them—that the forests were submerged and covered by detrital matter, which was upraised to form a foundation and a soil for another forest, to be in its turn submerged and converted into coal—and that thus the alternations which the vertical section of a coal-field exhibits are to be accounted for. The former views are maintained by Sir R. Murchison and other eminent geologists. The latter have been adopted by Sir Charles Lyell, in consequence mainly of the arrangements and structure observed in the remarkable coal-field of Nova Scotia, where he states that there is a range of perpendicular cliffs in the Bay of Fundy, composed of regular coal-measures, inclined at an angle between twenty-four and thirty degrees, whose united thickness is between four and five miles. By neither theory, perhaps, nor by any other yet advanced, is it possible to reconcile all the appearances which that singular compound, a COAL-FIELD exhibits—the various changes which the vegetable matter has undergone to convert it into lignite, jet, common coal, cannel coal, and anthracite, two or more of these varieties often occurring in the same coal-measures—in one quarter the clearest indications that the sea has let in its floods and mingled its spoils with those of the land, and in another quarter, through fourteen thousand feet, for example, of the drift accumulations in Nova Scotia, that there is not a trace even of any substance of a *marine* character, all appearing to have been deposited in fresh water. But while no explanation yet given of the phenomena can be regarded as satisfactory, while Nature withholds much, and ever will, of the wonderful processes through which she attains her ends, the vegetable source of the product cannot be questioned; nay, the origin of coal from the extinct forests, from the trees and plants of a former age, is so very probable, that some beds sound like wood under the beat of the hammer; and large areas, when thin slices are placed under the microscope, are found in every portion to retain the woody-fibrous structure.

III. The BOTANICAL CHARACTERS of the flora of the coal period form of themselves an interesting subject of study, and suggest some very important considerations as to the history and purpose of the formation. These will be best understood by a reference to the structure and habits of plants in general. Those of the coal, it will thence be seen, belong exclusively to one or two families,—as ferns, palms, and coniferæ,—which seem to have grown in every soil, and to have been adapted to every climate.

The most general divisions of existing plants are into the *vasculares* and *cellulares*. The former kinds all bear flowers, possess a system of spiral vessels, and are termed phonogamous. The latter, on the other hand, are flowerless, have no spiral vessels, and are denominated cryptogamous.

Another extensive subdivision of plants proceeds upon their anatomical structure, and the laws which regulate their mode of growth. Thus one class, it has been observed, increase in bulk by additional increments to the outside of all the parts which compose the plant, as the roots, stems, and branches; another, by additions to the inside of all these members: and for this reason the former are called exogenous, and the latter endogenous. In the one case the new or youngest growth is always exterior to the old; and if thus left unprotected, it will be readily admitted that the growth of all such plants would be greatly and constantly endangered by atmospheric as well as innumerable other causes. The remedy provided by nature against this, is a covering of the substance called bark, which is folded round the entire exterior, stem and branches, of the whole exogens, and within which the newly-formed tissue is all safely deposited. No plant, on the other hand, whose growth is from within, needs any such protection, and accordingly none of them—as all the grasses, corns, canes, and fungi—are possessed of bark, or any analogous membrane. The bark is an ephemeral substance, which lasts only for a year, and has annually to be renewed.

The additions to all exogenous plants are indicated in the stem or trunk, by concentric lines or circles. In the center there is a cellular substance called pith. When you take, therefore, a cross section of the trunk of this class, the structure and parts will be arranged thus—bark on the outside, pith in the center, and between these, concentric deposits of woody matter, and all connected into a solid mass by plates of comb-like tissue, radiating from the interior to the circumference, and termed medullary rays. A structure like this, so closely and firmly united, and filled up through all its parts, was surely intended for endurance; and yet out of this class of the vegetable tribes, nature has selected few of her carboniferous models. The plants of the period, as yet detected, are composed chiefly of cellular tissue, mixed up with the substance of the stem, and without pith, medullary rays, concentric woody deposits, or the binding ligament of bark. The hardy oak and tall slender cane may be taken as examples of the two modes of structure—the former allied to existing, the latter to extinct families.

Another ground of distinction among plants consists in the leaves or flattened expansions, from which they derive all their grace and symmetry. This is farther connected with the seed and rudimentary organs, and gives rise to the division into *cotyledonous* and *acotyledonous* plants. The non-flowering or cryptogamous are all of the latter kind. The flowering or phonogamous not only belong to the former, but are again subdivided into monocotyledonous or dicotyledonous, according as their seed-vessels are possessed of one or of two lobes. Where there are two lobes the expansion of the germ upon bursting from the ground terminates in two imperfect leaves, by which the botanist can at once determine the class to which it belongs. The corns and grasses have single cotyledons, from one extremity of which descend the roots, and from the other the stem springs up, terminated with a single leaf.

The leaves perform important functions in all those orders of plants with which they are connected, and serve as interesting guides in fossil botany, which seldom derives any assistance from the more destructible and "fleeting flower." The leaves of plants consist of a complicated net-work of vessels, filled up in the interstices by cellular tissue, and covered over with a thin epidermis or skin. Those belonging to the monocotyledonous sub-class are traversed by a number of parallel veins, while dicotyledonous leaves are divided into regular compartments, some of which upon withering display the most perfect and beautiful system of reticulation, rivaling in delicacy of texture the wing of the gossamer. Leaves which outlast the season, as in evergreens, are termed non-deciduous, and are covered or interwoven with a thin crust of silex, which at once serves to protect and communicate to these ornamental shrubs their bright enameled appearance. The grasses possess this property, and some of them can elaborate in their joints crystals of considerable magnitude. The leaves of ferns are called fronds, and differ from true leaves in bearing the reproductive organs on the surface, while the slightest inspection of their form and mode of expansion readily distinguishes them from all others. Fronds, properly so termed, originate in the stem and are part of it; there is no distinct line of demarkation between them: stem, leaf, and spori, or seed, are all as one body; and thus, as being of one piece, these membranous organs have been quaintly likened to a garment without a seam.

From this brief description it will be seen that all plants and trees arrange themselves under two great classes, namely, the soft and spongy, or the hard and fibrous-woody structure. The remains of such as have been detected in the carboniferous rocks belong almost exclusively to the former class, the cryptogamiæ and endogenæ, while of the three hundred and upward of fossil species which have been described and figured, not more than ten, and some of these still of doubtful characters, can be regarded as of exogenous and true woody growth. Ferns, mosses, palms, and gigantic succulent plants, now all allied to those of tropical climates, constitute the vast preponderancy of the fossil flora of the age in question. Are we to infer from this that the other families and tribes which at present so abundantly cover the earth were not then in existence? The botanist can now refer to his catalogue of eighty to a hundred thousand species of existing plants, growing in the different regions of the globe, and of widely distinguished habits and forms; and were few or none of these in being then? We possess not, as yet, sufficient data for the solution of this very interesting problem, although in the progress of geological discovery, every year is adding to the list, and giving us a more extended acquaintance with the vegetable products of the coal period. An important experiment recently made by Professor Lindley would seem to favor the probability that a far more numerically abundant flora had then existed. One hundred and seventy plants were thrown into a vessel containing fresh water, and among them were species belonging to all the natural orders of which the flora of the coal-measures consists, and also to other natural orders which it might have been expected would be found associated with them. In the course of two years, one hundred and twenty-one species had disappeared, being entirely decomposed, and of the fifty which remained, the most perfect specimens were those of coniferous plants, ferns, palms, lycopodiaceæ, and the like—the families, all of them, most allied to those preserved in the coal-measures.

Now the important fact to be attended to in this experiment is, the wide geographical distribution during the carboniferous era of those tribes of plants which enter most certainly and abundantly into the composition of the coal metals. Many others may, and doubtless did, flourish within the period of the formation. But that the plants, possessed of the most conservative vegetable qualities, and the most capable of resisting solution in water, should be precisely the kinds which had then a universal range over the earth's surface, can be ascribed to nothing else than to a wise predetermined purpose and arrangement. These plants were growing in every region. Every clime favored them—every soil nourished them. The bituminous product was intended for man's use, whose family was destined to inhabit the whole earth. How irresistible the conclusion, corroborative of all the proofs of design derived from the nature and structure of the coal-measures, that, anticipating his wants and providing for his improvement, nature purposely constructed such forms of vegetable life, possessed, like the watch, with a compensation balance so as to suit every condition, and to thrive in every land; or, what is equally probable and consonant to the requirements of the problem, that there was such a uniformity of climate and temperature, and other chemical adjustments, as were most adapted to the peculiar and prevailing vegetation of the period.

IV. The Organic Remains we proceed to consider more in detail, where a remarkable contrast will be observed between the vegetable and animal types presented, so far as they have been respectively fossilized and preserved. The vegetables are nearly all of terrestrial, the animals are as generally and predominantly of marine, characters. Is this the result of blind chance, or of contrivance and foresight?

The plants of the coal epoch consist chiefly of the cryptogamia, and of these the ferns are the most abundant, composing, according to the estimate of M. Brongniart, about two-thirds of the entire carboniferous flora.

The number of known existing ferns amounts to between seven and eight hundred, of which about fifty species belong to Great Britain, and upward of two hundred to the inter-tropical island of Jamaica. Nearly two hundred fossil species have been discovered in the British coal strata alone. The fossil genera most common to the district around, and occurring in every section of the great valley of the Scottish lowlands, are cyclopteris, neuropteris, pecop-

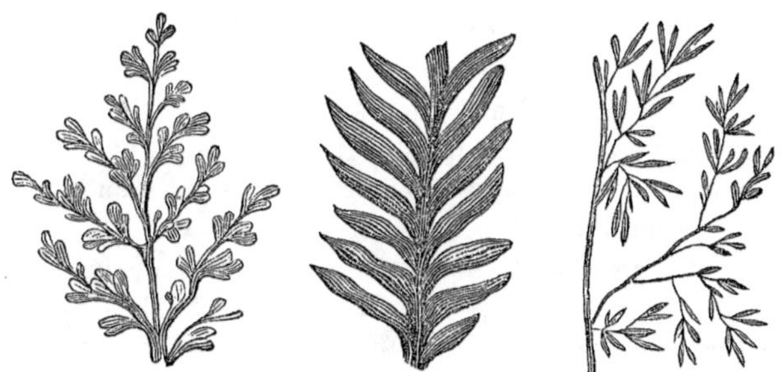

1. Sphenopteris linearis; 2. Pecopteris Mantelli; 3. Sphenopteris affinis.

teris, and sphenopteris. The shales and clay-ironstones in which these beautiful plants are detected, are generally of a dark brownish color, while the impressions are all of the deepest jet, bringing out in lively contrast the complete cast of the fronds. There is a great resemblance between the specimens of extinct ferns and the existing families of our filices, now growing on every hill, brae, or mountain corrie; and, if this were all the difference, nature would seem to have departed but little from her original models. But the presumption is that most, if not all, the ferns of the coal era were trees which attained to a great height, and similar to the tree-ferns now growing so abundantly in the islands of the Pacific. The decorticated stems and trunks are deeply indented with scars, the markings, it is supposed, of the fronds which dropped from their feathery sides. This inference is borne out by the additional circumstance, that the fossils are generally much flattened and compressed, as would necessarily happen to succulent plants and such trees as consisted of the cellular tissue of the endogenous class. What a striking change in the vegetation of our country, where purple heaths, and cheerful grasses, and luxuriant corns, and forests of every tint and structure, have replaced the long green stems, and dark somber hues of the fern-clad regions of the olden times! The remains of this tribe are so numerous as to have stinted, one would suppose, or utterly to have prevented the growth and increase of every other order of plants, bringing before the imagination the scenes of our Australian colonies, so wild and wondrous to European eyes—and carrying back the mind to the vision of primeval ages, through a long succession of times and their events, the vista of an infant world.

The lycopodia, or club-moss tribe, are also very widely distributed among the coal-measures, and attained in the earlier ages of the earth's history an equally gigantic size with the tree-ferns. At the present day, they are all weak, prostrate plants, of from two to three feet in length, and, following the same laws as the mosses and ferns, they are most abundant in hot, humid situations within the tropics, and especially in the smaller islands. As respects their botanical affinities, the lycopodiums are intermediate between ferns and coniferæ on the one hand, and ferns and mosses on the other; related to the first of those families in the abundance of annular ducts contained in their axis, and to the second in the whole aspect and outline of the stem of the larger kinds. Indeed, so great is the resemblance between lycopodia and certain coniferæ, that there is no other external character, except size, by which they can be distinguished; and, according to Professor Lindley, it is, at least, as probable that some of those specimens detected in the ancient flora of the world, which have been considered gigantic club-mosses, are really and truly pines, as that they are flowerless plants.

Another family of fossil plants abundant in the coal formation are the calamites, so named from their jointed reed-like structure. They attained to the size of trees, trunks upward of a foot in diameter being often met with, but still of such a soft succulent texture as to maintain the character of being, if reeds, easily shaken by the winds. These, and various specimens of the palm tribe, are to be found in every coal-field, and often in such vast masses as to show that they constituted no inconsiderable proportion of the flora of the period. Palms now only flourish within the regions of the tropics, where, from their various properties, as well as great productiveness as fruit-bearers, they constitute the chief source of dependence to the inhabitants for all their supplies of the necessaries, luxuries, and medicines of life. A single spathe of the date contains about 12,000 male flowers: another species has been computed to have 207,000 in a spathe, or 600,000 upon a single individual. The spathe constitutes the raceme or flower-stem of the tree, and on a single raceme of a Seje palm, Humboldt estimated the flowers at forty-four thousand, and the fruits at eight thousand. When these magnificent productions of nature covered the plains and marshes of our northern climes, there were no roaming tribes to gather their fruits, inhale their fragrance, or bask in their shades. And yet they were not formed in vain. Buried in the rocks, their collected remains now yield a product as useful and valuable to the human family—as contributive to intellectual improvement, as they would have been to mere animal enjoyment.

The genus sigillaria, one of the most common of the coal plants, possessed the singular properties of being apparently hollow in the center, yet with an inner woody axis floating in a woody succulent jelly, and inclosed in a thick outer coating of bark. The trunk is beautifully fluted with longitudinal parallel lines, regularly arranged along the surface, and dotted all over with small scars, as if impressed by the leaves penetrating through the bark into the central woody axis. The stigmariæ, once supposed to be a distinct genus, are now generally regarded as simply the roots of the sigillariæ; they are, for the most part, found resting in their natural position, in large clusters often; and forming with their dense matted fibers a floor of considerable thickness, on which, season after season, the leaves fell as the coaly matter accumulated. This tree grew to an enormous size, specimens of four feet in diameter by fifty feet in length being frequently met with; traces of a vascular and fibrous structure can be observed in the stems—also the annular wood layers are sometimes beautifully defined; and, combined with a coating of bark of an inch in thickness, the probability is, that the sigillaria belonged to the exogenous class of vegetables.

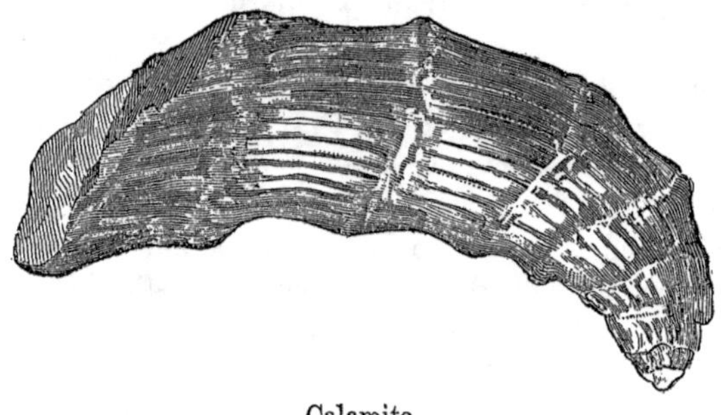

Calamite.

But of all the plants found in the coal-measures, the CONIFERÆ or pine tribe, distinguished by their punctated woody tissue, are the most interesting, whether we consider their characteristic properties, extensive distribution, antiquity, and consistency of habit through all the epochs and changes of creation. Unlike the tree-forms already noticed, the pines grow now as they grew before, inhabiting the same places, and preserving the same appearances in bulk and figure. In structure the coniferæ occupy a place intermediate between cellurares and vasculares, connected with the former through the lycopodiums, and with the latter by the myriceæ, or aromatic gale tribe. The scales of the cones are regarded by botanists as true foliage or reduced leaves, and in this respect they approximate to the genus zamia, of the order cycadeæ, where these organs are distinctly developed as carpellary leaves. Thus widely connected through the chain of vegetable life, the fossil pines, discovered in our coal-fields, form also the most interesting link between the present and the remote past, showing similar conditions of vegetable existence and forest landscape. No class of plants have been more useful to man than the whole pine family; none are more universal in their distribution over the face of the globe; none are possessed of such powers of endurance, existing through all time, and natives of every part of the world, from the perpetual snows of Arctic America, to the hottest regions of the Indian Archipelago. These trees differ as remarkably in form as in size, ranging through every gradation from the stinted juniper of the Grampians to the stately cedars of Lebanon. And the fossil specimens, huge in dimensions as those of Craigleith are, do not excel the existing races. The araucaria, or Norfolk Island pine, attains a height of two hundred feet; and in the Oregon territory of North-West America, there are species of the fir tribe (P. Lambertiana and P. Douglasii), which rise to even still more gigantic proportions. Figuratively, it is said of the cedar, that its branches shall cover the earth, and in the shadow thereof all fowl of every wing shall dwell: literally and truly we find, that members of the same family have existed in all lands, and flourished in the mountains through all ages.

Compared with the present condition of things, New Zealand bears the most striking resemblance in the character of its vegetation to the flora of the ancient carboniferous age. "The number of species of plants at present known is 632, of which 314 are dicotyledonous, and the rest, or 318, are monocotyledonous and cellular. The number of monocotyledonous is very small in comparison with the cellular; there are 76 species. The grasses have given way to ferns, for the ferns and fern-like plants are the most numerous in New Zealand, and cover immense districts. They replace the *gramineæ* or grasses of other countries, and give a character to all the open land of the hills and plains. Some of the arborescent species grow to thirty feet and more in height, and the variety and elegance of their forms, from the minutest species to the giants of their kind, are most remarkable."*

These few types of the flora of the ancient world clearly indicate the course and progress of creation. A dense vegetable covering already existed over all the earth. No grasses, indeed, as yet are found to have clothed the plains. But marsh plants grew luxuriantly in the waters. Fucoids and algæ abounded in the seas. The hills and mountains raised high in air their pines, palms, and fern-trees; nor would creepers and parasites be wanting, climbing to their topmost branches and mingling their bright

* Dr. Dieffenbach's New Zealand.

enlivening hues with the dark somber shades of the forest. Earth heard the voice of its Maker, and everything good and seasonable sprang from its teeming bosom.

The carboniferous limestones are everywhere loaded with ANIMAL remains. Every member of the series, the ironstones, sandstones, shales, and even the coal itself, all abound in relics of the past; and, as was to be expected, the fossils chiefly belong to marine forms of life. And in these there is no great departure, as might likewise be inferred, from the orders, and even generic types, we have been surveying in the lower formations. But there is an increase in the species of some of them, as well as the introduction of new and distinct creations altogether.

Thus the corals and encrinites remain with scarcely a change in outward form, but of increasing variety, and in countless myriads. The trilobites are nearly extinct, while the annelidæ, which appear not in the devonian system, return to the stage in greater numbers and diversity of structure. The conchiferæ are likewise enlarged in every order; as also the crustaceæ, which are more than quadrupled. Pteropodæ present four genera in the silurian group, decline to one in the devonian, which genus is not found in the carboniferous, but a new one takes its place. The brachiopodæ are again very abundant, as they were in the two former groups. The most characteristic shells of the order and period are the productus, spirifer, terebratula. One genus

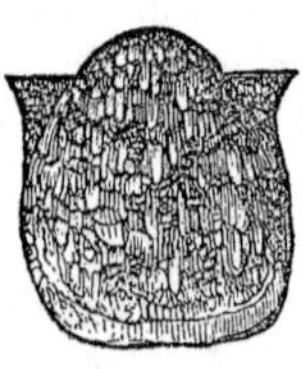

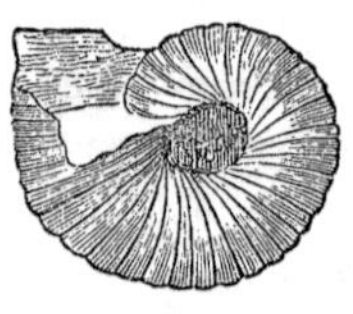

1. Product. scabriculus ; 2. Inoceramus vetustus; 3. Bellerophon tangentialis.

of heteropoda, the bellerophon, appeared in the silurian rocks, of which there were eleven species. Eight species occur in the devonian system along with a new genus, porcellia. The bellerophon numbers nineteen species in the carboniferous rocks, and the porcellia, which occurs also, contains three.

The cephalapods, the most predaceous of their kind, lose generically, while they multiply prodigiously in species during the latter epoch. Thus the goniatites alone amount to fifty-four, the nautili to forty-two, and the orthoceratites, which had declined to twelve in the devonian, swell to thirty-two species in the carboniferous series.

But the fishes in this group of rocks exhibit, unquestionably, the largest amount, both in number and form, of new types. Here the sharks and sauroids appear, for the first time, not small, or attenuated in bulk, but vigorous, robust specimens of their kind, strong and expert swimmers, armed with enlarged destructive organs, and every way equipped for maintaining the due proportion of numbers, and the free trade of the ocean. Thus of the order of placoids, there are twenty-eight genera, and ninety-four species; of ganoids there are five genera, and twelve species; and sauroids enumerate thirteen genera, and twenty-four distinct and entirely new specific creations. A specimen of reptilian life has here also been detected; and what is of still greater theoretic importance, in tracing the course of creation, the immediately overlying sandstones have yielded up impressions of the winged tribes that "fly in the open firmament of heaven." This interesting fact will, in its proper place in the order of superposition, be more fully alluded to.

The genus holoptychius, which began in the old red sandstone, again occurs in the carboniferous system, under eight new specific forms. Along with the megalichthys, afterward noticed, these constitute the two great natural families of fishes of carnivorous propensities, which give a marked character to the period. The prodigious increase of the shark-like creatures, of which not less than sixty species have been described from thousands of teeth, fins, detached vertebræ, and other fragments, is equally striking. Thus, in all, the faunæ of the carboniferous period amount to upward of a thousand species, which have been either figured or described.

In contemplating the period of creation under review, we are struck not more with the forms of life which actually existed, than with the absence of races which were afterward so abundant.

No quadruped or true terrestrial animal is found so low in the series of rocks, or mixed up in any way with all this profusion of marine exuviæ. Fossil insects and indications of other winged tribes have been detected; but no bone nor foot-print of beast, or inhabitant of land, has anywhere been discovered. The fact is all-important, as showing not only a plan, but a progress and succession in the work of creation. A vegetation, so rank and luxuriant as has been traced, trees towering hundreds of feet into the sky, and branches of the densest foliage stretching on every side, was amply fitted to afford shelter and food to families of terrestrial creatures of every kind. But in the circumstance, that during this period there were repeated alternations of marine and fresh water deposits, and consequently repeated submergence and elevation of land, we see a reason why the terrestrial races were not yet called into being. Great continents, comparatively speaking, did not exist; and there was no ark of safety provided to float them over the billows. Race after race would have violently perished during every shift or subsidence of the sea bottom: and hence, until the carboniferous series was completed and a statical equilibrium established between the land and waters, few or none of the races which afterward swarmed in our plains and forests were introduced upon the scene.

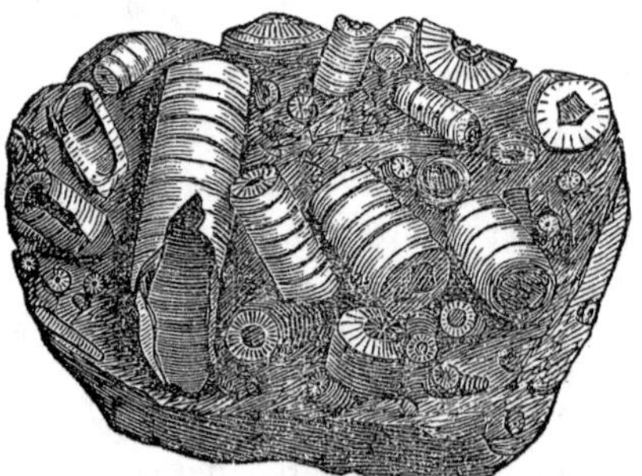

Fragment of Encrinital Limestone.

## CHAPTER VIII.

GEOGRAPHICAL DISTRIBUTION OF COAL—GREAT COAL FIELD OF PENNSYLVANIA, VIRGINIA AND OHIO—COAL DEPOSITS OF ILLINOIS, INDIANA AND KENTUCKY—ECONOMIC HISTORY—CONDITIONS OF FORMATION.

Considered mineralogically, and now demonstrated beyond a doubt, coal and the diamond are found to be one and the same in substance, and nearly also in their modes of formation. Newton detected the properties of the diamond in its refractive power over the rays of light, and inferred that, like amber, it was an unctuous body crystallized. In the crucible he reduced it to a state of pure carbon, burning, volatilizing, and resulting in the same elementary products as charcoal. Liebig goes a step farther, and declares the diamond to be a crystalline residuum from decayed vegetables. The action of fire could not produce the mineral, but would rather have the effect of drawing out its inflammable tendencies. "Science," he adds, "can point to no process capable of accounting for the origin and formation of diamonds, except that of decay. And there is the greatest reason for believing that they have been formed in a liquid." Sir David Brewster, in his beautiful optical analysis, has arrived at the same general conclusions.

Coal is also a product of vegetable decay, collected and formed in a liquid. It has not crystallized, and therefore wants the sparkle and the luster of the diamond. It retains all the carbon, and more of the hydrogen, and is in consequence infinitely more useful and valuable than even the precious gem. It is carefully incased and preserved among the rocks of the earth, and thereby in like manner akin to the glittering idol, whose true habitat has been found to be the sandstones* immediately overlying the carboniferous formation. Thus far the parallel can be traced between the two apparently very dissimilar and unequally prized minerals: in extent of substance and geographical distribution, the history of each stands apart.

I. The Geographical Distribution of the Coal Metals.—Our knowledge on this subject is increasing with every new geographical detail connected with the history of the earth. Until very recently the carboniferous system was supposed to be of very limited extent. The return of every vessel, engaged in a voyage of discovery or otherwise, brings tidings of some new island or continent on which it is found. The same tribes of plants and animals are everywhere observed to accompany the deposit—all presenting the same generic and often the same specific characters—and uniformly on the same great scale of development. This circumstance alone bespeaks a universal formation, when every region was capable of producing all the requisite conditions in climate, vegetables, corallines, and sea-bottom, and prepares the mind for the ready admission of the existence of the mineral in every unexplored quarter of the globe. Accordingly, all the great continents of the old world abound in coal. In Russia, the carboniferous system occupies, betwixt the Dnieper and the Don, an area of about eleven thousand square miles. India, China, and the Australian archipelago give up yearly more and more of the bituminous substance. Egypt is not destitute of the jetty mineral: for recently beds several feet thick have been discovered near Asuan, on the right bank of the Nile. The vast continent of America has it in proportion to its own vastness. And man, go where he will with the knowledge of the arts, and the diffusive blessings of religion and civilization, will always find that a wise

* The diamonds found in the Ural chain are supposed to be connected with the carbonaceous grits of the devonian and carboniferous periods, which have been transmuted into metamorphic micaceous rocks, and contain the diamonds between the flakes of mica, just as garnets occur in mica-schist. Captain Franklin discovered diamonds in Bundelkund, imbedded in sandstone, with coal beneath, and supposed to belong to the true carboniferous system.

Providence has anticipated his wants, and prepared the treasure for his use.

The coal formation in Scotland has been already traced as occupying the great central valley of the Lowlands, which separates the primitive crystalline and feldspathic rocks of the north from the silurian series of the southern border, and traversing the mainland from sea to sea. The middle and northern coal basins of England have an average uninterrupted stretch of about two hundred miles in length, by forty in breadth. The Bristol and Welsh coal-fields, are also very extensive. That of South Wales forms an immense double trough, comprised within a great oval elongated tract, betwixt St. Bride's Bay, and Pontypool, with an anticlinal axis ranging east and west, and embracing an area of one thousand and fifty-five square miles. This is the largest coal-field in Britain, in which there are sixty-four seams of coal, of all qualities, from the highest bituminous to the purest anthracite, and having an aggregate thickness of one hundred and ninety-feet. In Ireland the coal basins are comparatively small, and isolated from one another: the principal workable seams are in the counties of Kilkenny, Tipperary, Cork, Tyrone, and the northern extremity of Roscommon.

The coal metals immediately present themselves on the French coast at Boulogne, more inland at Mons, and in the central district at St. Etienne, betwixt the valleys of the Loire and Rhone. This last basin is of small extent, but possesses great geological interest from its position among the primary and metamorphic rocks, and the materials of which the series is composed. The metals are inclosed in a long narrow trough, of about twenty-five miles by less than a mile at its greatest breadth. Granite, gneiss, mica-slate, underlie them throughout: instead of shales, and sandstones of the usual kind, the coals are imbedded in micaceous grit, and the detrital alluvia of the crystalline rocks. It has been described as a self contained repository, with its own furnishings and equipments all, as it were, self-originating: the vegetable matter is of native growth, the trees are still vertical, and in one part of the field present the appearance of a suddenly petrified forest; the iron, too, is native, and seems to have been actually smelted on the spot, by subterranean self-combustion. The coal, underlying one of the bands of ironstone, has undergone fusion, and been changed into coke; while sulphur and crystals of sulphate of lime have been separated in the crucible by the process of sublimation, as if to complete this scene of marvels.

In the low countries, at Namur and Liege, and other places along the banks of the Meuse—in Germany, Silesia, Moravia, Poland, the Carpathian Mountains—on the banks of the Volga, the Dnieper, and the Don, the coal-measures are found to occupy tracts of greater or lesser extent. These are sometimes accompanied with the usual alternating series entire and unbroken, sometimes with the absence of one or more members. In Russia the metals are imbedded in the middle mountain limestone series in one field, while in another district they are situated in the lower part of the series, or beneath the calcareous deposit, as in the thin beds of Fifeshire. The Liege coal-basin is of a remarkably complex structure—the metals lying in small hollows of contorted strata, which are bent and twisted like a sapling—elevated into every varying position and degree of inclination—and thus, by obtaining cross or horizontal sections, you pass repeatedly over the edges of the same beds. An enterprising Scotchman has long been lessee of one of these coal-fields, out of whose iron bands he has molded cannon and ball for every nation in Europe; and whose locomotives, forged from the same strata, now ply in pleasure excursions along every railway of the Netherlands and vine-clad banks of the Rhine and Moselle.

The American coal-fields, like its interminable forests, endless rivers, and everything in that vast continent, are all on the gigantic scale. The basin of the Mississippi, extending from the Rocky Mountains to the Alleghanies, forms an area equal to two-thirds of the states of Europe, almost every part of which is covered with the carboniferous limestone, supporting the coal metals and the newer palæozoic rocks. The great coal-field of Pennsylvania, Virginia, and Ohio, extends, according to Sir Charles Lyell, continuously from north-east to south-west for a distance of 207 miles, its breadth being in some places 180 miles. The basin of Illinois, Indiana, and Kentucky, is not much inferior in dimensions to the whole of England, while another coal deposit, 170 by 100 miles, lies farther to the north, between lakes Michigan and Huron.

Mr. Logan, in his report on the geology of Canada, states that the coal-measures occupy nearly the whole of New Brunswick, a great part of Nova Scotia, Cape Breton island, and the south-west district of Newfoundland. And in the most remote northern regions, along the shores of the frozen sea, and the various rivers and their tributaries which fall into it, the carboniferous rocks with their inclosed beds of coal, some of considerable thickness, are found to prevail. A single seam, of an average thickness of ten feet, occurs in Pennsylvania, in the district of Pittsburgh, covering a superficial extent of about 14,000 square miles; which shows how inexhaustible the resources, and how limitless the means, of social advancement, of progress in the arts and sciences, garnered up for the generations to come in that mighty continent.

Upon the authority of Sir Charles Lyell we learn, that all the floral fossil phenomena are substantially the same as in Europe—a great preponderance of stigmariæ, ferns, lepidodendra, and calamites—some consisting of trees in an erect position, and of broken trunks, with their rootlets attached, and extending in all directions; and the same grits or sandstones, are found, as those used for building near Edinburgh and Newcastle. Of forty-eight species of fossil plants or trees, detected in the strata of Nova Scotia, thirty-seven are identical with those discovered in the British beds; and, in the United States, thirty-five out of fifty-three species are described as specifically the same with the European fossils. But the most remarkable of Sir Charles's discoveries is that, in the prodigious thickness and singular structure of the coal-basin in Nova Scotia, there are the remains of more than ten forests which rose up successively one over the other, and which, with their interposed layers of clays and solid stone, deposited at intervals, constitute a series of beds, whose vertical thickness is 14,570 feet.

II. The Economic History of Coal.—It does not appear, from any well authenticated records, at what precise period man availed himself of this useful mineral, either for the purposes of art, or of domestic comfort. The early history of nations is traditionary; but there is no tradition from very remote times, in any of them, as to the discovery of coal—no philosopher speculating about the importance of the fact and its bearings on the progress of civilization—no poet extolling the genius of the new Prometheus, that brought up the fiery combustible from the bowels of earth. The aborigines who dwelt amidst the primeval forests had no occasion to seek farther for fuel, when every hill and plain supplied them with all that was needed, and more than was convenient, as the cultivation of the soil engaged attention. Accident, doubtless, would first lead to the knowledge of the virtues of the hidden treasure. As the ground was cleared, and cities became populous, and the arts advanced, more diligence would be exercised in its search; and in proportion as it came, from the destruction of the woods, to be regarded as a necessary or luxury of life, coal would be sought for as an article of barter, or of commerce. Thus many ages might elapse before coal was introduced into general consumption, and though stored up specially for man, it was wisely ordered that the supplies and incumbrances on the surface should first be exhausted or removed, ere the inner chambers of his habitation were broken into and explored.

Bituminous matter, if not the carboniferous system itself, exists abundantly on the banks of the Euphrates. In the basin of the Nile coal has been recently detected. It occurs sparingly in some of the states of Greece: and Theophrastus, in his "History of Stones," refers to mineral coal (*lithanthrax*) being found in Liguria, and in Elis, and used by the smiths; the stones are earthy, he adds, but kindle and burn like wood coals (the *anthrax*). But by none of the oriental nations does it appear that the vast latent powers and virtues of the mineral were thus early discovered, so as to render it an object of commerce or of geological research. What the Romans termed *lapis ampelites*, is generally understood to mean our cannel coal, which they used not as fuel, but in making toys, bracelets, and other ornaments; while their *carbo*, which Pliny describes as "vehementer perlucet," was simply the petroleum or naphtha, which issues so abundantly from all the tertiary deposits. Coal is found in Syria, and the term frequently occurs in the sacred writings. But there is no reference anywhere in the inspired record as to digging or boring for the mineral—no directions for its use—no instructions as to its constituting a portion of the promised treasures of the land. In their burnt-offerings, wood appears uniformly to have been employed; in Leviticus, the term is used as synonymous with fire, where it is said that "the priests shall lay the parts in order upon the wood, that is, on the fire which is upon the altar." And in the same manner for all domestic purposes, wood and charcoal were invariably made use of. Doubtless the ancient Hebrews would be acquainted with *natural* coal, as in the mountains of Lebanon, whither they continually resorted for their timber, seams of coal near Beirout were seen to protrude through the superincumbent strata in various directions. Still there are no traces of pits or excavations into the rock to show that they duly appreciated the extent and uses of the article. Their term נחל, which properly signifies *charcoal*, appears to have passed into the northern languages, as in the Islandic *gloa;* the Danish *gloe;* the Welsh *glo*, a coal, *golen* to give light; the Irish *o-gual;* and the Cornish *kolan*—terms all expressive of the act of burning or of giving light.

For many reasons it would seem that, among modern nations, the primitive Britons were the first to avail themselves of the valuable combustible. The word by which it is designated is not of Saxon, but of British extraction, and is still employed to this day by the Irish, in their form of *o-gual*, and in that of *kolan* by the Cornish. In Yorkshire stone hammers and hatchets have been found in old mines, showing that the early Britons worked coals before the invasion of the Romans. Manchester,* which has risen upon the very ashes of the mineral, and grown to all its wealth and greatness under the influence of its heat and light, next claims the merit of the discovery. Portions of coal have been found under or imbedded in the sand of a Roman way, excavated some years ago for the construction of a house, and which, at the time, were ingeniously conjectured by the local antiquaries to have been collected for the use of the garrison, stationed on the route of these warlike invaders at Mancenion, or the Place of Tents. Certain it is, that fragments of coal are being constantly, in the district, washed out and brought down by the Medlock and other streams, which break from the mountains

* Westminster Review, No. LXXIX.

through the coal strata. The attention of the inhabitants would, in this way, be the more early and readily attracted by the glistening substance.

Nevertheless, for long after, coal was but little valued or appreciated, turf and wood being the common articles of consumption throughout the country. About the middle of the ninth century, a grant of land was made by the Abbey of Peterborough, under the restriction of certain payments in kind to the monastery, among which are specified sixty carts of wood, and as showing their comparative worth, only twelve carts of pit-coal. Toward the end of the thirteenth century, Newcastle is said to have traded in the article, and by a charter of Henry III, of date 1284, a license is granted to the burgesses to dig for the mineral. About this period, coals, for the first time, began to be imported into London, but were made use of only by smiths, brewers, dyers, and other artisans, when, in consequence of the smoke being regarded as very injurious to the public health, Parliament petitioned the king, Edward I, to prohibit the burning of coal, on the ground of being an intolerable nuisance. A proclamation was granted, conformable to the prayer of the petition ; and the most severe inquisitorial measures were adopted to restrict or altogether abolish the use of the combustible, by fine, imprisonment, and destruction of the furnaces and workshops! They were again brought into common use in the time of Charles I, and have continued to increase steadily with the extension of the arts and manufactures, and the advancing tide of population, until now, in the metropolis and suburbs, coals are annually consumed to the amount of about three millions of tons. The use of coal in Scotland seems to be connected with the rise of the monasteries, institutions which were admirably suited to the times, the conservators of learning, and pioneers of art and industry all over Europe, and in whose most rigorous exactions evidences can always be traced of a judicious and enlightened concern for the general improvement of the country. Under the regime of monastic rule at Dunfermline, coals were worked in the year 1291—at Dysart, and other places along the coast, about half a century later—and, generally, in the fourteenth and fifteenth centuries the inhabitants were assessed in coals to the churches and chapels, which, after the Reformation, have still continued to be paid in many parishes. Boëthius records that, in his time, the inhabitants of Fife and the Lothians dug "a black stone," which, when kindled, gave out a heat sufficient to melt iron.

How long will the coal-metals of the British isles last at the present, or even an increased expenditure of the fuel? So great has been the discrepancy, and so little understood the data on which to form a calculation, that the authorities variously estimate from two hundred to two thousand years. For home consumption the present rate is about THIRTY-TWO MILLIONS of tons annually. The export is about SIX MILLIONS: and yet such is the enormous mass of this combustible inclosed in one field alone, that no boundary can be fixed, even the most remote, for its exhaustion. The coal trade of Great Britain is nearly in the proportion of three to two of that of all the other nations of the world; while in superficial area her coal measures are to those of the United States only as 11,859 square miles to 133,132 square miles. What a vision of the future is hereby disclosed! If rightly employed, if the arts and progressive development of society at all keep pace with the means provided, the human race in the New World have a destiny to run, and a work of civilization to accomplish, to which the Old, in its brightest achievements, can furnish but a faint analogy. Scarcely two centuries have elapsed since coal was employed as an article of domestic use, or introduced upon the most limited scale into the manufactures; its now ascertained extent and boundless latent powers were not dreamt of or imagined even but half a century ago; and very recently the lamentation was general, that no coal-measures existed in the mighty continent of America. Who now can fancy a limit to the social movement with which that vast hemisphere is heaving all over—the advancing tide of its population spreading in every region—the forests cleared and covered with a net-work of railways, the rivers bridged from end to end with a navy of steamships—and all vivified and in motion through the agency of this long undiscovered product of the earth? Geological time rolled on, and the surface of our planet was replenished with the hidden treasure, and the man of science has no numbers to reckon the years that are past. More agreeable far to look through the vista of coming events, where a moral era has commenced out of which a mightier series of phenomena will emerge, the purposes of a wise Providence be illustrated in so transmuting and preserving the entombed relics of distant ages, and the glories of the latter day arise, when the desert place shall teem with a new life, and the wilderness give praise to the Creator of all.

III. Universal, and shall we add, synchronous as a formation, there is a very interesting question connected with this subject, namely, IS COAL NOW FORMING? The general opinion among geologists leans to the affirmative side of the question, and that here, as in all the other cosmical arrangements going forward on the earth's surface, time is the grand requisite. The necessary agencies are all at work, the other conditions are all admitted, and in the course of some future untold ages a new bituminous product will arise, similar in all respects to the old. The subject and the conclusions arrived at are not, however, free of many and great difficulties, to some of which we shall merely advert.

Reverting to all the circumstances connected with the geographical distribution of the coal metals, we are inclined to think that the era which produced them was not only peculiar in the wide geographical distribution of its families of plants, but equally, if not more so, in its limitation of all those physical conditions which were necessary for their conversion into coal. The basins, it will be observed, in which the vegetable matter was deposited, were, as compared with the existing ocean, small and shallow; for most of the plants and trees grew within their area or their immediate neighborhood, and are still found in their erect position, uninjured by roughing or transport in their smallest veinlets and even minute fructifications.

Then it is highly probable, that the great continents were not yet formed, but that a series of islands, barrier reefs, and inland seas, prevailed generally over the earth's surface, being still chiefly oceanic. Consequently no great rivers could, in such circumstances, be in existence, rolling down like the Ganges, Nile, and Mississippi more stony detritus and mud than arborescent matter, and all to be mixed and confounded in one indiscriminate mass. Atmospheric influences, too, must have been widely different from what they now are; for all the cast-off apparel of a summer's luxuriance is, we see year after year, speedily dissipated by the droughts, or absorbed back as *humus* into the earth, and when spring returns the ground is parched and bare. A difference of temperature must also be taken into the list of modifying causes; for the plants, during the coal era, are nearly of a class—a few great types with little variety of structure—one and the same in every region—and approaching the characters, most of them, of the existing tropical flora. The climate, according to Mr. Bunbury, was characterized by excessive moisture, by a mild and steady temperature, and the entire absence of frost; and it has been established by Mr. Darwin's interesting observations on Chiloe and other islands of the southern temperate zone, that extreme heat is not necessary to the existence of a very luxuriant and quasi-tropical vegetation. Mr. Austen, on the other hand, thinks that the temperature of Great Britain has not much changed since the coal period, because few of the fossil-ferns, found in the coal-measures, present any fructification, while those in more southern latitudes possess it; and, by experiments made by himself, it appears that the existing ferns of tropical climates would not fructify at a low temperature. Still, the great general fact remains unquestioned, that tree-ferns during the carboniferous age grew gigantically and in vast forests, where they do not grow at present over all the zones of the earth; and where now growing, in three out of the four zones, that the whole family are reduced to the size of small herbaceous plants.

Now, is it not a legitimate inference from all this, that, out of so many concurring circumstances, not one of which is similar in all respects now, a determinate effect was INTENDED to be produced, and which cannot, in the altered condition of things, be produced again? The argument is cumulative, and bears the strongest presumptive evidence on its side. The carboniferous series cannot be repeated—not for want of vegetable or animal matter, for there is a hundred times more of both at present on the surface of the earth than perhaps ever existed in any former period—but because there are so many new causes now in operation, so many changes in the relative position of sea and land, to modify its distribution and qualities, and to influence its place in the system generally, that the same conservative arrangements and chemical appliances cannot occur, nor any similar bituminous compound as a geological formation issue from Nature's laboratory.

Leonard Horner, in enumerating the difficulties connected with the formation of the coal deposit upon the theory of the whole of the matter, vegetable and earthy, being spread over the sea-bottom, says—"That the terrestrial vegetable matter, from which coal has been formed, has in very many instances been deposited in the sea, is unquestionable, from their alternations with limestones containing marine remains. Such deposits and alternations in an estuary at the mouth of a great river are conceivable; but whether such enormous beds of limestone, with the corals and molluscs which they contain, could be formed in an estuary, may admit of doubt. But it is not so easy to conceive the very distinct separation of the coal and the stony matter, if formed of drifted materials brought into the bay by a river. It has been said that the vegetable matter is brought down at intervals, in freshets, in masses united together, like the rafts in the Mississippi. But there could not be masses of matted vegetable matter of uniform thickness, 14,000 square miles in extent, like the Brownsville bed on the Monongahela and Ohio (the Pittsburgh seam): and freshets bring down gravel, and sand, and mud, as well as plants and trees. They must occur several times a year in every river; but many years must have elapsed during the gradual deposit of the sandstones and shales that separate the seams of coal. Humboldt tells us ("Cosmos," p. 295),—That in the forest lands of the temperate zone, the carbon contained in the trees on a given surface would not, on an average of a hundred years, form a layer over that surface more than seven lines in thickness. If this be a well-ascertained fact, what an enormous accumulation of vegetable matter must be required to form a coal-seam of even moderate dimensions! It is extremely improbable that the vegetable matter brought down by rivers could fall to the bottom of the sea in clear unmixed layers; it would form a confused mass with stones, sand, and mud. Again, how difficult to conceive, how extremely improbable in such circumstances, is the preservation of delicate plants, spread out with the most perfect arrangement of their parts, uninjured by the rude action of rapid streams and currents, carrying gravel and sand, and branches and trunks of trees?"

Nor, according to Mr. Horner, are the objections to the lacustrine theory, requiring so many oscillations of land and water, of less magnitude. "In the theory," he says, "which accounts for the formation of beds of coal, by supposing that they are the remains of trees and other plants that grew on the spot where the coal now exists, that the land was submerged to admit of the covering of sandstones or shale being deposited, and again elevated, so that the sandstone or shale might become the subsoil of a new growth, to be again submerged, and this process repeated as often as there are seams of coal in the series—these are demands on our assent of a most startling kind. The materials of each of these seams, however thin (and there are some not an inch thick, lying upon and covered by great depths of sandstones and shales), must, according to this theory, have grown on land, and the covering of each must have been deposited under water.—There must thus have been an equal number of successive upward and downward movements, and these so gentle, such soft heavings, as not to break the continuity, or disturb the parallelism of horizontal lines spread over hundreds of square miles; and the movements must, moreover, have been so nicely adjusted, that they should always be downward when a layer of vegetable matter was to be covered up; and, in the upward movements, the motion must always have ceased so soon as the last layers of sand or shale had reached the surface, to be immediately covered by the fresh vegetable growth; for otherwise we should have found evidence, in the series of successive deposits, of some being furrowed, broken up, or covered with pebbles or other detrital matter of land, long exposed to the waves breaking on a shore, and to meteoric agencies. These conditions, which seem to be inseparable from the theory in question, it would be difficult to find anything analogous to in any other case of changes in the relative level of sea and land with which we are acquainted."

While these statements show that we are still but imperfectly acquainted with all the conditions and circumstances under which coal was formed, two deductions may be made from them, not only as against the rival theories themselves, of Murchison and

Lyell, but still more strongly against the application of either theory to existing causes in the formation of the true bituminous product. In the first place, the vegetable matter brought down by the rivers, and spread over the bottom of the sea, does not amount to an infinitesimal fraction of what constitutes the enormous compound of the carboniferous age; and a different effect, according to the laws of nature of which we have experience, will necessarily result from the causes now in operation. Secondly, whatever, as a question of fact, it may have been with our coal-basins in the times gone by, certain it is that NOW there are no such oscillatory movements, causing the required changes in the relative level of sea and land, in those quarters of the globe the most densely covered with forests and jungle, and out of which the new coal-measures are expected to rise. The thin accumulations of woody residuum, observed by Sir Charles Lyell, in the sections exposed along the banks of rivers, railways, and other passages through American prairies and forests, are all unfavorably circumstanced—firm as the everlasting hills on their rocky foundations.

We may be reminded of the numberless ages required for the production of coal, that man's experience is but of yesterday, and himself an ephemeral of a moment as compared with the revolutions of time recorded on the fabric of the globe. This record, we have reason to think, should be vastly abridged. But grant it, for the sake of argument, in all its indefinite dimensions, and still the answer is, that a moment in a question of this kind is just as instructive as the lapse of a million of years. Time, while it witnesses change, does not create or of itself produce anything. It is rather a passive than an active agent. Time marks on its horoscope the effects of existing causes, but the causes themselves it neither fashions or eliminates. Geologists enter into minute calculations as to the annual decay of vegetables, and the transporting powers of water, the waste of forests and the uptearing of hurricanes. Grant them all to be correct, and the data in these respects to be unchallengeably sound, we again beg them to consider that the Mississippi bears on its bosom the earthy spoils of half a continent—that the Ganges mixes in its fabled flood the varied wreck of all the Himalaya,—and when all are duly borne onward by these and the mighty rivers elsewhere on the globe, that the arrangement of the mingled composite has yet to be effected—the clays, sands, coals, conglomerates, all in their serial superposition—the separation of the clean from the unclean—and where is the agency thus to dispose and to proportion? The deep says, it is not in me. The rivers show it is not in them. Are there any cosmical affinities in the things themselves to cause each to each, kind to kind, to take their respective places?

When we are told, that we know not what is going on in the depths of ocean, and other hollow places of the earth, our answer is two-fold. For first we reply, there were depths and hollows, lakes, estuaries, and seas, during all the *intermediate succeeding* epochs to the present age, and no true coal was produced: accumulation after accumulation of detrital alluvia followed, lapidified, and was distributed over extensive areas, and common to every region of the globe; but the real bituminous treasure has not been uniformly an accompaniment. A second answer is, that when and where vegetable matter, in any quantity, did accumulate, the result of the process was not COAL. The lignites of the tertiary deposits, and many of the oolites, have been subjected to the first and second stages only in those changes which plants undergo in their transition into the bituminous combustible. Nature in these instances, if we may use the expression, has made the effort, but the same results have not followed; the process is incomplete, and the product is only in patches. If we are reminded of the great oolitic deposit of Richmond, in Virginia, re-examined and pronounced to be so by Sir C. Lyell, some may still say non-content, that the problem is not yet solved as to the true position of the coal there. Many anomalies in geognostic arrangements occur in that vast continent: many of the intermediate series up to the chalk are absent altogether, and the sandstones, discriminating the new from the old red, are not fully determined. Lignite, in considerable quantity, exists among the tertiary deposits of the Alps, and has recently been found in the north-west provinces of India, in the vicinity of Kalibag; but all partaking of the usual qualities—wood, only partially altered by inhumation, and imperfectly adapted for domestic purposes.

One overwhelming consideration with us, in the discussion of this question, is the position which MAN occupies, and the part he now plays on the theater of creation. The beasts and quadrupeds of the earth do not appear to have been formed so early as the carboniferous epoch. Had they existed at the period it is impossible to say what effects would have resulted from their graminivorous propensities in modifying the amount of the vegetable exuviæ. But man has appeared, modifying, changing, controlling everything—the earth and all its stores under his dominion—and all submissive to his will. He has little influence, indeed, over the more solid departments or structure of the globe—the form of its continents—the direction of its oceanic currents—the rise of islands and depression of land—the movements of the earthquake, and fiery torrents of the volcano; but over all its living products, especially its vegetable and terrestrial animal tribes, his influence is immense—increasingly incalculable. And, the geologist says, had this new denizen left the earth to itself, and nature to her own arrangements—were there no tilling, draining, and reaping—were the jungle and the wilderness to be still uninvaded—the marsh and the lagoon to welter in their dreary desolation—a vast coal deposit would be preparing in all the great lakes and seas of the globe. These postulates and conditions, however, can no longer be granted. Every day and every season they are all curtailed and limited in their influences. Man cuts down the forest, and applies it in its green, woody state to his own use.—The waste is reclaimed. The desert he makes his habitation; a place of beauty and civilization. The moral triumphs over the material, the spiritual over the earthy, and his charter-right is to subdue all things to himself. Thus the geologist cannot, if he would, forget or overlook the remarkable human epoch in which his own lot has been cast. As regards the future, there is a new element to which a due place must be assigned in his speculations; and all the great revolutions, and after-phases of our globe, he must henceforth read and interpret in the REVEALED destiny of his own race.

Finally, let it be assumed, in the argument for the geologists, that vast masses of vegetable matter are already stored up and duly arranged over the sea-bottom, that more is continually accumulating, and that there is heat enough under the earth's crust to bituminize and indurate the whole. A new coal epoch is thus approaching, or rather, even now, we are living within its influences. But the question occurs, when completed, of what avail would it be to man, who would inevitably be swept off the earth in the elevation and breaking up of the strata from the depths beneath? Geology makes known the undoubted fact, that our planet has been subjected to many and most extensive changes before it was reduced to its present condition. These, from the beginning, have been all found subservient to the improvement and well-being of the human family. The next, upon a similar scale of magnitude, would inevitably prove the destruction of the race.

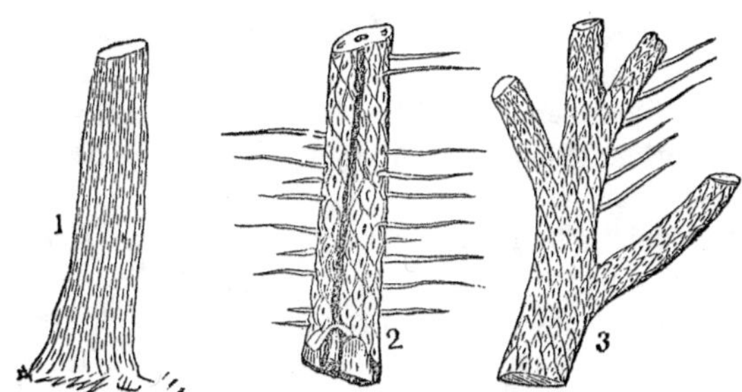


1. Sigillaria pachyderma. 2. Stigmaria ficoides. 3. Lepidodendron Sternbergii.

# CHAPTER IX.

## GEOLOGICAL STRUCTURE OF FIFESHIRE—DIVISIONS OF THE COAL-FIELD.

The general remarks on the coal deposit, in which we have been led to indulge in the two last chapters, may be verified by, as they all receive the most ample illustrations from, the admirable arrangement, position, and distribution of the metals in the counties of Fife, Clackmannan, Stirling, Lanark, and Renfrew, which are extensions of one great basin. Fifeshire alone contains an epitome of the system, divided as it is into numerous compartments, the encrinital limestone cropping out and marking their several boundaries. Indeed, the whole series of the carboniferous rocks are here laid open for examination on every hill-side, in the numerous ravines which intersect the district, and along the eastern and southern coast-lines. Approaching the coal-field from the north, a panoramic section at once fills the eye, and will rivet the attention, as, stepping from the strata of the antecedent epoch, you find, in immediate superposition as well as contrast of color, the multiplied and more diversified reliquiæ of the coal-measures.

The eruptive rocks will also be here studied to great advantage, where they have played no insignificant part in giving shape and outline to the landscape, and in laying open the inclosed minerals. It is impossible to convey any adequate idea, in mere description, of the marvelous display of plutonic action of which this peninsula has once been the theater: subterranean movements crushing and grinding into fragments the solid strata, parting and heaving them asunder, or crumpling into complicated folds the tougher and more unyielding beds, as if it had been some fabric of manufacture tossed and twisted by the wind. The bituminous breccia at Pettycur, Elie, Balcarras Den, and which appears again at the Rock and Spindle near St. Andrews, affords a remarkable instance of the action of the intrusive rocks in breaking, and transmuting into a composite paste, the series of beds constituting the coal-measures, in which every one of the strata has its representative in fragments, from the size of a garden pea to masses a foot in diameter or even upward. The storm lifts the ocean into lofty curling billows, leaving long narrow troughs and frightful yawning chasms beneath. Here, in like manner, and all over the surface, the crust has been broken up, and the minerals tossed about, or agitated like wreck upon the waves, and, upon subsiding, have been cast into the form of ridges, or broad tabular masses. The ridges, with their serrated outcrops, in the interior of the county, have been gradually rounded off and covered with soil; while, by the shore, they still present the effects of the violent commotions to which they have been subjected, exposed and laid bare by the action of the sea, upon the lower levels of the disrupted strata. The Ochils, Lammermuirs, and Pentlands, were already above the waters, calmly contemplating the troubled scene, as an inner circle of basalt and greenstone hills arose—the Lomonds, Largo Law, the Binn, and Binnarty, on the north; Stirling rock, Corstorphine hill, Arthur's Seat, Berwick Law, and the Bass, on the south—which were severally lifted into view, to be stationed as so many sentinels on the outposts of the field.

The coal metals shared in the general elevation of the hills, where they are either folded round their bases, or are depending, drapery-wise, from their tops. Thus the members of the inferior carboniferous series are raised about eleven hundred feet along the Lomond ridge, encompassing the east and west cones, and training westward by Binnarty and the Cleish hills. Largo and Kellie Laws have each their coal basins, of workable minerals, stretched along their eminences, and dipping toward the Teasses and Ceres basins. On the low grounds which skirt them on the south, the metals dip rapidly into the Forth, and are collected in various hollows or independent bands by the shore. The intermediate coal-fields, which occupy the center of the basin, are regulated in their strike and inclination by the dykes and outbursts of trap by which the strata have been invaded. A limestone traverses the county at right angles from north to south, emerging at Ravenscrag, which forms a line of demarkation betwixt the number of the coal seams on its opposite sides. The Lochgellie, Cowdenbeath, and Dunfermline basins, on the west, average about twelve to fourteen workable coal-bands, while on the east of the limestone, the Dysart, Wemyss, Teasses, and Ceres basins run from twenty to thirty-three of various quality and thickness. The Clackmannan coal-field recovers in numerical proportion, where there are twenty-four seams of coal, from two inches to nine feet thick, and two great slips, which raise the metals successively 700 and 1230 feet, as they abut against the Ochil range. In the Elgin basin there are twenty-seven beds of coal, with a thickness of fifty-six feet.

Fifeshire thus owes its diversified shape and contour, and access to all its vast mineral treasures, to the early disturbances by which it has been so thoroughly dislocated and furrowed. Every district has a section, separate and independent, of its own. The ground you tread on is, every foot of it, a cabinet of wonders—literally a necropolis, a city of the dead. Go where you will, chronicles of the olden time are before and around you, while everywhere—

"————————and at your side
Rises a mountain-rock in rugged pride,
And in that rock are shapes of shells, and forms
Of creatures in old worlds."

The cuttings of the Edinburgh and Perth Railway give excellent sections of the various minerals of the county, from the gray sandstone to the uppermost coverings of the coal-field. Entering Fifeshire from the west, your course lies deep among the detritus of the various members of the old red series already noticed. At the Newburgh Station, and under the cliffs of Clatchart, the gray sandstone and cornstone may be observed—the latter is regularly stratified; the former is embraced among the igneous rocks, broken, isolated, and inclined at every possible degree to the horizon. Clatchart Crag itself has been stirred to its foundations; the huge mass, reverberating now to the passage of other fires, rests on highly inclined beds of the gray sandstone; the black transverse dyke of basalt, a few hundred yards on the west, may be conjectured to have been the instrument of upheaval, as in fancy we can still discern in the half-raised, half-suspended position of the rock, the enormous pressure required for its elevation.

The Lomonds and Cults hills are conspicuous objects in the landscape. The line traverses for miles the yellow sandstone and overlaying grits which form their base. Greenstone and augitic trap in both ranges cap the summits, bursting through the coal metals, and elevating the various beds of limestone. The encrinital limestone sweeps round the peaks of the Lomonds, filling up the intermediate plateau, in some places bare of herbage or any covering of soil, and the fossils are lying exposed on the surface fresh as when washed by the waves, about eleven hundred feet above their ancient sea-bottom. A vein of galena occurs on the south side of the hill, intersecting the limestone at right angles to the plain of stratification, and is described in the notices of the period of its discovery as rich in silver ore. But it has no great claim, we believe, to be regarded as *argentiferous.* Two similar veins traverse the county, one already notice in Dura Den, and the other in the parish of Inverkeithing, situated among the same series of rocks, and having the same general line of bearing from nearly north-east by south-west. The lead ore in all of them is partly massive, and partly in regular hexahedral crystals. Lead, copper, cobalt, and silver are likewise found in the Ochil range, but in no great quantities, in the culminating heights betwixt Dollar, Bencleugh, and Dalmyat.

On approaching the river Leven at Markinch, the out-crop of the central coal-basin comes to the surface. After crossing the viaduct the line lies deep among the metals—a repetition of faults, upheavals, and depressions, where in succession the edges of the same beds are several times passed over. The dip is various, the strike generally to the south-east, and under the sea at Dysart the metals are wrought at the depth of several hundred feet.

The igneous rocks along the coast will not fail to call forth surprise and admiration, unrivaled as they probably are in the number of alternations with the deposits of the carboniferous series, and all the interesting phenomena which accompany their intrusion. No description, indeed, can do justice to the interlacings and alternations presented of the two classes of rocks, so different in their origin, as those of the traps and coal-measures; where, through the agency of the former, the latter series are bent, twisted, re-united, altered, and lying at every angle betwixt the horizontal and perpendicular. Nearing Kirkaldy the coal is split up, and the fused matter injected between the layers, converting them into cinder. Within the distance of a mile, from Seaforth to Kinghorn, there are from forty to fifty alternations of the igneous and sedimentary rocks; and again, on the west, toward Pittycur, there is a recurrence of as many, with examples of the jointed columnar basalt reposing on sandstones rendered quartzose, or converted into chert, and on shales baked into brick. The outburst at the Burntisland terminus, in three parallel ridges, throws up the strata, inclining them toward the north, whence trending round the town they dip under the Binn-hill. Orrock-hill, lying immediately to the north-east of Binn-hill, furnishes a beautiful example of jointed basalt: the entire rock, three hundred feet high, and nearly a mile long, by half-a-mile in breadth, is composed of regularly constructed columns, which divide into concretionary masses from one to three feet in length, and presenting generally the pentagonal or hexagonal form. The columns are grouped into distinct clusters, which, inclining at various angles, impart to the exposed face of the rock a pleasing picturesque effect. The erosive action of water, or swell of the ocean tide, is all that is required here to shape another Staffa—"that wondrous dome"—out of these magnificent materials.

A fresh-water, or rather perhaps an estuary, limestone is an object of considerable geological interest in this locality, mixed up and altered in many places by the igneous matter. The best sections occur a little back from Pittycur harbor, and on the western slope of Binn-hill, where it is extensively quarried. Scales of fishes and other ichthyolites are very abundant: also innumerable microscopic shells, belonging to the order of entomostraca and the genus cypris. Several species of palæonisucs have been found in good preservation, namely, P. ariolatis, P. ornatissimus, and P. Robisoni. The Pygopteris Jamesoni and specimens of the Eurynotus and Crenatis have likewise been detected in the deposit.

Vegetable remains are very plentiful, especially of the fern tribe and the lycopodiums: the impressions of the sphenopteris, of which there are several species, are extremely numerous, fresh, and beautiful. This limestone is of a dull, earthy aspect, acquired obviously from the bituminous matter diffused through the mass; not crystalline, though very compact in texture, and possessed of great hardness. Wardie beach, on the opposite shore, displays a bed having many points of resemblance, which abounds in nodular masses, inclosing coprolites and fishes; and inland, the celebrated Burdiehouse limestone is an extension of the Fifeshire deposit.

Thus varied and important is this small peninsula, a speck on the face of the globe, and affording so much room for speculation and detail. Inclosed between the estuaries of the Tay and Forth are to be found some of the most legible and remarkable chronicles of our planet's history. Fifeshire has been stirred and upheaved all over, abounding in all the life-moving and plutonic energies of the carboniferous age. The vegetable and animal kingdoms supply a vast proportion of the materials of the sedimentary rocks, while the fires of the interior have mainly contributed to the production of the rest. Shall we look across the waters, and replace them, in imagination, by the former continuity of land, when the center of the coal-basin was raised above them, and their numerous islets were high and dry upon the surface? Certain it is, that the erupted matter so abundantly scattered along the shores and piled up in such masses landward, would leave room for subsidence, while the outgoing of the deposits on both sides shows such an affinity in quality and strike as to demonstrate an ancient union and geological connection.

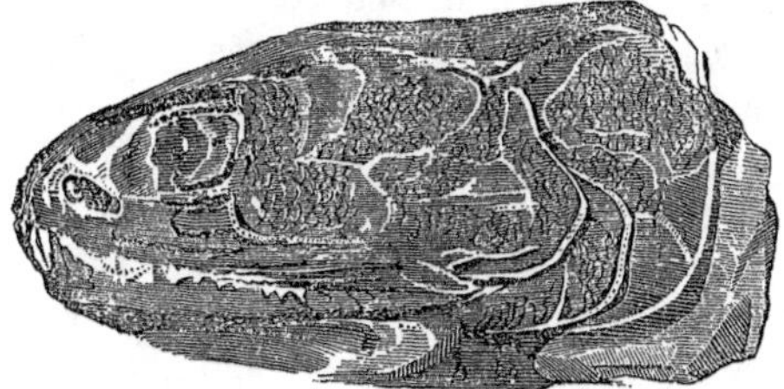

Diplopterus—new species.

# CHAPTER X.

## THE CARBONIFEROUS ROCKS—CONTINUED.

THE geology of the northern division of Scotland is, almost in every particular in the series of rocks that have been described, the counterpart of the southern, which now falls to be noticed. The fossils so richly imbedded in the former are here repeated, more sparingly in some, more abundantly in other families, and, in several instances, in the introduction of entirely new forms of organic life. Along the west and south border counties, the granites, with their associated crystalline group, are sparingly developed, stretching, at intervals, from the island of Arran through Galloway and Kirkcudbright into Dumfries-shire. The silurians follow in their order of superposition, occupying an extensive area from sea to sea across the island. The devonian system, chiefly in the upper and middle beds, wraps round the base of the older formation, and rests unconformably on its highly-inclined strata. The carboniferous deposits are widely distributed, some in isolated basins, and enveloped by the old red, and pregnant all of them with the fossils of the period. The ignigenous rocks, the traps and porphyries, are also very abundant, some in the form of detached cones, some in extensive ranges, and all demonstrative of their character as the agents that have lifted up, disrupted, and twisted the strata of the district.

In passing over this section of our course, it will not be necessary, therefore, to dwell in any minute or lengthened descriptions.

I. The geological student, in commencing his researches at Edinburgh, is immediately arrested by the more prominent objects that everywhere rise into view—the Castle Rock—the Calton Hill—Salisbury Crag—Arthur's Seat—and the Pentlands. A wondrous, glorious scene, every one involuntarily exclaims, upon reaching any of these heights, thrown, as if by the hand of an enchanter, in and around this lovely city. Geology here has its favorite residence—the birth-place and cradle of the HUTTONIAN THEORY—Arthur's seat there to attest its truth. What a history of bygone times recorded in these two words! What a revolution produced in the sentiments of mankind as to the science of world-making! And, still more, how deeply were men's minds agitated, and the foundations of religious truth stirred, by the novel views which were then announced! The assumption lying at the foundation of the rival, or Wernerian theory, is, that the materials of which the various strata of the globe consist were originally dissolved or suspended in water: they were thus in a condition to assume any form which their physical qualities and the laws of matter might determine; and, accordingly, in this fluid menstruum they were consolidated into various combinations, partly by means of crystallization, and partly by mechanical deposition. The Huttonian theory, on the other hand, employs the force of subterraneous fire as its principal machinery, which is placed at immense depths, and the materials on which it operates are under a vast pressure; and, consequently, while they are indurated into limestone, sandstone, and coal, along with their included fossils, their essential qualities are but very slightly affected, and the arrangement and disposition of their particles but little disturbed. The hills around, by which this theory was to be tested, and to whose singular structure it owed its origin, consist of an alternating series of tabular masses of trap and the sedimentary deposits, basalt forming generally the central nucleus, with tufa, greenstone, and sandstone variously disposed and folded over. All the conditions of upheaval, tortion, angularity, induration, fracture, and dislocation, are amply furnished; the columnar, jointed structure is well defined in Samson's Ribs; the very momentum of pressure, forcing the sandstone into the perpendicular, may be studied as a nice dynamical problem on the Castle rock; and when Sir James Hall brought from his crucible a reconstructed whinstone, regularly jointed and with no trace of vitreous fusion, the demonstration of the theory was felt and acknowledged, in its leading features, to be complete.

Palæontology has added its living wonders to the mere lithological speculations which were then in vogue and engrossed all attention. And geologists can now afford to smile at the misinterpretations, made by both parties, of established facts and well-ascertained things — nay, at the eagerness with which they irrelevantly pressed facts to bend to their conflicting views—the vehemence with which the Wernerian declared whinstone to contain organisms, and to be no exception to the law of mechanical deposition; while the Huttonian as deliberately set himself to prove that the nodules in chalk could only be the product of fire—the formation itself, as now determined, being merely a concretion of shells of the most perfect structure and undiminished luster. Truth, like light, emerges slowly, feeble in its dawnings when objects are obscurely seen or readily mistaken, a portion of the view half in shade, and half in brightness. And thus it has happened with both systems, as in the progress of the science errors have been detected and deficiencies supplied, peculiar to each. The acrimony of the contest, too, has passed away. Theology has been disentangled, and declared by the divine to be in no way affected by the issue. And while the scurrilities of the indiscreet abettors of both are utterly forgotten, the deductions of Hutton and the masterly expositions of his illustrator are in the main adopted as the basis of the only true system of geology.

II. In the general structure of the environs of the Scottish metropolis this plutonic machinery is deeply impressed, as it has been most vigorously exerted. There is everywhere the greatest derangement existing among the sedimentary deposits, everything is tossed out of its original place, and divided into small sections and detached groups. The connections and relative positions are very difficult to trace. Still, amidst all the disorder, the more general bearings of the different formations may be ascertained. Mr. Charles Maclaren, indeed, has examined everything with a pains-taking care, and described them with a minuteness and fidelity of detail, which cannot be surpassed, as they need scarcely be repeated. His "Geology of Fife and the Lothians," will be in every student's hands who desires to be acquainted with the structure of the district, conversant more especially as this learned geologist is with the position, fragments, and medal-stamp of every rock—their relations to each other, historical value, and bearings in the science—and illustrated with such diversity of section and diagram, that we feel as we accompany him,—

"Panditur interea domus Omnipotentis."

The general contour of the city, so picturesque and remarkable in its grouping of streets, may be taken as a pretty safe guide in determining the nature of the geology. The town is built over two parallel ridges, which completely expose the character of the inferior minerals. The northern division rests upon a series of beds, which appear immediately to underlie the true workable coal seams; the Old Town ridge and Castle rock bear up the lower members of the carboniferous deposit, while along the extended plateau on the south the yellow sandstone of the old red has been brought to the surface. The whole would thus seem to occupy the upraised floor of the great coal basin of Mid Lothian, dislocated and separated by the igneous matter of Arthur's Seat and the Calton, whence the metals all plunge to the eastward.—The flat, extending from Restalrig toward Granton and Craigleith, consists of the same series of beds as those upon which the New Town stands, and which have been elevated by the dykes and bosses of trap that so frequently intersect the strata.

The range of the yellow deposit, supposed to belong to the old red, is well defined; it commences on the northern slope and face of Salisbury Crags, and covers nearly the whole eastern side, depending to the Hunter's Bog. The same series of beds, readily distinguished by their reddish hue, train round by Samson's Ribs, thence proceeding by St. John's Hill, Heriot's Hospital, Burntsfield Links, they bear toward the New Cemetery on the estate of Grange. The beds here, exposed in several quarries, consist of an alternating series of marls, concretionary limestone, and sandstone, similar in all their lithological characters to the deposits of Dura Den and Glenvale. Not a fragment, indeed, of scale or organism has yet, so far as we know, been detected in the locality now defined, so as unequivocally to determine the position of the group in question. But is not the absence of the fossil test as fatal to its connection with the carboniferous series? while, considering its remote geographical distance from the undisputed domain of the new red, and its proximity to a surrounding belt of the true silurian, flanked with the old red, the presumption is that the deposit will yet be classed with the upper or yellow sandstone division of the devonian family. Still we merely indicate an unpresuming judgment, leaving it to so much gifted local research to confirm or disprove the correctness of the proposed classification.

III. The Mid Lothian coal-basin, so rich in minerals, forms part of the great carboniferous valley of Scotland, and may be considered as simply an extension of the coal-field of Fifeshire, the metals dipping on both sides toward the middle of the Frith. The out-crop rises toward the Lammermuirs and the Pentlands.—The area occupied by the coal-measures includes a space of about eighteen miles in length, by twelve in breadth. The series of beds composing the formation, are nearly five thousand feet thick, or about a mile in depth from the upper to the lower strata, and the whole fractured and dislocated in every part of the field. There are fifty-two slips, indeed, enumerated by the miners, which occasion a depression toward the north to the extent of 5,196 feet; the metals are again raised by a series of thirty-seven slips to the height of 2,412 feet; thereby causing a change of relative level in the strata, corresponding to the altitude of the highest points in the Lammermuir range, namely, 2,757 feet. The disturbances above and below thus approximate to each other. Have they been directed and modified by the same agencies, the silurian group rising higher and higher as the carboniferous subsided into the depressions occasioned by the evolution of the igneous matter? The Bass, North Berwick Law, and Arthur's Seat, are the products of the change, though indeed these scattered points of igneous rock on the surface can give no idea of its subterranean extent, since basalt and greenstone are met with at unvarying depths in a great portion of the coal district in question.

The whole field is prolific in organic remains. But BURDIEHOUSE LIMESTONE claims a separate notice, not only from the abundance but the very remarkable characters of the fossils contained in it, many of them met with for the first time in the progress of our sketches. This rock immediately underlies the encrinital limestone beds of Gilmerton, and is about twenty-seven feet thick, of a dark dingy color, arising from so much bituminous matter mixed up with the calcareous. The vegetable remains are very numerous, and in a state of beautiful preservation. Nowhere, indeed, in the best arranged herbarium, have we anything so graceful, so minutely and skillfully delineated, as are the figures of these plants upon the stone. There are several species of lycopodium; also stigmaria, sigillaria, equisetum, calamus, and cyclopteris, in great abundance. The fronds of the fossil sphenopteris furnish exquisite tracings of nature's penciling. Nor are the relics belonging to the animal kingdom less remarkable for their freshness and variety. Here are the extremes of organic life, microscopic shells innumerable, with the claws, eyes, slender feelers of their occupants, all entire; and the gigantic *Megalichthys*, with a body sixty feet long, teeth of four to six inches still sparkling with luster, and scales of corresponding magnitude brightly enameled. There are also the bones and plates of another huge creature, the *Gyracanthus*, along with the jaws of sauroid fishes, measuring from a foot to a foot and half in length, thickly studded with teeth. And there, too, lovely trout-like animals, the *Palæoniscus*—with all the fins and organs and body fresh and glistering, as if ready to leap to their prey, strewed in countless myriads around. Nor is the enumeration complete as to the kind and quality of the fossils of this curious deposit: there *coprolites* mark the habits of the predaceous monsters of the period—fæcal excrements composed of the remains of their victims—and in some places so numerous as to outweigh the calcareous matrix in which they are imbedded.

M. Agassiz, in his synoptical table of British fossil fishes, 1843, gives the following list belonging to the Burdiehouse limestone. In the Order of Placoids, *Ichthyodorulites*, there is a Ptychacanthus sublævis, Sphenacanthus serrulatus, and Gyracanthus formosus: of *Cestraciontes*, Ctenoptychius pectinatus and denticulatus, and Ctenodus Robertsoni: of *Hybodontes*, Cladodus acutus, parrus, and Hibberti, and Diplodus gibbosus, and minutus. In the

Order of Ganoids the following occur: of *Lepidoides*, Palæoniscus ornatissimus, Robisoni, and striolatus, and Eurynotus crenatus, and fimbriatus; of *Sauroids*, Megalichthys Hibberti, Diplopterus Robertsoni, Pygopterus Bucklandi and Jamesoni; of *Cœlacanthes*, Holoptychius Hibberti, sauroides, and striatus, Uronemus lobatus, and a Phyllolepis tenuissimus. Since this list was drawn up, many additional fossils have been obtained from the same locality; some of them exhibit characters which will establish, in all probability, new genera as well as species. The collection in the Edinburgh College Museum contains gigantic specimens in the highest condition of preservation, exciting our wonder at the strange forms which peopled our ancient seas, and admiration of those singular processes by which they have been embalmed by the chemistry of nature, surviving so many changes and disturbances in the history of our planet.

The comparative history of the fishes enumerated, in relation to the systems of rocks through which they extend, is both interesting and curious. For example, the genus ptychacanthus begins in the devonian and ends in the carboniferous period, one species peculiar to each formation. Palæoniscus begins in the carboniferous, and continues through the permian age, in five new specific forms. The megalichthys begins in the devonian and becomes extinct in the carboniferous types; diplopterus, holoptychius, and phyllolepis have each the same terms of existence; and again the pygopterus begins in the carboniferous, and survives, in two new species, through the permian era. Thus five genera are common to the devonian and carboniferous systems; two to the carboniferous and permian; eight belong exclusively to and become extinct in the carboniferous. These results clearly manifest an adaptation on the part of nature, as well as some arbitrary principle in the order of her creations, and all speak to the fact of progression in the course of events and of direct interposition in the successive origin of organic existence. Look again into these rocks. Consider the causes which so filled them with these memorials of warfare and death. Two families only, the least predaceous of their kind, survived the age which produced them—one wide revolution covered with its spoils the surface of the earth—the wreck is closed over and silted beneath the waves—and the carboniferous era, teeming with animal and vegetable life, forever passed away.

The deposit, so fruitful in these organisms, has, with much probability, been regarded as a fresh-water limestone, from the circumstance that it contains no corallines or marine shells. The plants, too, are all of a terrestrial or fluviatile kind, and so perfectly entire as to warrant the inference that they have not been tossed and drifted about in an ocean nor transported from a distance, but have perished *in situ,* and dropped amid still waters. It may have been an estuary on the borders of an ancient sea, whither the Megalichthys resembling the crocodile family in bulk, and the Gyracanthi akin to the sharks in voracity, may have roamed in quest of food, gamboled for pleasure amidst a luxuriance of tropical vegetation, or indolently reposed by the umbrageous shades of slimy lagoons. How different the scene over which they maintained undisputed sway from all that is now in these parts subject to man's dominion. Transpose the zones of the earth, and then only could there be an approximation to the more ancient condition of things.

Basin Form of Coal-fields. 1.1. Mountain Limestone.

IV. The Mid Lothian coal-basin is bounded on the west and north-west by the Pentlands, the Braid, and Blackford Hills. The Corstorphine Hills stand out in bold relief above the plain, and are remarkable of their kind; they consist of a sandstone basis, capped by an enormous mass of greenstone, in which the groovings and polish of diluvial or glacial action have long been familiar to the geologist. The carboniferous beds occupy, at intervals, the district toward Falkirk and Stirling, much broken and intersected by the igneous rocks. Stirling, like Edinburgh, is greatly indebted to its physical features, the Abbey-Crag, the dome-shaped and wooded rock of Cragforth, the Castle-Hill, and the Gillies Hill, overlooking and sharing in the glories of the plain of Bannockburn. These all consist of greenstone or dolerite trap, resting on sandstone, or often alternating in nearly conformable beds with sandstone, ironstone, and limestone. The Pentlands stretch about sixteen miles in length by six in their extreme breadth, the axis of the chain bearing almost due N. E. and S. W. The eastern division presents the different varieties of feldspathic rocks—in the center or middle group of hills the graywacke series are more developed—and on the west the old red sandstone and carboniferous deposits prevail. The axis of the chain in some of the higher points is capped with the sedimentary rocks, and along the entire range the phenomena of upheaval, dislocation, subsidence, and denudation all present themselves in turn, and in most instructive forms. The Carlops and Kaim-Valley coal-basin exhibits some remarkable appearances; within a trough-shaped, narrow space, beds of feldspar, porphyry, greenstone, and conglomerate are mixed up with the coal metals, all less or more denuded, separated by transverse openings, and irregularly broken off at their outcrop. Fossils, though sparingly, are found in the graywacke, as trilobites and orthoceratites. The Braid and Blackford Hills are outliers of the Pentlands, and present the same varieties of rock and general lithological structure.

Rapid and brief as the above sketch is, let the reader be assured there is much, very much, in the district to interest and instruct. Make the circuit of the Pentlands when he may, and he will not be satisfied until he has penetrated every valley, scaled every height, and become familiar as household words with every name and calling through the length and breadth of their varied range. Habbie's How, a very pastoral in the sound, Carlops, Kaim-Valley, Mount-Maw, Deerhoperigg, Dalmahoy-Crags, the Mendick Hills, how dear to every lover of nature in their sweet retreats and cool shady banks! And Tintock, rich in prophetic lore, to be understood must be ascended, the eye ranging over the whole central valley of Scotland, embracing both oceans in its field of vision, and numbering all over the lofty granite peaks of the Grampians. Resting-spots like these impart a delicious charm to the geologist amidst his wanderings. If pregnant with the materials of doubtful reasonings, perplexing arrangements, and intricate soundings, the science has its sunny sides and cheerful fields of recreation. And if compelled to traverse regions of dangerous stepping, dark profound abysses, he is speedily again by the side of sparkling rivers, among grassy holms and pastoral dales, redolent with the bracing airs of crag and mountain.

Nor are the moral influences of such speculations of a less healthful and refreshing kind. Geology, which deals with the cycles of time, is yet the youngest of the sciences. One exclusively of observation, all its objects lie scattered around the daily pathways of men. And still, but as yesterday, has it been looked upon with a favorable eye, as a means of investigating and establishing truth, and its truths themselves recognized as of good character and tendency. Herein, until very recently, the tree of knowledge was supposed to yield of its fruits of good and evil, most abundantly of the latter, and men long pertinaciously refused to partake of, or even to look at, the precious things that dropped from its numerous well-laden branches. Hume had attempted to demonstrate that there was no external world at all. Researches into the structure of mind, metaphysics, the domain of "common sense" as distinguished from the abstractions of the ideal philosophy, engaged and confounded alike the learned and the unlearned. Beneath, in the strata of the earth, lay the records and memorials, it was said, of vast untold ages, and all shrunk from an abyss on whose brink it was perilous to walk. The interior was literally regarded as unhallowed ground, from whose Pandora recesses, open who might, nothing but evils could issue, at utter variance with every fixed and established principle.

"Hic specus horrendum et sævi spiracula ditis."

Religion and science thus stood in direct antagonism to each other, divorced by general consent from an unnatural alliance; and men, in those days, in the Scottish metropolis, were grouped into coteries who eyed each other with a bitter jealousy. Some more liberal mind, indeed, a Blair and a Robertson, would pass occasionally into the hostile camp, but returned again to his own ranks, to be received with no very cordial embrace or flattering approval.

But now, were one of the sages of scarcely half a century ago permitted to rise from the dust, and to take his place among the intellectuals of the present time, nothing would be more likely to excite his wonder than the controversies, and their subjects, which figure in their works. Theory there is scarcely any among those who now give law in Modern Athens in letters and science.—Whether in the regions of mental philosophy, the walks of physical science, or the sacred precincts of religion, men's minds are nearly at one as to the objects and distinctive province of each. They do not fear or dread the pursuits in which they are respectively engaged, assured that skepticism, or any desire to maintain it, has now neither party nor standing; or come to what conclusion they may, the WISDOM FROM ABOVE will in its own pure and elevated region remain scathless against any or all the bolts with which it may be assailed. The everlasting hills are still there on their old foundations—the remarkable variety of structure, which, all around the city they so marvelously present, still speaks in impressive language of order and disruption, stability and change—and underneath, in the imperishable forms of buried generations, are the records of a history in which man has no part, and with which his destiny would seem in no wise concerned. But the language written thereon, and the leaves on which it is impressed, are divested of the awful sibylline mystery in which they were then involved. The saint is scared not away by the frightful characters and dark meanings which the sage pretends he can trace in them. Nor is the sage himself startled at the alchemy of his own art, and the singular forms he can summon to his presence from his subterranean domains.

A delightful repose all this from the fierce personal controversies of a few years ago. Healthful truths are brought to light. On one and the same page, penetrate as deep as they may, all professions and their abettors join alike in admiration of the ineffaceable impress of the order, wisdom, and goodness everywhere to be traced in the structure of the globe. There is no longer the metaphysician vainly attempting to resolve the whole concrete mass into the ideal; or ridiculously striving to raise a structure of materialism, on the assumption that all our ideas, whatever we know and all we excogitate about, are derived through the medium of our sensations. The regions of infinite space are explored, and the devotional tendencies of the age have become the more decided and intense in proportion as the mental vision has been enlarged. The mind seizes with a firmer grasp, and advances with a steadier pace over the fields of creation, because there *is* a Creator whose invisible Godhead is understood from the things which are made. And now, in search of truth, one and the same through all things, religion and science go hand in hand, sanctified and enlightened by the union, and imparting the most salutary lessons from the physical and moral revelations of Him whose path is in the deep places of the earth, and who for the display of his own glory has become the Instructor and Redeemer of the world.

## CHAPTER XI.

### THE LAMMERMUIRS—THE BORDER LAND—GENERAL STRUCTURE OF SCOTLAND.

THE interest which attaches to this division of our sketches of Scottish geology is in no degree impaired by the consideration that the rocks, all of them, belong to one or other of the systems which have already passed under review. A belt of undisputed Silurian deposit here meets us for the first time, flanked on all sides, and nearly throughout its length, by the old red sandstone. Porphyritic hills, greenstone bosses and dykes, and the various phenomena of trap intrusion and dislocation, are again presented in many and very striking illustrative details. "The border land," physically as well as morally, could not well be without its points of contention; and, accordingly, geologists have made "raide across the marches," and claimed as of Scottish origin an extensive domain of the English NEW RED sandstone, or Permian system. Corncockle Moor, too, and the quarries near Dumfries, unfold as curious a page in the history of the old world as does the Crigup Lynn, hewn out of the same family of rocks, of the stern warfare and fierce contendings which adorn, as they likewise disgrace, the annals of the seventeenth century.

The GENERAL STRUCTURE of the district, as now indicated, is determined in the main by the Lammermuirs, a high mountain-range of sedimentary rocks, which formed the northern barrier of an extensive inland basin or sea, and of which the Solway and Tweed occupy the central stretch or depression. The old red sandstone was herein deposited, the strata of which rest unconformably upon the older rocks. The carboniferous beds succeeded, but at a period when the floor of the basin was elevated, and the dimensions contracted; hence these beds, though reposing conformably for the most part on those of the old red and not separable on physical grounds, do not occupy the same extent of surface. Creeks and bays existed around the silurian shores, into which the materials of the sandstone were carried, and thus along the southern slope, from St. Abb's Head to Portpatrick, the old red is traceable in every opening and indentation, running up in long narrow tongues, or detached stripes, among the mountains. The coal series appear at various intervals in small isolated basins, forming on the west the coal-field of Whitehaven, which dips into the Solway, and on the east occupying from Kelso to Berwick, the valley of the Tweed, where the metals lie in very thin bands, and *underneath* the mountain limestone. Here are porphyries, which have disrupted and broken through the old red sandstone, and therefore, corresponding in age to those of the Sidlaws, Ochils, and Pentlands; and augite traps and greenstone, scattered over the coal-measures, which are as clearly the product of the movements that issued in the elevation of Arthur's Seat and the Lomonds.

The Lammermuirs have an extent of nearly one hundred and fifty miles in length, by an average breadth of twenty-five to thirty miles. The axis of the chain runs from E. N. E. to W. S. W., broken at intervals by rivers and their divergent valleys, and constituting the great frontier barrier of Scotland. The Lowthers, Corston-cone, Queensberry, and the high grounds along the upper right bank of the Nith, form outliers or extensions of the general mass. Long regarded as furnishing a true type of *Graywacke* rock, the Lammermuirs are now, by general consent, admitted into the family of SILURIANS, bearing affinities both to the upper and Lower series, and partaking likewise in some of the characteristics of the Cambrian group. The eastern division of the chain consists of very thick beds of a coarse brecciated rock, covered on the southern side by a fine-grained clay slate. In Kirkcudbrightshire, the slate-band and conglomerate, seen on the main land, and at white Bay, in Little Ross Island, are very closely allied in their mineralogical characters. And in the center division, about Innerleithen, the intrusive traps constitute a marked and interesting feature, more particularly as they there assume a subcrystalline granite structure, and convert the sedimentary deposits into hard flinty slates, or Lydian stone. The organic remains are not abundant: they are scattered, too, at wide intervals, but still sufficiently characteristic of the formation. They consist of graptolites, encrinites, trilobites, and several genera of shells. The list of conchiferæ, in some beds, is almost entirely Lower Silurian, while the *smooth Asaphi* would seem to connect this range of hills with the lower Silurian rocks of Tyrone and Fermanagh, in Ireland, which have furnished the only other specimens yet detected in Britain. The fossil localities are the lime quarries of Wrae, near Broughton, Greiston slate quarry, near Traquair, St. Mary's Isle, Kirkcudbright, Loch Ryan, and Little Ross Island; and in certain graywacke beds in Liddesdale, Mr. Nicol records the discovery of "fragments of plants, not unlike the broken reeds, and other imperfect vegetable remains, seen on some carboniferous sandstones." The collection of Lord Selkirk, from the vicinity of his residence, consists according to Mr. Salter, of—*Terebratula semisulcata*, *Leptæna sarcinulata*, *Atrypa reticularis*, *Bellerophon trilobatus*, *Natica*, *Turritellæ*, *Murchisonia*, *Avicula lineata*, *Orthonata cingulata*, *Phacops caudatus*, *Beyrichia tuberculata*, and *Graptolites ludensis*. These characteristic Upper Silurian fossils are accompanied by a *Leptæna sericea*, and *Orthoceras tenuicinctum* of Portlock, and appear to be of the date of Wenlock shale. Their latest historian, indeed, ascribes a vast indefinite antiquity to the whole range, and considers that the depository matter has been *twice* reduced to a muddy arenaceous state: that a chain of hills existed in these parts at an age long anterior to the Lammermuirs, and that another stratified formation has to be intercalated in this district, between the oldest existing strata and the parent rock, whence the sediment was derived. This opinion is founded chiefly on the circumstance, that in none of the beds have there ever been observed any fragments of granite, or the associated crystalline gneiss and schists, while fragments of clay-slate and graywacke are not uncommon amongst the conglomerate or coarser varieties. But, admitting the truth of the statement, does it warrant the inference deduced? The clay-slates and graywacke of the Highlands are equally destitute of the inclosed granitoid portions so abundant in the superimposed conglomerates of the old red; and, upon the supposition of an intensely but unequally heated sea-bottom, and partial outbursts of irruptive matter, these appearances in the Lammermuirs, where certain strata contain included fragments of similar consolidated rock, receive an intelligible and less extravagant explanation. We more willingly accede to the conclusion of Mr. Nicol, that we have still here much of the original shape and contour of this ancient land; that the rivers and valleys are all in their olden places, and that since the elevation of the group there has been no important change in their general character and physical outline. The Lammermuirs, too, connected as they are with the great silurian deposits of England, Wales, and Ireland, lend confirmation to the theory, repeatedly adverted to, that these mountains, as well as those of the preceding epoch, formed the land on which grew part at least of the exuberant vegetation entombed in the coal formations of Great Britain. It may have been a peninsula projecting into a sea, whose waves washed the Grampians on the north, covered all the midland and eastern districts of England on the south, and were bounded by the primary and silurian girdle of rocks on the west. Through these depths roamed the successive races of holoptychius, palæoniscus, gyracanthus, and megalichthys; the shallows and bottom teemed with swarms of molluscs, trilobites, cephalaspes, pamphracti; while the dense forests of ferns, palms, and pines, which clothed the shores and uplands, have been distributed among the various basins of the coal-measures.

Ascend the Eildons, or, as the route may be, Carterfell, Hartfell, or Criffel, and witness the changes, as the different systems of rocks were drifted into their places, and rose above that expanse of waters. Criffel, the loftiest mountain on the west, is composed of granite, and formed a solitary islet there, or one of a series of islands, of the primary crystalline formation. The silurian chains, in their respective positions, are next elevated to the surface. The old red sandstones collect and form along their bases, spreading over vast areas all around. These are lifted into day by the Eildons, and the numerous hills of claystone porphyry, which give such diversity of character through Liddesdale, Lauderdale, Cheviotdale, and the whole border landscape. Carterfell, which consists of a dark greenstone trap, resting on a white or light reddish sandstone, marks the upheaval of the carboniferous strata, and probable retirement of the sea from these districts, where we find no traces of any of the secondary or newer systems of rocks. Thus the line of the Scottish Border, from Annan to Roxburghshire, consists of the *under series* of the coal formation passing down the Tweed, by Kelso, Sprouston, Coldstream, to Berwick. The old red sandstone is largely developed by Chester, Hawick, Melrose, Greenlaw, Dunse; and again, after an interruption of trap and the coal-measures, it resumes its course by Chirnside, Foulden, and Mornington, to the sea. Scales of the Holoptychius and Dendrodus are found in the strata at Prestonhaugh, near Jedburgh, and likewise at the Knock Hill, in Berwickshire. On the higher grounds, from the Eildons to Hartfell and Peebles, the graywacke and slate beds everywhere prevail, presenting at St. Abb's Head, Selkirk, and Ettrick Bridge, interesting specimens of crumpled and bent strata. Remarkable veins of trap and calc-spar are to be observed near St. Mary's Loch; silver and other metallic ores are said to have been found in the neighboring hills: near Moffat, gypsum, pyritous graywacke, and alum slate, are very abundant—formations probably connected with the mineral waters of Moffat Well and Hartfell spa. At Glendinning, in the parish of Westerkirk, an antimony mine has been long wrought, which is about twenty inches wide, and once rich in the valuable mineral. A vein of galena or lead, lined with heavy-spar, crosses the Esk at Broomholm, below Langholm, and here the usual series of shales, limestone, sandstone, and thin bands of coal, are developed for miles, resting on the graywacke of Hermitage, Ernton, and Witterhope Burn hills.

The valley of the Nith, from the pass of Dalveen to Barjarg, incloses a space of nearly ten miles in length by four in breadth, filled with red sandstone and beds of limestone, and exhibits one of those original creeks or bays in the primary and silurian rocks which characterize this ancient belt. The lower basin, toward Dumfries and the Solway, presents the same series of extremely fine-grained strata. The small isolated basin of red sandstone near Lochmaben, and which contains the celebrated impressions of foot-marks in the beds at Corncockle Moor, as well as the very limited patch of sandstone in the vale of the Annan near Moffat, are probably referable to one and the same system with the above. And what is that system—the Devonian or Permian? The position of all these beds, and of others in Annandale, has long formed a fruitful subject of discussion with geologists and practical engineers, whether to regard them as an extension of the English new red, or to refer them to the predominant rock of the country. The latter view is borne out so far by the fact, that no borings, which have been both numerous and deep, have penetrated to the coal metals. On Greenough's map, on the other hand, the former theory is adopted, where the coal-measures are represented as extending *underneath* from Canobie, through Annandale to Arkit Muir, and as again emerging at Arbigland near Criffel. It has likewise been argued, that the foot-impressions on the slabs near Dumfries and at Corncockle Moor, have no analogues anywhere in the true old red of Scotland, while they are abundantly represented by the foot-prints of the newer sandstones of England and America. But now indeed such proofs are not wanting in America, that wide field of all organic things; the discovery has been made and assented to by the most competent authorities, that, in the old red sandstone of Pennsylvania, and 8,500 feet below the upper part of the coal formation, reptilian foot-prints are numerously and distinctly impressed, allied in form to the tread of the existing alligator. Then the larger orthoceræ and other testaceæ, found so plentifully in the limestones of Closeburn and Barjarg, also at Linburn and Shielgreen, would seem to claim very clearly and decidedly for the deposit in the middle basin of Nithsdale a Devonian origin.

We must refrain from entering upon the details of the extensive geological fields which have just been glanced at. A volume would not suffice to exhaust the subject. But, rapid as our sketch has necessarily been, enough has been advanced to show how intimately connected with the great fundamental principles of the science, and with the original configuration of our planet more especially, are all the deeply-interesting phenomena of the region in question. If at times the reader, as well as explorer, is apt to complain of the dryness of particulars, that the nomenclature is harsh and scholastic, how delightful to close, even in imagination, the day's excursion amid these lovely valleys, to be steeped in fairy lore by St. Mary's Loch, to dream of legends and minstrelsy until morning dawn by Newark's Tower. Nith, Gala, Ettrick, Yarrow, Teviot, silvery Tweed!—who, indeed, will ever associate with the minerals, sections, and technicalities of geology. Still how refreshing to lie down, traveled and weary-worn, by their green pastures and pure waters. How beautifully do these rivers, all of them with an origin so remote, hold on in their pebbly courses—winding and gathering from so many rills amidst the pastoral uplands — "making sweet music with th' enameled stones" — and anon with all their affluents sweeping in placid majesty to the main. Hither will men of all professions and pursuits,—the sportsman, poet, philosopher,—eagerly and rejoicingly resort, each with his own object or his own care. Finely, in imperishable verse, has the truth been expressed of that many-colored tide of human life on which all are embarked—

"Which, though it change in ceaseless flow,
Retains each grief, retains each crime"—

—but now these streams, dales, and hills retain no impress of strife or blood; and hence will the wish, age after age, breathe from many a heart—

"By Yarrow's stream still let me stray,
Though none should guide my feeble way:
Still feel the breeze down Ettrick break,
Although it chill my withered cheek;
Still lay my head by Teviot stone,
Though there forgotten and alone."

And so human life will glide away, a new epoch will come, and the development of man's immortal being will be accomplished in the new and brighter earth that is to arise.

We here close our review, over Scottish ground, of the earliest lessons to which we have access of the mineral structure of our globe. All the primary, palæozoic, and older class of the secondary rocks, are largely developed, leading us, indeed, a very little way into the inner chambers of the earth, but back through periods of time into the records of its history, for which the science itself furnishes no real standard of measurement. Vast, inconceivable cycles pass before the imagination, and fascinate the speculatist, while the sober inquirer pauses, doubts—nay, startles—at such remote undefined annals of creation. The legends and chronicles of Scotland are old indeed; but give geologists their own way, and what an antiquity would they assign to the mountains, valleys, and rivers of ancient Caledon! And yet, true it is, no rocks on the face of the earth can claim a deeper origin, an earlier arrangement, a more ancient ascent above the waters, than those whose nature and position we have so cursorily described.

Leaving for the present the question as to Time, geology has this advantage, in facilitating an acquaintance with its principles, that its lessons are as general as they are particular. Go where you will the record is before you, so that, generally speaking, what is observed of its subject in one district or country, or even continent, has its counterpart in some other place near or remote. The rocks of Scotland are all on the great scale, not solitary and individual specimens, but wide-spread formations along the face of the country. With scarcely a single exception, every class of rocks described in our course stretches from sea to sea over the island. The structure of Scotland is peculiar in this, that the bearing and the strike of the various strata, are correspondent and continuous. Hence the parallelism of the great straths and valleys. The principal rivers are observant of the same law. The several formations, from the primary crystalline to the coal and upper sandstones, have a common axis of elevation from nearly E. N. E. to W. S. W., partaking more of an equatorial than of a meridional direction. The porphyries and chains of the older traps maintain a similar direction. The greenstones and basalts, polygonal and jointed, or otherwise, are for the most part to be found *within* the area of the coal measures, or rising along the out-crop of the basins. Hence a description of any one locality will generally, in respect of the same series of rocks, be found applicable to another. The student may indifferently begin his researches as his convenience or sojourn for the time may direct. And whether it be the granite on the coasts of Aberdeen or of Arran—the schists of Glenisla or the Mull of Cantire—the silurian of St. Abb's Head or Portpatrick—the devonian of Stonehaven or Girvan—the porphyries of Dundee or Largs—the shales and limestones of St. Andrews, Glasgow, or Ayr—the columnar basalts of Earlsferry, Orrock, Campsie, or Staffa—the lesson throughout will be one and the same, either as respects the mineral texture or the geological position of the rocks examined. A section, therefore, commencing at Ben Nevis and terminating at Kirkcudbright on the Solway, would present the very same series in all the main phenomena of superposition, structure, dislocation, and fossil remains, as the section adopted from Ben-Mac-Dhui to the Cheviots. Granite, gneiss, quartz rock, mica schist, and clay slate, underlie the old red sandstone which traverses the upper district of Stirlingshire. The traps of the Campsie Hills have thrown up, and form the boundary of the great coal-basin, of which Glasgow constitutes the center, and within whose area and suburbs are exhibited all the most striking features of the basalt and greenstone family—the elevation at the Necropolis beautifully showing the effects of their intrusion, and the induration of the sedimentary deposits. On the south, the coal metals are again succeeded by the old red sandstone and the porphyries, which in their turn are replaced by the silurian or graywacke rocks of the border counties. The section throughout is of the most varied and instructive character, diversified by the grandest mountain scenery, the loveliest of the Scottish lakes, and a development of the arts and sciences over inexhaustible coal and iron treasures which has rendered the name of the western metropolis illustrious among the cities of the world.

Should the geologist desire to extend his researches along the western coast and among the islands, he will experience an additional interest, arising chiefly from the numerous junctions of the different formations or sets of rocks which the constant erosion of the Atlantic has everywhere exposed to view. Gigantic isolated portions of granite or syenite, bared all around, are to be seen on every headland. The twistings and flexures of gneiss and the schists are frequent and remarkable. Columnar basalt, similar to Staffa, fringes the base of every islet and promontory; and from appearances like these, he will invariably infer the presence of the carboniferous deposits, which, in small detached patches are of common occurrence. Here, likewise, are to be found the lias and oolites, in marginal stripes on several of the islands, easily distinguished by their characteristic fossils, and giving unequivocal indications of a far greater extension, and continuity with the main land, ere the inroads of the sea had broken up and parted so much of the aboriginal structure of the district. The *vi et sæpe cadendo* of geological agency—the convulsions of subterranean forces, and the destroying powers of water—are exhibited in all their grandeur, where, in the face of cliffs exposed to their foundations, the hardest rocks may be observed yielding to every wave, and the whole inner machinery of granitic and basaltic dykes which upheaved them from their basis traced in their most varying forms and complicity. Out of the Ægean a finer group of islands is nowhere to be threaded—some scarcely raised above sea-level—some towering into the clouds, as in the lofty peaks of Mull, Jura, and Rum, with an altitude almost equal to their length—most of them glorying in names soft and euphonious as the choicest of classic Greece—and yet, all fragmentary and disrupted, as if but yesterday shivered by the thunder cloud. Skye exhibits an epitome not of the islands only, but nearly of our whole British geology, in which there is every variety of trap, combined with the primary series—coal, white sandstone, and limestone—the lias and oolites of secondary formation—and mountains 3,300 feet in height, composed of Labrador feldspar and hypersthene, whose crystals in the dark composite mass rival in structure, if not in beauty, the stalactitic concretions of the Spar Cave itself. Rocks, too, are here, of metamorphic texture, to which a Macculloch did not venture to assign a name or position in his list. And the serrated jagged pinnacles of the Coolin ridge, with the black Coruisk inclosed as in a crater, who will attempt to describe—unlike to everything else in bleak, naked, precipitous grandeur! The poet of the Isles has sketched the picture—

> "Such are the scenes, where savage grandeur wakes
> An awful thrill that softens into sighs;
> Such feelings rouse them by dim Rannoch's lakes,
> In dark Glencoe such gloomy raptures rise:
> Or farther, where, beneath the northern skies,
> Chides wild Loch-Eribol, his caverns hoar—
> But, be the minstrel judge, they yield the prize
> Of desert dignity to that dread shore
> That sees grim Coolin rise, and hears Coriskin roar."

# ENGLAND.

## PART II.

### CHAPTER I.

#### ENGLAND—GENERAL SKETCH.

DIFFERING as England does in people, manners, language, laws, and institutions from Scotland, a still greater difference will be found to exist in the physical structure, the mineral qualities, the organic remains, and in all the other phenomena of her geological development. In the ascending series of rocks, Scotland furnishes only a few steps of the building—the lower courses of a gigantic pyramid; across the borders, strata upon strata follow each other in regular gradation, until they attain their apex of elevation in the center of the capital. Another distinction exists in the quantity and extent of those rocks which are common to both countries. All the primary, transition, and igneous formations are more abundant in the northern division of the island, constituting nearly three-fourths of its surface, while in the southern division they do not amount to a fiftieth part; but, on the other hand, the secondary and tertiary formations, which in Scotland are scarcely recognized, or only found in patches, form in England about two-thirds of its superficial area. Hence, on English ground, a new interest begins as a totally new series of mineral strata rises into view, and all charged with types and families of creatures of equally new and marvelous organization.

The new series of rocks to be described, are termed the Permian, triassic, oolitic, cretaceous, and tertiary systems. Some of these deposits are of vast thickness and extent. They all abound in fossils, some in the greatest profusion, others only in the rarest and most remarkable types. In consequence of these accumulations, England, as compared with her sister kingdom, may be described as the full organic form in bones, muscles, and fleshy appendages, plump and rounded all over, where one sees little of the framework or internal ossification. The great masses are so covered over, the ribs and members are so silted up, that the ridges and hills of the country, save on the outskirts, dwindle into insignificance. Every original depression has been concealed, new increments of matter are everywhere added, layer upon layer superinduced, until the older fabric is nearly obliterated, or only at wide intervals observed to rise above the surface. Scotland exhibits the huge trunk, stripped and laid bare; every yielding thing has been eroded and torn off; and little remains, except the giant skeleton, the lineamentary fragments of the primeval world.

What is common to the two countries, among the primary and crystalline rocks, occupies the whole western line of coast. The eastern shores of Ireland, correspond in mineralogical character with the opposite shores of Scotland, England, and Wales, where a great silurian belt covers, almost continuously, both lines of coast. These districts have thus all a common origin, are all of the same geological epoch, and were probably at one period more united than appearances now indicate. The Cumbrian group is isolated from the other portions of the system, and, as described by Professor Sedgwick, comprehends the lowest fossiliferous beds in the island, or perhaps as yet known in the crust of the globe. The elaborate work of Sir R. I. Murchison on "THE SILURIAN SYSTEM," has made every one acquainted with the extensive deposits in Wales and Cornwall, in which the divisions of the system are fully pointed out, their fossil contents amply detailed, and their relations to analogous deposits in other parts of the world satisfactorily demonstrated. Through all these regions, therefore, we are again carried back among the earlier records already noticed. Coincident with the same are the old red sandstone deposits which stretch along the base of the more highly-inclined silurians, covering the greater portion of Herefordshire and Devonshire; and here, as in Scotland, the sandstones and conglomerates are immediately succeeded by the rich treasures of the carboniferous age. In the rocks of the three families lie, in profuse abundance, the organic remains of the epochs which produced them—cast like wreck among the silts and sands now hardened and upheaved into mountains—the peaks of Skiddaw and Snowdon, of Plinlimmon and Helvellyn, once the beaches or floors of our ancient seas.

The Cumberland group of mountains, with its varied scenery and lakes, is surrounded with the carboniferous rocks—as bright and lovely a picture, set in a framework of jet or ebony, as the mind can contemplate. The great *scar*, or mountain limestone, constitutes the base of the coal series, resting on the old red conglomerate. This calcareous deposit is of vast thickness, range, and extent—a concrete mass of animal remains of five or six hundred feet. It presents the outline of a great coral reef which anciently fringed the center cluster of the lake mountains: and is still, with a few breaks, traceable along their wide and irregular circumference. The sublime gorge of Gordale, the fine gray precipices at the foot of Ingleborough, the caverns of Chapel-le-Dale and Clapham, the rocks of Kirby Londsdale Bridge, and the great white terrace of Whitbarrow, all derive their peculiar features from the effects of erosive action on this formation. Diverging from the great terminal group of the Cumbrians, the same deposit rises along the center of the district into an independent ridge, taking up the most commanding positions—the towering summit of Cross Fell on the one hand, and the celebrated High Peak of Derby on the other, with all its wondrous caves and sparkling fluor-crystals. The intermediate range of the Penine Alps, so denominated by the Romans, is chiefly composed of the formation. The caves of Kirkdale, the haunt of the British hyena and other extinct carnivora, are situated in the same limestone, which is also the repository of numerous lead mines, distinguished for their splendid metallic concretions and fluor-spars. And here, too, are rivers which are lost in its dark caverns; and that wonder of wonders, an astronomical paradox, where, from the peculiar conformation of the hills and ravines, the sun does not rise upon the inhabitants of Narrowdale, until he has passed his meridian, and, as if to repair the loss, twice sets upon their horizon in the course of every evening.

The coal-measures on the eastern side of this chain consist of the Northumberland, Durham, Yorkshire, Nottingham, and Derby fields; on the west and north, Whitehaven, Lancashire, Manchester, and North Stafford; and on the south lie the basins of Ashborne, Loughborough, Wolverhampton, and Dudley. The limestone skirts the out-crop of the metals in all these localities, and thus serves to define the relations of the several basins, and the cause of so many divisions in the field, occasioned by the net-work of coral reef with which it has been originally penetrated. The Wolverhampton basin is remarkable for the number of roots and stumps of fossil trees found "in situ;" in the Derby field the railway tunnel has exposed to view a group of sigillaria, forty in number, standing at right angles to the plane of the beds, and not more than three or four feet apart. Many of the tree fossils occupy a similar position in the Northumberland and Newcastle coal-measures, reminding us of the submerged forests of which, within the modern epoch, our sea-coasts furnish so many examples. The Newcastle coal-field embraces an area of nearly eight hundred square miles, being forty-eight miles in length by twenty-four in breadth; the depth of the shaft is about three hundred fathoms, from which are annually brought to the surface an average of six million tons of coal. Sixty thousand persons are employed in the mining operations; and fourteen hundred vessels are engaged in carrying the mineral to London and its environs. The iron trade, connected with the different English coal-fields, is upon a corresponding scale of magnitude, there being little short of a million and a half tons of the metal annually smelted and brought to the market, estimated to be worth, upon an average, twenty millions of pounds sterling, and comprising within the dimensions of this small island, as much as is exhumed by all the other nations of the globe. The Newcastle coal-measures have been singularly disturbed. A basaltic dyke, in some places eighteen yards wide, crosses the southern part of the field, throwing down the metals on one side ninety fathoms, and reducing the coal, at the distance of fifty yards, to a state of cinder. This great dyke is traceable through a course of seventy miles. As an example of the prodigious power with which these subterranean forces have acted in the district, suffice it to mention, that the limestone which underlies the coal metals has been elevated nearly to the summit of Cross Fell, a mountain three thousand feet in height; and estimating the thickness of the formation at four thousand feet, the limestone, it will thus appear, has been raised above its original position upward of six thousand feet.

The "green rock," or basaltic greenstone of the South Staffordshire coal-field, presents an interesting subject of geological research. The center of the formation, as also that of the eruptive agency of the tract, may be considered to be in the Rowley Hills, from which the latter diverges on all sides, setting off innumerable veins or vertical dykes, which are subdivided into smaller veins of a white color, and everywhere penetrating and altering the shales, sandstones, and coal metals. This igneous mass is more of an underground than super-surface rock, occupying an area of twenty-five square miles, and rising only into slightly-elevated and detached ridges. It corresponds, in mineral characters and position, with another extensive effusion of trap in the northern coal-fields, termed the "Whinsill." This consists of a bed of basalt, which has been injected among the strata of the coal-measures, or, as some conjecture, has been poured over them as a cotemporaneous formation—an overflood of lava produced during the deposition of the mountain limestone group, and overlaid in turn by the succeeding series of upper strata. Nearly the entire coal-measures of the north of England have been more or less influenced by the eruption of the whinsill, from which dykes are thrown off in every direction, accompanied by phenomena precisely similar to those exhibited in the coal districts of Scotland. In both countries the same agencies are thereby demonstrated to have been at work, originating in the same causes and producing similar effects, and doubtless cotemporaneous in their operations over these and other immense areas of the globe.

The rocks which constitute the SECONDARY and TERTIARY DIVISIONS in the great geological series remain to be described. These, generally, all range eastward from the older formations, to which they succeed in the order of superposition. The line of section of the whole bears from Whitehaven on the north-west, to Newhaven on the German Ocean by south-east, where, along this course, every formation in the island is intersected, ascending from the granite of the Cumbrian mountains through all the intermediate series to the London clay and upper tertiaries. The strata of which these formations consist are all, more or less, inclined to the horizon, dipping under each other, and emerging in succession to the surface. The outcrop is at right angles to the line of section, so that each class of rocks rises to and faces the north-west, meeting the eye of the geologist as they are in turn approached, and narrowing in extent and receding in proportion as they are vertically removed from the older systems.

Hence, were our researches to begin here, instead of in the Grampian range, the starting point would necessarily be in the Lake mountains. The crystalline primary rocks are developed, though sparingly, in this district; and these, again, are surrounded and overlaid by the lowest fossiliferous deposits, termed by their explorer and historian, "The Cumbrian System." All the driest details of the science are here too amply relieved by the charming and magnificent scenery amidst which they fall to be wrought out, where the inner and outer arrangements of Nature, in the disposition of her works, are alike fitted to call forth our admiration and delight. The author of "Elia," who had spent his days in a city life and had a prejudice against every other mode of consuming time, upon his first excursion so far into the country, describes Coleridge as "dwelling upon a small hill by the side of Keswick, in a comfortable house, quite enveloped on all sides by a net of mountains; great floundering bears and monsters they seemed, all couchant and asleep." It was enough; the soul of the man of genius was stirred. He clambered up to the top of Skiddaw; and he waded up the bed of the Lodore; and he satisfied himself, "that there is such a thing as tourists call *romantic*." But Lamb was never meant for a geologist, and for science of any kind he had no aptitude. The athletic Wordsworth is of a different mold, compacted of different elements, a mind stored with the loveliest images; an understanding capable of sounding the depths of any subject, and a thirst after knowledge from all and every source of visible creation; and yet, mark how disparagingly he pronounces judgment upon the student of unquestionably the most poetical of all the branches of physical inquiry—"that fellow-wanderer"—

> "He who with pocket hammer smites the edge
> Of luckless rock or prominent stone,
> The substance classes by some barbarous name,
> And hurries on;
> and thinks himself enriched,
> Wealthier, and doubtless wiser, than before."

But men, it would seem, can no more command their moods of thought than their prejudices. The poetical vein, like the geological, will burst through all restraints to illustrate and vindicate the principles of truth. We have often repeated, recalling them from memory, as the index of our own frame of mind, while searching in the crypts of the primeval world, the beautiful lines—a hymn to Nature's works, and the study of them—

> "These barren rocks, our stern inheritance,
> These fertile fields, that recompense our pains,
> The shadowy vale, the sunny mountain top,
> Woods waving in the wind their lofty heads,
> Or hushed; the roaring waters, and the still.
> They see the offering of my lifted hands—
> They hear my lips present their sacrifice—
> They know if I be silent, morn or even."

Nor does it rest here, for directly is our science under a deep debt of gratitude to the author of the "Excursion," who sought for and obtained the aid of the geologist's pencil to fill up the outline of his own sweet picture of the "Scenery of the Lakes." Read side by side, one may well ask, whether the descriptions of the poet, or the sketches of the philosopher, are the more buoyant in diction, diversified in illustration, or pregnant with devotional inspiration. The work of Wordsworth and Sedgwick as a companion of travel is without a rival, in which, and out of the darkest pages of creation, we see the light of science falling upon, as if intending in verity to produce, an illuminated volume, and over which, at one and the same moment imagination is throwing her gayer and softer colorings. The physical structure of the district, in fact, furnishes the key to all its picturesque and delicious scenery. The geology and the poetry are the counterparts of each other. Wordsworth has drank deep at the fountains, and told the story of the one: the lessons of the other have been read by a kindred spirit, who has heard the mighty voice muttered in the dark recesses of the earth, and, in his own eloquently impassioned diction, Sedgwick has recorded the truths "of wisdom, of inspiration, and of gladness; telling us of things unseen by vulgar eyes—of the mysteries of creation—of the records of God's will before man's being—of a spirit breathing over matter before a living soul was placed within it—of laws as unchangeable as the oracles of nature." And out of all the apparent confusion, and multiplicity of objects so blended together, he has brought "harmonies" to light, which are to have "their full consummation only in the end of time, when all the bonds of matter shall be cast away, and there shall begin the reign of knowledge and universal love."

Structure of the Cumbrian Group.

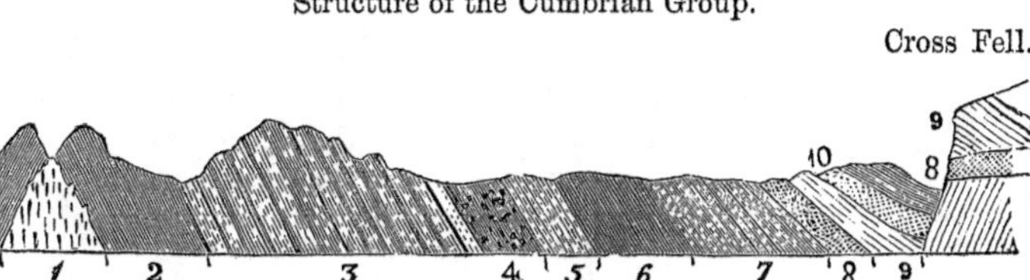


1. Granite.
2. Skiddaw Slate.
3. Green Roofing Slate, Porphyry, &c.
4. Coniston Limestone.
5. Silicious Grits.
6. Ireleth Slates.
7. Slaty Flagstone.
8. Old Red Sandstone.
9. Carboniferous Limestone.
10. Magnesian Limestone, and New Red Sandstone.

Thus, as seen in the preceding section, four geological systems are, in this charming district of lakes and mountains, all clustered together and rolled up for the convenient inspection of a few days' rambles: The Silurian, Devonian, Carboniferous, and Permian: and to these are to be added the Granites, Porphyries, and Plutonic family of greenstones and basalts.

## CHAPTER II.

### THE PERMIAN SYSTEM—NEW RED SANDSTONE.

THE geological formations described are succeeded in the ascending order by the PERMIAN system of deposits—a term borrowed from the department of Perm in Russia, where the strata cover an area about twice the size of France. This constitutes the new red sandstone of English geology, and has many equivalents in other countries. Thus, in the lower division of the group or true Permian, there occurs the Zechstein and Lower Bunter series of strata: in the upper or triassic division, the equivalents are the Upper Bunter and Grés Bigarré, or variegated sandstone, the Muschelkalk and Keuper of French and German authors. The system is largely developed in America, Africa, India and China; where, as in Britain, the deposits are of extremely varied mineral characters, consisting of grits, sandstones, marls, limestones, gypsum, and rock-salt, each presenting its own family types of vegetable and animal life.

The new red sandstone extends across England without interruption, through the medial or central counties, and ranges nearly north-east by south-west. The two great divisions of which it consists are everywhere well marked, the dolomitic or magnesian limestone forming the base, and giving character to the lower permian group; the upper triassic group is sufficiently distinguished by the rock-salt deposit which is wholly included in this part of the formation. Each, too, has its own peculiar set of fossils. Those of the former are allied to animals that flourished during the carboniferous period; two genera of fishes, the palæoniscus and pylopterus, are common to both. The fauna and flora of the triassic group are regarded as entirely new, neither borrowing from nor imparting anything to illustrate the organisms of the older families of rocks. The one series of strata thus represents the coming of a new, the other records the departure of a past state of things.

In the central counties of England this deposit expands into a great plain, surrounded on all sides by the coal-measures, while within its own area several basins—as those of Leicester, Warwick, and South Stafford—are included, being completely isolated by the new red. An interesting economic question hence arises—Do the coal minerals occupy the whole or any considerable portion, of the extensive area covered by this formation? An equally important geological problem is connected with the solution of the question—namely, What are the general relations of the older to the newer deposits of the district? The researches of Sir R. I. Murchison, and more recently, of the geological survey, have shown that the three groups of stratified rocks in South Staffordshire, the new red sandstone, coal-measures, and silurian beds, are each unconformable to the other—that the upper rests indifferently upon the two lower formations—and that where the old red occurs, the new is sometimes in immediate contact. It is inferred from this, that there was an uplifting of the silurian rocks, along with considerable denudation, previous to the deposition of the carboniferous strata. Mr. Jukes has observed pebbles of coal, in great abundance, in the lower beds of the new red sandstone, and thence deduces the following conclusions:— 1. That there was a movement and denudation of the coal-measures, amounting, in some localities, to their entire destruction and removal, before the deposition of the new red sandstone. 2. That, subsequently to the deposition of the new red sandstone, there was a very great movement of all these rocks, producing their present faults and inclined positions. 3. That the boundaries of the South Staffordshire coal-field, as far as examined, present examples of three kinds of relation between the coal-measures and new red sandstones; *i. e.*, by conformable succession; by fault, the coal-measures being present on the downcast side; and, thirdly, where the destruction of the coal-measures has brought the new red sandstone into immediate contact with the silurian strata. The author of this paper is farther of opinion that, while there is a great probability that the larger part of the new red sandstone plain conceals productive coal-measures, there is the presumption that these will not be found at a depth of less than 500 or 600 yards below the surface.

Corresponding with these views it will be remembered that, after the deposition of the coal-measures, there succeeded a period of violent plutonic action, whereby the formation was dislocated, broken up into smaller sections or basins, and pierced by the igneous rocks. There would, consequently, during this season of paroxysm, be a vast destruction of animal and vegetable life. The indurated crust would everywhere undergo great trituration. Gravel, sand, and mud of every quality would be cast along the shores, or silted up in the deeper hollows. And then again would come a term of general repose, as the angry elements subsided, exhausted by their own violence. The scene was actually or nearly as described; and, in the aspect of the older denuded and uplifted rocks, as above represented, there are the most striking evidences of the agitations of the period. The exuberant flora of the carboniferous age, suffered prodigiously, or became utterly extinct. Conglomerates were formed which exhibit few traces of organic life. To these succeeded the vast areas of the fine-grained sandstones, and gypseous and saliferous marls, everywhere nearly horizontal, and still undisturbed on their ancient beds. The tribes of animals were abridged in numbers, changed or modified in structure, so as to suit the altered state of things. The rain-drop, ripple-mark, and foot-print are all witnesses to be adduced of the mighty change, as they are all proofs of the doings of Him who holds the waters in the hollow of his hand, makes the clouds to distill in showers, issues his command to the hurricane and the earthquake, and restores in renovated beauty the face of nature.

The lowest bed of the formation is the magnesian limestone, which derives its name from the quantity of carbonate of magnesia distributed through the matter of the rock, amounting in some instances to as much as sixty per cent. It is likewise called the *dolomitic* limestone, from M. Dolomieu, who first investigated its granular crystalline structure. This limestone is generally of a yellow color, glimmering luster, passing occasionally into blue and brick-red varieties, and exfoliates in thin plates, or breaks up in large botryoidal masses. In this form it occurs at the cliffs of Durham, where it assumes the grouping and arrangement of chain-shot; and, as the beds are distinctly stratified, the face of the rock has a very striking and pleasing effect. In the more southern counties, this formation exists generally in the form of a conglomerate, supposed to be derived from the debris of the older carboniferous limestone united by a dolomitic paste; thus illustrating the source and mode of the deposit, while in the organic remains there has been traced a regular gradation between the types of the older sub-carboniferous and the successive newer strata.

Let us consider some of the more remarkable forms, tracings, and ingredients of the formation.

I. The Organic Remains are scanty as compared with those of the age immediately anterior. The vegetable forms, as yet detected, are new and distinct. The fishes consist of six or seven genera, and about as many different species. And here commences, it is supposed, the singular change in their ossification, for which science can assign no reason, as it cannot detect the least appearance of graduation into the now, for the first time, begun and completed change. The fishes of the formation present the homocercal—that is, the equally-lobed, or one-lobed tail-fin,—a structure peculiar to existing races, with the exception of the shark, sturgeon, and a few others, and form a striking contrast to those in the antecedent groups, which were all possessed of the Heterocercal, or unequally-lobed tail-fin.

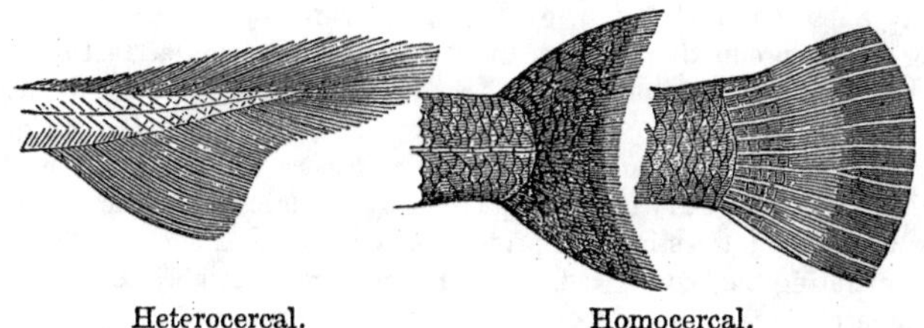

Heterocercal. Homocercal.

The Permian system of strata has hitherto been noted for the introduction of walking, air-breathing animals; hence it has been a canon of the science, that in these deposits lie entombed the last links of that ancient chain of organic life which prevailed from the beginning, and also the first terms of the new series which attained to such monstrosities and prolific exuberance in the succeeding epoch. Doubtful as to the existence of reptilian and ornithic creatures during the carboniferous period, both forms of creation are here distinctly manifested; and, in the higher members of the triassic group, birds and reptiles have left traces of their path. Thus remarkably defined, in an invariable chronological series, was the new red sandstone formation; all the ancient types of organic life were disappearing; completely new forms had just begun to replace them. But, while we are writing, the discovery has been announced that, so old as the devonian age, reptiles existed; alligator-like foot-prints, in regular alternating order, have been found impressed in the old red sandstone, near Pottsville in Pennsylvania, and by Mr. Lea, their discoverer and American conchologist, the animal which owned them has been named the SAUROPUS PRIMÆVUS. A revolution in geology is decreed in the words. Many divisions in the systems of rocks will have to be revised, many distinctions altogether obliterated, theories of development and of many other things are now sadly misplaced, and out of keeping with the newly-declared order and progress of organic life.*

* The strata in which these tracks occur have since been carefully investigated by Prof. H. D. Rogers, who has ascertained that they belong truly to the carboniferous red shale, and are, therefore, of an age essentially later than that attributed to them. In a communication made to the American Association, Prof. Rogers says :—They occur, indeed, in a geological horizon, only a few hundred feet below the conglomerate which marks the beginning of the productive coal series, in which series similar foot-prints, attributed to batrachian reptiles, had been previously met with in Western Pennsylvania. Instead, therefore, of constituting a register of the antique life earlier than any hitherto discovered, by at least a whole chapter in the geological book, they carry back its age only by a single leaf. The surfaces upon which these interesting foot-prints abound are the smooth, divisional plains separating the beds of red sandstone, and are invariably coated with a fine impalpable material of a once slimy and soft mud; and everything in the texture of these surfaces goes to prove that they were in contact with the air, and were the stages of rest between the alternate depositions of the strata. Many of them are covered with ripple-lines and water-marks, sug-

But without venturing at present to enter upon the consequences to palæontology involved in this important discovery, we proceed with the known and recognized history of the formation in question.

The organic remains contained in the upper, or triassic group, differ considerably from those of the lower division of beds.—While the same families of vegetable fossils are preserved which characterized the coal-measures, the particular species and genera have disappeared. About twenty species of ferns and coniferæ, a few calamites, several fucoid plants, and a gigantic genus named *Voltzia,* and resembling the Araucaria or Norfolk Island fir, comprise the thinly-scattered specimens of the flora of the period. The quarries at Coventry yield some undetermined stems of trees, and leaves like those of our thick-ribbed cabbages have been found in the strata near Liverpool. The animal remains are more numerous as well as varied in their structures ; some, indeed, altogether anomalous in their organization, and foot-prints of the most puzzling characters and dimensions. There are several new types of mollusca and crinoidea, among the latter the *Encrinus formosus,* one of the most beautiful forms in any department of the animal kingdom. The fishes of the placoid order consist of seven genera and fourteen species, of ganoids three genera and seven species. The REPTILIA supply the marvels of the period.

gestive of the shelving shore, and, with few exceptions, they are spotted over with little circular impressions, imputed to the pattering of rain. All over the successive floors of this ancient world, as delicate and impressible in their texture as so much wax or parchment, are the footsteps and the trails of various creeping things,—the prints of some unknown four-footed creature, thought to be reptilian in its nature, but of whose true affinities the Professor expressed his doubts, trails analogous to those of worms and molluscs, and various other marks, written in hieroglyphics too ancient to be interpreted. The larger foot-prints are, for the most part, five-toed, alternate in the steps, and with the fore-feet as large nearly as the hind ones; marks of the scratching and slipping of the feet, and the half effacing passage of the tail, or of some soft portion of the body, are often distinctly legible.

Prof. Agassiz stated his doubts as to the reptilian character of the foot-prints noticed, and, after describing the difference in the arrangement of the locomotive organs of the modern and the ancient fishes, gave it as his belief, that in those early periods there were fishes of a structure which permitted them to walk upon all fours.

Prof. Owen has described six distinct genera from these singular fossils, in which he has established an affinity to the batrachia. From the curiously-complicated texture of the teeth, the term *labyrinthodon* has been given to one genus, while the same authority suggests, that the foot-impressions to which the term *cheirotherium* had already been applied, might belong to this animal. The two genera, *claydyodon* and *rhyncosaurus*, are remarkable specimens of organic structure, the latter combining the lacertian type of skull, with edentulous jaws, which impart to the forepart of the head the profile of a parrot.

II. The Ichnolites, or foot-prints, constitute a marked feature of the formation. These geological phenomena were first introduced to the notice of the public, about twenty years ago, by the late Dr. Duncan of Ruthwell, when his announcement of the tracks and foot-marks of animals along the ancient shores of Dumfries-shire created a sensation among all classes hitherto unprecedented in the history of the fossil department of the science. Robinson Crusoe was not more moved at the discovery of a human foot-print on the sands of his lonely island in the distant main, than were men of science, that traces of organic life should thus be stereotyped in a deposit believed to be utterly destitute of fossil relics. The creatures which had traced them, so like to existing walking things, greatly increased the interest and the wonder excited by the picture—the tread in all the freshness of yesterday of the inhabitants of the antediluvian world! The phenomenon, however, is now one of very general and common occurrence, several quarries in the same locality—various places in England—in Saxony—in the states of Connecticut, Massachusetts, and Virginia—having since been found to yield the impressions in the greatest abundance, and of numerous types and forms. And so well delineated and perfect are the impressions, that, in the absence of any other reminiscence of the animal, these characters have supplied the same aid to the skillful palæontologist that the fragment of a bone, a fin, or a scale, did to Cuvier and Agassiz, in the reconstruction of their organic models, and determination of extinct genera and species. Birds and reptilian quadrupeds have all contributed their share in the production of these curious lithographs. Small toe-looking scratches, deep-palmy impressions, cloven hoof-like indentations, and large gigantic hollows, have all been pictured in clear distinct outline, covered up, and now again laid patent before you as by the removal of the coverlit of your album. The Boston "Journal of Natural History" communicates the following interesting account of the researches of Dr. Deane :—"I have in my possession," he says, "consecutive impressions of tridactyle feet, which measure eighteen inches in length, by fourteen in breadth, between the extremities of the lateral toes. Each footstep will hold half a gallon of water, and the stride is four feet. The original bird must have been four or five times larger than the African ostrich, and therefore could not have weighed less than 600 pounds. Every step the creature took sank deep, and the substrata bent beneath the enormous load. If an ox walk over stiffened clay, he would not sink so deeply as did this tremendous bird." Sir C. Lyell has examined most of the foot-print districts in America, and found the markings so numerous in some places as to resemble the puddled stand of a sheep-fold or market-place ; the very spots, doubtless, whither the animals had resorted to quench their thirst, or screen them at mid-day from the scorching heat. The various tracings become more distinct in proportion to the distance from the scene of common rendezvous, and the several routes by which they would return to their respective haunts, or fields of pasturage, are clearly defined.

A considerable doubt hung over the accounts from time to time detailed in the American journals and other publications, concerning these novel and extraordinary discoveries, until they were more than matched by the actual exhumation of the entire skeletons of the feathery tribes, far exceeding in dimensions anything hitherto dreamed of in the science of ornithology. The collections of Mr. Williams, and of Mr. W. Mantell, from the alluvial deposits of New Zealand, utterly confounded all previous calculations as to the size and bulk attainable by the bird tribe. The tibia of a Dinornis, in the collection of the University of Edinburgh, measures thirty-one inches in length, a femur seventeen inches, the average circumference of both being nearly twelve inches. From the foot to the top of the clavicle, the animal must have stood at least thirteen feet in height. With the strut of the turkey, or the pride of the peacock—head and neck of corresponding altitude—what a denizen for the wilds and forests of this region of the new world! When animals of similar dimensions, but of an earlier epoch, frequented the beaches of Great Britain, we have to imagine the Cumbrian mountains, the Penine chain, Derby Peak, and the lofty cliffs of Avon, surrounded by an inland sea stretching by central France, the Black Forest, and the Hartz mountains, and the shores all round silted with the materials which now constitute the triassic group. Tortoises, turtles, bird-headed lizards, birds themselves, salamander and frog-like creatures larger than crocodiles, resorted as now to the sea-shore, in the cool fresh of the evening or as tide-mark permitted, and regaled themselves at will on the food which an ever-bounteous element furnished to their various wants.

The science which, from such *indicia* as these, has succeeded in determining not only the class, but the very form and habits, of the animals which impressed them—no other traces remaining than those petrified footsteps, covered up and hidden for ages—presents subjects of study to the inquiring mind, which may well rank among the most valuable, as well as curious, of human research. Is it not wonderful enough, that organic impressions merely should have been transmitted so fresh and entire, as to admit of classification, equal in scientific precision to that of the families of living things? What matter of suggestive reflection, inscribed on every page of that history? The tribes which were created and flourished during the Permian-triassic age perished, their earthy parts in most cases were all again absorbed by the earth, dissipated or melted into the viewless air. Still there are memorials of their existence, enduring and indelible, not of bones and sinews, but of actions and habits, which the waters cannot obliterate, nor the floods wash away! Man, a being of a different mold,—and with him

> "Will all great Neptune's ocean wash this blood
> Clean from my hand?"

was the cry of instinctive dread—the foreboding of an assured conscience, that the foul and guilty deed could never be effaced from the memory, nor blotted from the records of creation.

The foot-tread of the robber has tracked him to his den; the minutest stain of blood has established the crime of murder; a dream or vision of the night has pointed to the mangled corse; a word uttered years after all was forgotten, or a rude ditty chanted, have recalled the pictures of infancy, and the wanderer to his home. Here we behold, stamped upon the rock, legible as the law upon the tablets of the heart, intimations of the great universal law, that an act once committed cannot be canceled; that a cause will be followed by a sequence of effects; indefinite and ever-extending; and that the Divine Spirit, which drew illustrations from the fields and taught wisdom among the rocks of Horeb, still points the moral in these ineffaceable memorials—that the recording angel so traces in the book of life the story of every age, of every generation, of every individual, never to be lost nor forgotten in that eternity whither their works do all follow them.

III. Other singular records of the age under review have been preserved in a similar manner; for the ocean itself has not failed to impress its own movements on the sands laved by its waters. Hence the RIPPLE-MARK has been detected, a recognized object of the science, and a phenomenon to be seen in the sandstones of all ages and in all countries. The new red, from the stiller waters perhaps in which it was formed, contains everywhere beautifully minute and perfect delineations of the kind. The *furrowed* sandstones form a class by themselves, being selected in the neighborhood of Brighton, as paving-stones for the streets, and in the stable-yards as a protection for the horses against slipping. The traces often of the more destructive violence of the sea, even of recent date, in leveling villages, sweeping down plains, undermining cliffs, overwhelming proud navies, are completely obliterated or forgotten, while here the records of its still voice are indelibly engraven on the rock.

Observe other markings as you walk along the sea-shore on a summer's eve; how every wavelet that breaks upon the beach leaves its tiny indentation, until the whole surface becomes furrowed as the reflex of the ever-shifting flood; there spring up on every side innumerable hillocks of sand, little blisters througn which you detect the movements of a creature within, and theh the trail of the sea-worm is visible all over. These were *vermes* and *annelides* burrowing in the sands, in those ancient times, with instincts and habits precisely the same. "We find," says Dr. Buckland, "on the surface of slabs, both of the calcareous grit, and Stonesfield slate, near Oxford, and on sandstones of the Wealden formation, in Sussex and Dorsetshire, perfectly-preserved and petrified castings of marine worms, at the upper extremity of holes bored by them in the sand, while it was yet soft at the bottom of the water; and within the sandstones, traces of tubular holes in which the worms resided." Nature here has changed little from her first models; the same element, which is now chaffing upon the same materials of sand and rock, has possessed through all time the same ingredients of life-stirring action.

IV. Nor has the atmosphere—that twin ocean of upper earth—failed to give evidence of the properties and laws by which it was then governed. The RAIN-DROP, a singular unmistakeable marking, has also been detected upon the sandstones of the period. These impressions have been described and adopted by men of science as the true veritable indices of the showers and cloud-falls of the old world. The very size of the drop may be measured, the thick pattering of the rain compared with the scanty or copious showers of the present day, and the very point detected from which the wind blew on the day that these showers fell. What a curious tale is thus disclosed, by a record, no modern version of which any one will stay to read a moment longer than he can escape to shelter from its influences. Astronomers tell us, upon the faith of the Herschels, the measurements of Strüve, Bessel, and Mädler, that, notwithstanding that light travels at the inconceivable speed of two hundred and thirteen thousand miles in a second, the light from Uranus, one of our own planetary system, does not reach our earth until two hours after it has been emitted from its orb; that, from the edge of the Milky Way, a star of the twelfth magnitude, careering in all the effulgence of that luminous ether, cannot be descried until four thousand years after the ray has begun its journeyings; and yet more, as the results of the most rigid induction, it is revealed to us that the spots of clouds, which under the resolving power of the best telescopes seem more oval flakes or small specks of whiteness, are really distinct and independent systems, floating at such an immeasurable distance that the light has to wander millions of years before it can break in its faintest morning-streak upon our horizon. Mark the analogy, therefore, ere you scoff at the credulity of the geologist, or the power of the rain-drop to transmit an image of itself through so many revolutions and ages of the earth's history. How impalpable a substance is light! how readily effaced its impressions, or intercepted its brilliant colorings, by the interposition of the frailest creation of matter—an insect's wing, the covering of a leaf, the disc of a flower-petal. But the light, thus easily obliterated or dimmed on earth, has been maintaining its own solitary independent course through every medium, every change, of upper and nether worlds. The moment of its efflux from remotest orb, in depth of infinite space, gave to every particle of that feebly or intensely luminous beam, a separate being and direction, with no return back to its parent source. And now, says the intelligent astronomer, as it drops gently into the searcher of his telescope, that is a ray from yon far distant unresolvable cluster of stars, or of astral systems, for millions of years traveling through these incalculable heights, when as yet the Chaldee sages had pointed no instrument to the heavens, nor the learned of Memphis recorded an observation. Can you deny to other matter, argues the geologist, a similar tenacity of self-preservation, the vitality of impress which merely records the uniformity of the laws and constitution of nature, and which intimates that, through all past time, there were showers to cheer and to refresh the products of the earth? Truth becomes more marvelous than fiction when traced in researches such as these—showing the illimitable range over time and space permitted to human inquiry—and producing, at the same time, things both of heaven and of earth scarcely to be dreamt of in human philosophy.

V. But the economic and practically useful, no less than the speculative or fanciful, form constituents of the new red sandstone formation. The strata are not only indented with impressions of strange and doubtful origin; they inclose, like those of the carboniferous system, treasures of the greatest value; and nature, in ceasing to abound in one kind of product, has been no less exuberant in others, equally contributive to the comfort and convenience of man. In this class of rocks are situated our great deposits of ROCK-SALT and gypsum, of the former of which, beside supplying the demands of the home market, the mines of Cheshire alone export from Liverpool upward of half a million of tons weight. The distribution of the saline mineral is very general over the earth, and by no means constant in its geognostic position; as, for example, in Galicia, it is found among the tertiary deposits; in New York, it occupies the middle of the silurians; while in Hungary, Poland, and England, it is uniformly associated with the new red sandstone. Rock-salt has been long known to and prized by mankind; it became an object of taxation or tribute six hundred and forty years before the Christian era, as narrated of Ancus Martius, "salinarum vectigal instituit;" and hence centuries afterward, when Great Britain was in possession of the Romans, the legions received salt as part of their pay or "salary." Our richest mines are in Cheshire, and along the districts watered by the Dee, the Weaver, and the Mersey. The beds, or rather masses, are imperfectly stratified, and vary in thickness from a few inches to 120 feet and upward: gypsum and variegated marls may be regarded as *constants* in the formation, the gypseous deposits sometimes attaining the enormous depth of 150 feet.

We speak of the beds of gypsum as *deposits*, in common with those of the sandstone matrix in which they are imbedded. It appears, however, on inquiring into the theory of their origin, that they are not strictly such in the true sense of deposits—originally as gypseous deposits—but altered limestones, metamorphosed by the action of gases which have escaped from beneath, and permeated the calcareous mass. The carbonates of lime have been converted into the sulphates of lime, by means of gaseous emanations produced in unknown volcanic depths. Even the dolomitic member of the group is supposed to have a like metamorphic origin; the needful elementary agencies having entered into the parent limestone, and converted it into the magnesian type. Why nature should not have done these things directly, at the first off-throw, science could not, perhaps, very satisfactorily answer the skeptically inquiring mind; but, as the ingredients are all chemically well known, and more especially as there is a vast laboratory ever at work, filled with all kinds of elements, in her subterranean regions, any hypothesis of formation is as rapidly established as it is conceived, and the interest of the subject humanly speaking augmented. The celebrated Berzelius, when questioned on the point, had his ready solution of the problem, easily derived from his unparalleled stores of chemical knowledge:—"Give me a substance containing sulphur—admit the presence of the vapors of sulphur, or sulphurous or sulph-hydrous vapors,—let limestone be also present, and water on the surface or in the atmosphere, AND WE SHALL READILY HAVE GYPSUM." The origin of the saltness of the ocean is still a mystery in science; equally involved in doubt and conjecture is that of the other member of the series, the rock-salt formation. The generally adopted theory, however, is, that it was dependent on volcanic agency for development, as it both contains, and is uniformly associated with, the acids, and other materials found in connection with volcanoes. The chlorides of sodium and gypsum, for example, are at present sublimed from volcanic vents; vapors charged with sulphuric acid are constantly issuing from the same sources; and these passing through or associated with the saline waters of the period, must have aided in the formation of rock-salt and gypsum, which occur more frequently in irregular masses than in true stratified deposits. An additional corroboration of the theory is inferred from the circumstance, that the gypsum accompanying the rock-salt is anhydrous, that is, free from water before exposure to the action of the atmosphere. Hence the conclusion, that the consolidation of both the rock-salt and the gypsum must have been effected by the agency of heat, as, by means of aqueous deposition, a hydrometric influence would have been sensibly perceived.

Wonderful certainly is all this—the inclosing, the consolidation, the arrangement of these remarkable substances. The sea, in the first instance, may readily and abundantly have supplied all the elements of the formation; but how collected and retained, crystallized and incrusted, layer upon layer, over the rocky bottom and volcanic inner chambers, are points still of nice geological inquiry. The celebrated salt mines of Cracow, in Poland, are wondrous operations of the art of man, into the still more wondrous products and recesses of nature. Here the entire arrangements of a city are almost perfected; the streets, market-place, chapel, rivers, reservoirs, grottoes, and all the requirements of comfort and safety gleaming in a blaze of saline crystals.

> "Scoop'd in the briny rock long streets extend
> Their hoary course, and glittering domes ascend;
> Down the bright steeps, emerging into day,
> Impetuous fountains burst their headlong way,
> O'er milk-white vales in ivory channels spread,
> And wondering seek their subterraneous bed.
> Long lines of lusters pour their trembling rays,
> And the bright vault returns the mingled blaze."

The deposit near Cracow is worked on four different levels or stories, divided into innumerable compartments, with thousands of excavations in every direction, and descending to the vast depth of one thousand feet below the surface. The length of the several passages, in their windings and turnings, is calculated to be nearly three hundred miles; about two thousand men are constantly employed in the mining operations; and, though the operations have been carrying on for the known period at least of six hundred years, the mass of rock-salt in the locality is still of inexhaustible extent.

The mines in our own land are equally remarkable after their kind, and cannot fail to interest, if not to astonish, the neophyte who ventures a descent. From the mode in which they are worked, the huge pillars left to support the roof, the thousand lights that illuminate the caverns, the reverberations from the blasting which at intervals ring through their depths, a grandeur and impressiveness are imparted to a scene which scarcely any other combination of objects could produce. And another world—a world of coal and iron—in all its magnificence and riches, lies interred under these glistering stores of lime and salt! How strangely contrasting in their qualities and structure the two formations. But except that a wise and far-seeing Providence collected and garnered up the waste and decay of both for man's use, no principle have we to guide us when speculating on their mineral properties and arrangement—no natural law certainly, self-acting upon matter and evolving new creations of its own, organic or inorganic, to reveal His inscrutable purposes.

## CHAPTER III.

### THE OOLITIC OR JURASSIC SYSTEM—AGE OF REPTILES.

When one is about to travel, or to undertake a journey of any distance from the daily beat of home, it is very seldom indeed that he puts into his pocket a book of science. Voyages, travels, a review at most, or the newest novel, may fill up a spare place in the portmanteau: anything that requires study, or would draw upon the reflective faculties, can be no fitting companion for the occasion, with at least nine-tenths of our moving public.

If the preceding pages have been perused with any attention at all, it is to be hoped that other things will be considered as worthy of a passing glance, as sure we are they cannot fail to be replete with lessons of instructive wisdom. On the ground of mere ephemeral curiosities by the way, geological matters claim consideration. They are exhaustless, too, and ever varying as you proceed. When you imagine that the last mountain rock or quarry contained the whole catalogue of Natural History, and showed you more than Goldsmith, or Buffon, you find that over the next ridge, or in the neighboring field, there are new subjects for study, and still renewing matters for wonder.

If you have taken up your abode for the night at classic Rugby, at sporting Melton-mowbray, or among the academic bowers of Oxford, there are objects all around, in every hill-side, ravine, or railway section, to fill you at once with admiration and astonishment. Go, inquire of that rock. It is the *lias limestone;* beyond it, and at no great distance, lies the *oolite;* and there, in the immediate vicinity of both, you have the *Stonesfield slate.* We invite you to examine any one of these common-place looking stones; and not in Gulliver, not in the history of the Knight of La Mancha, not in all the Mysteries of Udolpho, not in the

Romance of the Forest whose harmonious periods so charmed our youth, will you find anything to compare with the marvels therein to be disclosed. The machinery of a tale may require the aid of giants and genii, but here is "truth without fiction," more startling, marvelous, and so beyond the bounds of nature as now felt and seen, that the most daring fancy is utterly outstripped in its loftiest flights into the regions of the ideal. The series of beds which constitute the mineral features of this extensive district contains the full development of the reptilian type to which we were introduced in the last chapter. Animals there are in these rocks, with forms and features, so fantastic, and apparently disproportioned, that the tales of the most unscrupulous traveler would suffer in comparison. And in truth, there is no page in the book of nature—none, certainly, in all the works of man—so fraught with wonders, or remarkable for stirring incident, as the epoch of animal life whose history is there inscribed.

I. The Nature of the Rocks. The oolitic or Jurassic system, like that of the new red sandstone, comprises the subdivisions of two well-marked natural groups, in which the lias or lower series is included. In point of geographical range, the oolite formation is extensively distributed over the surface of the globe; in mineral character it is varied in every possible degree of texture and composition; in geognostic arrangement there are intercalations, without end, of marine and terrestrial detritus; the organic remains are in the greatest profusion, both as to diversity of type and increase of new creations; and, locally, such has been the appreciation of its various members, that there is scarcely a town or parish in the south-eastern part of England, that has not received from or given habitations and name to, some one of its numerous subdivisions.

Resting upon the triassic formation, there are bands of lias shales, limestones, sandy and ferruginous strata, and upper shales, including nodular concretions and beds of limestone. This series is distributed over the counties of York, Northampton, Somerset, and Dorset. The next are the lower oolites, which comprise an extensive series of calcareous, concretionary sands and sandstones, limestone, thin seams of coal and ligneous clays, and the Cornbrash limestone, which in many localities is a mere aggregation of shells and other marine exuviæ. The Stonesfield slate, the Forest marble, and the Fuller's earth beds, are included in the group, ranging along the Yorkshire coast, through Northampton, Oxford, and Gloucester shires; and in Scotland we have their equivalents in the Brora coal and oolitic limestone of Sutherlandshire, Skye, and the adjacent islands. The middle oolite succeeds, which includes the Oxford clay, the Kelloway rock, and the coral-rag, all more or less distinguished by their profusion and peculiarity of fossils, chiefly shells, echini, and corals. The whole formation terminates in two well known deposits, the Kimmeridge clay and Portland oolite, with its bands of green and red sands, layers of chert and drift-wood. This group prevails in Oxfordshire, Berks, Wilts, Bucks, and the Isle of Portland; the matrix of fossilized reptilia, fishes, and cycadeous plants.

The term OOLITE or roestone, as applied to the whole of the groups enumerated above, is derived from the resemblance between the small rounded grains of which the limestones are generally composed, and the roe of a fish. The Jura mountains, which divide France from Switzerland, consist mainly of these deposits, and hence Jurassic—the *Terrains Jurrassiques* of continental geologists. The word lias is simply a corruption of liers (layers), and has from time immemorial been applied to the rocks of this group. Their relation and order of superposition are fully brought out along the sections of the Great Western Railway from London to Bath. The Birmingham line from Derby by Rugby to the metropolis intersects nearly every member of the series, until they are covered about Wallingford by the chalk.

When one looks at these innumerable bands of rock, and the great diversity of earthy matter of which they are composed, the mind becomes utterly overwhelmed by the rapidity and vastness of the changes which, during this epoch, occurred upon the surface of the globe. A turbid, and often agitated, condition of the waters in which they were deposited is very clearly indicated. The animals of the period were manifestly of a class peculiarly adapted to the impregnated element, the slimy banks, and shallows which prevailed. The flora was abundant, of a kind, and produced in circumstances, favorable for the formation of a lignite coal. The spasmodic action which prevailed after the deposition of the carboniferous beds had not entirely subsided at the Permian period. The change was of too violent a kind to have been brought about without great internal, as well as external, commotion. We find, accordingly, in most districts, that the rocks of this class are upturned and disrupted. The detritus of the new red sandstone and magnesian limestone, thereby occasioned, would go to form new land during the submergence of such portions of the surface as were retained beneath the waters. The oscillations were numerous and frequent, corresponding with the aggregate of beds which compose the system; while the quality and arrangement of the sediment point to changes and alterations in sea-levels, river courses, land boundaries, estuaries, the size and distribution of the basins into which the alluvia were transported. The geographic extent, combined with the frequently insulated position of the oolitic series, clearly demonstrates a vast alteration in the bed of the ocean, as well as in the ridges and elevations which gave diversity to the land. The oolites, in fact, constitute vast calcareous reefs, raised upon the inverted strata of the older formations, which formed the cliffs and headlands of a sea swarming with lizards and crocodilians, and over whose thick umbrageous banks roamed the flying pterodactyle, watching or perhaps escaping from, the singular saurians that reposed in the thickets beneath. The substitution of the pyritous clays for the saliferous marls; the dark argillaceous oolites and blue mottled lias for the yellow crystalline dolomite, is in harmony and keeping with the plants and animals which now, for the first time, sprang into existence.

II. The Organic Remains are very abundant, and in both plants and animals there are various new kinds. Of the former are the cycadeæ, allied to the existing pine-apple; also the lilaceæ, and some other undescribed genera. With regard to animals, this has been emphatically called "the age of reptiles," along with which there are new families of fishes, crustacea, mollusca, and corals. The warm-blooded animals now for the first time appear, of which there are two genera, the *Amphitherium* and *Phas-*

*colotherium*, found in the Stonesfield slate near Oxford, and considered, by analogy of structure, to be allied to the marsupials that inhabit the Australian continent. The same interesting locality has furnished two new genera of insects, the *Prionus Ooliticus* and *Coccinella Wittsii;* in the lias, of different places, eleven genera and species have been discovered, but of which only wings and fragments have been obtained. A perfect specimen of this order has recently been found, by the Rev. P. B. Brodie, in the upper lias, near Cheltenham, resembling the genus *diplax;* but so shattered in the head, that its precise character cannot be determined. The reptilians supply alike new terrestrial and marine tortoises and turtles—lizards, whose arms and legs were provided with a filmy membrane, like bats, to enable them to fly—amphibious saurians, and water saurians unlike anything now in existence.

Contrast this catalogue with the few organic remains to be met with in the preceding period, and ask what called such a newly-inhabited world into being? The face of nature, so remarkably elaborated out of the waste and decay of these old stony materials, is moving all over with life—replenished, so far as yet discovered, with seventy-five generic and specific forms of new vegetation—a hundred and ten new forms of hard-working corallines—seven hundred and thirteen genera and species of the shelly tribes, from the simplest to the most complicated of the chambered orders—a hundred and sixty distinct races of fishes, placoids and ganoids—three varieties of the most strangely constructed mammalian quadrupeds, with thirteen kinds of insects to titillate and keep them in action—and all this array of organic life moving side by side with forty families of gigantic reptiles, herbivorous and carnivorous, creeping, swimming, and flying! The wonders of art have nothing to compare with this. The structure of a blade of grass will not suffer an atheist to live. During the six thousand years of man's existence, one new living thing, of any order or type, has not been called into being. Astronomy is daily adding to her achievements, and penetrating farther among the systems of the universe; but the nebular theory of creation is gone, and the new-world germs will not expand at its fanciful bidding. Geology nobly bears testimony in every page to the rule of one supreme intelligent Creator—an exuberance of life and forms which announces the authoritative interposition of Him

"Whose word leaps forth at once to its effect;
Who calls for things that are not—and they come."

And the mandate goes forth, in that awful simplicity of OMNIPOTENCE, which learning cannot mystify nor ignorance overlook.

This formation abounds in the remains of radiata, mollusca, and crustacea,—all of them differing specifically from those of the older secondary strata. The gigantic *crinoidea* of the carboniferous age have disappeared, succeeded only by a few dwarfish specimens of the *apiocrinite* and pentacrinite, while the *ammonites* mark an increase of nearly two hundred species, preserved in the most perfect state in the shales and limestones of the lias and oolite.

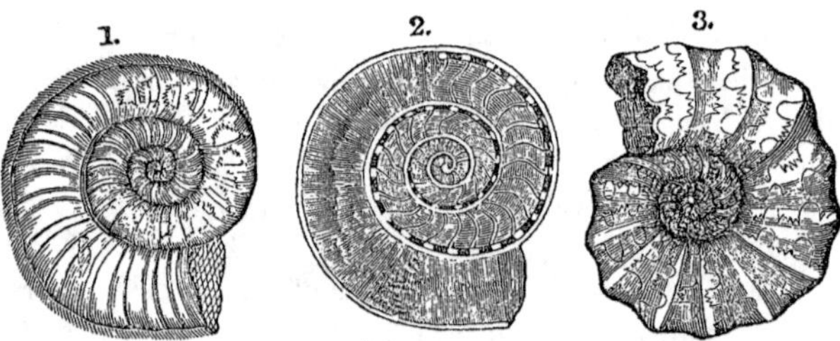


1. Ammonites obtusus; 2. Section of Ammonites obtusus, showing the interior chambers and siphuncle; 3. Ammonites nodosus.

The term Ammonite has been bestowed upon this remarkable shell-fish from its fancied resemblance to the curved horn on the head of the statue of Jupiter-Ammon. The spiral form of the shell is divided into several chambers or compartments, all of which are connected by means of an interior tube or siphuncle. It belongs to the order of Cephalopoda, among which are included ancyloceros, belemnites, nautilus, orthoceratite, and other many-chambered shells. Like the nautilus, the ammonite was gifted with a singular apparatus by which it could pursue its instincts either at the bottom or on the surface of the element in which it lived. The organs of motion were arranged round the head (hence the name *cephalopoda*); and, by the nicely adaptive arrangements of nature, the outer chamber of the shell was capable of retaining the entire body of the animal, while the interior chambers were hollow, thereby rendering the whole structure of nearly the same specific gravity with the waters in which it moved. An elastic tube passing through the siphuncle connected the cavity of the heart with the extremity of the shell, which enabled the animal to contract or expand itself as its exigencies required. Being filled with a dense fluid, excreted by the glandular organs, the creature, when alarmed or wishing to descend, withdrew itself within the outer chamber, whereby the contraction of the tube forced the fluid from the heart into the siphuncle, and increasing the gravity enabled it to descend to the bottom. Upon a reversal of the process—the simple projection of the arms of the head, and the consequent expansion of the body—the ammonite rose with equal facility to the surface, disporting itself at will in its native element. With a view to resist the pressure, when at the bottom, a provision was made by means of the *arch-form* in the structure of the shell; and, additionally, by the insertion of a series of transverse ribs, which comprise all the mechanical contrivances for giving strength and solidity which are sought by the divisions and subdivisions in the vaulted roofs of our Gothic architecture. The geographical distribution of the ammonite partakes of the universality so marked in the vegetable economy of the carboniferous age, the same species even being common to Europe, Asia, North and South America; and always, along with all its numerous congeners, manifesting the most striking examples of that adaptation of means to ends which prevails in every department of creation.

We shall now select a few details of the more remarkable of the reptilian types of this period, referring the reader to the ample and graphic descriptions of Buckland, Conybeare, Mantell, Phillips, and more especially to the Reports of Professor Owen, in the volumes published by the British Association in 1840–'1.

1. The first genus to be noticed is termed the Ichthyosaurus, which partakes at once of the characters of crocodiles, lizards, and fishes. So lavish has nature been in providing for the accommodation and wants of this anomalous creature, that to the paddles of a whale, is added the sternum of an *ornithorhynchus;* the

head of a lizard is joined to the vertebræ of a fish ; and the snout of a porpoise is combined with the jaws and teeth of a crocodile. The magnitude of the eye is prodigious, and the jaws, sometimes exceeding six feet in length, are studded with an apparatus of teeth, amounting in some instances, to a hundred and eighty. "From the quantity of light admitted in consequence of the prodigious size of the eye," says Dr. Buckland, "it must have possessed very great powers of vision: we have also evidence that it had both microscopic and telescopic properties. We find on the front of the orbital cavity, in which this eye was lodged,"—a cavity sometimes fourteen inches in diameter,—"a circular series of petrified thin bony plates, ranged round a central aperture, where once was placed the pupil ; the form and thickness of each of these plates very much resembles that of the scales of the artichoke. It also tends to associate the animal in which it existed, with the family of lizards, and exclude it from that of fishes." These bony plates gave strength to the surface of the eye-ball, which required protection above and below, from the dashing of

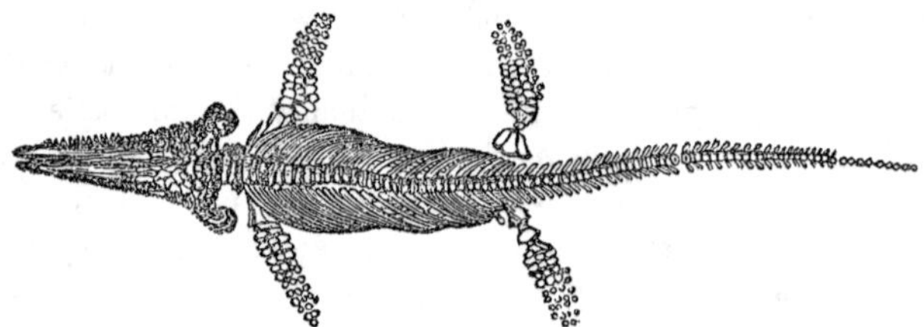

Ichthyosaurus communis.

the waves when it reared its head to the storm, and from the pressure of deep water when it scoured the bottom. The nostrils, it would seem, were placed so close to the anterior angle of the eye, as to render it impossible to breathe without raising the organs of sight to the surface of the water. An ocean, peopled with such monsters ! Imagine so many eyes, larger than a man's head studding its surface, and illuminating, as with fire-balls, their terrific jaws, glaring out from the briny flood ; and what a scene to gaze upon, so different from all that now covers these rich alluvial plains !

2. The Plesiosaurus is allied in some respects to the former, but in other points differs so materially, and possesses characters so strange, as to claim for it a degree of monstrosity unparalleled, even amid the ruins of the old world. Here we have the union of the serpent and chameleon, with a trunk and tail having the proportions of an ordinary quadruped. The mechanism of the lungs and ribs is peculiar, showing that the animal must have breathed with such force and rapidity, as to have rendered the color of the skin changeable, like the chameleon or dying dolphin.

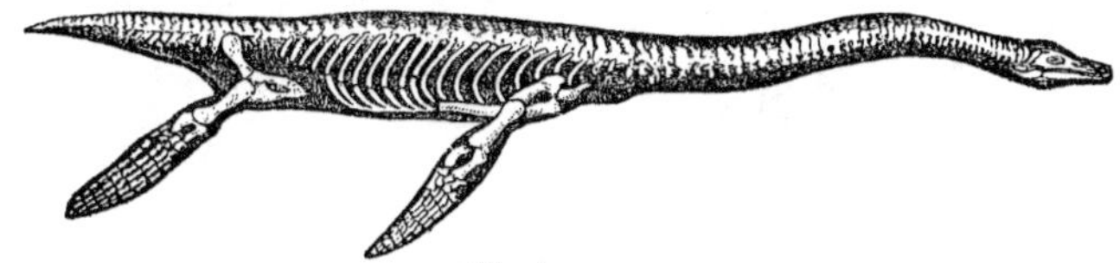

Plesiosaurus.

The neck bore a resemblance to that of the swan; the feet and motions were allied to those of the turtle; and, from the varied intensity of its inspirations, it is conjectured that the creature inhabited the shallow pools and marshy waters along the coast. The body would thus be concealed among the rank vegetable aquatics; while, with its long flexible neck, it would be prepared suddenly to pounce upon its prey. Mr. Conybeare compares the Plesiosaurus to a turtle stripped of its shell; and the ribs, being connected by transverse abdominal processes, present a close analogy to those of the chameleon. Ichthyosauri and Plesiosauri have been found in the secondary strata, from the lias to the chalk inclusive; of the former, twelve species are known and described, and nearly twenty of the latter. The most remarkable of the enalio-saurii or marine reptiles, is the Plesiosaurus-dolichodeirus, discovered in the lias of Lyme-Regis, and which is fertile in the remains of all the animals of that remote and wonder-producing epoch.

3. Another example, taken from the lias, is of its kind even more startling than either of the preceding. This consists of the remains of an animal called the Pterodactyle, or flying reptile, which, more than anything ever conceived or bred in poet's

brain, resembles what Milton must have intended, when to the great arch-fiend he gave a form and flexibility of body, that

"Swims, or sinks, or wades, or creeps, or flies."

Certainly each and one of all these evolutions the Pterodactyle could execute, and he was amply provided with the fitting instruments to perform them. This animal possessed a head intermediate betwixt that of a bird and a reptile, which in both cases is comparatively small, and offering the least resistance to the medium through which it passed, in quest whether of pleasure or subsistence. The hands were of the most prehensile character, adapted by the claws attached at once to fix and firmly grasp its prey, and, when needed for pursuit, to swing itself squirrel-like from branch to branch, and from tree to tree. The wings resembled those of the bat, but in length and size allied to nothing in existing nature, and finding their match only among the dragons of romance. Then, as to feet and limbs, these were of such a construction as to allow the animal safely to repose after its toils in a standing position on the ground, or to perch on trees, or to climb on rocks, or disport from cliff to cliff. The eyes were large; the wings terminated in fingers, from which projected long hooks; the beak was furnished with about sixty sharp piercing teeth. No

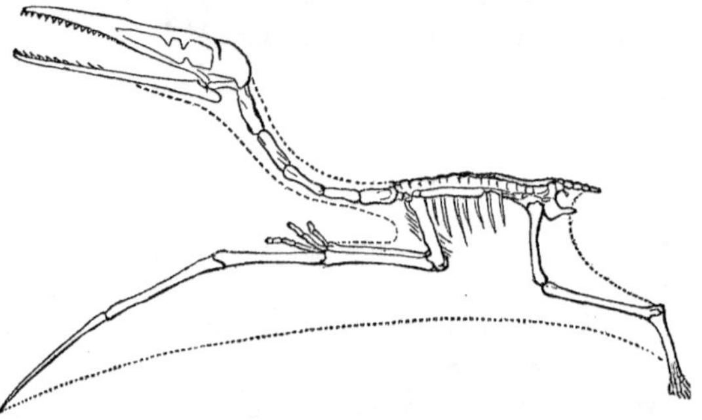

Pterodactyle.

wonder that naturalists were astonished at such heterogenous combinations, as they rose upon their sight—

> "That look not like the inhabitants o' the earth;
> And yet are on't;"

and knew not whether to ascribe them to the air, or the earth, or the domain of waters. But, in the hands of Cuvier, the entire structure and relations of the several parts of the framework have been explained and developed; the libellulæ and other insects on which they fed have been detected in the same rocks with their own relics; and out of that apparent mass of inconsistencies and contradictions, the genius of the skillful anatomist has produced one of the most striking examples of the harmony that pervades all nature, that has been extended through all ages, and that manifests the bounteous care of the common Creator in adapting all living things, each after its kind, to the conditions of its existence.

4. The Stonesfield strata belong to the lower division of the great oolite. The slate of the district has been long known and prized for roofing purposes. The village of Stonesfield lies about twelve miles to the north-west of Oxford, beautifully situated on the brow of a valley, both sides of which have been deeply excavated for the extraction of the slate. Woodstock and Blenheim are both in the vicinity, neither of whose remarkable heroes ever dreamed of the mighty wars, waged in a far distant age from their own, by the fierce assailants whose remains have now been disturbed by these operations. Here are abundant the remains of palms, aborescent ferns, seed-vessels, leaves, stems of several genera of coniferæ, and traces of reeds and grasses. Wings and their cases, the *elytra* of beetles, and other relics of insects, are mingled with the teeth, scales, fin-bones, rays of fishes, in the greatest profusion. And here, on the site of this ancient menagerie or battle-field, are the only known vestiges of mammalian animals in the secondary formations. One set of these remains resembles the Wombat, a marsupial didelphys of New South Wales; the other remains indicate a small insectivorous mammal, the Amphitherium, with thirty teeth in the lower jaw. Australia, therefore, supposed to furnish evidence of an entirely new order

of things, has been long anticipated in all its types of plants and animals by the denizens of our own land—our waters swarming with cestraceonts, trigoniæ, and terebratulæ — and our fields clothed with araucariæ and cycadeous plants—when perhaps but little of that continent rose above the waters.

5. The DINOSAURIA constitute a tribe or sub-order of the lacertians, characterized by the large development of the sacrum, the dorsal vertebræ, the bones of the extremities, which are all provided with large medullary cavities. Of this tribe there are three well established genera — the Megalosaurus, the Hylæosaurus, and the Iguanodon. These were the gigantic crocodile lizards of the dry land, whose peculiarities of osteological structure distinguish them as clearly from the modern terrestrial and amphibious sauria, as the opposite modifications for an aquatic life, characterize the extinct enaliosauria, or marine lizards. The Dinosaurians belong properly to the Wealden fresh water formations, which may be regarded as the true habitat of this order of terrestrial fossil reptiles.

The Megalosaurus was first described by Cuvier, and the family determined; he calculated the dimensions of the animal at from forty to fifty feet in length. Professor Owen, from better preserved specimens, has reduced it to thirty feet long: the head is five feet, the length of trunk with sacrum thirteen feet, and the tail about the same, allowing the Megalosaur to have had the same number of caudal vertebræ as the crocodile. The sacrum consisted of five anchylosed vertebræ, new in saurian anatomy: the hind-legs measure two yards, a metatarsal bone thirteen inches; the teeth are of corresponding dimensions, and curve backward in the form of a pruning-knife. The structure of the jaw indicates a long projecting snout, while the curvature of the teeth fitted them to retain like barbs the prey which they had once penetrated. All the organs of the monster declare the Megalosaur to have been a land animal, of carnivorous propensities, and in all probability performed, as headsman the same office upon the smaller herd of reptiles, sometimes making a snatch at a Plesiosaur, as both in turn did upon fishes and crustaceans. The sport of an Indian jungle is child's play compared to the onslaught of these grim kings amidst their ancient preserves. The remains occur in the deposits at Malton in Yorkshire, Cuckfield in Sussex, Bath, the Purbeck limestone, Tilgate Forest, and the Wealden.

The next genus of the land reptiles was remarkable for the size of the horny plates by which the body was protected. This is the Hylæosaurus—that is, forest-reptile—about twenty-five feet long, and covered with a series of large, flat, and pointed bones. These vary in length from five to seventeen inches, and are from three to seven and a half inches in breadth. In addition, as showing the kind of warfare to which he was exposed, a ridge of thick thorny scales pass along the back, and form an enormous dermal fringe, like the spines on the back of the living iguana tribes. The skeleton of the Hylæosaur has been found nearly entire, and all the parts in almost natural juxtaposition. The Wealden of Tilgate Forest, the deposits at Bolney and Battle of the same formation, contain the remains in considerable abundance.

What shall be said of the next figure that crosses the tragic stage, during this age of tyrant prodigies? The Iguanodon—a gigantic herbivorous lizard—is related to a family of harmless creatures (*Iguana*), which swarm in the West Indies, and in all the tropical forests of America, in certain peculiarities of the teeth greatly differing from those of other reptiles. The largest of living Iguanas, do not exceed five feet in length: the extinct genus attained a longitude of upward of twenty-eight to thirty feet. The caudal member was about thirteen, head three, trunk with sacrum twelve, and the girth of the body about fifteen feet. The teeth resemble the teeth of the rhinoceros as to bulk and general appearance, and, consisting as they do of incisors and molars, were recognized to belong to the order of herbivorous quadrupeds. The thigh-bone exceeds that of the largest-sized elephant, being from four to five feet in height, and presenting a circumference of nearly two feet in its smallest part. This animal, at its first discovery, was supposed to have attained the exaggerated proportions of nearly a hundred feet in length. But even under the reduced dimensions and more accurate deductions of Professor Owen, confirmed by those of Dr. Mantell, there is still size sufficient, as well as peculiarities of structure, to lead us to regard it as one of the wonders of geology. One femur of a recently-discovered Iguanodon is twenty-seven inches in circumference, and must have been nearly five feet in length; and a tibia, found with the same, is four feet long. Dr. Melville has established the important physiological fact, that the cervical and anterior dorsal vertebræ were convexo-concave,—that is, convex in front and concave behind, as in the existing pachyderms; while the reverse form, the concavo-convex, predominates in the existing crocodilians and lizards. It is farther established, that in the Iguanodon, as in many fossil and recent reptiles, the anterior extremities were much shorter and less bulky than the posterior. As in the existing family, so in the extinct, the huge body was ornamented with a horn of bone which projected from the nose. This nasal organ seems to have been worn more for decoration than for use; unless, perhaps, to assist in perforating its way through the thickets of vegetation on which it subsisted, to push aside an unwelcome intruder upon his pasturage, or as a mere set-off against the unprecedented length of tail. Imagine a herd of these monsters feeding in a prairie—the denizens of a period when all things partook of the gigantic! "The concurrence of peculiarities so remarkable," says Buckland, "as the union of this nasal horn with a mode of dentition of which there is no example, except in the Iguanas, affords one of the many proofs of the universality of the laws of co-existence, which prevailed no less constantly throughout the extinct genera and species of the fossil world, than they do among the living members of the animal kingdom." Professor Owen writes—"No reptile now exists which combines a complicated and thecodont dentition with limbs so proportionally large and strong, having such well-developed marrow-bones, and sustaining the weight of the trunk by *sychondrosis* or *anchylosis* to so long and complicated a sacrum, as in the order *Dinosauria*. The Megalosaurus and Iguanodons, rejoicing in these undeniably most perfect modifications of the reptilian type, attained the greatest bulk, and must have played the most conspicuous parts, in their respective characters as devourers of animals and feeders upon vegetables, that this earth has ever witnessed in oviparous and cold-blooded creatures. They were as superior in organization and in bulk to the crocodiles that preceded them as to those which came after them."

6. We close our enumeration of these fossils by simply stating, that the CROCODILIANS also flourished at this period. The living species are twelve in number, all remarkable for the size of their mouth, and their exuberant abundance of teeth. The extinct species were nearly as numerous, but all more allied to the gavials of New Holland than to the other members of the family. They seem chiefly to have subsisted on fishes, while their modern congeners are furnished with powers which enable them to prey upon mammalia and other quadrupeds. When Hobbes, the philosopher of Malmesbury—the old haunt of all these monsters—adopted the title "leviathan" for his political and anti-Christian views, he did it more in derision of the name than from any belief that such things as the term represents had ever or could ever have existed "in rerum natura." Persons, even now, to whom the subject is presented for the first time, will turn with aversion from its details under the influence of the very opposite feelings from those of the infidel metaphysician. The evidence of facts however, will yield neither to prejudices nor to theories. And, while we dream not of representing the patriarch of Uz as drawing his inferences from geology, still his mind was alive to convictions of the grandeur and diversity of the works of creation—to a sense of his own ignorance—and filled at the same time with awe and veneration at the unsearchable wisdom of the ways of Providence. "STAND STILL AND CONSIDER THE WONDROUS WORKS OF GOD. HAST THOU ENTERED INTO THE SPRINGS OF THE SEA? HAST THOU PERCEIVED THE BREADTH OF THE EARTH? DECLARE, IF THOU KNOWEST IT ALL."

# CHAPTER IV.

## THE WEALDEN FORMATION.

The Wealden formation is more local than any of the deposits we have yet considered. The term has a particular reference to the district features of Kent, Surrey, Sussex, and Hampshire, known as the *Wolds*, from the German *wald*, signifying a wood or forest: and as the geological position of the group is in immediate *superior* connection with the oolites, and *inferior* to the chalk, the character and history of the Wealden fall to be given in this place. The Speeton clay of Yorkshire, displayed along the cliffs adjoining Filey Bay, is considered to belong to the same series as the *gault* or blue and gray marls of Cambridge, Kent and Sussex; but it contains some characteristic indications of the Kimmeridge clay, and, therefore, we should expect that, in Yorkshire, these two strata are not separated as in the south of England.

I. Nature and Extent of the Deposit. The Wealden is a fresh water or estuary formation, as is clearly established by its fossils as well as by its lithology. The group consists of layers of clay, sand, shale, with subordinate beds of limestone, grit, and friable sandstone. The Hastings sands, Tilgate Forest beds, Tunbridge Wells deposits, and the Ashburn lignite shales and ferruginous sands, are all constituents of the series. The Dover Railway traverses the formation between Red Hill and Ashford: the branch leading to Tunbridge Wells affords excellent sections of the clay and sands. Thus occupying, in an irregular triangular form, the south-east of England, the wealden again emerges in the principality of Hanover, and other places in the north of Germany: continuing in the same course, it is again found on the British shores, occurring at Linksfield, near Elgin.

It would not be easy to restore, in imagination, the surrounding aspect of the superficial area now occupied by patches of the wealden formation. Take your station on the Peak of Derby, or Shotover Hill, or the heights of Ivanhoe—not so perilous adventure as that of the heroine of the tale on the battlements of Malvoisin—and you overlook a vast extent of vale and woodland, all then one broad expanse of water. This inland sea filled the whole intermediate district traced above, studded, in all probability, with islands, and fringed with shallows and rich arborescent headlands. Sharks prowled and darted in every direction; pterodactyles may be descried looming along the waste; while in terror or in joy, the plesiosaurus reared aloft his far-stretching neck, and then withdrew into his fenny retreats. The saurians, with their strong muscular jaws, are actively engaged, each according to his kind, by the shores or in the waters; while over the busy scene, the fierce-weltering ichthyosaurus looks in wild amazement, his large eyes leaping in their sockets, and spreading dismay among the tenants of the deep, as even now, when a kite enters a thorny brake, or pursues his stealthy flight over the meadows and green fields of timid nestling bird.

Nor would the land animals be less actively employed in maintaining the laws of their creation. No skeletons of birds have yet been detected; but their foot-prints, we have seen, are numerous. These clouds of insects, and other brilliant objects that flit with such rapidity across the sky, have all been stirred, and are leaping they know not whither, for the tread of a monster's feet is heard through the forest, mailed in plated horn thicker than Ajax's shield, and, pursued by another, presses and plunges onward in reckless haste. Imagine the many encounters during a single season between one set of the terrestrials only, the saurians: of the class, there are the remains of the megalosaurus, the great saurian—of the geosaurus, the land saurian—of the hylæosaurus, the forest saurian—of the teleosaurus, the perfect saurian,—all fitted with jaws and teeth, most cruelly bent on mischief, and restrained by no brotherly sympathies when accident or bold defiance bring them in the way of each other. The fell onslaughts of generous man, tribe against tribe, clan to clan, nation to nation, for some inconceivable nothing or unintended provocation, recorded within the brief historical epoch, may reconcile one to a picture of the irrationals similarly engaged, and throughout periods of time sufficient for the deposition of the entire oolitic series, before which the rule of earthly dynasties shrinks into utter insignificance.

These depositions accomplished, and successive races entombed within them, there is evidence that the floor of the ocean was raised above the waters, and that central Europe presented, all around, a breast of high land. There are various intercalations, in the series of marine and terrestrial deposits as well as of fresh and salt water fossils. Violent internal convulsions prevailed throughout the period, and the animals were all of a kind to care little for the war of the elements. Meanwhile a fresh water formation is completed in many places a thousand feet in thickness, and consisting of a series of beds; not continuous all round the shores of the oolitic detritus, but confined to a few localities, and characterized everywhere by its own group of organisms. This is the wealden formation. And the question arises, How this series of fresh water clays, and sands, and grits, was produced at a time when the sea prevailed so universally over the whole of continental Europe, and the eastern division of Great Britain? The solution is simpler than at first sight might appear, when viewed in connection with the existing distribution of all our great primary formations. The extent of dry land was such as to furnish water-shed for numerous rivers. The mountains supplied the detrital matter. This was brought to the river's mouth, where it formed deltas; or spread out on the floor of estuaries, where it received the few marine fossils which are found in the formation. Cast your eye along the geological map of western Europe, and—in the mountains of Wales, the silurian district of the north-west of France, the primary rocks of the tributaries of the Elbe, the Hartz mountains, and the gneiss and granites of Sutherland and Caithness—we have all the materials and requisites that are necessary for the silting process of the wealden, its accumulation, and geographical distribution as referred to in its range and extent.

The continuity of the coasts of France and England is herein supposed, and, upon geological data, this is a matter of far simpler inference than the framing even of a political constitution that will stand a decade of the years of our fleeting pilgrimage. The vision of Plato's Atlantis in the great ocean becomes in the geologist's creed a reality, who believes that a vast continent must have existed on our south and west, all now sunk and whelmed in the deep abyss. A chain of islands would just indicate the positions of the Alps, the Pyrenees, the Carpathians, and the Caucasian ranges, all then overlooking central and eastern Europe, not yet elevated above the waves. "At this period," says Professor Ansted, "it is most probable that no great east and west subterranean movement had acted on the part of the earth's crust now above the water in the northern hemisphere, and possibly the first intimation of such a disturbing force, may be traced, though faintly, in the existence of a considerable estuary, in which our wealden beds were deposited. From the condition of the upper Portland beds, we find, that, just at the close of the oolitic period, there were very numerous changes of level induced over a small area in the south-east of England, then, most likely, not far from the coast line of a large continent."

It may seem to many presumptuous, and beyond all the usual latitude of exaggerated description to attempt to dwell thus minutely on physical arrangements, and a vegetable and animal economy, so remote and beyond the sphere of observation. Remarkable enough that our great healing springs of Bath, Cheltenham, Leamington, Tunbridge, and Harwich, are all situated among, or have their origin in, the series of deposits we have been considering. But the judgment, more than the fancy, is employed in studying the geography of the ancient world, in looking out from the heights around, and trying again to unite the waters and the dry land, to recall the vanishing traces of former sea-marks, and from the disinterred remains of the remarkable races that inhabited the island, and swarmed around its coasts, to contemplate the ways and doings of

> "That Eternal Mind,
> Who built the spacious universe, and decked
> Each part so richly with whate'er pertains
> To life, to health, to pleasure."

And these three blessings all are striving to maintain, to restore, or to acquire. Life, health, pleasure—these are the great stimulants to all human exertion, and how best to promote them ought to be the aim of human study. The suite of rocks which compose the carboniferous system is one clearly of pre-arrangement, and designed for man's use. The strata, now beneath us, as undeniably evince a like beneficent purpose. The treasures of saline rock, gypseous marls, iron sands, and pyritous clays, may be mysterious all, in their origin: but their uses and their ends, human wants and frailties have long since established. The cravings of appetite satisfied, every creature has an instinct, which unerringly leads it to seek a remedy against injury and disease; and a provision for the one equally with the other, has been made by Him who notices the sparrow in his fall, and careth for the ravens of the desert. Slow of apprehension the mind, that cannot discern in the strata under review, a striking instance of foresight, a gift of benevolent wisdom, recesses long since stored with medicaments and restoratives for human frailties; and, though no angel now is there to trouble the waters, a kind Providence has designed them, and a good heart will use them, as tokens of its love.

II. The Organic Remains are chiefly of a fluviatile and terrestrial character. The beds in which they occur were deposited in the channel, or delta, of a river of great breadth, and demonstrate the existence of a large extent of neighboring country. These beds range from Hastings into Dorsetshire, but are not found to the north of the Thames. In Portland and the Isle of Wight they likewise exist with all their peculiar organisms in the greatest abundance. In the latter locality, the wealden beds form the cliffs between Atherfield Point and Compton Bay; they also overhang the Bay of Sandown. The Purbeck beds and sands are well displayed at Durdle Cove, Warbarrow, and Swanage Bays; and in the Vale of Wardour the same strata are developed. In every one of these beautiful, picturesque, accessible, and very limited districts, you have congregated specimens of the fauna and flora of rivers, groves, forests, and plains, which have no longer a place on the terraqueous globe. Compared with the living or extinct races they constitute a chapter in natural history nowhere else to be seen or studied.

Thus of eight genera of plants in the wealden, there are

only four common to it and the oolites, but not a single species. Of the hundreds of zoophytes in the older formation, not one occurs in the newer. Twenty genera of insects existed in the period of the wealden, one only of which is prolonged from the antecedent period of oolitic life; one new genus of Crustacean (the Cypris), and five species; while the conchifera have little in common, save the mytilus and unio, and both of which, generically, have been transmitted from the carboniferous era. The fishes of the wealden consist of seven genera, of which only one is new, the Sphenonchus. The reptilians amount to eleven genera, three of which present remains in the oolitic group, Cetiosaurus, Chelonia, and Megalosaurus—same species in both. The Cetiosaurus belongs to the whale race of animals, and it is singular to find the tribe exhibiting the same stupidity, or hardihood it may be, in forsaking, then as now, their briny element, and seeking a grave in the clays and sands of fresh water shoals! The Hylæosaurus and Iguanodon were both found in the Tilgate Forest beds, but have been noticed under the fauna of the oolite series, as probably living in the age of, as they approach so closely in structure and size to, the reptilian types of the deposit; frequenting the woods and pastures, while their mighty cotemporaries were following their instincts in the seas and lakes of the district.

It would thus appear that the close of the oolitic period of the earth's history resembles the close of the carboniferous period, in the sudden transition from an exuberant to a remarkably barren display of vegetable fossils. In the comparative scantiness of the sauroid family of fishes, by which the outgoing of the coal era is likewise distinguished, we may fancy another point of analogy in the diminution of the monstrous reptilians that appears to have taken place after this series of deposits. May it be inferred that these two periods enjoyed a higher degree of temperature than has prevailed, either before or since, generally over the earth's surface, and more certainly in these northern latitudes? Interred among the strata of both lie the remains of races, vegetable and animal, which have perished: and what we describe by kindred names are confined to climes and regions basking near the equator, and enlightened by other constellations. Then the alternating deposits of clay, lime, ironstone, coal, salt, gypsum, speak of lakes and estuaries, rolling rivers and high lands no longer existing in these parts. A few leaves of their annals are inscribed with forms of grotesque life, and stirring activities, which are there to attest the majesty of their revolutions. Geology, in little more than twenty years, has made the discovery, collected the facts, arranged and systematized the knowledge of the character and habits of the successive generations whose domain, whether of land or water, was so different from ours, and now all passed away.

A higher temperature, from central heat, will not explain these facts, for that should have prevailed more in the devonian, and still more in the silurian periods,—and of this we have no evidence. Appearances would rather support an opposite conclusion. The sweep of the comet again, resorted to upon occasions, may have destroyed, but could not maintain, such a state of things. A change of the polar axis, of the most inconsiderable extent, is demonstrated to be highly improbable, or almost impossible. And now, in the unwearied march of science, often baffled but never cast down, it has been announced as the probable solution of all the changes of the past, THE PROGRESSION OF THE WHOLE SOLAR SYSTEM, whereby the earth, and all the sister planets, are dragged through infinite space, and brought successively within the sphere of new constellations—now in a hotter and now in a milder efflux of ether—combining its own with a more general movement in a universal whirl—and thus constantly subjected, in all its parts, to ever-varying external influences! This, at least, is the ingenious theory of M. Poisson, which, he thinks, will account for the central heat of the globe, dipped for a time into a burning atmosphere, and cooling off more rapidly on the surface, and will give a no less plausible explanation as to the extent and frequency of change effected on the surface. Geology and astronomy become, when viewed in this light, correlative sciences, and impart an illustrative interest to the researches of each other. The lofty flights of the one are brought down, as it were, to more earthly things; while the geologist, on the other hand, is lifted from his miry pit and downward studies, to meditate on the "sweet influences and bands" that harmonize and link all the planets in their orbits, and rejoices to see his own earth taking part in the eternal music of the spheres. He is pleased to believe, according to the view of the astronomer, that this ball of stone and clay enjoys at times a vitality all over, which warms and cherishes into life natant forms, and creeping things, and flying dragons, whose development of powers could not have been sustained, on so great a scale, in the lower and less favored regions.

But while the cause may be adequate to the effect—and in the approximation to the truth there is a feeling of satisfaction, an elevation of vision and elasticity of thought, as

"Rays divine dart round the globe,"

—still the speculation referred to belongs rather to the poetry than to the philosophy of science, influencing the imagination more than the judgment, and trenching on relations that lie beyond the field of legitimate research.

## CHAPTER V.

### THE CRETACEOUS SYSTEM.

THE history of our globe during the deposition of the CHALK FORMATION, and the changes therewith connected, have now to be considered. By whatever causes effected—from whatever sources derived the materials—the line of demarkation is here complete. The sands of Africa, suddenly converted into or drifted over by the snows of the Alps, would not present a greater diversity of outline than is the transition to the geologist, when for the first time he steps into a chalk district, and marks the obvious contrast with all the surrounding scenery. From Gloucester into Wiltshire we pass, as it were, into a new zone of latitude.

The details contained in the two last chapters are in strict conformity with the laws of nature: the animals connected with the epoch possessed functions of life and an external adaptation of things suited to each other. Similar arrangements exist at present under nearly similar circumstances: the tropical animals bear a close affinity to the extinct races; and show that, however nature may contrive to display her exhaustless powers of invention in her forms of living creatures, she still conforms to a type, and has her limits of divergence. The past and the present so agree in all essential points as clearly to demonstrate a wise and controlling agency, a measure of enjoyment combined with an adjustment of figure, which, though approaching the marvelous, has resulted from design and the profoundest intelligence. Accordingly, the symptoms of the change we now witness are cotemporaneous. With the cretaceous system are introduced new mineral conditions, and along with these there are new forms of existence.

The animals of the chalk and oolite periods are essentially different—still generically shading, indeed, into each other—but so differing in species, and the appearance for the first time of new creations, as again to announce to us that we tread on sacred ground, and witness in its arrangement and contents the direct agency of Omnipotence. We can form no opinion, no notion whatever, in these changes, of the *modus operandi.* We remark simply the effects; and science, amidst all its otherwise barren and useless details, then achieves its loftiest purposes when it thus traces the footsteps and actings of the Great First Cause.

I. Range and Structure of the Chalk Formation. Considered mineralogically, this rock can never fail to arrest attention or inquiries, even among the least observant, as to its nature and origin. There is no trace of it in the northern portion of the island; and when one for the first time sees whole mountains of it, his sensations are not a little exciting. For our own part, we felt as if we entered a new world when we gazed upon hills, and their long-furrowed escarpments, of this calcareous snow-drift. Our acquaintance with the mineral had hitherto been limited to the fragments with which we were wont to trace the lines of our schoolboy pastimes. We got no deeper into its mysteries when, on a higher scale of action, we saw it delineate the diagram, or run over the fluxional problem on the black-board in academy and college-hall. But here! and half an island is covered with these stores of knowledge and of industry. Nine or ten counties on a stretch, from Dorset to Flamborough Head, and from Bridport to Deal, are covered over, and for hundreds of feet in depth, with the milk-white earth; and, whichever way you turn and bend toward the Capital, there are ample opportunities for the study of this curious page of geological history.

The chalk beds are not composed of one uniform compact mass of the useful mineral itself, which consists of nearly pure carbonate of lime, of soft earthy texture. Geologically considered, the cretaceous system comprises a series of green and ferruginous sands, clays, marls, gray and white limestones; and these again are arranged under three leading groups—chalk, gault, and green sand. The *chalk*—properly so called—is subdivided into the upper and lower,—containing in the upper numerous veins and nodules of flint, and varies in color through several intermediate hues, until, in its contact with trap, it assumes a deep red. The *gault* is an argillaceous deposit of stiff, dark blue clays, highly calcareous, and effervesces freely with acids. The *green sand* is a triple alternation of sands, cherty limestone, and friable sandstone, with beds, in some places of ocher and Fuller's earth. The whole series may be estimated at nearly two thousand feet in thickness, formed in a deep sea basin, the materials floating in very still waters, and aggregated successively through the combined influence of mechanical, chemical, and organic agencies.

The *mechanical* influence is very apparent in the sands and marls, which are evidently the spoils of islands and continents, washed down by currents and floods of fresh water, and deposited over an ancient ocean bed. The *chemical* composition of the flints or concretionary nodules, which give such a remarkable character and appearance often to the chalk, is equally demonstrable ; from fifty to a hundred beds of chalk, pure and beautifully white, will sometimes be seen alternating with as many bands of dark-colored flints, all regularly arranged as cannon-shot of all sizes on a floor, and presenting, for miles along the cliffs of the sea-shore, lines of beautifully defined fortifications. The *organic* agent is visible in the nucleus of these round masses, which consists of an animal or vegetable substance, as a coral, a shell, a piece of flustra, or sponge. The nodules assume various shapes, that seem to be molded according to the cavities of the matrix in which they are imbedded, but are actually the forms of the bodies or organic substances to which they are attached. The explanation given is, that a chemical attraction has taken place between the vegetable or animal remains, strewed abundantly through the waters, and the silicious matter held in solution. The silex in solution gradually incrusts, or incorporates with, the organized substance,—and thus were produced at once the flinty concretions and the wonderful petrifactions contained in them. Break any one of these nodular masses, and minute drops of moisture will, if immediately inspected, be seen to ooze out from its pores: thus clearly furnishing a proof of the state of solution in which it originally existed, and the watery menstruum in which it was produced.

The mineralogical history and arrangement of the chalk group of rocks are therefore in many respects very interesting. The chalk overlies the wealden, which was a mere delta at the river's mouth. The bed of the river suddenly disappears, and now there rests upon it a deep sea formation. How stupendous and overwhelming the forces of nature through all her operations! How vast her affluence and prodigality, which could so thoroughly alter all her exterior and interior arrangements, and fill the seas with this new matter.

II. THE ORGANIC REMAINS display the boundless profusion of animal life which prevailed during the cretaceous period. The wealden furnishes no grounds of comparison, as that is simply a local fresh water deposit, and consequently can furnish no test of the general condition of life upon the surface of the globe. But when we go back to the oolitic period we obtain a standard by which to measure the doings of nature in the interval, what new creations started into being, and what provisions were made for their subsistence. The state of the temperature cannot be determined, as the products, with the rarest possible exceptions, are wholly marine, and therefore affected by atmospheric influences in a very small degree. Neither can much be conjectured concerning the state of the land, as scarcely a fragment of true terrestrial life has been detected in the deposit; and yet, from the stillness and comparatively small dimensions of sea-basins into which the earthy ingredients were floated, the probability is that the land was both lofty and widely extended. One mammalian, and the remains of a solitary bird, and a meager sprinkling of vegetables, constitute the whole, and even dubious, amount of contributions from this department of nature. To Neptune, therefore, the palæontologist turns his undivided attention; and, comparing one period with another, he finds the following results:

The cretaceous deposits all lie WITHIN THE AREA of the oolites. They are *conformable* generally in position, and display, in proportion to their extent, a like superabundance of calcareous earth. Hence a return to polyp and shelly types of life, which we find so characteristic and diversified in both epochs.

Thus of the first order, Amorphozoa, the oolitic age produced only one genus; in the cretaceous we find thirteen genera, in the list Spongia, which is common to both. Of Zoophytes, there are twenty-three genera in the former, and seventeen in the latter—of which nine are common to both periods. The Echinodermata number eighteen in the oolite, and twenty-five in the chalk—five only common. The genus Foraminifera is entirely new in the latter formation, and consists of twelve ascertained genera, and nearly double the number of species. Of Annelida there are four genera in the oolite, and six in the chalk, in which the new order of Cirrhipeda occurs likewise. The Astacus is the only crustacean in the oolitic group: this and three new genera are found in the chalk. The Conchifera are very numerous in both deposits; forty-six in the older, and thirty-eight genera in the newer, of which eight are peculiar to the chalk. Monymaria are nearly in the same relative proportions. *Rudistes* occurs, as a new order, for the first time in the chalk, while again the Brachiopods, Gasteropods, and Cephalopods, are about equally abundant in both formations, with additions in the chalk to the generic models. And here too the new order Pteropoda, of a single genus and species, is introduced to our contemplation. Ammonites and Belemnites do not pass this age.

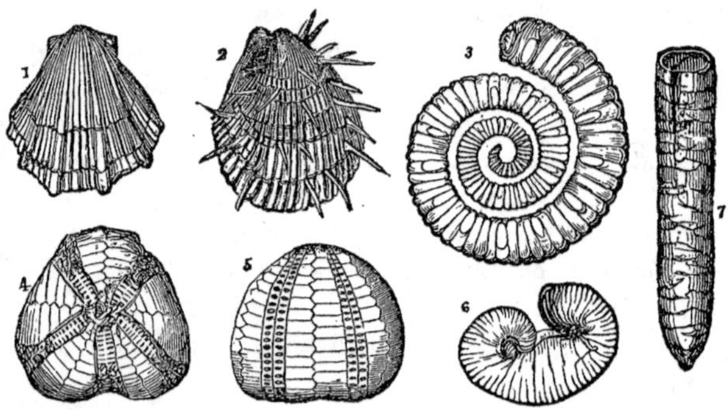


1. Pecten quinque-costatus.
2. Plagiostoma Spinosum.
3. Hamites intermedius.
4. Spatangus cor-anguinum.
5. Galerites albogalerus.
6. Scaphites Striatus.
7. Belemnites mucronatus.

The fishes of the two periods are equally striking in their contrasts; the two orders of Ganoids and Placoids are common to both, while the Ctenoids and Cycloids appear for the first time in the history of our planet, and which were afterward to contribute so largely to the sustenance and comforts of man. The Reptilians show a declension in the latter period in numbers, with the introduction, however, of four new genera—one of which (the Iguanodon Mantelli), is also found in the wealden.

The Cimoliornis Diomedeus, described by Professor Owen, is the only specimen of the order Aves or bird-tribe that as yet appears over this waste of waters. The term *cimoliornis* means simply the chalk-bird, and is allied, in some of its osseous processes, to the albatross, but also differs in too many points to be regarded as the ancestor of that courageous storm-braving animal. The claims of this fossil, indeed, to its true place in the system, have not yet been fully established. "Of the few actually fossilized remains of birds," says Professor Owen, "that have been discovered in England, the most complete and characteristic are those from the London clay. Some fragmentary Ornitholites have been discovered in the older pliocene crag, and in the newer pliocene fresh water deposits and bone caves. Extremely scanty have hitherto been the recognizable remains of birds from the chalk formations. The fossil from the wealden, which I formerly believed, with Cuvier and Dr. Mantell, to belong to a wading bird, I have since adduced reasons for referring to the extinct genus of flying reptiles called Pterodactyle." The fossil bones of the Cimoliornis were obtained by the Earl of Enniskillen from the chalk beds near Maidstone, and resemble the humerus of the albatros in form, proportions and size; there are no distinct traces of the attachments of the quill-feathers in any of the fragments; but in other points there are analogies to the osseous structure of birds; and there are bones so gigantic as will assign them a place, if the proofs are completed, among the enormous foot-print class of the permian age, and go almost to realize the fabulous "roc" of the Arabian romance.

Our attention in this group of deposits, however, is riveted more by the little than the great—by the microscopic than the gigantic forms of life. It is astounding, indeed, to contemplate the myriads of creatures which swarmed in the seas during this period. A fragment of chalk, the size of a garden pea, contains thousands of perfect shells; these shells inclose still, in many instances, the pulpy animal matter; and consist of a series of distinct well-defined chambers. In a cubic inch of the rock it is calculated that there are upward of a million of infusorial animalcules. Yet their orders are determined, their genera fixed, their very species are described, so perfect is the structure, and so thoroughly preserved all the parts of their minute shelly coverlets. The microscope has restored, under the action of certain dilute acids, the contour and shape of entire hosts of these creatures. Some specimens, so positively can it speak of them, appear to consist of tubes placed edgewise,—one projecting sometimes beyond another. Others are seen to possess a series of tubular organs placed parallel, and disposed in long lines of fragile reticulated riband. Some are oblong figures. Others are complicated, exhibiting numerous projecting processes, and of every variety of shape. Some resemble the shell of the nautilus; others are still detected with the skin adhering to the skeleton; while in the stomachs and digestive sacs of others the more minute infusoria, which the diminutive monster had swallowed, are made palpable to the sight.

All this may be called trifling, a misapplication of talent, a waste of ingenuity. What terms too grand to describe the lofty speculations of the astronomer, who points his telescope to some dark point in the blue sky, and descries in its infinite depths a cluster of closely aggregated shining particles, minute as the motes in the sunbeam, and hails it as the discovery of a new system of worlds. He cannot count them, for they are innumerable. He cannot measure them, for they have no dimensions. He cannot tell their relations, nor describe their orbits of motion, for a sparkling heap of star-dust is all that flits before the reflector. But the boundaries of knowledge are enlarged, and though man nor any of the arts may ever be benefited thereby, the fortunate discoverer will have his name inscribed in that distant region of the universe, and transmitted from generation to generation with increasing luster.

The discoveries of the geologist may be inferior in grandeur, but are they practically less illustrative in their bearings on existing arrangements? He sees the past in the present, the near and the distant in time brought together. A charm is thereby thrown over studies and speculations which would otherwise be useless. Thus, in the mineral structures resulting from the agencies of these invisible organic bodies, the mind is struck with the resemblance to similar processes that may be now going forward in the ocean: it sees in the discoloration of the waves, as the voyager steers his vessel over the main, a light by which to decipher the story of an age; and, while no voice issues from the countless myriads of animals which thicken the waters, rocks are elaborating and depositions made that will yet be raised into islands or continents. "On the coast of Chili, a few leagues north of Conception, the Beagle," says Dr. Darwin, "one day passed through great bands of muddy water, which, when taken up in a glass, was found to be slightly stained as if by red dust, and after leaving it for some time quiet, a cloud collected at the bottom. With a lens of one-fourth of an inch focal distance, small hyaline points could be seen, darting about with great rapidity, and frequently exploding. Examined with a much higher power, their shape was found to be oval, and contracted by a ring round the middle, from which line curved little setæ proceeded on all sides; and these were the organs of motion. The animals move with the narrow apex forward, by the aid of their vibratory cilia, and generally by rapid starts. Their numbers were infinite, and in one day we passed through two spaces of water thus stained, one of which alone must have extended over several square miles. The color of the water, as seen at some distance, was like that of a river which has flowed through a red clay district; but under the shade of the vessel's side, it was quite as dark as chocolate."

These are the foundation-builders of future islands, of the very color and size, it may be, as those which piled up these masses of the brick-red chalk. In an ounce of sea-sand, from three to four millions of these minute bodies have been enumerated. Twenty-two thousand can be placed side by side on a linear inch of surface. One single individual, in the course of a month in summer, will produce as many as 800,000,000. In a globule of water, a cubic inch contains more inhabitants than are now existing of the human family on the face of the globe. The skeletons of the animalcula are transported through the air in the form of a fine impalpable dust, covering the decks of vessels, and darkening the atmosphere many hundred miles distant at sea. The eye can trace nothing of structure—not even of granular form—and while clothes, rigging, and every crevice is filled and discolored with the organic nebulæ, it is not until the highest microscopic powers are applied, that it becomes resolvable and demonstrated to be a system of living creatures, moving through space, and fulfilling their destiny!

The views of nature thus opened up are boundless and infinite, in either terms of the scale, ascending or descending. The immensity of things on the one side, and their minuteness on the other, carry them equally beyond the reach of direct observation, and the intervention of means must in both cases be provided, ere they can become the subjects of human perception and examination. But what is it to me, some will reason, if there lie within the depths of space myriads of rolling worlds, when I see them not, and whose revolutions can in no way affect my condition on earth? These rocks around are but obstacles in my way, or stones for which I have no regard, as I can apply them to no useful purpose. I know that every blade of grass, every leaf in the forest, every drop of water, every grain of sand, teem with living creatures. And, in the air I breathe, systems more, beyond the ken of human view "both when we wake and when we sleep," revel in the irresponsible enjoyment of sentient existence. Science, viewed in this light, and calculated upon the rule of mere statistical enumeration, may be reckoned as utterly valueless, and knowledge as but a term for MATERIALISM.

But neither astronomy nor geology will permit our speculations thus to terminate. A principle of causation is involved in both, and to trace this through a chain of sequences and effects, whether in the great or little, in the remote or near, is the one grand aim of philosophy. If I can perceive no bounds to the vast expanse in which natural causes operate, and can fix no border or termination of the universe; and if I am equally at a loss to discern things in their elements, and to discover the limits which terminate the subdivisions of organic matter, my inquiries will not here cease. The mind will not be satisfied so to close and to shut up the thesis propounded. I am compelled to advance onward, even as the objects recede from the view, or expand in magnitude beyond the grasp of comprehension. The soul is filled with the idea of immensity, as it familiarizes itself to the thought of the highest mountains of the earth being but specks on its surface—the terraqueous globe as an atom compared with the sun—the sun itself dwindling to a star from some point in the distant fields of space—and even all the systems that sparkle in the clearest sky only as faint streaks of light, or not discernible even for millions of years after their creation, in the systems that replenish and shine in the still remoter void. Speculations, lofty as these, do leave something behind—something nobler than arithmetical calculation—and knowledge becomes SPIRITUALIZED by them.

The same result follows, when we descend in the scale of nature toward the other limit, when we perceive a like gradation from minute bodies to others incomprehensibly more minute, and are led as far below sensible measures of perception, as we were before carried beyond them, until vision is lost in utter vacuity and obliteration of all organic form. But the more attenuated and fragile the structure, the more the manifestation of Omnipotence and superintending care. If from microscopical observation we discover animals, thousands of which scarce form an atom perceptible to unassisted sense—each of which are endowed with a system of vessels, and fluids circulating in those vessels—if we can trace the propagation, nourishment, and growth of these animals—observe their motions, capacities of action, limits and conditions of existence—all this through countless millions and multiplications of tribes and generations—and, finally, after their term of being ended, now find them entombed in rocks, and elaborated into useful minerals;—knowledge thus pursued becomes again the handmaid of RELIGION, and terminates in the conviction, that we live in a universe over which the eye of Omniscience and love has been ever wakeful and predominant. The telescope leads to one verge of infinity, the microscope brings us to another; and in the discoveries of both there is the firmest assurance, that as nothing is too distant and vast for the Creator's control, so nothing is too minute for His wise and fatherly care.

# CHAPTER VI.

## THE TERTIARY SYSTEM.

The Tertiary System forms the last great subdivision of the rocky strata of the earth—the last in the creative, as well as geographical, distribution of organic and inorganic matter—antecedent to the human epoch. All the European and partly Asiatic chains of mountains were again farther elevated toward the close of the preceding period. Europe itself assumed a more distinctive shape and contour, a bolder coast-line, higher plateaux, deeper and more extensive lakes. Great Britain was rounded into form, settled upon new foundations, and already stood out, in her western and northern belt of granitic and primary rocks, the empress of the ocean.

In thus recalling the features of the old world, and marking the configuration of a newer state of things, geology furnishes indubitable evidence upon which to establish these and other more general conclusions. The physical geography of the globe is inseparably connected with the series of changes we have been contemplating. The elevation, small and isolated as it appears, of the formation termed the wealden, supplies a key by which to measure the rivers and deltas of our own island. The chalk, forming at the time the bed of the ocean, remained for a period in undisturbed repose, as evidenced by the hollows and erosive action seen on its surface. Then a series of convulsive movements, over a vast area, are indicated by the disrupted and altered position of the strata, when the bottom of the sea was lifted up, and its whole marine fauna completely changed. The secondary era passed away: the new tertiary arrangements, animate and inanimate, from henceforth commence.

Thus rolls on the mighty course of time. A continent is the

gift of one age: half a globe is shattered and wasted in the next. All living things become extinct and entombed in this quarter: in that, there are new and more abundant creations. The face of nature is again redolent with beauty: life, profusion, and enjoyment are everywhere abounding.

> "Look down on earth. What seest thou? Wondrous things,
> Terrestrial wonders that eclipse the skies.
> Nor can the eternal rocks His will withstand—
> What leveled mountains, and what lifted vales!
> High through mid air, here streams are taught to flow—
> Whole rivers there, laid by in basins, sleep—
> Here plains turn oceans; there vast oceans join,
> Through kingdoms, channel'd deep from shore to shore."

The geological district upon which we now enter, embraces London as nearly the center of its range, from which in every direction, along every line of railway, sections of the tertiary deposits are laid open: cabinets of conchology are to be met with in every pit for forty miles around; and what facilities to visit and examine them all with the speed of the wind. Not a spot but may be reached at a wish, sections more than can be numbered are in every locality, and in half the time one makes the ascent of Schehalion, he has taken the circuit of several counties.

London! what can it be likened or compared to? Nothing is so unlike as a simile, and we need not try to describe this emporium of the world by a comparison. It is not Rome nor Thebes, nor Nineveh, nor Babylon, but more than them all in the stirring activities of mere animal existence—more boundless in wealth—more dominant in conquests—more all-embracing in commerce; as deep in its sins, arrogant in its pride, haughty in its supremacy, as Queen City of the nations. About twelve hundred souls are every week added to that dense mass of human beings. As many, nearly, are every week blotted from the sum of mortal existence. No metropolis on this mundane scene ever stood in a similar relation to all other nations and cities of the world, whose every wish, for weal or woe, so affected the destinies of all the families of men. A part of every one of them is therein concentrated. Not a tribe but has its representative. Not a specimen or production of human skill but is borne thither. Genius, wit, industry, ingenuity, are in all their most beautiful creative efforts indelibly embalmed; and were that mighty pile to be ingulfed in the bosom of the waters, out of which its foundations were recently lifted up, the *genus homo* would, in all its entireness, be conserved together—the type and wonder of our own geological epoch.

This city, too, contains everything else that the world contains. A specimen of every living thing is here; and things which cannot live, but pine and die away from their native haunts, have been carefully preserved and skillfully arranged for the inspection of the curious. The kaleidoscope, in all its phantasmagoria of change and infinite diversity of hues, can display nothing half so various as the realities of nature; and types of the entire modern era, from the extinct Dodo to the recently-discovered Moas of Wanganui, are before you in all their diversified forms, from the misshapen and fantastic to the loveliest of earthly creations. When Adam gave names to the creatures of the field, they are simply said to have been "brought unto him to see what he would call them;" every tree pleasant to the sight grew out of the ground; and Eve, Milton beautifully represents

——"went forth among her fruits and flowers,
To visit how they prosper'd, bud and bloom,
Her nursery; they at her coming sprung."

Here are all things once more assembled, and as the tree of knowledge no longer bars from the tree of life, we can innocently search into all the mysteries, and see all the qualities and shapes, of every earthly object.

Nor is London less privileged and distinguished by its geological treasures and multifarious condition of things beneath. The capital stands on the tertiary *Eocene* strata, or last of the rocky series of the island. The pre-Adamic arrangements all here cease, the boundaries betwixt the old and the new world are here drawn. The age of HUMANITY dawns. And, interred in the deposits immediately below, lie the last of a series of monsters which preceded man's introduction upon the stage, and between whom and all his race an unequal war of merciless extermination must have prevailed. The reasoning animal, indeed, at once the most helpless and most potent of nature's offspring, could but ill have existed under a constitution of the elements which fostered the Palæotheriums and Chæropotami of the tertiary age.

Neither the romance of geology nor the era of prodigies, therefore, are yet over. The curtain once more requires to be lifted from the dark regions of the past, ere we approach the arrangements, forms, and distribution of animal and vegetable life, of the epoch in which our own lot has been cast.

I. The Tertiary Group consists of a series of well-marked and closely connected beds of clays, sands, gravel, brecciated conglomerate, marls, and limestones; some of which are of marine, and some of fresh water origin—points only to be determined by their respective fossil remains. Some lithological distinctions may also be established; the marine deposits are less minutely laminated than those of the fresh water; and also, in general, the beds are thicker, and their sediments more confused in their arrangement. "Limestones, and fine light-colored clays," says Mr. Phillips, "constitute the principal mass of the fresh water sediments; while sands, and blue and variously-colored clays, more particularly mark the marine depositions. The latter appear like the products of littoral agitation, as if the wearing of cliffs of older strata had furnished the materials of these newer rocks; while the former resemble the accumulations from the wasting surface of chalky and argillaceous countries."

These deposits lie in hollows and depressions of the chalk formation, and constitute what is termed the London basin. A similar series of materials occur in Hampshire, separated from the former by the upraised edges of the subjacent strata, which, cropping out in like manner on the south, inclose them also in a basin-shaped area. The same arrangement prevails across the channel, where a suite of rocks referable to the same age lie *within* the chalks, and constitute the well-known Paris basin, whose remarkable remains were first brought to light from their tomb of ages in Montmartre by M. Brongniart and Cuvier, upward of thirty years ago. The Auvergne basins, in central France, are equally well characterized. And, stretching onward through southern Europe, the tertiary deposits occupy positions nearly similar; and all composed, with slight local variations, of kindred fossils and sediments.

Geology has been compared to history. We also see how it embraces the whole range of physical geography, restoring the land-marks of the past, and presenting pictures of the earth's surface which the mere traveler can no longer detect. The rolling Thames, with town, spire, and villa nestling in every slope, and tunnel, bridges, and

> "Crowded ports,
> Where rising masts an endless prospect yield,"—

we seek in vain for on the geological map of the period. There were spice islands, with aromatic gales, palm trees, dates, turtles lazily pacing the sands, and crocodiles heavily climbing the banks, or plunging and gamboling in the deeper pools. A Polynesia, with a tropical climate and corresponding luxuriance of vegetable and animal life, occupied the intermediate regions of Europe and Western Asia. On the south and west a vast continent loomed over the main, whence, in part at least, the detrital matter of the several basins alluded to was derived; and there, too, in all probability, the source of the spasmodic action which successively elevated and depressed the bed of the sea on which were accumulating the tertiary deposits, and whose throes finally terminated in its own submergence, and upheaval of the south-east coast of Britain, and the whole of central Europe. Gulliver returned with a report of strange people, flying islands, and fertile descriptions of impossible monstrosities. Geology deals in a simple shifting of the scenes, new arrangements in the drama of creation, and is entitled to credit in its boldest assumptions, furnishing proof, as it abundantly does, from the existing wreck of those vanished realities to which it now assigns local habitation and name. London occupies the bottom of an ancient sea, whose spoils, six or seven hundred feet in thickness, are there to attest the fact; and for miles around, every excavation into the marine mass multiplies the evidence, and repeats the story of its existence.

The plastic and London clays constitute the lower beds of the series immediately above the chalk, and are nearly co-extensive in their range. From Reading on the west, these sediments stretch eastward through the valley of the Thames along the right bank to Margate; on the left, they cover the entire district to Ipswich; and constitute a very large part of the soil of the adjacent counties from Norfolk to Hampshire, prevailing more especially through the central and eastern districts. Mr. Prestwick has recently shown, that the lower English tertiaries form several distinct subdivisions, each marked by different conditions, and these conditions indicating ancient hydrographical and palæontological changes of importance. A conglomerate bed of round flint pebbles, mixed with yellow, green, or ferruginous sands, extends almost uninterruptedly from the Isle of Wight to Woodbridge, in Suffolk; this bed underlies the London clay, intercalated betwixt it and the plastic clay, and forms a well-marked geological horizon, dividing this formation from the older Eocene deposits. It contains thirty known, and eight or ten still undescribed species of testacea, twenty of which are not found in the lower deposits, while all are nearly identical with those of the superior and London clay beds. The plastic formation thus embraces the London clay, as the chalk does both, which again in its turn is embraced by the oolites; whence the older and *inferior systems* all widen, and extend successively as the bed of the sea was elevated; and hence the basins were gradually narrowed and contracted as they approached the last and closing ante-human epoch.

A kind of convergency in all this can be distinctly traced in the superficies of the earth to the state which it has now assumed. A similar approximation in its living inhabitants, as will immediately appear, can as clearly be pointed out to its present occupants. Intelligent will and design are equally manifest in the arrangements; for, however great the amount of change, the restraining hand of foresight is visibly present in them all, and, in every successive advance to the present order of things, a purpose is discernible in making the more effectual provision for the permanent stability of the human system.

II. The Organic Remains of the tertiary deposits, if they possess not so much of antiquity as those which have already passed in review, are all the more interesting and worthy of attention, as they admit of a closer comparison with the established order of things, and the laws now regulating the distribution of animal and vegetable life. The locality most fertile in the organic remains of this period is the small island of Sheppey, situated near the mouth of the Thames, which is not more welcomely descried by the home-bound mariner as a Pharos of light and safety from the howling waste of waters, than it has proved to the palæontologist a repository and beacon-light for determining the most recondite mysteries connected with almost every living thing, in sea or land, during the Eocene age. It consists entirely of the London clay deposit, of an average thickness of five hundred feet, and displaying in the cliffs vertical faces two hundred feet high. The fossils in both localities are almost identical; in the isle of Sheppey they are more abundant, as well as accessible; and, in consequence, they have been more minutely and generally described.

1. The shells are very abundant. A few genera have survived the changes and disturbances succeeding the upheaval of the chalk, and a single species of Gasteropodes (Actæon elongatus), is common to both formations. The Belemnites and Ammonites, swarming in the seas of the secondary period, are now entirely withdrawn. The Nautilus is but sparingly represented. The new genus Cerithium is introduced, a long, tapering, spiral-formed shell, and apparently of strong predaceous habits. Lobsters resembling existing species are very abundant. The Nummulites, of which entire rocks were formed during the secondary age, still survive. And, as an index to the state of temperature, it requires to be mentioned, that many species, now found only in tropical seas, are mixed with the testaceous fossils of these localities.

2. The fishes are equally peculiar and characteristic of the era upon which we enter. Nothing can more strikingly show the violence and universality of the change that was cotemporaneous with the tertiary arrangements, than the total disappearance of the old tribes of fishes, and their replacement by entirely new specific, and a large infusion likewise of new generic, types. The change is no less remarkable when viewed in its relation to existing races, every one of which, with the solitary exception of the salmon family, have here their representatives. Perch, cod, herring, mackerel, eels, had all become occupants of the seas of this

period, and their remains deposited in the clays of Sheppey are in the greatest profusion. "The number of fossil fish from the London clay," says Agassiz, "amounts to ninety-two in the one single locality of Sheppey, without counting ten species to which I have not yet assigned names, not having hitherto been able to characterize them in a satisfactory manner." The difficulty arises from two causes—the imperfect and fragmentary state of the fossils themselves, and the new principle adopted by him for their classification.

Most of the fishes belonging to the tertiary era are of the Cycloid and Ctenoid orders, with thin fragile scales, which, unlike the Ganoids whose cuirassed bodies were protected by a thick covering of plates, have been unable to preserve the integrity of their form and outline. The greater number of these interesting remains, accordingly, have rotted in the matrix, their bones separating, and the soft parts all replaced by clay. The scales are *disaggregated* (leur sécailles désagrégées), and the cranium alone of the osseous structure remaining entire, owing to the soldering of the pieces composing it, the ingenious naturalist has adopted this single organ as the basis of the new system. "The characteristic features of the skulls of the mammàlia and reptilia are known; the variations which such a bone, such a crest, such a groove may undergo in such and such a family are understood; and already, at the first glance, it is possible to ascertain whether the animal under consideration is carnivorous, ruminant, or solipedal. But nothing is more variable than the forms of the cranium and of the heads of fish. The multitude of bones and of spines which serve for the attachment of the muscles, the infinite variety of forms in the families themselves, impart such a diversity to the crania of the fish, that the ichthyologist frequently despairs of being able to reduce them to their respective types, and in fact a comparative craniology of fish does not exist. There is no one, that I know, who can tell at first sight, whether such and such a cranium belongs to a percoid, to a sparoid, or to a chetodontal type." *

Isolated crania and detached vertebræ are nearly all that remain

---

* Rapport sur les Poissons Fossiles de l'Argile de Londres.

of the Sheppey fossils, and the conclusions established from them by M. Agassiz, are as follows, throwing new and important light upon the two last great and approximating geological epochs.

The English coasts, at present, are inhabited by one hundred and sixty-three species of fish, of which there are eighty-one genera, divided among six predominant families, while two or three are only occasionally domiciled. Sixty species belong to the order of Ctenoids, fifty to that of the Cycloids, and eleven to the Ganoids. The fossil distribution establishes the following results: of Ctenoids twelve species, eleven genera, and three families, of which the perch tribe is the most numerous; three genera of the Teuthiæ, a family essentially meridional, and occurring only in southern seas, a fact which shows a higher climatic condition of temperature than now exists in this latitude; thirty-two species of the Cycloid order, twenty-six genera, and eleven families—of these the cod and mackerel tribes are the most numerous. While no trace of the family Salmonidæ has been detected in the tertiary deposit, a family exclusively tropical, the Characidæ, is found to have had congeners of very considerable size in the more ancient epoch. The haddock, cod, and ling races are very abundant—a fact, says Agassiz, which proves that, notwithstanding the more meridional physiognomy of the Sheppey deposit as a whole, there is nevertheless already an approximation in the fish of this interesting locality toward the actual character of the ichthyological fauna of England.

The living representatives of most of these fossils are, if anywhere, to be looked for in southern and tropical latitudes; for, notwithstanding of an approximation, there is not much of real identity of type between the existing and extinct races of the British seas. In fact, there are but four genera, *Megalops*, *Cybium*, *Tetrapterus*, and *Myripristis*, whose families are still known in the current epoch; and but very few species, from the rich prolific beds of Sheppey, have been as yet rendered into living forms.—The fishes most nearly related to the present inhabitants of warmer climes are those which are obtained from the fossil tertiary deposits of Monte Bolca in northern Italy, and in the little explored region of Mount Lebanon. Much remains to be done, therefore, before wider generalizations can be fully established.

The knowledge already acquired in this department of ichthyology confirms every previous inference relating to periodic physical changes of the globe, and their convergency to the order and arrangements of nature which now prevail over the earth.

3. The reptiles and semi-natants of the tertiary period lead to the same general conclusions. The intercourse now so closely established betwixt this country and Borneo throws new light, every day more and more, upon the ancient condition of our island. The resemblance, both in the fauna and flora of these remote places, is striking throughout; when, for *space* on the one hand we substitute *time* on the other, we have nearly a transcript of their respective conditions. The northern swarmed with the crocodiles of the southern hemisphere: the boa constrictor has his representatives in the serpents of the London clay; and turtles, both of marine and fresh water characters, are equally abundant. The Pythonic monster is also there, represented by reptilians which now only inhabit tropical countries, and prey on quadrupeds and birds, both of which became abundant during the tertiary age.

4. The mammalia consisted of large pachyderms or thick-skinned animals, now represented by the rhinoceros, tapir, and elephant. Wolves, foxes, and raccoons, mice, rats, rabbits, hogs, even monkeys, began also to flit over the stage of stirring life. The existence of the order Quadrumana and the ape genus Macacus, during the earlier tertiary period, was determined by the discovery of the fragment of a lower jaw, including the socket of the last molar tooth, in a stratum of blue clay in Suffolk, and described in the "Magazine of Natural History," for 1839, by Professor Owen. Other remains have been detected of the same animal in France, the East Indies, and South America, establishing beyond a doubt the co-existence of four different genera of apes and monkeys with the extinct mammalians of the English tertiary deposits.—That these creatures were anterior to Man, in point of creation, is in accordance with all geological evidence regarding the animal kingdom. The progressive development theory avails itself of the fact, but can establish less upon it than if it took the example of the bat—which, in anatomical structure, resembles the human family scarcely less than the monkey! But geographically

considered, it furnishes a striking instance of the wonderful revolution which this island has undergone since the comparatively recent epoch of the tertiary formation. Images and pictures of life are thus called up in the vista of the past, which at once transport the mind into the bosom of the wilderness or remote Afric forest; and long ere man had betaken himself to cities, or a stone of all that huge capital had been dug out of the earth, or a sail of all its vast commercial greatness had been wafted over the waters, the very spot on which he has developed the greatest resources of his power, enterprise, and genius, was tenanted by those tribes which approach him nearest in form, which philosophers have mistaken for his type, but in which the semblance of external figure is lamentably contrasted by the absence of all that moral framework, mind, and spirit, which pre-eminently distinguish and glorify the human race!

A remarkable peculiarity in the mammalian remains of the tertiary period is the total absence of the ruminating animals, which do not appear until the modern epoch, when we recognize them at once as the companions and useful contributors to the comforts of man. These still retain "the names" which Adam bestowed upon them. The more ancient creations rejoice in the mythical nomenclature of science, of which between fifty and sixty species have been determined. The greater proportion are from the Paris basin; but the district under review contains, in its lower and middle divisions, the remains of some of the more remarkable of the group—as the *Palæotherium, Anoplotherium, Lophiodon, Chæropotamus, Didelphis, Balænodon,* and the huge *Mastodon.*—These animals are specifically different from everything now in existence; even Macacus Eocenus will find no lineal descendant in Ceylon, Madagascar, or the Cape; and no Celtic pedigree will meet the case. The race have left our island, and departed from the earth; and to restore them in imagination, we must seek their nearest analogies in the impenetrable fastnesses and prairies of unreclaimed nature.

5. BIRDS are distinctly traceable in this formation. The Eocene clays of the Isle of Sheppey have produced materials sufficiently indicative of the class, in which the true affinities of the aerial inhabitants are detected, and a new genus completely established.

The specimens found bear a resemblance to the osteology of the smaller kinds of vultures, and one has been designated Lithornis Vulturinus. The 'Icones fossilium sectiles' of Kœnig contains a description of some other ornitholites found in the same locality, considered by the author as belonging to a natatorial or long-toed bird, and denominated Bucklandium Diluvii. The Paris basin is more fruitful in these fossils than the London; from these several species have been determined—more or less allied to the pelican, the sea-lark, curlew, woodcock, buzzard, owl, and quail; thus clearly establishing the link in the chain of being, but still at a wide interval from the gay choristers and domesticated tribes which minister so much to the solace and happiness of man. The geologist traces the connection, and sees in the expanse of ages, as race after race emerge upon the scene, a gradual preparation and tendency of all things to a final result; sea, earth, and air successively possessed by creatures approximating as they advance to those of the human epoch; and man proudly or presumptuously concludes, that all has been "worked solely for his good." But as the poet has sung—may we not ask, and ask concerning the humblest life which man often despises and as often terribly destroys, but which is never overlooked by Him who made man and all things, and whose tender care is over all his works?—

> "Is it for thee, the lark ascends and sings?
> Joy tunes his voice, joy elevates his wings.
> Is it for thee, the linnet pours his throat?
> Loves of his own, and raptures swell the note.
> Is thine alone, the seed that strews the plain?
> The birds of Heaven shall vindicate their grain."

6. And in the Flora which then decked the plains, fringed the marshes, or clothed the heights, "the birds of heaven" had ample provision in seed, fruit, and herbage for all their wants. Remarkable indeed the adaptation of the animal tribes referred to in the previous section to the lacustrine condition of the surface which still so generally prevailed. The plants of the period are such as are now exclusively confined to warm or tropical latitudes. The palms and cocoa-nut bearing trees are abundant and

of different kinds. One family belongs to the *Nipadites*, which are found in Japan and the Spice Islands, generally in the estuaries of rivers, or along the tracts of damp marshy grounds. The lovely Acacia was here naturalized. Pepper, dates, and cucumbers added to the variety of the sylvan banquet, which tall branching pines shaded from the scorching heat. If we are no longer in possession of the luxurious fruits and condiment-bearing plants of this early age, the change has led to other and better productions. For deep lakes we have these verdant meadows and corn plains; the stagnant marshes are drained of their mephitic vapors; the theroid monsters are supplanted by the laboring ox and the industrial horse; and with all the arts flourishing, and carried to the highest pitch along her borders, the proudest achievements of science wafted on her bosom — the "fruitful Thame" may challenge the nations of the earth for every product which climate yields or genial suns ripen.

Such was the dawn or introduction to the present order of things. In the language of geology it is called the EOCENE AGE of the world, because it approaches in its organic productions to those which are now existing, and containing a very few recent species, not more than three or four per cent. Nature did not all at once leap from one epoch to another. In the tertiary deposits there is evidence of successive creations, rests and pauses, as it were, before the final and crowning consummation of her works. More and more analogies begin to manifest themselves in the ascending series of the group. The Miocene, or middle period, developes a yet larger proportion, though not a majority, of the present inhabitants of the sea. The Pleiocene arrangements follow; and in the shells and terrestrial products of this group the modern characters and types are still more clearly discernible. When we reach the highest members, the difficulties of separation from the modern deposits begin to multiply; the mineral qualities and mere earthy beds are not distinguishable; while, on the other hand, in all the animal forms and huge colossal proportions of Mastodons and Theriums, there are the unequivocal markings of an extinct anterior age.

## CHAPTER VII.

### THE MAMMOTH PERIOD.

The tertiary deposits are referable to three great divisions, containing subdivisions, some of marine, some of fresh water origin, and severally characterized by their fossil remains. The terms Eocene, Miocene, and Pleiocene, are applied to them in their respective order of superposition, as the lower, middle, and upper groups. The London basin belongs to the first of these divisions. When these congeries of beds were completed, and the bottom of the sea was elevated, a fresh water occupation of the district appears to have prevailed. And during the supremacy of this reign of the Naïads it was, that England was tenanted by herds of large quadrupeds, tigers, hyenas, and the companions of the untamable class, whose haunts are now in the Indian jungle, or the forests and prairies of America.

This has been denominated the Mammoth Epoch, when the elephant race literally swarmed over northern Europe, from Italy to the Arctic regions. Great Britain at this era formed part of the continent, or rather of the great series of lakes and marshy swamps which then prevailed. Hence only can geologists account for the identity of fossils scattered over this area. The organisms are all of a type, all of the remarkable orders now confined to warmer climes. And when we find these fossils cast up in every field from the same series of deposits—in Switzerland, on the banks of the Danube, through the plains of Siberia, and northern Russia—in the basins of the Rhine, and the whole of lower Germany—in the Netherlands, over central and northern France, the entire south and east coasts of England—we decipher in all this, not only the organic characters of the same period of time, but the connecting links of one and the same superficial portion of the globe.

This is a very remarkable chapter in the history of our island, whether we consider the mineral or animal arrangements that prevailed, and their relations to continental Europe. Here we contemplate the relics of herds of the larger mammals which then ranged over a quarter of the earth's surface, all now extinct; while, toward the close of the epoch, everything conspires to favor the notion, that our insular position was then, for the first time, established.

The type of the period is the Mammoth, or the Elephas Primogenius. There are only two existing species, namely, the Asiatic, which is limited to within 31° north latitude, and the African, whose range extends to the shores of the Pacific, as far south as the Cape of Good Hope. America, through all its forests and boundless wastes, possesses not a single individual of the modern family, while the remains of the extinct race are to be found in every prairie, along the banks of the Missouri, and abundantly in the great salt marshes, whither they had resorted in vast herds in quest of the salt, and been mired, as heavy animals are frequently at the present day. The intertropical plains of the new world, and the polar regions of the old, were equally congenial to their habits. Nay, so adaptive were they in their nature and tastes—these gigantic pachyderms of the middle tertiary period—that in every intermediate country, they have left in their huge skeletons unequivocal traces of their sojourn or migration.

From the British strata alone, no less than three thousand and upward of fossil teeth have been dug up belonging to this colossal animal. These are found chiefly in the drift along the east coast of England, from Robin Hood's Bay, near Whitby, to Holderness. In a period of little more than thirteen years, the fishermen of the village of Happisburgh have dragged up more than two thousand grinders of the mammoth. In the valley of the Thames the relics have been discovered very numerously, at Sheppey, Woolwich, the Isle of Dogs, Lewisham,—in the gravel beneath the streets of London,—at Kensington, Kew, Wallingford, Oxford,—and all around the south-east coast from Brighton to Lyme-Regis, in Dorsetshire. The central counties of Stafford,

Northampton, Warwick, and York, are everywhere strewed a few feet under ground with these remains. At Stroud, a railway section laid open a tusk, measuring nine feet in length; and everywhere in the British Channel the fishery of the extinct quadruped is as ardently pursued, and often is as remunerative, as the fishery of the finny tribes themselves now existing on our shores.

These animals, once filling the plains of England with herds equaled only by those of the buffalo race which now darken the prairies of America, have fulfilled their destiny, and have perished from the earth. "The difference," says Professor Owen, "between the extinct and existing species of elephant in regard to the structure of the teeth, has been more or less manifested by every specimen of fossil elephant's tooth that I have hitherto seen from the British strata; and those now amount to upward of three thousand. Very few of them could be mistaken, by a comparative anatomist, for the tooth of an Asiatic elephant, and they are all obviously distinct from the peculiar molars of the African elephant." Cuvier ascertained like distinctions between the extinct and the existing Indian elephants; and concluded, from the reconstruction of the complete framework, that the mammoth type is no longer in being.

The proof that the elephant race actually inhabited this country is as satisfactory, and as well established, as that the species were different from any now existing. Little, indeed, can it be wondered at, upon the first discovery of their remains, that the accounts given by geologists and others were received with the greatest distrust. Their appearance, in these high latitudes, was attributed to the inroad of armies rather than to any indigenous connection with the soil that covers them. Cæsar, it was remembered, brought many elephants with him into Gaul. According to Polinæus, one at least was transported across the channel into Britain: hence an easy and ready explanation of the fossils, as Voltaire, in his time, fancied the shells found on mountain tops to be the stray specimens dropped by pious pilgrims or superstitious monks on their journeyings. But as their numbers increased—some from Ireland where the soldiers of Rome never set foot, along with the bones of the rhinoceros and hippopotamus which could be instructed in no military tactics, and all over the length and breadth of the land bones and entire skeletons began to be exhumed — all grounds for skepticism against their aboriginal national descent were forever swept away. And Britain, it was admitted, literally and truly, had once been stocked, among its most recently extinct families, with these monster tenants of the wilderness.

An entire carcass, it is well known, covered with long woolly hair, was found at the mouth of the river Lena, as far north as the 74th degree of latitude, imbedded in ice. This discovery opened up more enlarged and correct views as to the history and habits of these animals. Subsequent years increased prodigiously the stock of fossils, entire and perfect in hide and fleshy muscle; and now, so abundant are the remains of the fossil mammalia in the arctic regions, that they have not only become an article of commercial traffic to man, but serve as an unfailing repository of food to the present denizens of those countries, the hordes of marauding wolves, foxes, and bears, which prey amid the polar regions and sterility. It has farther been ascertained that, where the lichen and the scanty moss now only grow, a rich arboreal vegetation once flourished in these latitudes; birch trees, of large dimensions, are everywhere imbedded in the sandy cliffs; and it is conjectured, with the greatest probability, that herds of elephants migrated from the warm interior, during the summer months, to the embouchures of the rivers and borders of the arctic sea, covered as they were with sheltering forests, or shrubby brushwood steppes. "As we advance," says Murchison, "into the plains of Siberia, or descend into the valleys of Tobol and the Obe, the bones are in greater quantities, and in a better state of preservation; and the farther the Siberian rivers are followed to their mouths, the more do the mammalian remains increase, until at length whole skeletons, and even carcasses, are found. The single fact of the very wide diffusion of the mammoth bones, over enormous regions, in itself indicates that those creatures had long been inhabitants of such countries, living and dying there for ages; while their final destruction may have resulted from aqueous débacles dependent on oscillations of the land, the elevation of mountain-chains, and the formation of much local detritus."

The same causes will account for their destruction in this country—causes, whose effects are still traceable over the whole of continental Europe. Doubtless, these causes extended across the channel, and may have been cotemporaneous with the movements which resulted in separating us from France, occasioning débacles by the alternate upheaval and depression of the sea-bottom, which even the largest animals would be unable to contend against. In the midst of these movements, multitudes would resort to the higher protected grounds, in quest of food, or retire for shelter to caves and other concealments that were elevated above the waters. Remains, accordingly, of nearly all the quadrupeds of the period, the rhinoceros, hippopotamus, lion, tiger, hyena, bear, elk, are to be found in such places, associated with bones of the elephant family, and mixed, for the most part, with the alluvia and detrital gravel of the district. These animals appear not to have perished simultaneously or suddenly; but from the condition of the celebrated Kirkdale caves, when first discovered, it would rather seem that they had long haunted these places, the caverns being generally at a considerable elevation, with an entrance on the side of the valley. The floors were entirely covered with mud, teeth, bones, and stalagmitic incrustations, several feet deep—a den of monsters that were devouring each other, while the common enemy of destruction was approaching to seal the fate of all! The "Reliquiæ Diluvianæ" of Buckland, which first introduced the notice of these caves to the public, assumed the Mosaic deluge as the cause of the catastrophe: other hypotheses have been resorted to, as that certainly would not apply to all the circumstances of the case. Bones of a species of hare or rabbit, the water-rat, mouse, weasel, with fragments of the skeletons of ravens, pigeons, larks, and ducks, are also included among the relics of the fiercer tribes; and many have supposed that these were drifted in by subaqueous currents, or dropped through the fissures, which are both numerous and large in the limestone in which the caverns, for the most part, are situated.

The Mastodon, that is, the mammillary-toothed elephant, was another of the extinct pachyderm class then inhabiting the island. Remains of this animal have been found in the Norwich Crag; there are several species, all of gigantic proportions, some of which have been detected in North America only, and others in Europe. The tigers of the period were larger than the largest of the Bengal race, as is proved by the fossil teeth and bones of the extremities that have been discovered, both at Kirkdale and other places. And so, generally, of all the extinct carnivora, in the qualities of strength and size, superior to all existing types, and cast in the mold of, as they had to contend with, the mammoths and monster theria among which their destiny was cast.

And again, and again, will the questions recur to every curious reader of these details—when, and how, were these huge quadrupeds exterminated, or driven from this island, some of them now utterly extinct, and some of them only generically allied to existing tropical races? The epoch of their rule, according to the geological testimony, verges on the human age, if it does not actually run into it. Terror-stricken, shall we suppose, by the terrene and subaqueous movements which severed Great Britain from the continent — the rush of waters — the rending of the rocks—and the drying up of lakes, consequent on the change—they sought a refuge above the general wreck, where the weak were preyed upon by the strong, and a fierce carnival, for a season, was maintained? On the continent, while similar alterations were taking place over large superficial areas, and the tertiary deposits were being drifted up, many of the animals, and whole families, would escape into southern and warmer countries, and some of the species, in consequence, might long survive the destruction of others. But here, insulated and deprived of the means of performing their annual migrations, the races of every kind would all more speedily perish, preying more easily upon each other, and weakened by alteration of habits, and the great physical changes to which they were subjected. On the Ararat of Yorkshire, and other favored heights, they found a temporary resting-place! But, it was only temporary; for, as the island approximated to its present condition, it proved no longer a suitable dwelling to creatures of their mold—their course was run—and a new creation was to occupy their place.

In closing these sketches of the geology of Great Britain, one may well marvel at the vast changes over the face of this island

and of all its productions, as read in the varied and multiform disclosures which the interior structure, formation upon formation, makes known to us.

1. Mark the distinct character of the geological evidence of all the changes, organic and inorganic, to which the island and its inhabitants have been subjected. The evidence rests upon direct observation. The registers are graven as with a pen of iron, and in characters which to be understood have only to be read. The historical period, beyond two decades of centuries, is an utter blank. When Cæsar came into the island, painted savages peopled the land, Druids immolated in thousands their human victims, and, the brief occupation of the invaders past, we are again involved in the darkness of barbarous annals and exterminating wars of unknown tribes. Whence the migrations of its first inhabitants? who were the Cymri that spoke the language of Cwm Llewelyn, and of Cefn y Bêdd? who were the Silures, the Trinobantes, the Cantii, and the Atribates? and whither and what the ever-conflicting lines betwixt the territories of Picts, Celts, and Scots?—questions these that will ever puzzle and disturb the slumbers of the unhappy wight who deals in chronicle lore and archæological history. What now of the oldest civilized states of the old world who gave law, literature, science, art, language, and blood, to all the families of the earth, as the tide of population rolled westward, and the Quadrumana and the Bimana contended for mastery amid the dense aboriginal forests on the banks of the Danube, the Rhine, the Rhone, the Seine, the Thames, the mountains of Cambria and Caledonia? Rome sits in ruined majesty by the waters of the Tiber. Greece knows not, and mourns not, the buried ashes of her mighty dead. Carthage *has* been blotted out. Tyre has fulfilled her destiny—"a place for the spreading of nets in the midst of the sea." The shepherd kings of the pyramids have not a name even among men; and Thebes, Luxor, and Carnac, lie as fossils in the desert. What of Babylon and her Tower on the plains of Shinar, that was to reach unto the heavens? and of Nineveh, "a city of three days' journey" to be compassed? Mounds of earth and rubbish, over which the Arab has pitched his rude tent, and into which the prying antiquary, at the risk of his life, digs for fragments, while the Tigris and

Euphrates pursue their heedless course through the waste slimy borders of Uz and Mesopotamia. Thus mark how many illustrious heroes, scholars, lawgivers, who once filled the world with their fame, have, with all their splendid or useful benefactions to their race, passed under the thick cloud of oblivion! The very names of the most noted of them is matter of dispute. And of the multitudes who panted after glory in these ancient days, not an incident in the life of millions has reached the present times.

But geology, as HISTORY, is truthful in the oldest as in the most recent of its narrations. How generally accurate in its family genealogies: their relations, kindreds, alliances, and individual peculiarities; the length and strength of body, contour of face, size, structure, and capacity of head, eye, and stomach—all as precisely determined and described in regard to the "habitans" of the most ancient fossiliferous rocks, as the living possessors of earth, sea, or air. Look into our museums, cabinets, monographs, and palæontological lists, and types of organic life are there, from which not only to number the tribes, but to tell of their own varying states and conditions. Wonders there are in geology. But its most seeming fables are realities. The placoids and ganoids of the silurian and devonian age, the exuberant flora of the carboniferous, the giant birds of the triassic, the matchless reptilian forms of the oolite, the microscopic organisms of the chalk, the colossal mammoths and mammalia of the tertiaries, were all as veritable productions of the island as the most familiar grains, grasses, and domesticated breeds which minister to our daily wants. How obscure, uncertain, and limited the range of human history! How extensive, and boundless, and minute the pursuits of geology, which touches on the history of all creatures that ever lived through all their species, genera, orders, and classes, and even remounts to the primeval condition of the planet itself during all the periods, phases, and revolutions of its existence! But of man there is no trace. No voice from the past, issuing out of the solid framework of the globe, intimates the existence of the human family anterior to the last of those great physical changes which we have been contemplating, and over the wreck of whose organic tribes the epoch of the tertiary sections of its crust closes.

2. The teachings of this science in physical geography are no

less definite than the astounding disclosures which it makes in history—shadowing out, where mountain chains now rise, the seats of ancient sea bottoms—creeks and bays by lines of mudstones and conglomerates—continents that have been formed from islands, and islands disrupted from continents—lakes, estuaries, and rivers displaced and silted up, and now become the richest depositories of our mineral treasures. The connection of Great Britain with France is a matter almost of demonstration. A zone of primary crystalline rocks encompasses the western coast of both countries, whence geology follows them from Wales and Cornwall into Britanny and Normandy. The silurian, devonian, and carboniferous systems are arranged in the same order on both sides of the channel. Their chalk coasts are identical. A succession of elevating movements, depressions, and dislocations, is traceable everywhere along the southern counties of England, where the line of disturbance, from east to west, has separated the chalk on the north and south, and elevated the Wealden into an anticlinal axis on the Sussex coast. The Isle of Wight has been so shaken by the convulsion, as to have been literally tumbled over, the whole cretaceous formation, and every inferior deposit subjacent to the tertiaries, being in an inverted position. The existence, too, of a vast connecting stretch of land in the Atlantic is far from being improbable, whence the rivers of the Wealden may have issued, as well as much of the detrital matter been transported which now constitutes, with their remarkable and varied organic exuviæ, the basins of London, Hampshire, and Paris.

Very recently botany has come to the assistance of geology, in a manner as remarkable as it was unsuspected. It appears that, along the coast line of Great Britain and Ireland, there are several distinct floras or groups of plants, and all geographically related to existing families on the opposite coasts of the Continent. The flora of the west of Ireland corresponds to that on the north-west of Spain—the south-west of England, and also of Ireland, presents groups allied to those on the north-west of France,—and, again, one is common to the north coast line of France, and south-east of England,—while the fourth and fifth have their types in the alpine flora developed in the Scottish and Welsh mountains, and the mixed and diversified tribes more generally distributed over Ireland, England, and Germany. The assumption implied in this botanic speculation is, that these are the remains of a state of things no longer enduring, proofs of the existence of hotter or colder climates than now prevail, and the indications of a configuration of land and sea when a great mountain barrier extended across the Atlantic from Ireland to Spain. The distribution of the second and third sets of vegetation depended on the connection of England with France and Germany, when a sea covered a large portion of the south of Europe, and the upheaval of whose bed, which constitutes the latest of the tertiary deposits, gave rise to a vast continent, comprising Spain, Ireland, the north of Africa, the Azores, and the Canaries. The alpine flora of Scotland and Wales was effected during the glacial period—to be afterward noticed—when the mountain summits of Britain were low islands or members of an archipelago extending over the Frozen Ocean, and clothed with an arctic vegetation which, in the gradual upheaval of those islands and consequent change of climate, became limited to the summits of the still existing mountains. Professor Edward Forbes, adopting in this curious speculation the views of Mr. Hewet Watson, finds a corroboration of them in the peculiar distribution of *endemic* animals, especially of the marine and terrestrial mollusca. And he justly concludes that all the changes required for the events which he would connect with the distribution of the British flora, are borne out by the geological phenomena that prevailed during the epoch of the several tertiary deposits.

3. Geology, moreover, in deciphering the evidences of those stupendous operations which resulted in the statical, mineral, and organic arrangements merging in the modern epoch, inculcates some important truths connected with the science of natural theology. The mind, indeed, can never escape, in these investigations, from theistic conclusions. Step by step, as we ascended through the component strata of the globe, witnessed the modifications to which they were subjected, and observed the successive introduction and extinction of so many types of animal and vegetable life, we were just furnished with so many incontestable proofs of the direct interposition of Almighty power. If, indeed,

I can read anything more clearly than another in these constantly recurring geological phenomena, termed epochs and formations, it is that of INTERFERENCE with the established order of things. I am conscious that matter did not originate itself. I can see no power in what is termed a law of matter to constitute organic bodies. The originator of matter must be the disposer of all its forms. And when I see these forms so repeatedly changed, assuming new shapes, and giving new scope for varied and multiplied degrees of enjoyment, I have only the more evidences and illustrations before me, that creation and change are, in these instances, correlative terms. The quadrupeds of the tertiary age are like nothing that preceded them in any of the orders or sections of animal existence. Their size, structure, and abundance, equally rivet the attention. And, however long or short the period assigned them on earth, they constitute a group of organic statuary, too remarkable to have been slid in and out by the simple operations of material law. The geological fact, of formation after formation, and of life after life, lies at the foundation of the sublime truth, that God is potentially in, arranging and disposing anew, the entire series of his works: and when I see this mundane scene shifted in all its parts, one system subverted, and another so very different introduced; and, again, the organic and inorganic condition of things readjusted, and in keeping as before, I at once rise in the contemplation of the change "from nature up to nature's God."

Geology, I should thus conclude, admits us a step nearer than any of the other sciences, even than astronomy itself, to the actings of the divine Architect. The revolution of every season demonstrates a providence—the workings of a perpetual miracle—in its sustaining energies. But geology shows us, not the mere annual renovation of things already existing, but the circumstances under which they BEGAN to exist. The fiat of Omnipotence peals through the bounds of creation. The earth and the seas obey. We see new things starting into being. We are present, as it were, at the moment of their birth. We see the molds out of which they are fashioned, and the first provision made to sustain them. Geology, in a word, hangs up before us one of the brightest and most diversified pages in the book of nature, inducing habits of thinking, and constantly reminding us of the facts and relations, that bodily and vividly keep before the mind the ever-active impress of the Divinity at whose bidding—

> "Awakening nature hears
> The new creating word, and starts to life
> In every heighten'd form."

# FRANCE AND SWITZERLAND.

## PART III.

### CHAPTER I.

GEOLOGICAL STRUCTURE OF FRANCE—BASIN OF PARIS. ORGANIC REMAINS.

On the continental side of the Channel it will not be necessary to dwell, in minute details, upon any of the systems of rocks which are here presented. What is France? The tourist will say—A two hours' voyage from the sister isle—a salt lake separates them—a pleasure trip is the measure of their estrangement. The geologist will add—And when safely landed, one finds himself among the sights and objects, the rocks and fossils, which engaged his attention on the coast of Albion, the cliffs and downs of both countries being composed of the self-same materials.

I. The Physical Union of France and England, although already adverted to, falls again to be noticed.

The geographical distribution of the respective rocks of France and Great Britain forms a remarkable coincidence in giving shape and contour to their general outline. Thus, the primary systems in both stretch along their western shores, presenting a vast barrier-wall of the oldest and hardest rock against the incessant encroachments of the Atlantic. Britanny and Normandy consist almost entirely of granite, gneiss, mica-schist, and silurian rocks; on these repose the upper suites of the secondary strata,—the lias, oolite, and chalk—training to the south and east. On the tertiary formations rest the secondary, narrowing in their basins, and preserving the same general line of bearing with the English beds, and in both cases reaching their maximum of thickness and exuberance of fossils around the capitals of Paris and London. The old red sandstone is not indicated on the maps, nor is it clearly ascertained to possess a habitat in the district in question. The coal-measures are of very limited dimensions, but in their due order of position at Hardinger, near Boulogne, and passing under the chalk and green sand, continue in an easterly direction by Valenciennes, Mons, Namur, and Liege, to Eschweiler, near Aix-la-Chapelle. The new red sandstone, of both divisions, is amply developed along the eastern boundaries from Semoy in Ardennes to Langrés and the borders of Switzerland. On the west again, the tertiaries prevail from the mouth of the Gironde to Bayonne on the Adour, where they are exposed to the constant tearing and erosion of the rude surges of the Bay of Biscay, while in the interior, and over the district of Auvergne, the granites and gneiss are widely overlaid by the overflowings of the most recent extinct volcanoes; the oldest and the newest plutonic rocks thus lying in immediate superposition and contact.

The rocks on this side of the channel are not indeed everywhere so well displayed, nor do they crop out with the same successive regularity as in Britain. Over extensive districts some disappear altogether, while in other places patches are seen lying out of their due order of superposition; not that in these instances the order is ever violated, but that some of the intermediate members seem to be wanting, and the remoter ones are in consequence found in contact. Still they conform to each other in their great line of section, and occupy the same constant relative position in their respective basins. Here, as in England, the Oolitic system embraces the Cretaceous, and extends in a larger semicircle round Paris as a common center, stretching from Ardennes to Normandy. The Lias, again, is inferior to the Oolite, and, filling a wider space, reposes on the transition slates of Virreville on the western coast. The Plastic clay, London Clay, and freshwater beds emerge in succession, and maintain each their corresponding dimensions. A remarkable grouping of rocks, illustrative of the order of superposition, occurs within the circuit of a few miles in the immediate vicinity of Boulogne, where resting upon the mountain limestone the following series may be observed: Coal, Oolitic marble, Purbeck and Portland stone, Iron-sand, Wealden clay, Chalk marl, Green sand, and Chalk. The Plastic clay reposes upon the chalk at Calais on the east of this group, and on the west stretches along the coast from Etaples to Treport.

The period during which the two countries continued to be united superficially, extended down at least to the last great upheaval of the bed of the ocean, subsequent to the Pleiocene deposits, and probably even after the establishment of the current epoch. The different formations we have been tracing are geologically connected over vast tracts of country; these tracts once formed basins or inland seas, into which their several suites of materials were drifted; the extensive regions of the older formations were amply fitted to inclose them; and, when the *uppermost* or pleiocene series of the English beds were deposited, one and the same shores and waters must have been common to the two countries—to the now insular as well as to the continental basins of the closing tertiary age.

One feels a real and enhanced pleasure in his researches, and his speculations assume a wider and a loftier range, as he casts a glance back to the white shores of Britain, and around upon the aspect of the country before him, and sees that he is still treading the same soil, threading his way among the same rocks, ascending and descending the slopes and valleys of the same earthy accumulations, varied only by slight local causes. Embarked upon the Seine, and along the banks of that lovely river, there is laid open for inspection a series of deposits, with every one of which we are already acquainted. The resemblance is even more striking when we examine the vast undulating plains around, and find the depressions, elevations, hills, and general outline of surface all of a class; and when we observe also the rocky foundations beneath to be one and the same—extensions merely of the same series of deposits, and forming at no very distant geological period integral portions of one great continent.

Combined with the subterranean movements which occasioned the dislocations, and inversions often, of the strata on both sides of the channel, the action of oceanic currents and incessant beating of the waves may be looked to as the instruments which produced their severance. The proofs are ample of the encroachments of the sea upon the eastern coast of England, the sites of towns, villages, and extensive fields, as marked on maps, now forming sand-banks, islands, and marshy swamps. The promontories and cliffs of Yorkshire, Norfolk, and Suffolk are still, as they were in Pennant's time, "perpetually preyed on by the fury of the German sea;" the whole site of ancient Cromer is now under its waves; the towns of Shipden, Wimpwell, and Eccles, have entirely disappeared; large manors and even parishes have, piece after piece, been swallowed up; nor has there been any intermission, from time immemorial, in the inroads of the sea along a line of coast twenty miles in length, in which these places stood.* The ravages, from the same cause, have been equally if not more violent on the shores of the channel, the Straits of Dover, and the whole south coast; where slips of enormous magnitude are frequently recorded, cliffs undermined, and lands of considerable extent carried into the sea. The Isle of Wight, the peninsulas of Purbeck and Portland, the promontories of Devonshire and Cornwall, have all received their shape from the destructive agency, as they are still preyed upon and consumed by the tides and currents to which they are incessantly exposed. The French coast bears similar testimony to the inroads of the sea. From Calais to Cherbourg, with its magnificent dock-yard, the line of shore is everywhere indented and stripped bare, the strata undermined, and huge masses toppling over the abyss or rising into lofty pyramids of the most grotesque and varied forms. Britanny lies open, on every side, to the full swell of the Atlantic, where very recent as well as more ancient history attests the ravages of the waters in the destruction of towns and woods, the inundation of whole parishes, the severance of the hill of St. Michael from the main land, and, according to tradition, in the obliteration of the south-western district, of unknown extent.

Familiarized to facts such as these, and their necessary deductions, the mind no longer startles at the notion of the former physical union of the two countries. The agency seen in operation

* Lyell's Principles of Geology, vol. i, p. 269.

is demonstrably adequate to the effect. The straits are narrow. Their greatest depth between Dover and Calais is twenty-nine fathoms. The bed throughout is composed of the same stratum of chalk-rock, while a submarine chain extending from Boulogne to Folkestone is only a few fathoms under low water. Accordingly the wave of the mighty "ocean stream," parted on the western coast, met tide after tide on the opposite banks of the connecting peninsula or narrow tongue of land, the one portion winding round by the Orcades and rolling up the German Sea, and the other portion beating on the line of cliffs facing to the west. The softer sedimentary deposits of the tertiaries would rapidly yield to the constant erosive action; the harder strata of the chalk, bared and undermined, would speedily follow; and thus, in a period comparatively short, the entire mass would be carried away, and the gulf of separation be irrevocably effected.

As a proof that France and England were united, and that these operations were continued *within* the human epoch, M. Desmarest, in his prize essay on this subject, proposed in 1753 by a society at Amiens, adduces the fact, that the noxious animals in both countries are identical, creatures which were not fitted to swim across the straits, and were not of a kind to be willingly introduced by man. But Desmarest in this only followed the views of an older writer, and from whose work, "Restitution of Decayed Intelligence," all his facts and reasonings are obviously borrowed. This curious volume is the production of Richard Verstegan, written about two hundred and fifty years ago, and dedicated to James I. of Great Britain. The principal object of the author is to trace out the origin of the western nations, and more especially of "the most noble and renowned English nation," as discoverable in their language and other antiquities. The fourth chapter of this quaint work is entitled, "How the Isle of Albion is showed to have been continent or firm land with Gallia, now named France, since the Flood of Noah." Verstegan holds the doctrine that "in whatever manner and form it pleased Almighty God, in the beginning of the world, to divide the sea from the dry land, is unto us wholly unknown; but altogether unlikely it is that there were any *isles* before the deluge;" and to this event he ascribes the disruption of much of the dry land and the formation of islands. The connection of France and England continued long after this, and their severance, he believes, was produced by the operation of existing causes. The narrow isthmus by which they were conjoined extended across the Straits of Dover, just as Africa is united to Asia by the Isthmus of Suez, or North and South America by the Isthmus of Panama. This isthmus was breached by the action of the sea on both sides, but the sea being *lower* on the west side, the current swept with greater violence through this new channel, "toward the most huge Western Ocean, the greater divider of Europe and Africa, from the late found America." He notices the identity of cliffs on the opposite sides of the straits, the submarine ridge which extends from Folkestone to Boulogne, the existence of marine shells all over the Netherlands and adjacent countries, and their consequent submergence before the sea was permitted to retreat through the new course produced in the isthmus, "and no way is there else to be found or imagined, whereby these seas might be drained or drawn away." He refers to the identity also of the noxious animals in England and France, when our isle, continuing since the flood fastened by nature to the great continent, these wicked beasts did of themselves pass over; nor is the earthquake omitted by the writer, in his enumeration of causes whereby the sea, first breaking through, might afterward by little and little enlarge her passage; and the labor of man, too, had its share, when the inhabitants of the one side or the other by occasion of war did cut it, thereby to be sequestered and freed from their enemies.

Such is the train of illustration employed by Richard Verstegan, at a time when the state of the science of geology could furnish him with few helps; and but little indeed has been added by subsequent observers, except a few additional facts and inferences, which serve to confirm his conclusions. He remarks that such too had been the opinions of others, as of Antonius Volscus, Marius Niger, Servius Honoratus, the French poet Bartas, and our own countrymen, John Twin and Dr. Richard White; but these simply held the connection of the two countries as a matter of opinion, without laboring to find out "by sundry frequent reasons, that so it was indeed." * England long dominated in France, crowned her princes Sovereigns of Navarre and the adjacent provinces, and Agincourt, Cressy, and Poictiers tell where man waged war against his fellow-man, over the remains of races long extinct, denizens of the same land, and propelled by instincts fierce alike for mastery or destruction. What a moral effect has been produced by the physical severance of the two nations, not only to themselves, but to the rest of the world! Great Britain, freed from the connection, can well afford to repose in peaceful majesty on her own shores, improving the arts, extending her commerce, and communicating, as the most noble and renowned nation the blessings of religion to the remotest parts of the globe.

II. Organic Remains. There are three districts in France which claim the special consideration of the geologist. The first comprises the basin of the Seine, of which Paris may be regarded as the center; the second is the basin of the Loire, extending in the direction of the rivers Gironde and Adour; the third is the volcanic district of Auvergne, embracing the tertiary and lacustrine formations, which have excited much geological speculation. The Silurian beds of Britanny are in many places absolutely loaded with Trilobites, which have found an able expositor in M. Marie Rouault; and the New Red Sandstone, which skirts the Vosges mountains, is equally remarkable for the fossils, vegetable and animal, peculiar to the Permian system.

The Basin of the Seine. The series of rocks included in this district, are described as the Paris basin formation, where, amidst their fossiliferous remains, the genius of Cuvier shone forth and captivated the world by his wonderful disclosures in the science of comparative anatomy. The deposits occupy a depression in the chalk upon which they rest unconformably, like those of the London basin: they agree generally in their organisms, but differ considerably in the quality of their respective materials. Blue clay with imbedded calcareous and argillaceous bands characterize the London formation, while that of Paris is distin-

* Restitution of Decayed Intelligence, by Richard Verstegan. London, 8vo, 1605. Noticed in "Chambers' Journal," June, 1846.

guished by a superabundance of white limestones, marls, and gypsum. These rocks range over a vast extent of superficial area, being in their greatest length from N. E. to S. W. about one hundred and eighty miles, and from E. to W. about ninety miles. They belong to the Eocene period, consist of alternating groups of marine and fresh water strata, and have been arranged in the following order, according to the corrected diagram of M. Constant Prevost, who has considerably modified the earlier tabular arrangements of Cuvier and Brongniart:—Plastic clay, Calcaire grossier, Calcaire silicieux, Gypsum, Marls, Marine and fresh water strata.

*The plastic clay and sand* consist of intercalating argillaceous and gritty beds, containing a considerable quantity of lignite and fresh water shells. This deposit is not continuous throughout the basin, nor is it always lowest in position. In some places it rests upon a marine calcaire grossier, and in other places it is mixed up and imbedded in it, clearly showing that a river charged with argillaceous sediment entered a bay of the sea and drifted down, from time to time, wood and fresh water shells. No remains of mammalia have been detected in the plastic clay reposing on the chalk. *The Calcaire grossier* is composed of a coarse limestone, often passing into sand, and extremely rich in testacea, a locality near Gignon alone furnishing about four hundred distinct species. *The Calcaire silicieux* is a compact silicious limestone, almost destitute of organisms, and from its strong resemblance to the precipitates of mineral springs, as well as the fact that the few fossils contained in it are all of the land and fresh water species, it is justly inferred that the deposit is of fresh water origin. *The Gypsum,* with its associated *Marls,* is a saccharoid rock of considerable thickness, and constitutes the hill of Montmartre and other elevations toward the center of the basin. Here occur the remarkable variety as well as abundance of those organic remains which have given so much celebrity to the Paris basin. Fishes, reptiles, crocodiles, tortoises, birds, bats, mice, squirrels, opossums, gigantic mammoths, Anoplotheriums, and palm-wood, are all interred in this receptacle of the extinct dead. The remains of about fifty species of quadrupeds alone have been detected in the deposit, some of them, to the minutest organ, in the highest state of preservation—all of them extinct—and nearly four-fifths belonging to a division Pachydermata or thick-skinned animals. Immediately above the gypseous formation is an oyster-bed, of great superficial extent; this is succeeded by beds of sand, entirely destitute of fossils, forming a suitable covering to the countless millions which lie interred beneath.

Reader! pause and reflect upon this enumeration of the rocky strata, and their contents, which compose the Paris basin. What vast accumulations, now of terrestrial floods, now of inroads from the ocean—here a deposit, testifying to the fact of some great inland lake, with huge monsters browsing on its banks or reposing in its shallows—there another, bearing witness to "the strength of a mountain river," combating with the waves of an estuary, and each wearying of the conflict and mingling their spoils from land and sea in one common mass. Neptune is again triumphant, and leaves as the trophies of victory whole families and tribes of his own domains. Silvanus now asserts and establishes his reign, and the Genet, Raccoon, Opossom, the Squirrel, Woodcock, and Buzzard are there to proclaim his sway. The Nereids too had their doings, and both genera and species of seven extinct nondescript fishes show their powers. And, last of all, come the Naïads of the streams, presenting you with their offering in the Quail, Curlew, and Pelican, along with Tortoises and Crocodilians. Count and enter upon your list, as found in the gypseous formation alone, eleven or twelve species of the Palæotherium, an animal partaking of the respective structures of the rhinoceros, the horse, and the tapir; of the Anoplotherium five species, commingling the light and graceful form of the gazelle with the conformation of the camel; fifteen species of the Lophiodon, closely allied to the former, but partaking also of the qualities of the hippopotamus; seven species of the Anthracotherium, a creature whose dimensions through the various members of the family swell out from the size of the hog to that of the hippopotamus; the Chæropotamus, allied to the suidæ, and forming a link between the Anoplotherium and the existing Peccary; and, lastly, as closing the list of this remarkable race of thick-skinned animals, we are presented with specimens of the Adapis, of hedgehog appearance, but in size three times larger, and uniting in characters the insectivorous carnivora with the Pachydermata.

It is recorded of Newton, that, toward the close of his wonderful calculations, when it seemed that the arithmetical results were to be in harmony with the dynamical problem to be solved, when he felt on the verge of determining one of the most important laws ever discovered by man, and which forever would bind the heavens to the earth—the nerves of the calculator gave way for a time, and he was unable to finish his task. He called in the aid of a friend, pacing the room in tumultuous agitation while the few last terms were being added. It is impossible for any other mind to realize the intensity of the geometer's feelings when the result was announced! Knowing how trifling a novelty will at times agitate the finest minds, no wonder need be that Newton was affected by an uncontrollable tremor, when he saw that the discovery was made and tested, not only of the law that binds together the particles of matter which compose our earth, but also that which unites the heavenly orbs in all their majesty with the simplest of terrestrial phenomena; and demonstrates that, over the descent of a leaf in the forest—the drooping of a blade of grass—a pebble tossed upon the shore—a mote rising and falling in the sunbeam—a drop issuing from the rain-cloud—there is the same regulating power as that which retains the planets in their orbits, and determines their course through infinite space. Cuvier, in simple but eloquent words, has recorded, in the Introduction to his "Ossemens Fossiles," the state of *his* feelings as he established his discoveries, and proceeded in his task of reconstructing his singular menagerie from the dry bones of Montmartre in the basin of Paris. "I at length," he says, "found myself as if placed in a charnel-house, surrounded by mutilated fragments of many hundred skeletons, of more than twenty kinds of animals, piled confusedly around me; and the task assigned me was to restore them all to their original position. At the voice of comparative anatomy, every bone and fragment of a bone resumed its place. I cannot find words to express the pleasure I experienced in seeing, as I discovered ONE CHARACTER, how all the consequences which I predicted from it were successively confirmed; the feet were found in accordance with the characters announced by the teeth; the teeth in harmony with those indicated beforehand by the feet; the bones of the legs and thighs, and every connecting portion of the extremities, were found set together precisely as I had arranged them before my conjectures were verified by the discovery of the parts entire; in short, each species was, as it were, reconstructed from a single one of its component elements."

Cuvier proceeded upon the principle, that every organized individual forms an entire system of its own, all the parts of which mutually correspond, and that none of these separate parts can change their forms without a corresponding change on the other parts of the same individual body. Where the viscera, for example, are so constructed as only to be fitted for the digestion of recent flesh, it is requisite that the jaws should be so formed as to fit them for devouring prey—the claws for seizing and tearing it to pieces—the teeth for cutting and dividing its flesh—the limbs or organs of motion for pursuing and overtaking it—and the organs of sense for discovering it at a distance. But under this general principle in the structure of carnivorous animals, the ingenious anatomist further discovered that there are several particular modifications, depending upon the size, the manners, and the haunts of prey for which each species is destined or fitted by nature; and that, from each of these particular modifications, there result certain differences in the more minute conformations of particular parts. Hence it follows, that there will exist distinct indications in every one of their parts, not only of the classes and orders of animals, but also of their genera and species.

Thus, in order that the jaw may be well adapted for laying hold of objects, it is necessary that its condyle should have a certain form; that the resistance, the moving power, and the fulcrum, should all have a certain relative position with respect to each other. To enable the animal to carry off its prey when seized, a corresponding force is requisite in the muscles which elevate the head; and this again gives rise to a determinate form of the vertebræ to which these muscles are attached, and of the occiput into which they are inserted. The teeth of a carnivorous animal require to be sharp, in proportion to the greater or less quantity of flesh that they have to cut; their roots to be solid and strong, in proportion to the quantity and the size of the bones that have to be broken; and these conditions of structure will necessarily influence the development and form of the several parts that contribute to move the jaws.

The strength of the claws, in like manner, and the mobility of the paws and toes, have a necessary relation to the forms of the bones in the feet, and the distribution of the muscles and tendons by which they are moved. As the bones of the forearm are articulated with the humerus, no change can be made in the form and structure of the former without occasioning correspondent changes in the form of the latter. The shoulder-blade also, or scapula, requires a correspondent degree of strength in all carnivorous animals, while the play and action of the several parts are dependent on the muscles which set them in motion, and the impressions formed by these muscles still further determine the forms of all these bones. Again, the shape and structure of the teeth regulate the forms of the condyle, of the scapula, and of the claws, in the same manner as the equation of a curve regulates all its other properties;—and, as in regard to any particular curve, all its properties may be ascertained by assuming each separate property as the foundation of a particular equation, in the same manner a claw, a shoulder-blade, a condyle, a leg or arm bone, or any other bone separately considered, leads to the discovery of the characters of teeth to which they have belonged; and reciprocally from the teeth we are enabled to discover the structure and forms of the other bones.

Thus, conducting his investigations by a careful survey of the bones and organs individually and separately, the skillful anatomist was enabled to reconstruct the whole animal to which they severally had belonged. The orders likewise and subdivisions of herbivorous, ruminant, hoofed, and cloven-hoofed animals, he determined with equal precision, and found to result from the same constant laws of organization. By employing the method of observation, where theory was no longer able to direct his views, Cuvier was furnished with other astonishing results. The smallest fragment of bone, even the most apparently insignificant apophysis, he found to possess a fixed and determinate character, relative to the class, order, and genus of the animal to which it belonged; insomuch that, when he observed merely the articulating extremity of a well-preserved bone, he could at once ascertain the species as certainly as if the entire animal had been before him. Proceeding after this method, assisted by analogy and exact comparison, Cuvier has been enabled to determine the fossil remains of seventy-eight different quadrupeds, in the viviparous and oviparous classes. Of these, forty-nine are distinct species hitherto unknown, twenty-seven of which are referable to seven new genera, and the other twenty-two new species belong to sixteen genera, or sub-genera, already known; while the whole number of genera and sub-genera, to which the fossil remains of quadrupeds investigated belong, are thirty-six, including those both of known and unknown species; some hoofed animals not ruminant, and some ruminant—others *gnawers* and others carnivorous—two, of the sloth genus, toothless—and two, amphibious animals, of two distinct genera.

Such are the triumphs of science, which always lead to a profounder admiration of the works of Nature, in the immensity and constancy of those laws that have prevailed through all time, and where her wisdom and foresight are demonstrated by a series of systematic contrivances and mutual adaptations to which she invariably adheres. In the remote invisible depths of space, slight oscillations have from time to time been detected, and following up the researches, astronomy, as announced beforehand, is rewarded by the discovery of a new planet. The earth gives up its dead, entombed for ages in its stony matrix. At the bidding of science their figures are restored, their habits determined, their very food ascertained, their characters for ferocity or otherwise brought to light, and they are all, each after their kind, called by their names. What a mastery in all this over the extinct forms of organic nature, as Newton manifested in a different way in his wonderful deductions and calculations respecting the molecules of inorganic nature and the physical heavens!

III. The Paris basin, which consists of the lower or eocene series of the tertiary system, is inclosed nearly on all sides by the middle or miocene group of strata. These, however, are most fully developed along the district of the Loire and its tributaries, as the former are chiefly confined to the water-shed of the Seine and the environs of Paris. We thus advance a step upward in the Course of Creation, while so far as geology has been able to mark the progress, the last stages of the stupendous work, prior to the introduction of its noblest inhabitant, are to be discovered in the PLEIOCENE deposits that immediately succeed, stretching over the western shores from Bordeaux to Bayonne.

THE BASIN OF THE LOIRE. The rocks which compose these upper layers of the earth's crust, have all a family resemblance to the tertiaries already described. In the district of the Loire the *miocene* beds consist generally of quartzose sand, gravel, and broken shells, mostly loose and earthy, but in many places agglutinated by a calcareous or ferruginous cement, so as to be fit for building purposes. The "faluns," as they are provincially termed, resemble the crag of England, abounding in shells, and mammiferous remains incrusted with serpulæ, flustra, and balani. The deposit is seldom above seventy feet in its greatest thickness. Betwixt Sologne and the sea, patches are found to rest successively upon gneiss, clayslate, the coal-measures, Jura limestone, greenstone trap, chalk, and the upper beds of the eocene series. The *pleiocene* beds are not materially different in their lithological characters from those of the miocene group: blue clays, marls, and osseous breccias are among the prevailing strata; and siltings of sand and gravel, only distinguishable by their organic remains from the alluvia and superficial drifts of the current era. Volcanic products are often largely mixed up with these pleiocene beds, and in districts where, in addition to the fossil evidence, they clearly establish that they belong to the class of extinct volcanoes, as the sedimentary deposits are themselves determined to belong to the pleiocene age.

The interesting peculiarity connected with these two groups of the tertiary system is, that here all animal as well as vegetable life approaches a step nearer to the existing family types. Analogous species of molluscs are more numerous, the testacea in many instances being identical with those of our modern seas. The mammalia are likewise more akin to those of our domesticated tribes, where the horse is strikingly prefigured in the hippotherium, the dog in the agnotherium, and the cat in feline forms as large as lions. The glutton and the bear have also their compeers, nor are the fox, hare, and mouse, without their representatives. But the marvel of the formation is the Dinotherium or gigantic tapir, whose dimensions in every organ and member are

Restored Form of Dinotherium.

stupendous. The dinotherium was seemingly possessed of powers which enabled him at once to exercise the digging propensities of the mole and amphibious habits of the walrus, a trunk projecting nearly as long as that of the elephant, and two enormous tusks depending from the lower jaw. This animal was partly terrestrial and partly aquatic, and hence, says Dr. Buckland, the tusks may also have been applied to hook on the head to the bank, with the nostrils sustained above the water, so as to breathe securely during sleep, while the body remained floating at ease beneath the surface. Thus would he repose, moored to the margin of a lake or river—the huge body, of eighteen feet in length, with a corresponding thickness, indolently basking in the sun-beams, or quietly cooling after exertion in the limpid wave — and these enormous tusks, ready to release him at a bound, when attacked by the enemy beneath. The dinotherium existed during the miocene period, and constitutes an intermediate link between the tapir and the mastodon. It has left abundant remains in the basin of the Rhine, in Bavaria and Austria, and in several districts of the formation in France.

The tertiaries have a wide geographical distribution, and cover a vast extent of superficial area. Stretching from the Rhone to the Danube, they are found in every part of central and southern Europe, along the Julian Alps, and over the interior of Italy, from Ancona to Turin. The eocene group is ascertained, from the character of its fossils, and especially by its nummulites and echinoderms, to extend from the Mediterranean, through Egypt, Asia-Minor, and Persia, to Hindostan, and there to occupy large regions forming the western and northern limits of British India. This enormous mass of tertiary strata was drifted into lakes or estuaries, whereby the mind is carried back to a period when Europe was chiefly lacustrine, and all these countries eastward were as yet submerged in their waters. What explanation can geology give of their elevation to the surface ? A scene of volcanic agency, now and *before* the modern epoch extinct, remains to be noticed, which in part at least will furnish a probable solution of the changes then in operation or completed.

Central France, consisting of the districts of Auvergne, Velay, and Viverais, is universally admitted by geologists to be of volcanic origin. The most cursory glance at the dome-shaped hills, the basalt, trachyte, and scoriaceous ingredients of which they are composed, at once satisfies the student of nature as to the class of rocks among which he here treads. This region lies upon the river Rhone, nearly in the angle formed by it with the Mediterranean, and covers an area of forty or fifty leagues in diameter. Here are associated, perhaps, the earliest and the latest products of Plutonic action, the primary granites, and the basaltic lavas of comparatively recent times. The granite is flanked on the south and west by immense overliers of gneiss. It may be described as the highlands of the country, whence all the great rivers, the Seine, the Loire, the Gironde, and their principal feeders, take their rise. The mountains, though not remarkable for elevation, now that we are approaching true Alpine peaks, reach the height of four, five, and six thousand, and the Aurillac group to nearly seven thousand feet above the level of the sea; but what a geological series of events is embraced within the period of their physical history! The great depository arrangements of the globe have, one and all, succeeded to those paroxysmal movements that raised their tops above the primeval seas. Race after race of living creatures have enjoyed their span of existence, to be mixed up with the strata which during the interval have been collected and arranged in their various systems. The crust of the earth from time to time was disrupted. The depressions and fissures were as repeatedly replaced with new matter. The tertiary period dawned upon Creation, when plain, lake, and seas, were all teeming with an exuberance of terrestrial and aquatic life,—and when again all in the region of Central France was disturbed, and these newer molten rocks were erupted from beneath. The subterranean fires, wherever seated, were thus, after the lapse of geological epochs, still glowing with intense vigor. And, just bordering on the advent of man, the two classes of rocks would seem to have been placed in the closest proximity, as if to remind him, that the same Omnipotent agency which created every single atom of his earthly habitation, likewise determines every movement and advance of the structure, and makes the near and the remote equally manifest the thunder of his power.

There cannot exist a doubt that the district in question was the seat of an extensive chain of lakes, imbosomed amidst the primary rocks, and silted up during the currency of the tertiary age, partly by sedimentary and partly by igneous matter. The unstratified masses which encircled their waters, still stand out in bold relief from the well-defined strata that now occupy their basins. A walk up any one of these valleys—and they are innumerable—or among the cones, hundreds of which are scattered over the high grounds in the vicinity of Gergovia, will present to you in striking contrast these extremes of natural masonry. One can almost trace, in some localities, the very fissures which opened in the sides of the granite rocks, whence issued the molten flood that first perturbed the waters of the pure silent lakes. No straining of the imagination is indeed required to trace the whole progress of their silting—now in the dark lava-current from the bowels of the earth, and now in the collected debris from the mountain sides, hurried down by the torrent or by their own convulsive throes—here the fine comminuted sand, gently carried in by the stream, and there the waste of animal life forming entire beds of calcareous marls of still unsullied freshness. In the whole range of geology there is not, in fact, to be found anything more instructive and interesting than is displayed in these lacustrine deposits, the extreme thinness often of the beds, and the beautiful regularity of their superposition. The lavas intermix, and alternate repeatedly, with the alluvial and organic strata. A myriad of trickling rills fling themselves from the upheaved ridges, so green and flowery to their summits; they are collected into streams in the different ravines, and sweeping through the deep-cut gorges, lay open the interior to the depth of many hundred feet. Here the various igneous and aqueous groups can be read and studied in detail, as they were quietly deposited or violently strewn upon one another.

The hill of La Roche, in the Puy de Jussat, presents a face of a variegated quartzose grit of nearly seven hundred feet in thickness. At Chamalières, near Clermont, the same deposit is equally well exposed. Green and white foliated marls are very abundant, attaining a thickness sometimes of six to seven hundred feet, and consisting chiefly throughout this immense depth of the shells of *Cypris,* a genus which comprises several species, some of which are recent, and still existing in the waters of our stagnant pools and ditches. The structure of these beds, in this volcanic region, is as remarkable as the materials of their composition. The strata divide into plates thin as paper, which are piled up into laminated masses of several hundred feet, of various colors, but the white and green prevailing, and the whole sometimes covered by rocky currents of trachytic or basaltic lava. Gypseous marls, similar to those of Montmartre, have also contributed to the silting up of the lakes, where, as at St. Romain, they are worked, and extensively used for ornamental purposes. A remarkable deposit occurs among the series, termed the *indusial limestone,* from the circumstance of its containing the cases or *inducia* of a tubular-form species of insects; a creature that not only assisted individually toward the increment of the rock, but possessed the power, like its existing analogues, of attaching to its body a load of shelly molluscs, in some cases no less than a hundred of these minute shells being arranged around one tube, while ten or twelve tubes are packed within the compass of a cubic inch. Some beds of this limestone are six feet thick, and may be traced over a considerable area, showing the countless number of insects and molluscs which contributed their integuments and shells to compose this singularly constructed rock. The fibular coralline rocks of the Keelan islands bear some faint resemblance to these ancient organic deposits, where the insects build from beneath, and gradually mount to the surface of the ocean when their work is done, and they perish. The *Phryganeæ* of the tertiary age enjoyed their brief hour in the sunshine, fulfilled their destiny, sank into the waters, and contributed to form rocks over their bottom. They weaved not, like the existing races of builders, their own shroud, though the materials in which they are entombed are mainly of their own construction—concretionary plates of the finest texture, and indestructible as marble.

The lacustrine deposits in the department of the Haute Loire are nearly identical with those now described, but concealed very much by the lava and scoriæ that have flowed out in immense quantities in the trough of the river. The best sections are exposed near the town of Le Puy, where the sedimentary and erupted rocks are beautifully interstratified. The Aurillac basin, in Cantal, is filled with similar materials, although there is a greater proportion of silicious strata mixed with the calcareous marls. Indeed, so much in this district does the silex predominate, that a bed of tertiary limestone is covered with nodules of flint, and resembling in appearance the upper chalks of England. The fossil remains, however, clearly mark the distinction, where we have the shells of the *Planorbis* for those of the *Echinus*, and other fresh water testacea instead of the marine types of the Cretaceous formation.

IV. General Conlcusions. This district has been the theater of great volcanic action. The epoch of its activity is clearly determined by the undoubted tertiary character of the formations with which its porous lavas and scoriæ are intermixed. Basalts and trachytes, of the same age, texture, and qualities, are to be found in the various countries through which the deposits have been traced. The granites, porphyries, and greenstones we have seen successively employed in raising up the symmetrical rocks of the grand palæozoic systems, and thereby giving shape, stability, and access to the economic and gradually-augmenting volume of the crust of the globe. Can we see in these last extinct throes of the interior, the operations of the same great FINAL CAUSE—the overruling hand of power, wisdom, and goodness in the mineral arrangements and diversified ingredients of our earthly habitation?

Take a glance at the extent and geographical situation of this family of rocks. Everywhere among the Andes and Cordilleras, there are evidences of the elevation of large mountain-tracts, through the agency of volcanoes now extinct, and probably of the age in question. A volcanic region in the north of Spain, extending over twenty square leagues, from Amer to Massanet in Catalonia, is situated among the lower beds of the system, penetrating a nummulitic limestone and other strata, conjectured to belong to the age of our green sand and chalk. The Drachenfels on the Rhine and the Eifel chain of hills near Bonn, are likewise referable to this class of volcanic ejections. The Katakekaumene tract of mountains, in Asia-Minor, is composed of comparatively recent volcanoes, where Mr. Hamilton conceives the great cones of Mont Dore, the Cantal, and Mont Mezen in central France are represented by Ak Dàgh, Morad Dàgh, the trachytic hills east of Takmak, Hassan Dàgh, and Mount Argæus. Similar eruptive indications have been traced by Mr. Grant in the district of Cutch, situated near the eastern branch of the Indus, and consisting of large tracts of tertiary deposits. The elevated regions of the Tyrol, the flanks of the Bernese and Swiss Alps, have been the scene of violent disturbance, during and since the deposition of the tertiary formations; and, in the peninsula of Italy, there are numerous groups of volcanic origin, as in Tuscany the igneous rocks of Radicofani, Viterbo, and Aquapendente, and those of the Campagna di Roma, which are of the same chronological series, or probably not later than the pleiocene period. The West India Islands, the Azores, Iceland, Owhyhee where the peaks of Mauna-Roa and Mouna-Kaa rise to the height of between 15,000 and 16,000 feet above the sea, belong to the same class of phenomena. Thus in every quarter of the globe there have existed Phlegræan fields of ancient as well as of modern date, whose convulsions anterior to all historic records are still traceable in the submergence and closing up of lakes, the drainage of large tracts of land, the upheaval of mountains, and the reduction of the earth to existing superficial arrangements.

The products of these tertiary extinct volcanoes are indeed vastly inferior in amount to the ejections of the more ancient periods, whose stupendous monuments are seen in the primary and secondary mountain-chains of granite, porphyry, and greenstone; but still they had force enough to influence very extensive tracts of country, to convulse and move large portions of the crust of the earth. Even now it is impossible to guess through how wide an extent, in the subterranean regions, the shock of earthquakes is simultaneously felt. Not less than 100,000 square miles of country were permanently elevated by the Chili earthquake of 1822, from two to six feet above its former level, and part of the bottom of the sea remained dry at high water, with beds of oysters, muscles, and other shells adhering to the rocks on which they grew. The contemplation of volcanic phenomena in South America, has led Mr. Darwin to remark that, in order to comprehend the vast surface which was affected by the earthquake in Chili, and which destroyed Conception, in February 1835, it had a north and south range equal in extent to the distance between the North Sea and the Mediterranean—that we must imagine the eastern coast of England to be permanently raised, and a train of volcanoes to become active in the southern extremity of Norway—also that a submarine volcano burst forth near the northern extremity of Ireland—and that the long dormant volcanoes of the Cantal and Auvergne, each sent up a column of smoke. It need, therefore, excite no wonder that geologists have felt themselves warranted to ascribe the elevation not only of the sedimentary formations in central France to the volcanic movements of the district, but likewise those of the Paris and London basins, as well as the general rise and dislocation of the strata along the southern and eastern coasts of England. The cause, as compared with recent and still daily observed phenomena, was abundantly adequate to effect the results. Other districts would be simultaneously influenced; the tertiary deposits in their various successive groups were all arranged under similar circumstances and exposed to similar changes; and hence a doubt can scarcely exist, that all these geological basins, and this vast superficies of tertiary matter, were cotemporaneously elevated, as well as subjected to one and the same range of subterranean convulsion.

As an approximation to the period when this district was last subject to volcanic action, it may be noticed that the craters of Auvergne and the Cantal had all ceased to emit fire or were just expiring, when those of Etna and Vesuvius *began* their operations. From whatever cause, it would appear that the incandescent elements had here parted with their caloric or had shifted their position, and that new vents were opened for them in the basin of the Mediterranean. These latter volcanoes may have been in activity *before* the historical epoch, although the evidence must still be regarded as inconclusive, and the violent efforts to fasten a collision upon revelation have utterly failed. But in Auvergne, on the contrary, little doubt exists of the priority of all the volcanic emissions to the human epoch. When Cæsar encamped among these narrow defiles, his Commentary is silent as to any eruptions save the irruption of his own legions. The inhabitants, as now, were cultivating the vine or peacefully engaged in rural occupations, as little dreaming of any disturbances from the interior, as they were unprepared to resist the torrent of mail-clad warriors that poured through their valleys and devastated their fields. The poet Sidonius Apollinaris had his residence on the borders of Lake Aidat, but he sung not of the "sublime" in these upthroes of his native province. Nevertheless, an immense degree of historic interest must ever attach to these volcanic rocks, inasmuch as they are infinitely modern when compared with the primary and secondary formations, the granites and the traps of Britain. They keep continually, too, before our eyes the fact of a succession of igneous operations, and remind us that plutonic agencies have prevailed through all time, and over regions which have only recently been liberated from their ravages; that at any moment, and at any place, they may again burst forth, when islands will be raised, continents submerged, the fertile plain laid waste, and lakes, estuaries, and seas converted into dry land.

Nor are there evidences wanting, in existing volcanoes, of the intensity of the fires which still glow within the interior of our earth. There are at present more than TWO HUNDRED volcanoes in active operation; these are not confined to any particular zone, but are distributed like those of the older families through the different quarters of the world. The greater centers of action are situated in the mountain-ranges of South America, along the western coast of North America, and in the numerous islands of the Southern Pacific; but at the same time there is scarcely a portion of the earth's crust that is not subjected to the shock of volcanic influence and the movement of earthquakes. There are two theories by which all volcanic phenomena are attempted to be explained. The more prevailing one among geologists is that which connects them with one great source of central heat—interior lakes of molten stone—the residue of that incandescent condition in which the globe originally appeared, and out of which the primary crystalline strata were formed. The other mode of explanation is that which supposes the internal heat to be the result of chemical and galvanic action among the materials composing the earth's crust. The metallic and earthy bases, upon contact with water, everywhere transmitted through fissures and apertures on the surface, burn, melt, and are converted into lava-form matter, and which acting again as fuel, serve to fuse the rocks among which they occur. Hence various gases will be generated sufficient to occasion much local disturbance; though certainly not upon a scale to correspond with the magnitude, universality, and perpetuity of those changes that have resulted in the igneous products of the primary, secondary, or even tertiary formations.

But whatever be the source or cause, the heat and the elements of heat have been in constant activity, volcanoes and earthquakes, like the hurricane and disease, subserving important necessary purposes in the economy of nature. Humboldt was the first to remark the linear distribution of volcanic domes, which he considered as vents placed along the edge of vast fissures, communicating with reservoirs of igneous matter, and extending across whole continents. Lyell, considering that the earthquake and the volcano are probably the effects of the same subterranean process, and that the subterranean movements are least violent in the immediate proximity of volcanic vents, observes, "that if the fused matter has failed several times to reach the surface, the consolidation of the lava first raised and congealed will strengthen the earth's crust, and become an additional obstacle to the protrusion of other fused matter during subsequent convulsions." Thus, needful in all past time, these igneous phenomena are needful still—in supplying and indurating new lands—in repairing the waste and continual encroachments of the sea—in keeping up a salutary degree of heat over the earth's crust, and thereby perhaps essential toward maintaining the necessary volume of the earth's bulk. Nor will the fires within have fulfilled their law and purpose of inclosure until the ordinance of Heaven in its creation be completed, when the earth and the works therein shall be burnt up.

## CHAPTER II.

### THE ALPS—MONT BLANC.

The Pennine or Western Alps constitute the loftiest group of mountains in Europe. They consist of a vast chain of isolated peaks, all of which are elevated above the region of perpetual snow. Mont Blanc, Mont Cervin, and Mont Combin attain respectively to the heights of fifteen thousand seven hundred and thirty-two feet, fourteen thousand eight hundred and fifty-five feet, and fourteen thousand one hundred and twenty-five feet, above the level of the sea. This group is succeeded by that of the Bernese Alps, of which the Jungfrau is the most conspicuous, reaching the altitude of thirteen thousand seven hundred and eighteen feet. The Helvetian Alps lie to the east and south of these two ranges, rising in Mont Rosa to the height of fifteen thousand one hundred and fifty feet into the same aerial frozen regions. The rivers Rhine and Rhone spring from the glaciers which occupy the valleys intermediate betwixt the Bernese and Helvetian mountains, while the Po, rising among the Cottian Alps on the south-west, derives its principal tributaries from the same alpine sources with its larger twin-sisters.

Switzerland, thus bounded on the south, is walled in along the entire northern frontier by the range of the Jura mountains, whose loftiest point, the Le Reculet, is five thousand six hundred and twenty-seven feet above the sea level. The mountains of Savoy stretch along the left bank of the Lake of Geneva. Mont Pilatus, the Rigi, and other noted hills of tourists, occupy the eastern central division of the country, among which are situated the largest cluster as well as the most celebrated of the lakes. The great valley of Switzerland, the territory proper of the cantons Vaud, Fribourg, Berne, and Soleure—within which lie all the principal towns, those of the old Roman and all of modern times—forms an extended plateau or basin, inclosed by an amphitheater of mountain land, diversified at intervals by low swelling ridges, undulating hills, precipitous ravines, the deep-set channels of turbid streams, and lovely lakes imbosomed in orchards, vineyards, and meadows of the most luxuriant pasturage.

The two great rivers, embracing the entire drainage of the country and of all the lakes, debouch through narrow gorges at opposite sides of the Swiss territory, and pursue, nearly at right angles to each other, their respective courses until they mingle their waters—the one in the Mediterranean, and the other in the Northern Ocean.

The little town of Neufchâtel, so often alluded to, lies on the north bank of the lake of the same name, the Jura mountains gently sloping up behind. In the suburbs, forming one of a row of detached unpretending houses, is situated the neat château of M. Agassiz in the middle of a small garden, which rests against the hills, and is bounded on the south by the waters of the lake. A most fitting habitation for the great ichthyologist, surrounded as it is with the noblest scenery, and replete in every locality with the richest treasures of his favorite study. I visited the place in the autumn of 1846, unfortunately when M. Agassiz had just left for America: in a beautiful evening strolled through the garden and adjoining inclosures, and was pleased to observe numerous traces in the rocks, and in some fossil relics lying about, of his studies and researches.

The geology of the Alps, the last stage in our self-elected course, is of the most complicated character. The researches of Studer, Escher, and Brunner, natives of the country, have served to establish the general superposition and normal arrangement of the various groups of strata, as those of the illustrious De Saussure had long before been directed to determine their mineral distinctions, and chiefly their classification upon mineralogical principles, into separate crystalline masses. The labors again of Brongniart, Deshayes, Agassiz, D'Orbigny, and Brown, have been mainly employed upon their organic remains, with a view to ascertain the geological epochs within which the several suites of rocks have originated. Our own countrymen, Buckland, Lyell,

Sedgwick, and Murchison, have attempted to systematize still further the alpine deposits, as well as those of Italy and Germany, by showing their relations to the well-marked divisions of our British systems; and the result is, that over all these widely-extended regions, and amidst all the metamorphism, contortion, dislocation, and upheaval of such lofty ranges, there is a true transition from the Silurian, Devonian, and Carboniferous rocks existing in the eastern Alps into the higher secondary and tertiary strata of the western or Swiss Alps.

It would be impossible within our limits to furnish even a moiety of the details and evidences by which the intricate structure of the Alps has been so successfully unraveled, and the arrangement of nature in the due order of superposition so persistently maintained. We shall simply advert to the equivalents of the English strata which have been satisfactorily ascertained, and shall then consider some of the more interesting phenomena connected with the age, elevation, erratic blocks, and glaciers of this Alpine country.

I. General Structure. The great central axis of the Alpine region, stretching from the Rhone to the Danube, consists mainly of the primary crystalline rocks. The granite is everywhere accompanied by gneiss, mica-schist, chlorite-schist, silicious and serpentine limestones. The upper silurian, devonian, and carboniferous systems are distinctly represented in the eastern Alps; but no traces of the Permian deposits have been detected in them or in any part of southern Europe; while again in following the central parts of the chain from Austria into Switzerland and Savoy, all fossil evidences of the four sedimentary systems disappear. The conclusion arrived at by geologists, therefore, is that for these palæozoic and triassic formations there exist no representatives among any of the vast piles of strata of the western Alps; or, if they ever had a place in this part of the chain, that they have been obliterated by the powerful transmuting action of metamorphism, or plunged to inaccessible depths beneath the upraised edges of the primary series. Coal plants, and anthracite coal itself, have both indeed been found in the valley of the Arve in Savoy, at Tarentaise, Maurienne, and along the base of Mont

Blanc; but as they occur in connection with belemnites, these beds have been referred by M. E. de Beaumont and others to the Lias formation, which is clearly determined by its numerous animal fossils to exist in this part of the chain. The remarkable picturesque rocks of Varennes, Duron, and the Col de Balme belong to the lias deposit—the grandest specimens, perhaps, of natural architecture anywhere to be seen.

But, making allowance for all the uncertainties of their lithological complement, and quitting all points of a doubtful character, it has been satisfactorily established that the flanks of the Swiss Alps are covered by a series of sedimentary deposits of vast thickness, which form a true transition from the newer secondary into the older tertiary strata. The normal arrangement of rocks within these limits is complete, beginning with the lias and terminating in distinctly recognized beds of the tertiary pleiocene group.

The lias formation is largely developed along the northern, eastern, and south-western side of the chain, forming an immense belt from near the foot of the Jungfrau, in the central district of Switzerland, to Savona in the Gulf of Genoa. The oolitic formation succeeds, on a scale of still greater magnitude, having a continuous stretch from the Mediterranean at Toulon to Vienna, on the Danube; again constituting an enormous deposit along the Jura range of mountains; and then by Ulm, Altmuhl, and Amberg, to Beyruth, with its celebrated bone caves, in the heart of Germany. The Oxfordian group are represented by the "Neocomian" limestones, a series of hard subcrystalline strata, abounding in fossils of the gault and upper green-sand. To these succeed beds of red, gray, and white marly limestones, containing *Gryphææ*, *Inocerami*, and *Ananchytes*, and regarded as the equivalents, as they are undoubtedly in the position, of the white chalks of England. A supercretaceous group, consisting of nummulitic and shelly rocks, the "flysch" of the Swiss, constitutes the close of the secondary, and graduates conformably and insensibly upward, by mineral and zoological passages, into the eocene system. The vast beds of strata, which are termed the "molasse" and "nagelflue," contain in the *lower* series a large proportion of living species of marine shells, while the associated and *over-*

*laying* strata of terrestrial origin are loaded with forms all of which are extinct. In this group there is nevertheless shadowed forth a type of rocks characteristic both of a miocene and pleiocene age ; but so anomalous is their arrangement, that the younger are often found to dip under the older rocks out of which they have been formed. And as of these, so generally of the entire Alpine series now referred to, the position of the various groups in particular localities can only be unraveled in their flexures, dislocations, and displacements, by means of the organic remains with which they severally abound.

II. The Superficial Accumulations embrace a wide-spread class of geological phenomena. These have originated in causes some of which are still in active operation, others are dormant, and others again may be considered as belonging to agencies which may be termed extraordinary, or permitted only at intervals to display themselves. The effects of their operations are visible, less or more, in every part of the surface of the globe. They have been termed the Pleistocene group, and consist of both marine and fresh water materials. To these are referred the bowlder-clay formation, the vast depôsits of sand and gravel heaped up in valleys, the erratic blocks spread over hill-tops, and the various kinds of detrital matter which, although often laminated, is loose and unstratified, and clearly distinguishable from the more indurated and subjacent beds composing the earth's crust. Nor in gathering up the links of this extended field of review, will it be possible to omit all mention of glaciers and their moraines, so intimately connected with Alpine scenery.

The sand, gravel, and drift accumulations of every kind are common to every country where waters flow or valleys exist. They cover the great straths of Scotland, the low steppes of Russia, the lofty gorges of the Himalaya, the desert wastes of Africa, and the elevated plateaux of North and South America. Among the Rocky Mountains they are of the most varied character, and are spread over extensive areas in those sterile regions, high up among the sources of the great American rivers. Wherever a stream falls into another stream, a stream into a lake, a lake into a river, or a river into the sea, bars, gravelly shoals, and deltas are found to exist, or to be in the act of formation. Accumulations of this class, therefore, are to be regarded as of various periods, as they are evidently the results of causes of continual operation, ordinary as well as extraordinary. Many of such phenomena, however, are as clearly the indication of a state of things which no longer exists. Whether by a subsidence in the sea-bottom, or an elevation of the land, they are now raised far above the influence of the element within which they were collected, and to whose abrading powers they owe their laminated structure. Such, in particular, are those regular-shaped terraces as well as detached hillocks of sand and gravel, several hundred feet in depth, so common in the straths of Scotland and valleys of Switzerland, through which arms of the sea or of great inland lakes once penetrated, and over whose shores and bottoms the debris of the mountains gradually accumulated. "The Sea Margins," the work of the accomplished Robert Chambers, contains a minute and interesting detail of these facts, gleaned from varied sources of reading and most extensive personal observation, and clearly warranting the inference that the sea at no very remote period covered vast districts of country from which it has now receded.

The Bowlder Clay immediately underlies the gravelly beds which have been noticed. Betwixt the two classes of drift there is a clear line of demarkation, although both sand and gravel are often in considerable masses included in the plastic mud which chiefly characterizes the bowlder clay. This formation is of great extent, covering the whole of the north of Europe, a large portion of northern Asia, and in America extending from the Arctic Sea to Boston; massed up in every ravine, and ranging from the lowest valleys to two thousand feet on the mountain slopes, where it is often accumulated to a great depth. One striking peculiarity of the bowlder clay is, that huge blocks of stones of all ages are imbedded in the mass in every region and country where it is found: hence the name. The bowlders are not always of local origin; on the contrary, the parent rock is more generally situated at remote distances, even from five to eight hundred miles. Thus the Scottish Grampians furnish the greater proportion of the huge blocks which are scattered over the lowland and midland counties of Scotland. The Lammermuirs, the Cheviots, the Lake Mountains of Cumberland, have strewed their wreck over the vales of the Tweed and Northumberland, through Yorkshire and the midland plains of England. The chalks of Denmark and Norway are spread out on every shoal and bank in the German Ocean to the British shores; while again, through all Friesland and central Germany, the primary rocks of Scandinavia are as distinctly to be traced. The erratic-block family have in like manner traveled over France, those of Britanny and Normandy penetrating to the basin of the Loire; the Cantal down even to the shores of the Mediterranean. Switzerland, perhaps, contains the most interesting specimens of this universal drift-wreck; as, on the sides of the Jura, at an elevation of four thousand feet, at Monthey, where they give a feature to the landscape, and on the east bank of the lake of Geneva, lies the celebrated *Pierre de Gouté*, which figures in the Huttonian controversy, measuring about ten feet in height by fifteen to twenty in breadth and length. Mont Blanc is conjectured to have been the source of most of these *pierres roulés*, which have been transported across the valley of the Rhone, or lifted sheer over the mountains of Savoy, and are now at the distance of sixty and seventy miles, lying in all the passes and ridges of the Jura.

Various explanations have been given of the origin and deposition of the bowlder-clay formation, as well as of the erratic block-drift, for the two can scarcely be separated in the question of cause and effect. The bowlders, for example, are sometimes in the mass of clay itself, sometimes they are lying loose on the surface, in many instances they are spread over areas where no clay exists; but in most cases maintaining their unmistakable character of being water-worn, rounded, and covered with striæ. Both classes of phenomena, therefore, are supposed to be referable to the same period of time, as they probably have originated in the same series of causes. One theory advanced in explanation of both, is the agency of powerful currents that swept over Britain and the adjacent continents, generally in a north and north-westerly direction, bearing along with them soil, gravel, and the larger debris of rocks; and as obstructions occurred, or the violence of the currents subsided, the heterogenous materials were deposited in the various countries and at the different elevations in which they are found. The direction of the currents, often from different centers, is indicated clearly by the position and lithology of the mountains from which the blocks have been transported, no less than by the fact that the greatest accumulations of drift and bowlders are to be observed at the south-eastern extremities of such gorges and valleys as were open to the diluvial action. But the hypothesis fails in giving a satisfactory account of the transport of the larger blocks, often of sixty to a hundred tons weight, over a course of many hundreds of miles, plunging through hollows, and now stranded on mountain-slopes several thousand feet above. The theory of icebergs, as the transporting agency, meets this difficulty; and accordingly, in one form or other, such a cause or agent, of widely-prevailing influence, is almost universally adopted into the creed of geologists. This theory implies, that those portions of Europe now covered with the bowlder-clay formation were submerged after the deposition and consolidation of the tertiary strata—that this submergence was the result of a change in the earth's axis or some extraordinary alteration in its planetary relations—that a great arctic glacial continent subsided and disappeared beneath the waters—and that vast floating masses of ice, inclosing rock loosened from the sinking land, penetrated southward, grazing and polishing the harder substances that lay in their course, or carrying along with them the more yielding and transportable materials. Admit all or even a limited number of such assumptions, and we know from what is occurring in recent times, that the cause is quite adequate to the production of the effect. Sir James Ross, in his late humane exploratory expedition, encountered in the polar regions icebergs from a hundred to three hundred feet in height, and from a quarter to half a mile in length. Two-thirds of every iceberg float beneath the water. What a carrier power, at once for erosion and transport, in every one of these frozen floating mountains! The Polar ocean still maintains its great southward current to the equatorial seas, modified by the headlands and inequalities of bottom which occur in its progress; and then, as now, the icebergs driven along this highway of waters would drop, at intervals, portions of their stony load, to take up at other stations whatever was prepared to adhere to them. Hence the difficulty vanishes as to the large detached blocks so often found on the elevated sides of mountains. Hence, too, the explanation of those collected groups which are entirely free from any admixture of clay. And hence, upon the retreat of the waters and the elevation of the land, it is reasonable to infer that many districts would be swept bare again of their mud, while the bowlders would remain, and that in other quarters ridges and the deeper accumulations would be formed. "Both theories," however, as stated by Mr. Page in his excellent treatise, "Rudiments of Geology," "are beset with difficulties; and though the latter accounts more satisfactorily for most of the phenomena of the erratic block group, still there are many points respecting the distribution and extent of the deposit to be investigated before either can be finally adopted. All that can be affirmed in the present state of the science is the composition and nature of the clay, gravel, and bowlders—the course of the currents concerned in their deposition—the fact of the land having a configuration of hill and valley, not differing much from what now exists—and the peculiar scantiness, if not total absence, of organic remains."

Whether this mysterious cataclysm occurred before or within the modern epoch is a question which, as yet, has not by any means been determined. The few organic remains detected in the deposit are of marine origin—one or two species of shells—but all identical with species now existing. The presumption is that the climate which prevailed over these northern regions during the period was extremely low. But how long it lasted, and why there are no types preserved, in all that congeries of materials of the *terrestrial* fauna and flora of the period, are points both of them of a very perplexing kind. Whether just dawning upon the advent of man, or within the actual era of his history, certain it is that these are the results of a chaotic condition over a large portion of our planet, of which, if we except the deluge, we have no record nor memorials in any of the after changes and modifications of its surface. Shall we add, as indicative of a FINAL CAUSE appearing in and overruling the tumultuous agitation, that to this source is to be traced great part of the soil which covers the valleys and mountain sides of all the submerged districts? that hereby extensive lakes were silted up, the flinty rock concealed by fertile earth, and the steep acclivity made accessible to the husbandman? One thing is clear, that all the latest tertiary strata in this alpine region have, after their consolidation, been disturbed and broken up: it is upon their inverted edges that the superficial accumulations have been deposited and now rest: and whether the submergence of Europe, and other parts of the globe, was simultaneous or not with the cause of their movement and overthrow, a superintending wisdom and purpose are unquestionably discernible in those accessions of soil and other economic arrangements that resulted from the change.

There is another theory, however, which has been applied to the explanation of these phenomena — namely, the THEORY OF GLACIERS, as illustrated in the works of Venetz, Charpentier, Agassiz, and Forbes.

A glacier is a moving stream of ice formed in the transverse valleys and furrowed gorges of alpine chains. They are of great depth and indefinite length; and as they proceed slowly but progressively in their courses they carry along with them all the loose and prehensible mountain debris with which they come in contact. On their surface they bear every falling splinter, small and great, from the overhanging rocks. The sides and bottom of the ravines through which they pass are stripped, polished, and striated. The avalanche breaks upon them with its accumulated load; and every mountain rill, upon the melting of the snows in summer, deposits over their flanks the materials with which they are charged. Immense masses of matter are, in these various ways, collected and transported from the higher into the lower valleys: these at the outgoing of the glacier generally assume a ridge-shaped form, and are termed *moraines*. The underlying blocks are all rounded and grooved: those borne on the surface are sharp and angular, until they are swept away by the torrents into the rivers, where they are in turn subjected to their smoothing operations. There can be no doubt, therefore, either as to the disintegrating or transporting power of this mighty agent. When I stood upon the Mer de Glace I saw before me, in one gorge of the mountain, a continuous stretch of icy machinery fourteen miles in length by two to three in breadth, and several hundred feet in depth. The whole was in motion; and, whether we adopt as the principle of translation the mechanical pressure of Agassiz, or the hydraulic law of Forbes, the instrument of an incalculable carriage-power was there. And yet, upon the first glance, it shrank into a span, or appeared but as a small lake, as we viewed the glacier pouring down that deep gorge of Mont Blanc; a sheer depth of dark perpendicular rocks rising on its edges many thousand feet in height; several of the sharp-pointed Aiguilles, the Grandes Mullets, and above all, the Peak de Dru, unrivaled in symmetrical grandeur, penetrating still higher into the clear sky above. How many such glaciers are dispersed through that vast alpine chain; and how immense, upon any rule of calculation, have been the earthy and rocky materials which they have borne downward in the lapse of time!

Familiarized to such gigantic operations among his native Alps, M. Agassiz came to the conclusion that not only the bowlder drift of Switzerland, but nearly all the superficial accumulations of northern Europe, were to be ascribed to glacial action. In the straths and glens of Scotland he fancied a moraine in every talus of a mountain, and in every bar of a river. He saw the polishing of glaciers in the pass of Killiecrankie, on the sides of Ben Nevis, and the steep promontories of Morven. The parallel roads of Glenroy originated in the same cause. From the Mediterranean to the Arctic zone a polar climate universally prevailed, and the whole was covered with a mantle of ice; vast fields of ice, too, depending from the mountains penetrated into the adjacent valleys; the plains in succession were invaded, and erratic blocks were scattered in every direction; when at last, upon a change of temperature consequent upon other changes in the planetary relations of the earth, all these erosive influences were for a time increased, and the glacial power attained its maximum. Not only the upper and transverse furrows in the Alps but all the lower and great longitudinal valleys of the Cantons were the seats of glaciers during this period. Along the passes of the Rhine, the Rhone, the Drance, the Doire, the Arve, and the Isêre, the irrepressible tide of ice maintained its course, leaving portions of the drift at different elevations, and dropping bowlders on the intermediate hills and on the more distant and loftier barriers of the Jura. Sir R. Murchison opposes all these speculations of Agassiz and others. The elevation of the alpine chain, of which there is abundant evidence in comparatively recent times, he regards as cotemporaneous with the translation of the bowlder-drift, and considers that during the sub-aqueous condition of northern Europe, the Alps and the Jura were from two to three thousand feet below their present altitude. He finds that the famous blocks of Monthey opposite Bex are composed exclusively of the granite of Mont Blanc—that they have been transported on ice-rafts through the gorge of St. Maurice to their present locality—and reasons with justice that had they formed part of a moraine the debris of all the intervening rocks, along the valley through which the glacier passed, must have been associated with them. None of the glaciers of the Alps, he thinks, could have been of the extent implied in the transport through their agency of the Jura blocks, nor have ever the upper longitudinal and flanking valleys around Mont Blanc been filled with general ice-streams. The materials, likewise, of true glacier moraines he conceives can be readily distinguished, on the one hand, from the more ancient alluvia, and, on the other, from tumultuous accumulations of gravel bowlders and far-transported erratic blocks. And, looking at the various causes which have affected the surface, Sir Roderick concludes, that all the chief difficulties of the bowlder-clay formation are removed, when it is admitted that frequent and vast changes of the land and waters have taken place since the distribution of large erratics—that a great northern glacial continent has subsided—that the bottom of the sea over Britain and the adjacent continent has been raised into dry land, while the Alps and Jura, formerly at lower levels, have been considerably and irregularly elevated.

The elevation of this stupendous chain of rocks, not by one but by a succession of upheavals and depressions ere they assumed their present position and grouping, is a point generally admitted, and not difficult to demonstrate. The Alps, for example, are folded all round with successive belts or zones of sedimentary matter, marking, as so many milestones at different points of altitude, the measure of increment attained during the intervals of their deposition. These belts contain each their own peculiar class of fossils which determine their relative ages. In succession, the several suites or families of rocks rest upon the inverted outcrop or inclined edges of the older groups. Thus the history of organic life upon the globe, the incoming of new races and the extinction of old ones, as contained in these deposits, becomes a scale of measurement of the elevations, disruptions, and ever-varying conditions of the inorganic crust, while in the inverted, dislocated state of the crust itself, we mark the several throes by which it was lifted above the waters. Not one of the fossiliferous beds enveloping the granitic and crystalline nucleus of the chain of the Alps but has been shifted out of its original horizontal position, and the shift of the subjacent having always preceded the deposition of the overlying formation, it follows that, in addition to the intumescence of the chain, there must have been a series of oscillatory and elevatory movements before attaining its final altitude. But after the consolidation of the whole rocky strata, and while the waters were still many thousands of feet in depth, the superficial accumulations were being deposited—the bowlder drift, and erratic blocks, either by icebergs or other causes, were floated into position—and it was not until every one of these traveled stones, fresh even now as when torn from the living rock, were quietly settled down into the bottom of the sea, that Mont Blanc had displayed a moiety of its massive outline, or towered to one-half of its present colossal grandeur. The elevation of Ben-Mac-Dhui dates from the era of the old red sandstone formation. Mont Blanc was invaded on all sides by a sea that received the latest of the tertiary deposits. Both were submerged during the cataclysm which produced the bowlder clay ; but as no increment to its bulk was derived from this cause, Ben-Mac-Dhui falls geologically to be reckoned a completed, and therefore a far older, mountain than Mont Blanc, which had not attained its full altitude and bulk until the expiration of the Pleiocene age !

Such are the mighty agencies contemplated by the geologist in the various later changes which have affected the surface of our globe. The rill, the river, the torrent, the glacier, the earthquake, the volcano, are still in operation, but only as faint images of the enormous powers which in the more ancient times have been at work. That the earth has been repeatedly encroached upon by the waters every principle of his science goes to establish; but out of every convulsion he sees a better and more stable condition of things to have emerged. If the bowlder drift and the cold plastic clay formation point to a continuance of sunless, lifeless seasons, he forgets not, as the products of the period, that two-thirds of the soil of Great Britain and of the grain-bearing lands of the continent, have been derived from these accumulations—the industrial monuments of their invasion in every quarter of the world.

## CHAPTER III.

### THICKNESS OF THE EARTH'S CRUST—CENTRAL HEAT.

THE question arises, Since upon geological grounds it is demonstrable that the crust of the earth has been repeatedly upheaved and broken, have we reason to conclude that similar states of paroxysm and convulsion may not again return? This brings us to the consideration of two very interesting problems, namely,—THE THICKNESS OF THE EARTH'S CRUST—And THE DOCTRINE OF CENTRAL HEAT. Have we any means of determining either of these points? The doctrine of the igneous origin of granite and other rocks proceeds upon the assumption of a vast reservoir of heat existing somewhere within the interior; and the question to be solved is—What is the thickness of the solid crust beneath which the molten rocks have their origin? and what the cause of their fusion?

I. An opinion has long prevailed among geologists of a certain school, that the crust of the earth is of very limited dimensions. A thin coating of primary crystalline rock is interposed betwixt the sedimentary strata above, and the intensely incandescent mass of which the interior is composed. The experiments of Fourier establish a formula of increasing temperature of the strata in a descending series, and from the rate of this increase, it is inferred, that about one hundred miles below the surface the entire nucleus is in a state of complete fusion. Some have even assumed the melting point to be less than thirty miles, when "the next contiguous matter is in a state of fusion, at a temperature probably higher than any that man can produce by artificial means, or any natural heat that can exist on the surface."* Sir John Leslie

* Dr. Pye Smith on Scripture Geology.

attempted a demonstration of the ultimate resolution of the materials into light, as the only element capable of resisting the vast pressure of the outer crust; and, erroneously assuming the *modulus* of compressibility of air, water, the metals, and all known earthy substances to be invariable, however greatly the pressure may be increased, this ingenious philosopher came to the conclusion, that, instead of Tartarean darkness, the offspring of superstition, the inner chambers of the earth are filled with luminous ether, the most pure, concentrated, and resplendent. Darwin believes that much of the vast continent of South America is suspended over an inner sea of liquid fire, and says, that, "daily it is forced home on the mind of the geologist, that nothing, not even the wind that blows, is so unstable as the level of the crust of the earth."

With the fires of Etna and Vesuvius raging on the one side, and the recent though extinct volcanoes of Auvergne and the Cantal seated so near on the other side, what security is there, amidst so many undoubted facts of the mobility of the land, that these vast piles of Alpine mountains may not again, through mere mechanical weight, break through the film of crust on which they rest, and sink into the abyss from which they so lately emerged! The doctrine of central heat, it may be replied, does not necessarily imply the universal *fluidity* of the central mass, an opinion supported by Lyell, Poisson, and other eminent philosophers; while there is reason to infer, as repeatedly stated, that there is no identity of scale and mechanism between volcanoes now active, and the igneous causes which gave birth to these and other stupendous mountain-chains.

But astronomy gives a different and more comfortable solution of the problem. The influence of the moon alone, it would appear, acting upon our planet, requires a thickness of crust of at least ONE THOUSAND MILES, to prevent the fabric of the globe from being severed into fragments. The earth, considered in connection with its own planetary system, has three distinct motions in space, a fact in science usually illustrated by the movements of the common spinning-top. A more striking illustration may be seen in the steam-vapor which has aided you onward, that living cloud of light and heat which towers and floats away in these beautifully curling wreaths. Like the trail of the comet, how gracefully it sweeps over the plains in its forward movement: then it turns to the right or left in the direction of the wind: and then, in a third convolution, every globule of the airy mass is twirling on an axis of its own. Equally buoyant is the earth, hung upon nothing, and cleaving the liquid firmament. It turns on its axis, causing the vicissitude of day and night; it moves through its orbit, making the circuit of the sun and the diversity of the seasons; and, in addition, there is an oscillatory motion like the unsteady zig-zag twistings of the carriage-train, occasioned by the excess of the equatorial over the polar diameter. This excess amounts to about a three-hundredth part. But, small as it is, it exerts an assignable influence over the cohesion or attraction of the solid framework. Now, by a nice mathematical demonstration, resting on the sun and moon's attraction, Mr. Hopkins infers, as indicated by the phenomena of *precession and nutation*, that the minimum thickness of the earth's crust cannot be less than one-fourth or one-fifth of the earth's radius. The theorem is of too abstract a nature to be here introduced; but it appears from it that the observed amount of *precession* requires this degree of solid matter, which gives a clear depth of solid arch over either vacuum, resplendent light, or fiery fluid, of from eight hundred to a thousand miles. This may well allay the fears of the most timid as to the stability of the ground beneath his feet, whatever be the state of the interior, or under whatever modifications the materials therein may exist.

II. But if this thickness of crust is required now, it must have been equally required in all past time: hence, it may be argued, no security is thereby afforded against the bursting out of the pent-up fires, or disruption of the outer crust? Now, it has been questioned whether there be such a thing as a CENTRAL fluid heat at all, while the solidity of the earth throughout has been maintained as more in unison with the principles of established science.

The doctrine of a central heat is as old as the days of Bishop Burnet, who imagined that the internal fire, pre-existent in the bowels of the earth, was the agent employed in breaking up the fountains of the deep for the production of the deluge. Leibnitz and Buffon regarded the earth as an extinguished sun or vitrified globe, which, according to the calculations of the latter, required seventy-five thousand years to cool down to its present temperature; and that, in ninety-eight thousand years more, the heat will be utterly exhausted, and productive nature extinguished. Whiston fancied that the earth was created from the atmosphere of one blazing comet, and deluged by the humid tail of another. And Whitehurst, one of the oldest of modern geologists, regarded all the strata of every formation, as concentrically arranged over the surface of the globe, and then employed the expansive agency of internal fire to account for their upheaved disrupted condition. These cosmogonies, it is needless to remark, all now rank with the speculations of the alchemists, and that Behmen and their authors are considered as of equal authority in the sciences of chemistry and geology.

The searching tests of experiment, as already noticed, have been brought to illustrate the subject of internal heat, but the results have not been decisive, nor very satisfactory. It has been stated, as a general rule in the mines examined, that, in proportion to their depth, the heat increases as we descend; and the mean result of all the best observations, as given by Cordier, amounts to one degree of heat for every forty-five feet of depth. Different mines, however, it has been ascertained, vary in their degrees of downward temperature; as in the Durham and Newcastle coal-pits, the increase is estimated at one degree for every forty-four feet,—in the Cornwall iron-mines at one in seventy-five feet,—and in Saxony some of the mines give an increase of only one degree in one hundred and eighty or one hundred and ninety feet of perpendicular descent. Much of this difference may, indeed, be readily accounted for by the nature of the contents of the mines themselves, their position in the system, and the quality of the rocks among which they are situated. But a difficulty will remain, how to dispose of the increasing ratio of temperature, and the changes that must necessarily result from it in the bowels of the earth. Thus, assuming it to be a uniformly increasing ratio in proportion to the depth, it will follow from this law of increase that we reach a point, about twenty-four miles down, hot enough to melt iron: at double that distance, such a heat as will fuse every substance with which we are acquainted: and at a hundred miles, that a temperature will exist, of whose resolving powers we have no experience, and cannot even conjecture. The astronomical theory of a thousand miles of crust melts into airy nothing in its presence, and the formula of Fourier, before it has reached the required hundred, will have found a nucleus in complete fusion, acting intensely upon the thin external crust, and seeking through every crevice of these "flagrantia mœnia mundi," to issue forth in torrents of fire.

It has been farther objected to a central fluidity, that such a fluid must be in constant circulation by the cooling of its exterior— a fact ascertained in the case of all fused metals. Tides too, it has been argued, would be produced in the fluid matter, however deeply seated, through the influence of the sun and moon, and which *tides* would necessarily occasion such oscillatory and expansive movements as astronomy has neither noticed nor accounted for. Again, the supposition of a central heat of the earth, prevailing from the beginning and through all the phases of its history, implies that its cooling is still going on; and that, in consequence, a contraction in the mass or bulk of the earth will follow the law observed by all other bodies in parting with their heat. Hence this contraction might lead to the shortening of the day and other mechanical results. But Laplace satisfied himself, by reference to ancient astronomical records, that there had been no alteration in the length of the day, even to the smallest calculable degree or point of a second; and that thence, the hypothesis of a fluid, or even primitive heat of the earth, had here no confirmation.

An objection to the theory has likewise been urged, from the well-known property and tendency of heat to become equally diffused through all the particles of any body in which it exists. Thus, it is an established principle, that heat not only diffuses itself on all sides, but passes continually from bodies in which the temperature is greater to those in which it is less; and that if a body be placed in a medium having a temperature different from its own, the momentary variations of its temperature will be as the differences between the temperature of the body and of the medium. Hence, when the heat beneath the surface of the earth, at whatever depth, becomes of sufficient intensity to melt iron, it cannot pass beyond this until the whole surrounding mass is heated to the same degree of intensity. The law of increment and transmission of caloric, it is argued, must be the same below as above; and, assuming the nucleus of the earth to be fluid, no solid crust could thus be formed upon the surface until every particle of the heated fluid mass was cooled down to the point of consolidation. This principle is well understood in the formation of a crust of ice upon water. If extendible to other bodies, and to subterranean distances, then the simple fact of an existing outer crust, solid and cooled down to the existing temperature, militates against the probability of a central fire, and is utterly repugnant to the hypothesis of a liquid central mass.

It is maintained, however, on the other hand, that the central caloric, however intense at any depth, has long ago arrived at the point at which the conducting power of the rocky crust has either entirely ceased or permits no further sensible decrease; that this point was reached some time before the creation of man, when the process of cooling had acquired a maximum or stationary condition, and that it formed a part of the processes by which the earth was adapted to its high destination among the works of God. But may not the adaptation have been effected by the gradual conduction of the heat outwardly, not by suffering it to remain and glow in opposition to its known properties in the inner regions? It may be maintained as a safe principle in physical science, that if there be heat in the center of the globe, it must have the properties of heat and none other. No geologist hesitates to admit, upon evidence amounting to demonstration, that a vast source of heat exists in the interior of the earth, widely spread beneath the stony pavement, and that it has existed at all times. But whether that heat is local or generally diffused—whether it is central or infra-superficial—whether it is constantly maintained, or is excited at intervals by certain combinations—are questions as yet of mere speculation, and for the solution of which we have no data to lead us, beyond probable inferences.

Upon the whole, as the known density of the earth is considerably greater than that of a solid sphere, composed of any such rocks as we are acquainted with, the presumption is, that heavier materials, in an increasing ratio, than any constituting the superficial crust, enter into the composition and structure of the central parts. All the great mountain systems in the different zones of the globe are the product of palæozoic times. The fires which cast them out have gradually diminished by every succeeding effort. A steadier equilibrium betwixt the conflicting elements of the upper and the lower world, appears to have taken place—once only disturbed, at the deluge, since man's occupation—and for the repetition of which there exists no preparation in the established course of nature. The very convulsions which have shattered the earth to its foundations, while they are evidences of benevolent wisdom, furnish, at the same time, the best guarantee against blind fortuitous derangements to come; the result, as they are, of periodical causes, acting in a way and with an intensity of which we have no experience, and for which, indeed, we have no expression in any of the sciences.

# GENERAL PRINCIPLES.

## PART IV.

## CHAPTER I.

### RÉSUMÉ.

GEOLOGY, as will be seen from the preceding details, is among the most comprehensive of the sciences. It invades the province of every one of them, and lays them all under contribution while following out its own peculiar researches. A dry description of rocks, in their simple mineral qualities, does not limit or exhaust its ample resources. Botany, zoology, meteorology—a part, in short, of every branch of natural history, as well as chemistry, physics, and astronomy, are severally enlisted in its service, and all give interest and importance to its discursive investigations. And thus, receiving gifts from every walk of science, geology gives back in turn, and imparts to each, illustrations new and rare, from its own wonderful storehouse.

Geology, considered in itself, may be pursued in three different ways, as it resolves into three great leading branches of investigation. Observing the arrangement and superposition of rocks, as exhibited in the crust of the earth, along with their mineral distinctions and fossil contents, we embrace all the objects included in *descriptive* or *phenomenal* geology. The exposition, again, of the general principles by which such phenomena can be produced, constitutes what has been termed *geological dynamics*,—by which are traced the laws of action of known causes, and their relation to such changes as those which geology considers. The last branch leads to a consideration of the causes in which the phenomena have originated and the doctrines deducible from them. This has been called *physical geology*, and embraces all that is theoretic in the science. These three branches, while thus definitively distinct in themselves, are yet frequently combined in the works of writers on the subject; nor is it easy, or even possible, in practice, to separate them, as few will be content to describe without attempting also to explain.

It has been no part of our vocation in these investigations to inquire into the *origin* of a material universe;—what was its pre-existent state, and by what process this globe at first was brought into an earthy concrete form. Astronomy has tried various solutions. But whether by the splintering of other worlds, or the evolution of matter from a Saturnian ring, or by the condensation of gaseous star-dust diffused through infinite space, no astronomical hypothesis has proved satisfactory. Geology is better employed when she assumes a beginning to her researches upon the visible crust of the globe. The mystery of *creation* is not within the range of her legitimate territory; and, while the investigation of laws and of the influence of secondary causes falls within the province of both, it may be safely admitted that neither astronomy nor geology are, of themselves, capable of giving us any real or precise account of the origin of the universe, or of any of its parts.

That we have begun with the primary rocks of the Grampians, as the most ancient division of systematic lithology, was more with a view to have some 'principia' for description than assumptions for theory, and because no geological research has penetrated deeper. The crust of the earth, as far as observation extends, is proved to consist in its lower parts of a series of crystalline rocks, some of which are stratified, and others unstratified, intercalating one with another, and maintaining the same relative position, each to each, as a system, in every region of the globe. Granite, gneiss, micha-scist, quartz-rock, and limestone, constitute these first outwork courses of creation; one uniform cause acting simultaneously over the earth, appears to have placed them all in position; and as no breathing animal or blossoming plant witnessed this morn-dawn of nature, the rocks belonging to the period are termed the primary or azoic series. The fossiliferous deposits follow in their due order of superposition, arranged into groups and systems according to the organic remains by which they are respectively characterized, and preserving, in their geographical distribution, the same uniform and persistent vertical arrangement as the former. Amorphous rocks, of all ages and extent, are distributed among the stratified portions of the crust, whether crystalline or sedimentary, whereby the latter are dislocated and upheaved, and the inequalities of the surface, and all the pleasing diversity of plain, hill, and mountain have been produced. It is the special object of descriptive or phenomenal geology to note all the facts connected with these appearances and changes, to collate and compare them one with another, and finally, to systematize them according to their natural affinities and relations.

Dynamical and theoretical geology, again, inquires into the supposed principles and causes in which all these arrangements have originated, and by which they have been modified. The agencies, processes, and changes which we now observe in the existing course of nature, furnish the grounds and analogies by which alone we can speculate respecting the past condition of things, subject always to the consideration that, in proportion to the difference of effects and changes in the two periods, so are the causes and agencies which produced them, as well in relation to time as to force. The enormous magnitude of the results witnessed during the more ancient geological epochs, demonstrates the intensity of the causes then in operation; and, admitting these causes to be the same in kind with such as prevail at present, we are yet warranted to infer their more violent activity, as likewise to assume a more rapid increment in their effects. Thus the geologist, from observation of the laws of crystallization now manifested in the aggregation of the elementary particles of bodies, reverts to the existence of similar forces, whatever they be, which produced the crystalline texture of the primary rocks, their fissile structure, and the separation of all those materials which exist among them in the form of gems, agates and metalliferous veins. Igneous causes he still finds in operation, as volcanoes, earthquakes, and chemical agencies closely connected with both; and the same forces he hesitates not to connect with the elevation of mountain-chains, the vast masses of plutonic matter everywhere diffused through the earth's crust, and the disturbance, dislocation, and other changes produced upon all the stratified rocks through which this matter has penetrated. A mighty power in continual action, he further perceives in the waters of the ocean, of the atmosphere, of the rills and rivers that issue from the mountains' side: and to such aqueous causes, operative in the past as in the present day, he refers the transport, lamination, and detrital structure of the materials of all the sedimentary deposits. Nor does he leave out of estimation the effect of assumed cosmical changes upon the temperature of the planet, and the laws that regulate the distribution of heat over the surface: causes such as these the geologist sees greatly to influence, at present, the conditions of organic life in every quarter of the globe; and hence, he justly calls for their assistance in explaining the history of those remarkable organic remains which characterize the several geological epochs.

When the geologist proceeds systematically to trace the series of these phenomena, to ascertain their causes, and to connect together all the indications of change that are found in the organic and inorganic kingdoms of nature, he attempts the structure of a THEORY OF CREATION, which shall embrace the whole course of the world, from the earliest to the present times; and which, it may reasonably be concluded, may be resolved into one great cycle, yet unfinished. But for this the materials of the science are by no means prepared, nor is its progress sufficiently advanced.

The history of organic remains forms an interesting branch of descriptive geology, where, it may be said, we find the medal-stamps of creation in the first forms of organic life that came from the hands of the Creator. The fact is all-important, and the science is prepared to announce it, that in the lowest fossiliferous strata of the earth, VEGETABLES appear among the first of all living things : the impressions of plants, and entire beds of carbonaceous matter, are found in the most ancient strata of the Silurian group of rocks. Nor less important is the fact, that the fossils which next arrest the attention are the remains of marine animals, myriads of shells, and vast numbers of fishes. Then, in the ascending series of strata, the foot-prints of birds are lower down than the impressions of the beasts of the earth. The sea, it is next discovered, swarmed with huge reptilian bodies, before mammalian quadrupeds and cattle had yet a place on dry land; and man, the noblest specimen of organic structure, the crowning apex of the pyramid of terrestrial being, is, according to the geological narrative, precisely in his place—no bone nor fragment of his kind, having been detected in the solid frame of the globe.

Such is the vista into the past opened up through these rocky entablatures of the globe. Compared with other branches of knowledge, in point of mere exciting topics of interest, geology occupies a distinguished position. Nay, the truth here, to those not conversant with the science, is even more incredible than fiction. As a study into the records of creation, geology has disclosed views, and elicited discoveries, of the works of the Divine Architect of the world, which the religious inquirer will as cordially embrace, as ignorance only can overlook or misapprehend.—Newton imagined, so porous is all earthy matter, that this terrene globe could be crushed into the size of two or three cubic inches of solid substance. Geology now shows that the most concrete rocks, chains of hills and even of mountains, the soft clays of Virginia, and loose floating deserts of sand, are many of them composed of the shields and skeletons of animalcules; evidences, through all past time, of the wondrous prodigality of nature, and of the superabundant goodness of its Author. Nothing, indeed, at first sight can appear more barren of every point of interesting illustration than the rocky masses of the earth. Tear off the grassy covering which conceals, while it freshens, the outer crust of the globe, and to mere disorder and confusion there seems to be superadded the more repulsive features of sterility and death. But examine a little deeper, and you will see order, symmetry, and beauty; what is now frigid and motionless, was once animated with the breath of life; these stony chambers beneath, the necropolis of a buried world. The study of the Course of Creation, therefore, when read aright—whether in its organic or inorganic lessons—cannot fail to present the most varied and sublime illustrations of the power, wisdom, and goodness of Him who reared the stupendous fabric, and made our earth one of the bright rolling planets of the universe.

There are many points, however, and questions of the deepest importance, that are far from being satisfactorily determined.— The progress of vegetable and animal life, for example, is supposed to correspond with the varying conditions and changes of the earth's surface, when the races are summoned into existence, not at once, nor after short intervals, but successively, and after ages of unfathomable extent. The record, even as a chronicle of mere life and death, is a marvelous one, full of singular revelations, and disclosing types of organized being that have long been obliterated. But when as yet there was no rational head in this mundane scene, the assumption is, that the inferior tribes were for MILLIONS of years the sole living occupants of the planet! Can all the data be sound, rightly understood, and properly interpreted, that lead to such conclusions? The epic of this lengthened series of events is yet, it may be said, without a hero. The tragedy of wild revolution and carnage lacks romance in the very monotony of its devastation. And destitute alike of a *moral*, and of a fitting audience, the brilliancy of the representation loses half its attractions in losing all its humanity.

One established principle of the science connected with this point is, that there are certain groups of animal species found fossil in the different sets of strata which compose the earth's crust, and that these demonstrate something like a series of distinct faunas corresponding to the number of formations. Seven or eight sets of rocks, at least, are as distinctly characterized by particular sets of fossils. But the exceptions to the law are likewise very numerous, inasmuch as both species and genera have been carried forward, and are identically the same, from one formation and epoch into another. Hence, points neither of difference nor of resemblance, from age to age, are absolute, and cannot very minutely be applied as regards the several formations and their organic contents. The types of one formation are repeatedly mingled with those of another. And the value of all the evidence collected from fossil remains, while it establishes undeniably a succession in the mineral deposits, leaves the question as to the limits of the epochs, and their relation to Time, still partially undetermined. The theory too of progressive development, or that of independent acts of creation—the causes of the extinction of old, and the introduction of new races—the extent of time implied or indicated in the whole series of events—and the all-important point involved in this chronology, whether all or any of the geological series are alluded to in the Mosaic account of creation—are questions that necessarily press upon the attention, as we would solve or not the inquiries suggested. The sounding-line of geology is not to be despised, or cast at once aside, should it fail in furnishing a just estimate and measure of such profound investigations. Every failure will only prove a stimulus to renewed exertion, as every discovered path of error leads one step in advance toward the path of truth, and that in turn to harmony with the Book of ALL TRUTH.

## CHAPTER II.

### THEORIES OF ORGANIC LIFE.

AFTER inquiring into their *order* of succession, the *relation* which organic fossils have to each other, as genera and species, falls naturally to be considered. How have these various families of creatures, brought to light by geology, been formed? In what manner have they become extinct? Have they all proceeded from a few original types, which have been modified by circumstances, increased in variety, and perfected in form, as they advance from the older to the newer formations? And does geology furnish any data on which to build a theory of their extinction as the higher and succeeding kinds emerged into being? A learned author, Professor Pictet of Geneva, has spoken of these speculations in terms of a rule or law, as follows:—"*The faunas of the most ancient formations are made up of the less perfectly organized animals, and the degree of perfection increases as we approach the more recent epochs.*"

This was long held as a favorite dogma among geologists, when, in proportion to the scantiness of facts, there was an increasing eagerness to magnify their value, and to build upon them the widest generalizations. But now, since accurate observations are more and more multiplied, and the principles of palæontology are better understood, the doctrine of a gradual advance of animal organization toward higher and more perfect forms as we ascend through the successive deposits of the earth's crust, is daily losing ground among the cultivators of the science. The notion is based upon the theory of *a scale of beings*, in which all animals are supposed to form a series, or to constitute links of an unbroken chain, whereof each species is more perfect than that which precedes it, and the varying degrees of perfection constantly increasing until they reach their maximum in man, the highest link in the chain. M. Pictet himself regards this theory as vague and unsupported by facts, as well in the organization of the extinct as of the existing races of animals. These beings, he says, are divided into a certain number of groups, each of which exhibits a peculiar type ; but while some of the groups are manifestly superior to others when we consider their organization generally, it happens also that the result of a comparison sometimes fails to establish any real superiority. The faunas of the more ancient formations he holds to be far less imperfect than has been often supposed, where the vertebrate type is represented by the fishes, and whose structure is as complicated and finished as the most recent of their kind ; while the invertebrate again furnishes numerous examples of fossilized gasteropoda and cephalopoda, the most perfect orders of the molluscous class. As with these, so with the relics of every succeeding epoch, in which all the types, the genera, and species of every family of the animal kingdom, are represented by organic structures as perfect as those of the present day.

We quote the following important cautionary remark by the same author :—"We ought not," says Professor Pictet, "to be too hasty in assuming the absence of certain more perfect types in the older faunas, merely because we have not yet discovered any remains of them. We hardly know anything of these faunas, except with regard to some of the inhabitants of the sea ; and it is well known, that in the present condition of the globe, those animals living on land exhibit the higher forms of structure. Is it not possible that in these first ages of the world, terrestrial animals also existed, more highly organized than their marine cotemporaries, although their remains either have not been preserved, or are still to be discovered ? The existence of didelphine mammals in the oolites has been made out by the discovery of a very small number of fragments ; and the remains of land animals generally are hardly fossilized, except by sudden deluges and inundations, which are always trifling in their results, compared with the slow but unceasing deposits from the water of the sea. May we not yet expect new discoveries in these ancient strata, revealing to us the existence of primeval animals at present little suspected?"

The same mode of reasoning may be extended to the ancient floras, or terrestrial plants of the primeval ages. What a revelation, for instance, is made in the recently discovered coal deposits of Oporto and the Upper Douro, where, along with the orthides, trilobites, and graptolites of the lower silurian rocks, are found vegetable impressions strongly resembling the ferns of the carboniferous age? The Cromarty fossil pine, from the lower old red sandstone, has been already noticed. While these pages have been passing through the press we have to record the discovery of a specimen, nearly two feet in length and half a foot in thickness, from the beds of the middle old red and immediately underlying the yellow sandstone of Dura Den. This fossil is considerably flattened and furred with the scars or markings so characteristic of the decorticated trees belonging to the coal formation. Does not this warrant the expectation of a richer harvest to be yet gleaned in these ancient fields than the marine fuci and algæ that have hitherto been mainly gathered in by the geological sickle?

Another mode of accounting for the succession of organized beings on the surface of the globe, and consequently also their successive extinction and outgoing, as seen in the fossiliferous rocks, is that which is termed THE THEORY OF DEVELOPMENT, or the doctrine of the transmutation of species. The same has been a very ancient and favorite notion among mankind. Early in this century it assumed the form of a system, under the adaptive principle of Lamarck, who conceived that animals, according to the circumstances in which they are placed, by the use or disuse of certain organs, the frequency and degree of exertion or strain upon particular parts of the body, were themselves the agents in inducing all the variety of structures by which they are distinguished into so many orders and families. The aquatic fowl, for example, is attracted to the waters in quest of food, and so in time becomes web-footed. The heron dislikes to plunge into the flood, or will only venture into the shoals, and hence he becomes a wader, and is equipped with long legs. The woodpecker rejoices in those little aphides and creatures that nestle under the bark of trees, and thus, from constant exercise, acquires his strength of bill. The eagle seeks the blaze of the sun, and soars to the gates of heaven, and hence his penetrating eye and speed of descent upon his all-unconscious victim beneath. And, in like manner, through the whole range of animated nature, and in all past ages, genera and species have all acquired their adaptive powers, and distinctive forms of organization, arising from a certain plastic character in their different constitutions, and their own voluntary attempts to supply their constantly increasing wants. There were a few great leading stamps or dies of nature's own molding; but all the rest—even man himself—are merely offsets from the primitive type, with such extension of organs and modification of excrescences as were required in each particular case; succeeding races always retaining a strong affinity to their immediate predecessors, and a tendency to impress their own features on their kindred which succeed them. There is a limit of divergence; but within that limit, the human family have their place assigned them among the monkeys and wild men of the woods.

It is the same extravagant idea, *that of a constant progression toward animal perfection,* which has become so popularized in "The Vestiges of the Natural History of Creation." This author, indeed, has taken a wider and bolder flight than even the French philosopher, M. Lamarck. He brings the rudimentary elements and molecular forms of all creation before him. He expatiates through infinite space, and amidst the original fire-mist of the astral worlds. He finds but one grand law pervading the whole universe of being, operating in the self-same way in the production of planets and suns, as in the germination of insects and animalcules, the life-impregnating principle in the one being only a modification of the aggregating and rotary tendencies that rule in the other—the blind and casual evolution of some agency of a material system, substituted for the creative will of an intelligent ever-active First Cause. "A nucleated vesicle" is the fundamental form of all organization, as nuclei of luminous matter are the sources of the stars; this is the meeting point between the organic and the inorganic, the end of the mineral and beginning of the vegetable and animal kingdoms; whence they start in different directions, but in a general parallelism and analogy. Assuming the vast indefinite periods of the geological epochs to be correct, the author makes great account of time, and the mighty changes which will be produced in the lapse of countless ages, and thus rebuts the argument against his theory that is so obviously furnished from the fixed unaltered characters of organization that have prevailed throughout the entire modern epoch. This he argues is merely a point, an infinitesimal fraction, when compared with the epochs of geology. The eye detects not the changes which all specific forms are slowly but unceasingly undergoing within limited portions of time, even as the nicest instruments cannot always enable the astronomer to note the changes of position among the heavenly bodies. Hence the *appearance* of so many of the stars as unchangingly fixed in their relations to each other. The whole solar system, too, upon the ground of imperfect unrecording vision, *seems* to be anchored in one portion of space. And hence likewise the argument against the motion of the earth itself, which so long prevailed, derived from the fact of there being no sensible parallax, and now so easily accounted for by the insignificant smallness of its orbit, as compared with the remoteness of the stars. Limited, in like manner, to the narrow field of observation afforded within the human period, the modifications of species and their transmutations into the higher grades of animals are not appreciable, *because* its six thousand years are as a moment, in comparison with those incalculable ages of geology which have been concerned in the phenomenon!

Thus does the author of the "Vestiges" revel amidst the sublimities and copious materials of his subject. Time and space, the elements of the astral heavens and the earth, are alike indefinitely in his grasp. That he has failed to frame a better system of things than the one we see actually around us, is a necessary consequence of the restraints imposed on human investigation. Facts will not be supplanted by any heights, or depths, or ingenuities of speculation. And as existing nature is all against the doctrine of transmutation and development, so the discoveries of geology through all its formations are equally opposed to such views of creation. A short sketch of both will abundantly illustrate this.

As to the course of living nature, the development theory is there at once repudiated in the now clearly established fact, that the first germinal vesicles are different in the different tribes of animals. A non-identity of type is discoverable in the minutest microscopical beginnings of organic life. And "by no change of conditions can two ova of animals of the same species be developed into different animal species; neither by any provision of identical conditions can two ova of different species be developed into animals of the same kind." Corresponding to these differences in their fœtal forms, there are in all the stages toward parturition a similarity of progress in the various organs and appendages in the same kinds of animals. Fishes, birds, quadrupeds, all manifest a divergence from each other in the first action of the respirating organs—in the nervous system—and in all the apparatus connected with the movements of the heart and blood-vessels. There is no structural interchange, in the minutest part, that distinguishes the orders of the perfect animal in any of the antecedent fœtal conditions; the organic contrivances within the egg being as complete and as thoroughly prospective to the future use and habits of the bird, as are the petals of the flower inclosed within the bud, the arms of the giant oak within the acorn, or man in his evolving capacity toward intellectual being.

What is thus true in all the rudimentary stages of organic development is strikingly confirmed by the unalterable condition of all living nature. Plants and animals never diverge, beyond small ascertained limits, from the fixed characters of their families, resisting the effects of every kind of influence, whether proceeding from natural causes or human interference. The lapse of three thousand years has left the embalmed carcasses of men and animals, in Egypt, wrapped and swathed in a material woven from the same species of plants which still flourish on the banks of the Nile. The crocodile and the ibis still drink of its waters. Nothing changed in form or appearance, the swarthy Arab repairs to its cooling fountains to quench his thirst. Nature has been tortured in a thousand ways, to cause her to depart from her long beaten paths; but she is obdurate on every point. Man would improve her kinds, and hybrids are produced; but there the variety ends. Crosses are constantly attempted; but "the hitherto and no farther" is soon approached. Our fruit-bearing trees are coaxed with all the appliances of horticultural skill; and yet in all their seminal and floral organs, the texture of their leaves and bark, the structure of their roots and stem, the rudimentary stock remains one and the same. Domestication has, indeed, wrought wonderful changes and improvements in the breed of many creatures. Horses, oxen, sheep, pigs, dogs, and poultry of all sorts, are increased in bulk, tamed, ameliorated in habit and disposition. But the skeletons of all continue essentially as they were in their natural state; and even the individuals the most widely removed from the primitive type, as exemplified in the canine race, never present any real difference of form in the important organs.—When again abandoned to their own guidance, and the restraints imposed by man are removed, the domesticated animals, one and all, return to their former condition, and speedily resume the instincts and appearance of the jungle and the forest.

If such are the unvarying laws of physiology now, the presumption is that they have been the same in all past ages. Creatures are brought from the extremities of the earth—the polar, temperate, and tropical denizens, all mixed up and crossed with each other—food, climate, and treatment, all changed—and, through all, the type of every species continues as before—no transmutation of one kind into another under all the violent tutoring agencies to which they have been subjected. For thousands of years such has been the unswerving course of nature. Would it not clearly be a solecism in reasoning to argue differently over the geological epochs, however indefinite in extent, because, in the far-off regions of space, our eyes can note no change in the relative position of the stars? The things will not compare. Time and space are not co-ordinate terms. And an appeal from positive knowledge to supposed, assumed ignorance does not meet the question.

Meanwhile, the amplitude of the current epoch, if we may so speak, gives scope and verge enough for all the requirements of the problem to be solved, the conditions of the argument to be established, the process of reasoning to be employed. An experience not merely of six thousand years, but an experience embracing a uniformity of results in all the hundreds of thousands of instances into which animate nature is divided, in all the countless species of plants and animals which have existed successively throughout the whole of that period, furnishes proof of such a cumulative kind as approaches, if not to demonstration, at least to the nearest possible degree of certainty. There is no instance of a single transmutation of a vegetable species into another species, of algæ into fuci or conversely, of grasses into cereals, of endogens into exogens, of the pine into the oak; and the same of animal species, where, through all the living tribes, the fixity of family law has maintained its steady, unchanging course since Adam gave names to them, down to the present hour. What link in the chain is wanting? The course of creation is verified and complete. The exception would be a miracle. And we are not at liberty, upon just principles of ratiocination, to refuse our assent, where all the facts, indefinite as to number, are exclusively on one side, and none upon the other. Our belief in the case is defined and restrained by the absolute uniformity of stubborn, unbending nature; and an appeal from the known to the unknown, from the human to the geological epochs, is just to relinquish reason for the dominion of imagination, the evidences of the senses for the visions of fancy. The shark, rapacious as ever, holds the empire of the seas—the lion, the domain of the forest—the eagle, the region of the air—and man, progressive man, alone looks unto the heavens and blesses his Maker.

Hume was so impressed with the force of this argument, as to maintain, upon the ground of it, the absolute impossibility of establishing the truth of a single *miraculous* event, or of any event that did not harmonize with the existing course of nature. The Laws of Nature have been so uniform, within the entire range of human experience, as that no testimony or reasoning of man, says that subtile dialectitian, can invalidate their authority, or render credible any alleged case of discrepancy or of deviation.—The author of the "Vestiges," for the first time, has cast the whole weight of this evidence aside, or holds it as even scarcely relevant in a question of proof. And thus outstripping, as he does, both the measure and the requirements of the Christian's faith, he may be safely left to the logic of its most merciless adversary in dealing with the phenomenal or imaginary transmutations of the geological epochs.

But the facts of geology, from its remotest periods, are in themselves no less strongly opposed to this extravagant, untenable hypothesis. This might be presumed from the distinct teachings of geology, as already stated, against the theory of a scale of beings becoming more perfect as we ascend from the faunas of the older to those of the newer formations. The families of the various formations are distinct, and consist of real non-interchanging forms of structure, whether they die out and disappear with a particular formation, or are carried forward and intermixed with the fossils of another. The fishes of the silurian rocks, are as perfect after their kind as those of the Devonian, Carboniferous, or Cretaceous deposits ; and not less perfect than they are genuine types of all their successors. The *sauroids* of the old red sandstone have reptilian resemblances, but yet the *saurians* of the oolite age have no affinities of true kindred descent ; while, again, of all the mammalia of the tertiary period, there is not one that boasts a likeness, in habit or organization, to a single creature of an antecedent or posterior epoch. "Thus between the *palæotherium* and the species of our own days," says Cuvier, "we should be able to discover some intermediate forms : and yet no such discovery has ever been made. Since the bowels of the earth have not preserved monuments of this strange genealogy, we have a right to conclude, that the ancient and now extinct species were as permanent in their forms and characters as those which exist at present : or at least, that the catastrophe which destroyed them did not leave sufficient time for the production of the changes that are alleged to have taken place." Agassiz, in his own department of fishes, is equally opposed in all his deductions to the transformation of species from one formation to another, which he asserts, "the imagination invents with as much facility as the reason refutes." Professor Owen, after minutely examining the organic structure of the nine orders of fossil reptiles, declares no less strongly against the theory, and adds—"The nearest approximation to the organization of fishes is made by the *Ichthyosaurus*, an extinct genus which appears to have been introduced into the ancient seas subsequent to the deposition of the strata inclosing the remains of the thecodont lizards. But by no known forms of the fossil animals can we diminish the wide interval which divides the most sauroid of fishes from an *Ichthyosaurus*."*

The development theory is not more at fault in the rudimentary structure and primitive size of animals, as brought to light by the deepest researches of geology, than it is in the perfection and complication of the several organs with which they were endowed. These organs in the earlier types ought, upon the principles of this theory, to have all partaken of the simplicity and sameness of the germinal vesicles; varying, indeed, in their complexity, as in their completeness, in proportion as we ascend among the fossiliferous strata. But the facts are not so. Nay, so far otherwise, that in the very earliest specimens of Nature's workmanship we find the mechanism of the parts as minute, varied, and multiplied, as in those of her most recent productions. Examine the eye of the Trilobite, the oldest of crustaceans, and the distinguishing type of the lowest of the fossiliferous rocks. These creatures swarmed in the Silurian seas. Their destiny was not fulfilled by the close of the tertiary periods, for they still exist. But in none of her subsequent creations has Nature displayed greater elaboration in the parts, or more skillful adaptive contrivance in their arrangement, than in the visual organ of this palæozoic family. The eye of the trilobite is formed of four hundred spherical lenses, arranged in distinct compartments on the surface of the cornea, which again projects conically upward, so as to enable the animal while resting, or seeking its food at the bottom of the waters, to take in the largest possible field of view—this, as it might require, either for the purpose of defense or attack. Fishes, birds, and mammals, have all, it is well known, an optical apparatus precisely adjusted to their respective habits and the element in which they live. Fishes and fowls have their eyes differently constructed.—

* This branch of the argument has also been minutely and ingeniously extended in the last work of Mr. Hugh Miller, "Foot-prints of the Creator," where the author dwells particularly on the comparative measurements of the different fossils found in different formations; a masterly and felicitous addition to the side of truth.

The bat, which preys in the dark,—the eagle, which soars in the blaze of the sun,—and the mole, which burrows in the earth, have each peculiar and appropriate organisms. But in none is there greater complication or perfection, than what is manifested in the eye of these earliest and still living tribes of the waters.

The number of plates or cylinders which compose the eyes of insects, a higher and more gifted class, differs in different species, amounting in the ant, so provident and wise, to only fifty, in the house-fly to eight thousand, and in the mordella to the amazing number of twenty-five thousand and eighty-eight. And yet how much is all this surpassed by the astounding mechanism displayed in the eye of the cod-fish, in whose crystalline lens there have been detected about five million fibers, every fiber containing about twelve thousand five hundred teeth; and the total number of these teeth or processes reaching the numerical, though to us utterly inconceivable, amount of sixty-two billions five hundred thousand millions! But more than all this. Look at the multiplied appliances furnished to the humblest and lowest of all living creatures for performing the functions of an existence scarcely removed above the vegetable. "The tentacula of polypi," says Dr. Roget, "are exquisitely sensible, and are frequently seen, either singly or altogether, bending their extremities toward the mouth, when any minute floating body comes in contact with them. When a polypi is expanded, a constant current of water is observed to take place, directed toward the mouth. These currents are never produced by the motions of the tentacula themselves; but are invariably the effects of the rapid vibrations of the cilia placed on the tentacula. Now, of these organs a single *flustra foliacœa* has been calculated to possess about 400,000,000." Thus much for the Zoophyte class of animals—placed on the extreme verge of organized bodies—and members of a system of being, according to the development theory, whose primitive productions are of the simplest kind, the monads of a germinating vesicle!

Nor will the development theory do better, when it would account for the diversity of instincts which prevail in the animal kingdom. The instincts, indeed, it assumes as the cause of all their diversity of structural organization. But this is to beg the whole question. Geology carries us back to the beginnings of organic life, when animals, each after their kind, were already perfected, and endowed with a ready-made apparatus for the particular sphere of existence assigned them. The polypi are still a distinct race, unvarying in their instincts, not the least improved in the building art, still piling up reefs, and doing the same thing which they did when first created. The nautilus has lived through all time, swimming his fragile bark as dextrously over the Silurian seas as he now does amidst the breakers of the Pacific. The cephalopoda and the finny tribes then warred against each other, and ever since they meet in mortal conflict. The same with all the great families which were successively brought upon the stage: species and genera have changed, the old withdrawn, and new ones introduced; but in their respective orders—reptiles, insects, birds, and quadrupeds—the type ever continues, and the instincts remain; and there is no nearer an approximation to or crossing of each other's domains now, than when first summoned into being. Were the development theory true in nature, and the epochs of geology the myriads of ages assumed, the presumption would be, that the old primitive forms would have been all obliterated and figures of creatures substituted, all of the most remote and indistinct analogies. The *monodal* races, why have they not all passed away? Had the reptiles sprung from fishes, why, upon the principle of progression, should there be fishes still? Had man derived his parentage from the monkey, why are there so many species of the one class, and only a single great family of the other? The vegetable tribes have been equally true to their kind—the fucoids and algæ, still abundant in the seas—the pines of Mar forest, rivaling in coniferous qualities the most gigantic of the oldest relics—and the palms and fern trees of Australia maintaining the very types that flourished in the carboniferous era.

The scheme of creation, moreover, implied in the development theory, proceeds, as it appears to us, upon an inconsistency of assumption that is completely at variance with its own leading cardinal principle, namely, a continuous progression from the less to the more perfect forms of organic existence. If this be true with the *particulars*, why not also in the *generals* of all that is endowed with the mystery of life? Every great type or class of being, whose remains are detected in the most ancient rocks of the earth, has still its representatives in living nature. The two ends of the chain, the infusorial and mammalian families, are still produced distinct, and each perfect after its kind. The course of creation is thus always, through indefinite time, returning upon itself like the fallacy in dialectics of reasoning in a circle, instead of advancing from the successively higher standards of the perfected models to still more varied and perfect degrees of excellence. The circumstances and conditions, too, of the planet are different from what they were in the palæozoic times, and yet the tribes developed then are all developed still; different in the species and genera, but of the same forms and families; not larger, but more frequently less, in size, and not of better or more complex workmanship. The principle is, therefore, inconsistent with itself, while it leaves unexplained its own assumption of progression in *one* particular direction only, instead, as it ought to be, in all the primitive types of organic existence. The theory is imperfect beside, in attempting no explanation of the inorganic structures of creation; for the original molecules of matter which assimilated, aggregated, and produced the primary rocks of granite, gneiss, schist, limestone, should have had their law in this direction as well as in the other, of progressive perfection. But these rocks, in no such sense as this, have been repeated or reproduced: matter, essentially the same, according to the theory of the "Vestiges," whether organic or inorganic, has here retrograded rather than progressed; and if we would contemplate its most elaborate and beautiful forms, either igneous or sedimentary, we must go, not to the secondary and tertiary formations for our specimens, but to the crystalline groups of the primary epoch.

Whatever it may have been with Lamarck, it is certain, in the case of the author of the "Vestiges," that the speculations originating in the nebular hypothesis lie at the foundation of all his philosophy. This Essay would never have been executed, as it could not even have been imagined, but for the data so abundantly supplied by a universal star-dust lettering, filling all space and inscribed over all time. But change the names, and it is only the atoms of Democritus and the vortices of Descartes that constitute the elements, one and all, of the modern cosmogony. Cicero in his first and second books "De Natura Deorum," has given a full and ample refutation of the former; and his merit is the greater, when it is considered that the inductive methods of philosophizing were not in use nor even guessed at in his time. The argument, as quaintly translated in Ray's "Wisdom of Creation," is thus stated—"If the works of nature are better, more exact and perfect, than the works of art, and art effects nothing without reason, neither can the works of nature be thought to be effected without reason; for is it not absurd and incongruous, that when thou beholdest a statue or curious picture, thou shouldst acknowledge that art was used to the making of it; or, when thou seest the course of a ship upon the waters thou shouldst not doubt but the motion of it is regulated and directed by reason and art; or, when thou considerest a SUN-DIAL or CLOCK, thou shouldst understand presently, that the hours are shown by art and not by chance; and yet imagine or believe, that the world, which comprehends all these arts and artificers, was made without counsel or reason? If one should carry into Scythia or Britain such a sphere as our friend Posidonius lately made, each of whose conversions did the same thing in the sun and moon and other five planets, which we see effected every night and day in the heavens, who among those barbarians would doubt that that sphere was composed by reason and art?"

The inhabitants of this island are no longer the "barbarians." The Scythians still are so, and have ever been. Upon the development hypothesis, might we not pause to ask, has our intellectual, and moral, and social progress affected our physical condition so as in aught to change the organic relation of the two nations, barbarous both in the time of Cicero?

But we proceed:—"A wonder then it must needs be," continues the philosopher, "that there should be any man found so stupid and forsaken of reason, as to persuade himself that this most beautiful and adorned world was or could be produced by the fortuitous concourse of atoms. He that can prevail with himself to believe this, I do not see why he may not as well admit, that if there were made innumerable figures of the one-and-twenty letters,—in gold suppose or any other metal,—and these well shaken and mixed together, and thrown down from some high place to the ground, they, when they lighted upon the earth, would be so disposed and ranked, that a man might see and read in them Ennius's Annals; whereas, it were a great chance if he should find one verse thereof among them all: for if this concourse of atoms could make a WHOLE WORLD, why may it not sometimes make, and hath it not somewhere or other in the earth made, a temple, or a gallery, or a portico, or a house, or a city? which yet it is so far from doing, and every man so far from believing, that should any one of us be cast, suppose upon a desolate island, and find there a magnificent palace, artificially contrived according to the exactest rules of architecture, and curiously adorned and furnished, it would never once enter into his head that this was done by an earthquake, or the fortuitous shuffling together of its component materials, or that it had stood there ever since the construction of the world, or first cohesion of atoms; but would presently conclude that there had been some intelligent architect there, the effect of whose art and skill it was. Or, should he find there but one single sheet of parchment or paper, an epistle or oration written full of profound sense, expressed in proper and significant words, illustrated and adorned with elegant phrase,—it were beyond the possibility of the wit of man to persuade him that this was done by the temerarious dashes of an unguided pen, or by the rude scattering of ink upon the paper, or by the lucky projection of so many letters at all adventures; but he would be convinced, by the evidence of the thing at first sight, that there had been not only some man, but some scholar, there."

Now, here let there be but the substitution of a few terms—"fortuitous concourse" for the "nucleated vesicle"—"atoms" that whirl in mazy dance through indefinite time, for the "star-dust" revolving through infinite space—"transmutation of species" for "the lucky projection of so many letters"—and the overthrow of the one hypothesis is as ruinously complete as the demolition of the other.

Thus geology, while it reveals a succession of animal types, pronounces each after its kind perfect in its own degree and measure of organic development. The oldest known fossil fish (the Onchus Murchisoni, and inhumed in the lowest fossiliferous beds), belongs to the highest type of the Cestraciont division of the vertebrata. What they were made at first, they all vindicate their capacity of continuing to the end. The various tribes and orders had their own limits of organization, their own sphere within which the functions of each were to be performed, and adapted to the condition in which they were placed, each reaped the full enjoyment that divine benevolence had appointed. Man was the last in the course of successive creation, endowed with the highest and most enlarged capacities, and, allied to none, was constituted the priest of nature, that he might collect the silent praises of the universe, and offer them to the Creator in intelligent devotion.

But here it is, when we have reached this link of the chain, that the most vitiating element in the whole doctrine of progressive development is manifested. The anti-theism and materialism, involved inevitably and undisguisedly in the noxious dogma, are brought out in bold relief. This dogma implies, that the cosmical arrangements and all the organic transmutations of living types, are none of them directly the result of any personal, immediate creative actings on the part of Deity. These arrangements, from the beginning, are all dependent on one unchanging law, applicable alike to organic and inorganic bodies, to the mysterious principle of life, and to things inanimate,—to mind as to matter. The simple effect of this may appear to be, the removal of the Creator merely a step farther from his own works, which he can still hold in the hollow of his hand, and bend whither He will. But the statement goes a great deal farther. It strikes directly at the root of all moral distinctions as well as of all revealed truth. The creature man, upon this hypothesis, the last link in the terrestrial chain, comes not from his Maker's hands "made in his own likeness." He too is the product of a natural law, evolved after a long series of metamorphoses, to whose operation the moral and the physical are equally subject,—the soul and the body alike the result of its rigid inflexible agency. From the fire-mist and electro-nebulous matter, which is assumed to have originally filled all space, Man, along with suns and stars, and all planetary bodies, derived the first germ of his being. At first gaseous, it became in process of time concrete. There was no life until the electric spark, struck in some mysterious way from the dance of atoms and wild whirl of the elements, vivified the germ with this newly-developed principle. Then the germinal vesicle became a self-moving, self-acting thing—not at first, but after a series of changes, adapted into the type of the human family, whose life was but the life for ages of the animals that have perished, and are now fossilized in their various formations. THE PRINCIPLE OF LIFE, in short, as implied in this account of its origin, is the same essentially with the light and heat that sparkle and glow in the rolling orbs which deck the firmament!

Much of the development theory is built upon the influence of the instincts as manifested in the lower tribes. Let its abettors listen to the indignant cry of THE WHOLE FAMILY OF MAN against this theory of his origin; and say, if there is not an instinct here, peculiar and distinct, to vindicate his claim to a separate and distinct position in the great system of being. "Quanta ad eam rem vis," says Cicero, "ut in suo quoque genere permaneat."

The continental philosophy, at no time for the last century, has partaken of a religious, healthy tone. It has been profoundly subtile in its speculations and analysis, but never truly spiritual. The author of the "Vestiges," from his own turn of mind, has been all the more enamored of it, and, unwittingly dragged into its vortex, has been carried far beyond the ken of all rightful philosophies. These are not the subjects of legitimate investigation. Man has no plummet-line, in all his armory of science, wherewith to sound them. Grant that in the manner now described, the human race originated, and became living creatures—destined, it may be, to undergo new changes and to ascend into new orders of being—the animal nature to be perfected in the progressive modifications of his type. But the divine ethereal spark, as men vulgarly dream of themselves, what account is given of this? The soul, what? and whence derived? The thinking principle of mind,—where its place, and what provision made for its efflux, in the nebulous ether? The inference unquestionably is, that if such be its source, the human UNDERSTANDING must be of the essence of matter out of which it evolved,—glorious as the sun and fair as the moon,—but not the heavenly element, animate with the immaterial, incorruptible being of Divinity. But this is not the teaching of geology. Through all the story of its undefinable epochs, and in the myriad sarcophagi of its extinct generations, there is no record, no trace of man. He stands, utterly and far apart, from every fossilized thing, while—

> "The most distant star's invisible beam,
> Or comet on his farthest journeyings,
> Or all the extent which philosophic ken
> Has given to infinite space, the elastic soul
> Springs over"———

and claims kindred with the image of the heavenly, whence it came, and whither it seeks and aspires to return.

While, therefore, to wild speculations like these nature and geology give no countenance, but demonstrate the reverse to have been the course of creation in all the present, and in every past epoch,—that races, like individuals, have their terms of existence,—that all die out or are violently exterminated,—and that new families are created, adapted to the changes which have taken place, and organically distinct from all that preceded them,—there is, at the same time, a theory of progression and development distinctly traceable in all the divine actings in this world. This view of things is in every stage of it visibly dependent upon His will, as it emanates directly from His appointment, and stands in pleasing contrast to the rationalist phasis of creation.

> ———"Wisdom's artful aim
> Disposing every part, and gaining still
> By means proportioned, her benignant end."

## CHAPTER III.

### ANALOGICAL ORDER—PHYSICAL AND MORAL—OF PROGRESSION.

THE author of the "Vestiges" devotes two chapters to what he terms general and particular considerations respecting the origin of the animated tribes. He regards it as a thing completely demonstrated, or as requiring so little proof as to be taken for granted, that the inorganic elements all took together by a process of natural law, which Deity was not required to superintend, but simply to begin. He supposes, hypothetically, that this also would be the case with the organic structures, that, in the originating of the first tribes, God supplied the materials, and that natural law assimilated and fashioned them into their different orders and families. This might be predicated of the Creator, he fancies, as the mode in which he *would* act; and by removing him a step away from his own works, and allowing all the subsequent genera and species of the epochs of geology to go out and to come in according to the same process, his special interference in such arrangements is rendered unnecessary; and the greater honor is reflected upon operations in themselves so complicated and vast, and yet all so minutely, orderly, and prospectively ordained.

We need not employ more than a sentence in reply to this mode of reasoning. Hypothetically I would say, if God was to create a world at all, and to store it with living creatures, he would do all these things *directly* of Himself. He created every individual particle of the original matter, in all their infinitesimally minute and myriad atoms. We do not know how, nor the manner thereof. But every one of them required his *special* interference singly, as in combination and a whole; and had not Deity so specially acted with the parts as with the mass in willing them into being, none of them, of any kind or quality, would have been in existence.—Why not the same *manner* of creating as to the species, genera, and orders of the animated tribes? These required not less His direct personal interference than the elementary particles and minims out of which they were formed; and superintendence in the one case is as dignified, if the term may be so applied, as in the other. Admit the omnipotence, omniscience, and omnipresence of Deity—and the author admits them all—and any other mode of reasoning is wholly nugatory—as useless in science as it is inadmissible in fact—as inconsistent with the subtilties of the profoundest analysis as with the conclusions of the most confiding theology.

But the creation of the world by God being admitted, it is no less true, and it is equally a necessary truth, that the arrangement and disposition of its parts, the order and succession of its events, are each immediately an effect of the great First Cause. As no material substance could originate itself, so neither could it impart the principle of life, or construct the organization through which that principle is manifested and maintained in the exercise of its functions. Equally impossible is it for the course of events, the motion of the elements, the growth of plants and animals, and all those subtile processes in nature by which objects are produced and distinguished, each after their kind, to be the results of chance, or of any inherent, underived properties existing in the things themselves. Whether God acts *mediately* by a course of nature originally established, or *immediately* and *constantly*, by the same divine agency which produced all things at first, and impressed upon each its peculiar properties, may be a question in philosophy, but none in theology. We indeed may speculate respecting the manner of the Divine acting, and may speak of that manner as the laws according to which the system of nature proceeds; but we cannot doubt the source whence the chain of events takes its rise, or wherefore it is that there are order and regularity in the arrangements of the universe. And while everything is of God, and the course of nature precisely such as He intends upon whom the whole is dependent, it is interesting to find the closest analogy subsisting between the actings of the Divine Being in every department of his supreme and universal government. The scheme of revelation manifests itself to be of God, not only by the peculiar testimony of prophesy and miracle to which it appeals, but by the resemblance which it bears, in the order and character of its dispensations, to the established constitution of creation and providence;—so intimate and striking as, in fact, to leave no doubt, in every impartial mind, that the author of the one must be the author of both.

We have already stated that a progression is manifested in the order and arrangement of the rocky masses which compose the earth's crust—in the nature and qualities of its mineral contents—and in the various revolutions which are indicated by the fossil organic remains that lie entombed in the strata of the interior. Take the most useful of all the sections of the earth's crust, namely, what is denominated the carboniferous or coal formation, here we have a regular sequence or series of beds resting one upon another, and all so disposed, from the lowest to the highest, as to be most suitably adapted for reaching and bringing to the surface the inclosed treasure. Nor did nature all at once bring to maturity those prodigious masses of plants and vegetables of which this wonderful deposit is composed. Her flora seems to have been upon a limited scale at first, until the earth, being prepared for its accumulation and preservation, throws from its teeming bosom, with a profusion unknown before or since, the vegetable matter out of which our coal is formed. Consider, again, the dip and dislocation of the strata connected with it, and you have a proof of a new order of causes being brought, subsequently, into operation, before coal could be available for man's use. Examine, next, the vast accumulations which repose upon the coal—the curious relics which are imbedded in them—the evidences thereby afforded of relative changes in the sea and land—of the elevation of mountains, the denudation and formation of valleys—and you cannot fail to infer, from all this, that the surface of the earth was not always as it now is; that there was a period when man could not have existed on it; and that for him who was the last in the order of all God's creations, it was gradually and progressively prepared as a suitable habitation.

When, again, we advert to the *course* of creation, there is a gradual progression from the little to the great, from the insignificant, if we may apply such a term comparatively to any of the works of God, to the noble and the grand. Each of the links that compose the mighty chain is perfect in its kind ; each serves to connect and illustrate the link that borders next to it ; each is adapted to its place in the system, so that the lowest could not be exalted, nor could the highest be brought down, to answer the purposes of any inferior member of the series. A pebble has more attraction to the eye than any of the colorless particles which compose the soil ; but from the pebble the fruits of the earth can derive no nourishment. The lichen or the moss which adheres to the solid rock may be inferior in beauty and attraction to the lily of the valley, or the lofty cedars of Lebanon ; but the latter will not grow in the barren regions of the north, and without the former, hundreds of insect and animal tribes would perish. Man constitutes the principal link in the chain of visible creation ; he is higher than the highest of the animal race ; and do not the superior endowments and blessings of man, however eminent in themselves, appear still more eminent and valuable by contrasting them with the inferior powers, the ruder enjoyments, the meaner and more sordid passions, of the lower creatures ? which yet amply display the wisdom and goodness of their Author, both in their frame and state, in the relation which they have, and the connection which they hold with the orders above and below them. Looking upward, again, what is man but a lower link of that chain of beings which, like its Author, reacheth through immensity ? Thousands, nay, millions of spiritual orders may possibly fill up the chasm, if that be possible, between the human and Divine nature, and who, by the very contrast with man's estate, may have a juster knowledge and a more grateful relish of their own refined and spiritual natures. Take away, indeed, "the human face divine," and there would be one note of praise less in the great temple of Jehovah ; but, while angels could not fulfill the purposes of man in the order of creation, the perfections of the Godhead are infinitely more exalted by their activity in a purer sphere — their keener visions and juster apprehensions — their unclouded faculties—and their sublime and lofty contemplations, all corresponding with the clearer manifestations of divine truth, light, and glory, vouchsafed to them.

Descend, in short, as low, or rise as high as we may, in the scale of being, we will still find something inferior, something superior; and not more remote from each other in the extreme points are the minims of nature intimated to us by the microscope, and the magnificent systems above which the telescope has disclosed to view, than are the wonderful differences and infinite range subsisting among living organized substances, from the vegetable to the animal, from the irrational to the intellectual, and from the intellectual to the spiritual and divine. But one class cannot complain of the superior advantages of the class above it. The constitutions of all are precisely adapted to their respective places in the scheme of things, and the desires of all, according to their various capacities, are suitably gratified. Each is happy in its sphere, and still subservient to the higher happiness of others. The garden is the insect's paradise, man is lord of the brute creation, angels are principalities and powers when compared to the knowledge and the happiness of man. "Consider," says the author of "Paradise Lost,"

> ———————————— "that great
> Or bright infers not excellence: the earth
> Though, in comparison of heaven, so small,
> Nor glistering, may of solid good contain
> More plenty than the sun that barren shines:
> Whose virtue on itself works no effect,
> But on the fruitful earth."

When we turn to the *dispensations of providence*, we find the same principle prevailing in the communication of all its gifts — of them all, whether evolved in the natural or moral course of events. The many blessings which the mere diffusion of the solar rays imparts are not obtained all at once; the early dawn, the meridian splendor, the softening shades of twilight, are each accompanied with distinct and peculiar enjoyments to man and beast. Observe the course of the seasons: after winter come the gentle zephyrs of spring, the glowing heat of summer, to be again succeeded by the rich though milder beams of autumn. The seed which is deposited in the ground scarcely at first exhibits signs of life; but from that seed the green stalk gradually ascends, the ear is formed, the corn is produced in the ear, and man gathers from it his daily bread. Behold the new-born infant—the most helpless and imbecile of all nature's productions — what labor, watchfulness, and care, before he comes to the maturity of manhood! how slowly do the powers of intellect expand! what diligence requisite for the moral culture of the heart! how gradual and progressive the whole steps by which he has been trained for the business and enterprises of life! Look now into the crowded city, where thousands and tens of thousands of rational beings have passed, and are all passing, through a similar process of discipline; consider how many generations have passed away before it attained to its present greatness; its wealth, its buildings, its schools of instruction, its temples of solemn worship; its philosophers, poets, orators, and statesmen; its laws, manners, sciences, and fine arts, are the accumulation, the work, and the growth of centuries. It is the same with nations as with individuals, and with all nations and countries as with one; the blessings of civilization are gradually diffused, sometimes retarded, and often buried for ages beneath the inroads of barbarism; but again emerging in greater abundance, taking a firmer step, and advancing onward and wider than before. And at last, from the favored position on which we have been placed, we see before us the certain prospect, in the increased facilities and means of communication which are now opened up, that they will be still more universally imparted, until truth, righteousness, and peace, cover the face of the whole earth.

Consider now, under the same progressive aspect, the *scheme of revelation.* Here we find the same analogy prevailing from the less to the greater, from the smallest tokens of the Divine favor, to the full and boundless manifestations of inexhaustible love and mercy.

From the fall to the restoration of man, the expressions of God's interest in our condition are limited and obscure; but the plan is defined and the means arranged in the only way that was proper to display his goodness and make us sensible of his mercies. The blessings conferred upon the people of God, before the law and under the law, were chiefly temporal. Hence the rites and ceremonies of their worship were purposely of such a nature, and so multiplied, as principally to operate through the medium of the senses. Hence the various symbols of the Divine presence, when God personally, as it were, descended among them, and over-awed them by his visible glory. Hence the giving of the law amidst thunders, and lightnings, and shakings of the mountains, when external nature under its most appalling aspects bore testimony to the severe justice of the Divine character, and seemed to intimate, in a way which even the most hardened sinners would understand, how dreadful must be the judgments of their incensed and supreme Lawgiver. The Israelites were not sufficiently removed from their natural state to be as yet capable of a religion purely spiritual, like the Christian; and hence it was, that every later dispensation of God excelled the former, even as the trumpet on Mount Sinai "waxed louder and louder," every succeeding blast transcending those that went before. The prophets rose above the ritual law, and showed men a more excellent way of worshiping God than by external performances, thereby preparing their minds for the reception of the Gospel. The tabernacle was no longer used after Solomon's temple was built, but was laid aside, as the temple itself was "when the fullness of the time was come;" and as the sanctuary and tabernacle preceded the temple, so the glory of the latter was to be greater than that of the former, by the appearance of Him who was greater than the temple, whose mission was distinguished by more numerous miracles, and by sublimer and more important truths than had been before manifested to the world. Behold a higher dispensation still, when, after the state of grace ends, the state of glory shall commence; where all knowledge shall be imparted and all truth unvailed, where imperfection and sin shall no more adhere to us, and where, after the experience of millions of ages spent in the enjoyment of heavenly happiness, we shall be still advancing in glory and felicity, and attaining to higher measures of the increasing strength and ever-growing splendor of the sons of God.

These analogies may be extended. The wisdom and goodness of a God, for example, equally appear in the late and partial promulgation of Christianity, which is sometimes considered an objection against its truth, but which, in fact, is in perfect accordance with the same principle of progression which we have been illustrating in the general economy and arrangements of all God's proceedings.

The gifts of nature are not imparted universally, nor in the same measure to all. The discoveries of science are the result of long and patient investigation. Herbs have been allowed to run waste for centuries upon centuries, of which the medicinal virtues have only recently been discovered. Through how many ages had mankind been left in ignorance of the properties of the magnet, and the simple apparatus of the compass-box, braving all the perils, and tossed about on the unknown wastes of the ocean? How much did the progress of knowledge and education suffer, during the lapse of so many generations, for want of the printing-press? What oppressions and cruelties have been practiced upon the different nations of the earth, through means of bad laws and bad government, of which even yet many are learning but the elements? And how is it that of one and all these things—the truths of science, the art of healing, the principles of navigation, the discipline of wholesome instruction, the enactment of good laws, and the various blessings of civilized life—more than two-thirds of the human race are in these latter ages still entirely destitute? God governs both in the kingdom of nature and in the kingdom of grace, and any objection, therefore, against the truth of revelation that may be built upon these grounds, goes equally to dethrone the Almighty from any share of interest in the government of the universe. But the Gospel, in fact, would have been premature before the actual time of its appearance; the history of providence in former ages could not have been appealed to, the sacrifice of the Redeemer had not been understood without the legal sacrifices preceding, the prophesies would have been unfulfilled, and the world would have been unprepared for a worship so pure and spiritual, a morality so searching and uncompromising, and a faith so lofty and exalted, had there not been much previous training and discipline, through the instrumentality of patriarchs, prophets, and legislators. One of the most striking proofs, in short, of the Divine wisdom in the dispensation of grace, is its harmonizing so exactly with the established course of nature. This is manifested more especially in the manner in which the heavenly blessings with which it is fraught have been communicated—slowly, gradually, and partially at first, more fully and generally diffused as men were prepared to receive them, and, when "the fullness of the time" had arrived, imparted freely and in the richest abundance unto all; light after light, truth after truth, and mercy upon mercy, all in such order of succession, that the former illustrate and recommend the latter, while the last are only a preparation for future and still greater mercies.

And so it has been with the whole Course of Creation—the succession of strata, of animal and vegetable tribes, and with man and the adaptive provision for his higher destiny. This is a doctrine of development and of progression, widely different from that of the "Vestiges," more in unison with the Creator's wisdom and the Creator's care:—a speculation worthy of a separate treatise, namely, the progress and development of man's intelligent, moral, and spiritual being as indicated in THE COURSE OF REVELATION.

## CHAPTER IV.

### CAUSES OF EXTINCTION OF ORGANIC LIFE.

WHEN the palæontologist has completely established his position, that all the organic phenomena of primeval times have resulted from the impress of original structure, in opposition to the theory of progressive development and transmutation of species; and when he can trace, also, corresponding changes in the mineral formations in which the fossil remains are imbedded, the important inquiry has still to be made into the causes of the extinction of so many races of the animal and vegetable kingdoms. Introduced successively upon the surface of the earth, was there always a physical and necessary relation betwixt the living tribes and the varying conditions of the surrounding media in which their lot was cast? And do the differences in the one explain the changes in the organic functions of the other?

When we look back to the earliest of the fossiliferous rocks we can discover something in the nature of their materials themselves which would cause the destruction of their organic tribes. The Silurian strata have been violently disturbed, and much molten matter, during the period of their deposition, injected among them; and by causes such as these, life would suffer greatly, and whole races be suddenly destroyed. Even the strong incased ganoids and placoids of the Devonian period could not always be able to subsist and bear up against the spasmodic throes that produced the conglomerates. Animals preyed likewise upon each other, and by this means kept up then, as now, the general average and balance of life. But in none of these modes can anything like a LAW be inferred, any stated provision be detected, for the outgoing and the incoming of the different genera and species which successively peopled the globe. The rocks differ, as the organisms differ, age to age, from each other: but the series of changes traced in the one class of phenomena, furnish only a few data by which to determine as to the alterations that would be produced in the class cotemporaneous.

No land animals have been found in any of the formations beneath the new red sandstone. No quadrupeds existed before the tertiary age. And the monster lizards which so exuberantly sprang into existence during the middle secondary epoch, had all disappeared when these terrestrials occupied the stage. Wisdom we can trace in all the arrangements; care and goodness are everywhere apparent. The seas swarmed with marine animals, while the terrestrials could scarcely have subsisted on an upheaving earth and new forming land. Quadrupeds roamed not over fields so diversified by the lakes and slimy lagoons in which the Saurians found their convenient habitation. And beyond the simple fact, that Divine will so ordained that such things should be, both in the animal and mineral changes in the history of our planet, we have only a ray of light to guide us in interpreting the revolutions and destructions which are therein so indelibly recorded.

The mollusca and shell families appear and depart along with the calcareous deposits which inclose their remains; but we know as much of the source of the one as of the range and limit of, or the causes which destroyed, the other. Orthoceræ and nautili have survived all changes, and have maintained in the types by which they are represented their old instincts and predaceous propensities. The holoptychii and dipteri perished, just as the materials of the new red sandstone were being deposited, and whose identity, in all essential mineral qualities, differs in nothing from the old red in which they are entombed. The flora of the carboniferous age came and went with the suddenness and entireness of an eastern dynasty, the gorgeous spoils of which are all that remain to attest its former greatness. The mammoths, dinotheriums, and kindred pachyderms of the tertiary groups had all left the earth on the dawn of the human epoch. And now, since the commencement of that epoch, we find that entire families have become extirpated, that species of others have been driven from their former localities, and that generally, both of vegetables and animals, the geographical distribution is being, year by year, greatly modified. During the last century, the introduction into Germany of some new species of insects, and their multiplication, utterly destroyed forests of vast extent; and every year, in some quarter of the globe, we hear of equally mighty catastrophes produced by equally minute insidious causes.

The organic things of earth, it would thus appear, have their terms of existence of longer and shorter duration, and the race at last dies out equally with the individuals which compose it. No better reason for this can be assigned, than that such is, and has always been, the course of nature. Particular families of plants and animals are cotemporaneous with particular groups of rocks: with these they are observed for the first time; at the close of the deposit, all farther traces of their remains are lost; and, in so far, there is ground for arguing that the same general causes were concerned in effecting the successive changes, organic as well as inorganic, of the periods and formations in question. What these causes were, it may never be permitted to science fully to determine. It was indeed, the opinion of Cuvier, that in the mammoth epoch a change of climate effected the destruction of this giant family of pachyderms. This change of climate has been accounted for by Murchison and others, especially in Siberia, where so many remains are found, by an elevation of the country to the height of one or two hundred feet above its former level. And doubtless, by such a change, animal as well as vegetable life must, in many specific forms, have been greatly affected.

There can be little doubt, however, of the most perfect adaptive arrangements prevailing through all the geological epochs, some of which have been plausibly conjectured. As reptiles, for instance, differ from birds and mammals, in having a lower and simpler structure of the lungs and heart, and therefore a less active performance of the respiratory functions, they become less dependent on the atmosphere or oxygen for existence. "Hence," says Professor Owen, "from their extraordinary prevalence in the secondary periods, under varied modifications of size and structure, severally adapting them to the performance of those tasks in the economy of organic nature which are now assigned to the warm-blooded and quick-breathing classes, the physiologist is led to conjecture that the atmosphere had not undergone those changes, which the consolidation and concentration of certain of its elements in subsequent additions to the earth's crust may have occasioned during the long lapse of ages during which the extinction of so large a proportion of the reptilian class took place. And if the chemist, by wide and extended views of his science in relation to geology, and mineralogy, should demonstrate, as the botanist from considerations of the peculiar features of the extinct flora has been led to suspect, that the atmosphere of this globe formerly contained more carbon and less oxygen than at present, then the anatomist might, *à priori*, have concluded that the highest classes of animals suited to the respiration of such a medium must have been the cold-blooded fishes and reptiles. And beside, the probability of such a condition of the zoological series being connected with the chemical modifications of the air, the terrestrial reptiles, from the inferior energy of their muscular contractions, and still more from the greater irritability of the fibers and power of continuing their actions, would constitute the highest organized species, best adapted to exist under greater atmospheric pressure than operates on the surface of the earth at the present time."

By parity of reasoning it may be inferred, that as great changes would be effected in the waters of the globe as in the constituents of the atmosphere; and, while thus preparing for the introduction of new families of animals, the destruction of already existing tribes may be as conclusively imagined. The various calcareous deposits in the mountain limestone, magnesian, oolite, and chalk periods, would imply very different qualities in the condition of the ocean; an infusion or abstraction of ingredients as favorable to the existence of one kind of animal life as they would be destructive of another. A period of great plutonic action, too, when vast masses of melted matter, charged with metallic and other substances, were poured over the bed of the sea, could not fail to have considerable influence upon many of the inhabitants of the deep; and while providence was making arrangements for an increase, or diversity, or for higher types of animal life, the existence of other forms and classes was ordained to terminate.

The introduction of new and higher races upon the earth has

thus been accounted for. "Through such a medium as the air," says the authority quoted above, "approaching in a corresponding degree to the physical properties of water, a cold-blooded animal might even rise above the surface, and wing its heavy flight, since this would demand less energetic muscular actions than are now requisite for such a kind of locomotion: and thus we may conceive why the atmosphere of our planet, during the earlier oolite periods, may have been traversed by creatures of no higher organization than saurians. If we may presume to conjecture that atmospheric pressure has been diminished, by a change in the composition, as well as by a diminution of the general mass of the air, the beautiful adaptation of the structure of birds to a medium thus rendered both lighter and more invigorating, by the abstraction of carbon and an increase of oxygen, must be appreciable by every physiologist. And it is not without interest to observe, that the period when such change would be thus indicated by the first appearance of birds in the Wealden strata, is likewise characterized by the prevalence of those dinosaurian reptiles, which in structure most nearly approach mammalia, and which in all probability, from their correspondence with crocodiles in the anatomy of the thorax, enjoyed a circulation as complete as that of the crocodile when breathing freely on dry land."

Again, it is conjectured—"The first indications of the warm-blooded classes would appear, if introduced into the reptilian era, under the form of such small insectivorous mammals as are known at the present day to have a lower amount of respiration than the rest of the class; and the earliest discovered remains of mammalia,—as, for example, those in the Stonesfield oolite,—are actually the jaws of such species, with which are combined the characters of that order, Marsupialia, which is most nearly related to the oviparous vertebrata."

It has been seen that igneous and aqueous agents have remodeled, from time to time, the physical geography of the globe. Can it admit of a doubt that changes in the physical structure of the earth's surface will be accompanied with other changes in the organic productions of extensive areas? Species, it is well known, both of plants and animals, are limited to particular localities of variable, and often of no great, extent. If marine, an alteration in the sea bottom will prove fatal to many. If terrestrial, an increase of altitude, the conversion of dry land into marshes and lakes, or of lakes and marshes into meadow and arid loamy soil, will completely alter the flora and fauna of the district in question. Look into any estuary or rocky pool along the shore of the ocean, swarming with testacea, and crustacea; every bowlder incrusted with corallines; the rocks carpeted all over with fuci, waving with every ripple their long graceful branches, or smoothing and polishing their sides in the violent currents; creeping things, too, innumerable shy stealthy creatures, darting amid the shingle, or burrowing in the sands; and the finny tribes, of all forms, glancing and sparkling like living gems in the dark green thickets. This is one description only of tens of thousands of such phenomena around the islands of Great Britain. An elevation of a few feet, and what myriads of animals, whose only habitat are these ocean caves, would perish, and their races be forever blotted from the things that were! These shores have witnessed many such upheavals. Not a plain, hill, or rock, in the whole continent of Europe, but once formed the bed of the sea. Even now, what a vast influence does mineralogical structure alone exercise over the economy of life, both as to the number of individuals and the character of species frequenting particular localities. Trees as well as plants have an adaptation to certain kinds of soil, and once firmly rooted, birds, insects, and creeping things, will also resort thither in quest of shelter or of food. Aquatic fowl, the waders and swimmers of our sea-shores, have their favorite haunt among the breakers or calm bays, whose submarine rocks furnish pasturage and shelter to molluscs, crustaceans, and fishes; while, again, over the marshy, the oozy, the sandy, the gravelly, or the rocky beach, other families, both terrestrial and marine, maintain their respective ascendency.

M. Agassiz is just now pursuing his favorite researches in exploring the lakes and rivers of America, where he has already detected many things new and old to enlighten the western *savans* in the boundless riches of their mighty dominions. He has succeeded in capturing, on Lake Superior, species of fishes hitherto unnamed. He has likewise been able to dredge up from the same deep waters, specimens of the garpike (*Lepidosteus*), whose representatives have been found in the oldest palæozoic deposits, and in the deposits of all succeeding times. Suppose these lakes to be suddenly drained of their waters—and which, according to the chronometrical details of Niagara, must one day come to pass—and many species of animals and plants would cease to exist, not merely by the violence of the action, but by the simple alteration of the aqueous character of the districts. Many animals, indeed, will be able to escape, and to betake themselves to other localities amidst slow or even rapid superficial changes. The camels and antelopes of the desert may sink under the sirocco and be buried in the sand; but, in other circumstances, they will be able to bear up and carry themselves to fertile lands, as the steady, irresistible march of the sand-flood invades their former pastures. The Sahara of Africa has been gradually extending and widening in its desolating sterility, until it now covers a region of about 582,000 square miles; how many, in consequence, of the vegetable and animal races, have thus been deprived of their appropriate nutriment, and become extinct? How many examples of similar devastations, but upon a far greater scale, does almost every one of the geological epochs furnish? The central region of France abounded with lakes, attracting to their arborescent banks the huge pachyderms of the tertiary age, when the Auvergne cones blazed out, pouring floods of lava over lake, marsh, and plain; and thus obliterating and silting up entire races, the great and the small, terrestrial and lacustrine, and now constituting the pictorial wonders of the age that produced, and the convulsions that destroyed them.

There is reason to believe that species in the ancient world were possessed of a wider geographical range than in after periods. But the causes of extirpation were also of wider operation. The old formations are all greater than the new, receding in extent as they descend in time. And if we are to regard alterations of climate, changes in the constituents of the atmosphere, subsidence of land and elevation of sea-bottom, intrusion of igneous rocks, the escape and circulation of noxious gaseous matter, as among the *causes* which have led to the extinction of the successive organic tribes in the several geological epochs, so do we find the *effects* approximating to a scale of corresponding magnitude. But the real terms and boundaries of all are in the hands of Him who made them. We see but a part, and know only in part, of the secondary means of destruction.

## CHAPTER V.

### TIME, AND THE GEOLOGICAL EPOCHS.

THE speculations of geology respecting the arrangement and position of the mineral masses of the earth are matters of direct observation, falling immediately under the cognizance of the senses, and whose verifications are both numerous and conclusive. But a question thereupon arises which is not so easily dealt with, namely, as to the periods of time that have elapsed during the various successive epochs or formations described. Looking at the current operations of the laws of nature, and supposing their uniformity in past ages, a scale of increment is laid down for the several deposits of which the earth's crust is composed. An approximation is made as to the number of years required for each, and the result is, that the geological estimate embraces an inconceivably lengthened and bewildering series. The calculation proceeds not by hundreds, or thousands, but by millions of the terms of our numerical notation: and, as the fossiliferous strata alone are reckoned at about seven or eight miles in thickness, the time that has elapsed since the first appearance of life upon the planet, has also been made a matter of measurement. Accuracy as to any precise definite amount, is not, indeed, pretended; but no estimate, it is said, made upon purely geological data, falls short of vast enormous periods, which will only bear to be compared with the cycles of astronomical phenomena, and not with the brief fleeting days of man's existence.

What account, then, is to be made of this reckoning according to the popular opinions respecting the origin of the world? Will it be accepted by the Christian, who confides in the Mosaic chronology of the work of creation? What is that chronology? Can the geological and the sacred be compared or reconciled with one another?

I. There is one important deduction to be established from these investigations which meets us at the threshold of the inquiry, namely, that geology clearly and distinctly shows there is a BEGINNING to the course of creation as respects the crust of the earth and its organic forms of life. The stratified rocks all manifest succession in their order of deposition, and, therefore, also succession in time. Some are prior to and older in formation than others; and all of every class and quality, demonstrate principles of arrangement in conformity with law and design. We never, for example, get back to a period, however deep we go into the interior, in which we find the matter of the earth assuming, as it were, different modes of existence, or arranging itself according to affinities of which we have no experience. Over every material substance, the rocks of the oldest as of the newest formation, the same physical forces are seen to be operative. The granites, with all the molten amorphous masses of every age, are composed of ingredients brought together and aggregated in proportional quantities, and according to definite principles of attraction. But throughout the whole series and succession of deposits, we never come to a point at which matter has been formless, or free from the operation of law, endlessly quiescent, or when no controlling designing hand was rendering it plastic and obedient to its will.—As with the arrangements of matter, therefore, so likewise with its origin. We revert in both cases to a necessarily prior cause. And geology, vast and inconceivably great as may be its cycles, proclaims over all its past antecedents and depths of accumulation, that TIME, not eternity, is indelibly recorded.

This truth is rendered still more apparent and intelligible, when we consider the various families of plants and animals of which the earth has been the theater. These organic structures at once speak to the mind of creative interference. No principle that we know of inherent in nature could, of itself, originate these forms. The first thing of life indicates an intelligent Creator. But epoch after epoch passes away, and along with them their living tribes generally perish. Succeeding races, of different characters and habits, are called into existence. The earth is again peopled—again to be swept of all its garniture—the land and ocean to change places—creatures of another mold, suited to both, again to be brought into existence. These phenomena all speak, not only of a beginning, of successive periods of time, but also of direct superintendence over the course of events from age to age.

It is the same with the formations themselves in which the organic things are imbedded. The course of creation progresses, but always under such breaks and renewals as clearly to manifest, that the same power which watches over the organic, is operative also in respect of the inorganic structures of the earth. Various are the genera and species of once animate forms, imbedded in the different strata beneath our feet; but equally various are the strata themselves; as a new race arises, so are there new forms of rocks produced along with them. And when we compare the two extremes of the fossiliferous strata, the silurian and the tertiary, or any of the intermediate—the old red sandstone and the oolites, the carboniferous and the chalk—we find that the rocks are just as various in quality, structure, and appearance, as are the animals which existed and perished during their respective epochs. The lines of demarkation are distinct. They may sometimes run into each other, so as to leave it doubtful where the one series ends and the other begins; but so it is with the organic remains themselves, a few of an antecedent epoch living into and invading the province of another, when the limit is reached, and the family altogether disappears. The same law holds in the great mineral masses of the earth's crust. Rocks are of different families, even as plants and animals are; and over the entire surface of the globe, they display in their various suites such changes and diversities as demonstrate an interfering hand and a new creative energy. Indeed, there is, it may be avowed, a much greater diversity of type in the mineral groups themselves than in their organisms, the living genera and species of one formation differing, often, less from each other than do the rocky matrices in which their remains are imbedded.

II. But, in estimating *the time* that elapsed during the formation of the various sedimentary strata, are geologists warranted in assuming such principles of calculation as have been adopted?—There are two aspects under which the subject may be approached—the one, as respects the formative process of rocks—the other, the probable duration of life in the different epochs, or rather, as connected with the formations which indicate the epochs.

1. Of the Formative Process. How long the earth existed before being brought into a habitable condition for either vegetable or animal bodies, geology has no means of determining. The primary crystalline beds are the oldest rocks of which we have any knowledge: we can penetrate at least to no antecedent matter, bearing the record of its own age, out of which these rocks were produced. We are warranted, therefore, in accounting for their origin, to remount at once to the initial creative act which called them into being, and the presumption is, that no great length of time was occupied in this arrangement. The Divine will commanded, every particle obeyed, and all took their places. The eruptive rocks are of comparatively sudden growth: they are not the result of a gradual deposition, but of igneous fusion in the interior of the earth, and elevated to the surface through the operation of forces of rapid activity. How long our planet was in thus assuming form, and the dry land appearing, we have no certain means of judging, except by looking to the end of its creation, and assuming that the "void" was not permitted indefinitely to continue. The occupancy of life at once exalts the work and illustrates its purpose.

The fossiliferous strata were formed in different circumstances and under different conditions, when the course of nature, if we may so speak, was fully established, and the train of events under the operation of physical law commenced its onward march. The oldest of the fossiliferous deposits is the Silurian. It likewise constitutes one of the greatest depth, as well as of extent, on the surface of the globe. The position, generally, of the silurian beds, is along the line of the great mountain-chains, except in Russia, where they spread over the interior, and thin out into smaller dimensions, and where, from the absence of the intrusive rocks, they are only semi-indurated. This system of rocks was, therefore, formed in circumstances the most favorable for rapid accumulation, amidst such primal operations of nature as have never been repeated upon the same scale of magnitude. The first shaping-out, if we may so speak, of the earth's surface, in the elevation of its mountain-ranges and corresponding depressions of the sea-bottom, bears all the marks of a single cotemporaneous act, not completed in a moment of time indeed, but continued through a period of unparalleled spasmodic agency. Every region shared in the convulsive movements, and the whole earth, in one and the same age, was begirt with mountains. These violent throes were accompanied everywhere with violent action upon the already consolidated masses. Disintegration would keep pace upon them with the rate of uprise. And as the bare jagged rocks unprotected with herbage, friable and just rending from the fire, were lifted suddenly above the waters, the waters in turn would dash violently upon their sides and broken serrated crests, and so become as rapidly filled again with all the waste and spoils of the period. The changes now going on, and the rate of increment of the land above sea-level, the occasional appearance and disappearance of an island, the slow but constant action of the waves upon the coast, and the detrital matter borne down by the rivers, can be no measure of the effects of forces and agencies such as were then in operation. The Mississippi, within a quarter of a century, it has been ascertained, brings down little more than a half of its former spoils. The organic remains, accordingly, which have survived the silurian period, belong chiefly to the molluscous classes, and thin filmy fucoid vegetables; the structures, in short, which were best calculated to live during the period in question, and to remain undestroyed throughout its agitations.

The old red sandstone series is likewise of vast extent, both in depth and superficial area. The scale of its mass corresponds with the scale of the forces which produced it—the magnificent operations amidst which it was accumulated. This was a period of great and frequent trappean eruption. Hence the conglomerate red offers a splendid specimen of rapid formation. This member of the devonian suite consists of large masses of gneiss, quartz, mica-slate, and hornblende rock, cemented in a paste of silicious sand, probably the debris of dissolved granite. The included portions bear all the marks of attrition, of violent tossing about in a troubled sea. Estimate the thickness of the whole deposit at its maximum of nearly ten thousand feet—consider what vast agencies were still at work, in tearing up and carrying off the spoils of the mountains—probably with but little pause or intermission in the violence of the action—and thus, not so much in the light of remote antecedents as of comparatively associated formations, will we be warranted in regarding these early courses in the work of creation. The fishes of the period all speak of its spasmodic character, mailed, plated, and completely inclosed in strong horny integuments; their heads, some of them, of entire uncovered bone, and their caudal fins propelling with the whole force of the vertebral column,—conditions of structure which give indications of the stormy seas whose waves they had to buffet, and of the conserving properties by which their forms and outlines have been transmitted to us so wonderfully entire.

The carboniferous class of rocks have all the marks of a very peculiar formation, constructed for a special purpose, and elaborated amidst an extraordinary state of things. Here we meet with vast accumulations of vegetable, calcareous, and metallic substances, for which we detect no anterior preparations. The coming on and the outgoing of the whole coal series are as distinct as they are surprising. To what are we to compare them? By what scale of time are we to adjust the terms of their growth? Proceeding upon the existing laws of nature, calculations have been made as to the rate of increase, for a year, of pure vegetable matter, over a given area. The Ganges, Nile, Amazon, Mississippi, La Plata, and the other mighty rivers of the earth, have been appealed to as to the quantities with which they are annually charged. The forests, with their load of every revolving season, have been weighed, when their decadence of leaves, fruits, branches, and all the gatherings from the flood and storm have been duly taken into account. The result is, according to this method of solving the problem, that about six hundred thousand years were occupied in the production of the whole coal series.—It must be admitted, in any attempt to reduce this number, that the violent forces of the antecedent periods cannot be admitted as data of circulation; throughout the whole of the carboniferous era, a state of repose seems to have universally prevailed. But then all the living productive powers of nature were just as violently in operation as the others were quiescent, and the result in the one case bears a proportion to the result in the other. If inorganic matter was rapidly collected by the action of violent causes, so under an extraordinary state of things, of climate, moisture, atmosphere, and other physical arrangements, organized bodies, vegetable and animal, would multiply as rapidly. A condition of nature that produced uniformity of vegetation over the entire surface of the globe, as the coal deposit everywhere manifests, and all of gigantic dimensions in every family of plants, is not merely to be denominated *tropical,* and its results calculated by a scale of existing weights and measures. In many places of the earth, even now, several harvests are reaped within the year. Who can set bounds to their number, or guess the prodigious increase, when the whole earth was covered with a flora, not only of unrivaled exuberance, but of uniform distribution nearly on every part of its surface? But a test of indisputable value, for ascertaining the rate of increase in the sandstones and shales embraced within the coal-measures, occurs in the case of those fossil trees which are so frequently found in an upright position, or but little inclined to the plane of stratification. These are numerous in every coal-field, and are often traced through several layers or beds of rock. The fossil trees of Craigleith and Granton were about fifty feet in length, and lying at an angle of scarcely twenty degrees to the strata in which they were imbedded. Their passage through the solid rock, therefore, cannot be estimated at less than fifteen to twenty feet, that is, a mass of sandstone of corresponding depth must have been formed, during the comparatively short period that trees of lofty stature were able to resist the destroying action of the elements, to say nothing of the chances of currents, hurricanes, and other agents breaking them in pieces. This *instantia crucis* may be extended to every sandstone bed of the formation, and thus serve to exercise a salutary restraint upon the mind in its imaginary conceptions of the enormous periods of time required for the accumulation of the whole series.

The carboniferous epoch was immediately succeeded by a period of great violence and of vast disturbance in the solid crust of the earth. Hence the broken inclined position of the coal strata, and the injection of so much igneous matter, forming often ridges and hills of considerable elevation. The new red sandstone, the overlying deposits, would share in all the activity of the time. A celerity of increase, on a scale of more rapid accumulation than existing causes could produce, must consequently fall to be admitted to the rocks of this family : so much, indeed, was the plutonic agency then in force, that the rock-salt and gypseous beds are ascribed to its influence. From this period downward, the formations are all of more contracted dimensions, the basins narrowing in superficial area to the upper tertiaries, which partake of the character of local rather than of universal deposits; while the evidences here are innumerable that, until the globe settled into its present form, and assumed its present arrangement of seas, continents, and mountains, the land and water were continually changing places, the crust and framework subject to constant upheaval. The Cordilleras and Himalaya constituted, in those days, the bed of the ocean. What law of nature was not in violent activity ere they attained their sublime altitudes! How many rivers changed their courses! how many mountains were washed to their summits! how many hills melted like wax at the voice of their Creator, amidst convulsions which swept the earth so repeatedly of its living tribes, and bared as often the bosom of the great deep!

We have not, in this enumeration of the mineral strata of the earth's crust, as yet spoken of any of the calcareous deposits. They are very numerous, some of them of prodigious thickness, and belong to the formations of every epoch. There is not one, but many, alternations of limestone connected with every such formation. Whence the source of all this material? The primary beds are not in sufficient mass to have furnished supplies for every succeeding age. The mountain limestone alone, of the middle secondary epoch, contains more calcareous matter than is to be found in the three antecedent periods. The lias, oolites, and chalks are likewise of vast thickness. The beds of the tertiary group are less considerable; but in the gypseous marls, and numerous alternating bands throughout the clays and sands of the formation, there is the clearest evidence that the stores of nature were still abundant. Nor are they yet exhausted. What supplies in every river, sea, and ocean of the world! What countless myriads of living animals are now employed in elaborating the material! And when we again inquire, whence is it all? the answer is, that throughout all time, a wise and bountiful Providence has thereby provided the pabulum for its successive creations of organized bodies—the law of their nature is to pile up rocks—and in all the monuments of the past, we discern the style and architecture of the builders of the present. Look, then, to your still active, living, working chronometer. With what incredible swiftness do these minute creatures ply their labors! how many fathoms of coral reef will they rear in a season! When the hapless mariner returns, after a brief short interval, what hazards to run from structures which now for the first time appall him with their formidable barriers! Millions of years! Not even thousands are needed to construct islands, and to pillar the floor of the ocean, over vast expanded areas, with broad, massive, indurated rock.*

2. THE PROBABLE DURATION OF LIFE IN THE DIFFERENT EPOCHS. The geologist will tell us not to look at one but at the various families, of all kinds and of all habits, which his science has brought to light, and so many of whose remains he has disinterred from the earth. Every formation abounds with them. They flourished through every epoch. The epochs are many. The tribes which existed and perished in them are many. To allow time for the coming in and the going out, and the fulfillment of their various destinies, what an untold, incalculable amount of ages must

---

* "There is no doubt that coral, under favorable conditions of growth, increases to an enormous extent, and very rapidly: and although there are many instances on record of reefs which have not increased for many years, there are others telling a very different tale. The case of Matilda Atoll, described by Captain Beechy, is quoted as an example of this latter kind, this atoll having been converted in thirty-four years from being a reef of rocks into a lagoon island, fourteen miles in length, with one of its sides covered nearly all the way with high trees. Some experiments were also mentioned, in which it has been attempted to measure the rate of increase of different kinds of corals, and as one result of these, is an instance of a growth of two feet thick of coral, accumulated on the copper bottom of a vessel in the course of twenty months."—*Geology of the Voyage of the Beagle, by Charles Darwin.*

have elapsed! Now, give the millions of years supposed, and the wonder some may not hesitate to confess is, that there are so few, and not so many, of the former creatures of the earth which have re-appeared in our geological catalogues. The fossil regions of Great Britain, an epitome of the world, have been well explored, and the statement of fact stands nearly as follows:—Leaving out of consideration all the shelly and lime-building tribes, the numbers of the other families of animals hitherto found and described are, in the various groups of the silurian system, eight genera of only one order of fishes; in the devonian, of two orders, there are under forty genera, and not many more species of fishes. in the carboniferous, of three orders, there are about fifty genera, and a hundred species of fishes; in the permian and triassic, of three orders, there are twenty genera, and fifty species of fishes and reptiles; in the oolitic, of four orders, there are sixty genera, and two hundred and twenty species of fishes, reptiles, and mammals; in the wealden, there are, of three orders, twenty-five genera, and thirty-eight species of fishes and reptiles; in the cretaceous, of six orders, there are fifty genera, and eighty species of fishes, reptiles, and birds; in the tertiaries, of seven orders, the genera are about one hundred and fifty, and two hundred and twenty species of fishes, reptiles, birds, and mammals: thus making in all about four hundred genera, and seven hundred species of the larger families of living creatures during the whole currency of the geological epochs. The current epoch contains, exclusive of microscopic organisms, nearly two millions of species of vegetable and animal bodies existing on the terraqueous globe; and of which there are about eight thousand species of fish alone existing in our present seas.

When we take, instead of Great Britain, the whole explored geological field of the world, the result, so far as the argument is concerned, will be strengthened, not weakened. The formations of other lands are simply, with slight variations, a repetition of our own. The same genera of animals are everywhere prevalent The specific types are likewise in many instances identical. The silurian organisms of Russia are so like those in our own island, that "no English geologist," says Murchison, "acquainted with the organic contents of the Wenlock limestone, can view the Calymena Blumenbachii, C. macrophthalma, C. variolaria, and other Trilobites associated with the Leptœna depressa, L. euglypha, Terebratula reticularis, and many corals most familiar to him, without at once recognizing in the upper strata the distinct representative of that British formation." Various other fossiliferous identities are farther alluded to, when it is added—"In taking leave of Scandinavia, we must specially advert to the close relations which exist between its lower and upper silurian groups, and those of Great Britain and distant parts of the world. Of 133 silurian fossils which we brought back or noted on the spot, at least eighty-four are British, and from twenty-five to twenty-seven are North American species. In this comparison the identity of the upper silurian groups of the Baltic and Great Britain is, indeed, most surprising; for, among seventy-four Scandinavian species, upward of sixty are common to the strata of this age in both countries, and of these, fifteen to sixteen species are also found in the upper silurian rocks of America." The devonian fossils are equally striking in their resemblances and extensive geographical distribution. Similar representatives are detected, and still more abundantly, in the carboniferous formation—universal specific types of the fauna of the epoch. One remarkable instance has been stated—upon the authority of M. L. Von Buch—that the *Leptœna lata,* so typical of the silurian rocks of Britain, is spcifically the same with the *Leptœna sarcinulata,* which is no less prevalent in the Russian carboniferous strata, and continued even throughout its uppermost members. Our field of review, therefore, contains a fair proportion of the various fossils of the world, specific and generic. The formations lying before us throughout our base-line, give a true indication of the state and conditions of life during the several epochs, while in number and variety of individual forms they are above the average.

Need it then be urged, that no such incalculable cycles of ages would be required for the whole of this catalogue of animals fulfilling in their several epochs their allotted destiny upon the earth? Compared with the mass of inorganic matter in which they are entombed, their relics are literally as nothing. Only here and there, of certain classes, at remote intervals often, there is a fossil or its impression. And so entire and well-preserved are these organisms, that we have reason to presume there has been no great obliteration, absorption, or utter waste of the races to which they belonged. On the contrary, as their distribution is so persistent in their respective formations throughout the globe,—the same genera and species being common to the four quarters of the world, — the presumption is, that specimens of nearly all the tribes that ever dwelt on the earth or swarmed in its waters have been handed down to us; and thus the number of the actual relics found becomes, as it were, a chronometer or measure of the ages during which they subsisted.

Look again at the demands of geology. Upward of SIXTEEN MILLIONS OF YEARS* are supposed to have elapsed since the creation of life upon the earth. The lowest of the rocks, in which that life has found its grave, have been reached. Their contents, upward, have been examined and catalogued. How many generations of animals must have subsisted within that period? How many individual skeletons must have been entombed and preserved, seeing that things of the filmiest texture, plants and animals, have been inclosed and handed down to us entire? Quadruple the ages of every one of the existing denizens of sea and land, and still, what countless millions of generations, succeeding each other, have lived and died during the eras that were to run? Geology presents us with her list, her whole lengthened organic roll, of scarcely four hundred generic, and less than eight hundred specific forms, gathered out of all the past cemeteries of the dead. The cemeteries themselves, of such vast walls and dimensions, may, according to the present mordant powers of the elements and the capacity of rivers for the transport of mud, have required the calculations usually assigned for their erection. But where, the question will ever recur, where is there anything like a corresponding amount of animal exuviæ apart from the calcareous supplies, to be found in the successive formations, conforming in any approximation to the existing powers and capacities of parturient nature? The fossil remains, inclosed from the beginning to the end of the inconceivable cycles of time, are the remains only of a few great families: their skeletons are admirably pre-

* Mrs. Somerville's Physical Geography.

served, or their casts are minutely and accurately engraven on the rock; and do they not look as if they were the *identical individuals* which rose in the dawn and were buried in the setting of their own geological epoch!

If we go still farther into details, the results will be found startling enough. Let us select one of the periods, the old red sandstone, for illustrating our views. The period assigned for this formation embraces a term of about, we shall suppose, according to the geological distribution of time, a million or two of years. This formation consists of three great subdivisions, every one of which contains their distinct specific forms, and hence their separation into the lower, middle, and upper groups. This was preeminently the fish epoch—finners which roamed in undisturbed possession of every sea on the surface of the globe. Dropping into the waters, and speedily silted up in the sands, the skeletons were in the best of all possible circumstances for preservation; and accordingly, the specimens of the period constitute the wonder of the geologist, for their enameled freshness and perfect outline of figure. The productiveness of fish is prodigious, the cod-fish multiplying at the rate of three millions and a-half, mackerel at about half a million, and most of the other tribes at a corresponding high ratio. Count now how many generations, of every one of the species of the separate groups of the old red sandstone series, would exist and multiply during a period of so many hundred thousand years. The modern epoch and its breeders have scarcely reached their six thousand. When six times six have been added, and sixty times more have been added to these, they will still be a third short of the term allotted to the favored denizens of the olden time. And where, amidst the well-protected few that have yielded up their remains, are the traces of the myriads upon myriads that perished and were buried along with them? To the genus Homo, the head of creation, few think of the earth, as it now is, being the abode for periods reckoned by millions of years. Nay, within his as yet brief period, how many of his cotemporaries have already passed from the stage, extirpated, many of them, by his own direct agency? The dodo, and his fellow islander the solitaire, and other brevipennate birds,—probably, too, the elk and the urus,—certainly from this island the beaver, the wolf, and the bear, and just as certainly, at no distant day, the extinction of many other races will follow in the onward progress of civilization. But as now, so in all past ages, superior power, or a more dextrous instinct, have led to their extirpation. Their destiny was fulfilled, and the race perished. And as we are reasoning upon the known laws of nature, whence the geologist only seeks a footing for his vast cycles of time, so, we venture to affirm, is he bound to abide by the test of his own selection, and to read therein the terms of life granted to the families of earth. The modern epoch shows the outgoing of genera as well as of species within the limited compass of a few thousand years — gives reasonable indications of the probable extinction, speedily and at no distant period, of hundreds of others, — these families possessed, all of them, of as enduring structures, and of higher types of existence, than those of the older epochs,—and, therefore, upon every fair ground of analogy, are we justified in concluding that there can be no such diversity of ages, under one and the same system of nature, as that of hundreds of thousands of years to the living tribes of earth.

When such premises are made the grounds of such inferences, and, again, when the geologist reiterates the statement that these great periods of time correspond wonderfully with the gradual increase of animal life, and the successive creation and extinction of numberless orders of being, and with the incredible quantity of organic remains buried in the crust of the earth, we have just to remind him that betwixt *great* periods of time, and the *gradual* increase of animal life, there is no necessary connection. However long and indefinite the time connected with the rocky formations, certain it is that the successive organic tribes were created within a period that admits, and can admit, of no calculation whatever, not even of any analogical illustration from experience or the known laws of nature. The species, however numerous, of every epoch were called at once into being, not gradually but instantly, by the fiat of an all-creative act. Their multiplication and increase depended upon the law of their nature; but how long they were to be privileged to multiply, in one unvarying specific form, according to that law, is a point that comes legitimately within the range of experience and the calculations of existing life. Let not things which differ, therefore, be mixed together. The organic and the inorganic types, in the act of formation, cannot be compared. And no argument can be adduced from the fact of the mere numbers of animal species, or of their individual increase, in support of the assumed length of any geological epoch. Species as well as individuals have perished, and gone out within the narrow limits of our own epoch, and yet have multiplied in progeny through countless myriads.

The same course of argument applies to every one of the formations, to some of them of vast thickness, even more conclusively, where we find the same species persistent throughout the group, and the same genus often extending over two or three entire formations, embracing periods of geological time of as many millions of years. Thus the *Leptæna lata* of the Silurian age lives on to the close of the Carboniferous; the *trilobite*, earliest of living creatures, has its representatives still in our modern seas; the mail-clad *holoptychius* existed through the whole of the Devonian and Carboniferous eras; and equally remarkable is the fact that the *Onchus Murchisoni*, the oldest fish yet detected in the rocks of the earth, is a creature more allied to the existing genus *Spinax* (the dog-fish) than to any other family of relics inclosed in all the intermediate ascending series of deposits. Among the infusoria it is ascertained that there are two kinds of living *Gallionellæ* identical with the fossil species in the Richmond clays of Virginia; while again, in geological botany, we have all the types of the coal formation still flourishing with the same gigantic forms in the continents and islands washed by the Pacific.

3. THE SUPERFICIAL ACCUMULATIONS. The argument of the geologists, for their indefinite periods of time, proceeds mainly upon the assumption that the present and the past operations of the laws of nature are nearly uniform; or, in other words, that the existing rate of increment of detrital and alluvial matter, in seas, deltas, and rivers, is to be taken as the standard throughout the various geological epochs. Tried by the test of the superficial accumulations, the subject is brought within a manageable compass, the definite is substituted for the indefinite, and the scale of accumulative power in the ancient will be in the ratio of its

erosive and transporting agency in the modern epoch. The products of volcanoes also fall to be considered in estimating the effects of causes now in operation.

The *bowlder clay* comes first and legitimately within the scope of this estimate; for, whatever theory of its formation be adopted, whether by the sudden submergence of a vast arctic continent and consequent upbreaking of the icy regions of the polar seas, by the sweep of a universal deluge, or a violent upheaval of the bed of the ocean, certain it is that the materials were brought together by rapid spasmodic action. This deposit covers the whole of Northern Europe, much of Asia, and extends over the vast continent of North America, as far as the 42° of latitude: it varies from a hundred to several hundred feet in depth: and thus, so far as quantity and extent of superficial area are concerned, the bowlder clay formation may be compared with any of the older rocky formations of the interior. But no geologist has ventured to speculate about an indefinite cycle of years, as the condition of the planet during the drift and accumulation of these rude and plastic materials.

The *sands* and *gravels* which succeed are likewise of great depth, spread over extensive valleys, and rise on the acclivities of hills five and six hundred feet above the level of the sea. This may be regarded, all of it, as the collect of the current epoch; and within the period of civilization and history and the arts, what sand-floods have been carried to every quarter of the globe, covering entire regions, devastating cities, and obliterating the very traces of man's dominion over countries once subject to his use. Nor would fossils be wanting to complete the analogy, as the *dunes* along the shores of every continent, and especially on the coast of the North Sea in Norway, Denmark, Holland and Belgium, only require consolidation in order to represent with living instead of extinct species, the fossiliferous deposits of anterior times; more particularly the Molasse and Nagelflue of the Swiss Alps. Near Tours, in France, there is a bed of oyster-shells which is twenty-seven miles long, with a corresponding breadth, and twenty feet thick. And in the United States there are beds far exceeding this: a stratum, nearly continuous, has been traced from the Eutaw Springs in South Carolina, to the

Chickasaw country—being six hundred miles in length by ten to a hundred miles in breadth.

When we descend from the land to *the sea* we find equally extensive accumulations, spread over the bottom, or raised along the tide-level in the form of bars, shoals, and banks. The whole eastern coast of the United States * is bordered throughout by a line of sand-banks and islands, of various forms and outline, but very uniform in their mineral ingredients, being composed for the most part of a fine, white, and quartzose sand. On the coasts of the southern states, the Carolinas and Virginia, they form a chain of low islands, separated from the coast by a series of lagoons; while higher up, on the southern coasts of New England, they occur as submarine ridges, parallel to the coast, and separated from each other by wide channels. To the north, these arenaceous deposits are still more extensive, forming vast submarine plateaux, such as the St. George and Newfoundland banks. And at the bottom of all the bays and creeks of that much indented land, prodigious *siltings* are going forward, not under the form of narrow ridges, but as broad connected strata or flats; consisting seaward of very fine sand, and more inward of a coarse gravel, and in not a few instances of *calcareous mud,* where the deposit takes place in the vicinity of coral reefs. The same processes are in operation around every island and by the shores of every continent where tidal action favors the deposition of the materials—the result as now ascertained, not so much of rivers, as of oceanic currents. The depth of these sands it is impossible to determine; but thousands of feet may not reach their soundings. And as to organic remains, they are most favorably situated and composed for attracting and sustaining every kind of marine creature: it is upon the banks that border the coast of North America that the most extensive fisheries are carried on, because these are the abodes of those myriads of invertebral animals—the molluscs, annelides, and zoophytes, types of the older formations—which serve for the food of fishes, the ctenoids and cycloids of maritime enterprise. And thus, co-extensive with the littoral territories of the ocean, we have all the elements and ingredients of a FORMA-

* Mr. Davis.

TION, completing within the human epoch, that may almost rival the Old Red Sandstone itself.

Nor does the analogy terminate in the production, whether of one or many beds, of sand and gravel deposits. Simultaneously with these, there will be siltings and accumulations of various kinds of materials arranging themselves, at different depths, over the bottom of the ocean. The beds, too, will have their edges slid over each other, and where maintaining a degree of parallelism, the inclination of the more remote members of the suite will correspond with the increasing depth of the sea bottom. Then the imbedded remains will be as various as the different kinds, genera, and species of animals that frequent the different localities; nor will eruptive matter be always wanting to give diversity to the scene, indurating, dislocating, and disarranging the relative position of the deposits: Until we have formed, *within our present seas*, the whole complement of a geological formation—the calcareous, muddy, sandy, gravelly suites, cotemporaneous in origin and growth, with all their diversity of fossils, living and imbedded at the same period—some beds consisting entirely of microscopic or other marine bodies—some composed of vegetable and other mixed materials—some where the land and waters have mingled their spoils together—and all to be united and agglutinated into one great composite system by the dykes and eruptions of submarine volcanoes.

These processes are all now in active operation; and, without straining the argument, the clear undeniable inference is, that, as the amount of materials accumulated and arranged in the modern, so will be the ratio of increase in the more ancient periods of the earth's history and revolutions. And hence thousands, not millions of years, would, upon such inductions, be the scale of reckoning as to time.

But to state the argument in this form is vastly to underrate the forces of nature in the primeval times. There are, on the contrary, the strongest reasons for believing that the two classes of phenomena can bear no proportion to each other, either as to the manner of or the periods occupied in their formation. The bulk of dry land, compared with water, was then, as all geological appearances testify, perhaps only a twentieth instead of a third part, as now, of the supermarine area of the globe. How infinitely greater, therefore, would be the action of the waters over all the materials subject to their disintegrating power, whether upon the islands and continents already raised above their waves, or upon the immense submarine tracks of rock just lifting up their peaks and waiting to be elevated into air? Nor in alluding to volcanic products can we fail to perceive how immensely inferior are the modern to those of the palæozoic ages, when all the great mountain-ranges were bursting into position; the American continent, not as now with a few isolated eruptive centers, but rending all over, as the mighty Andes and Cordilleras were rising above the deep and assuming outline; and in every quarter of the globe the plutonic, erosive, and denuding agencies were upon a scale of corresponding magnitude. Leibnitz, in his "Protogæa," has long ago anticipated these views, where, in the masterly sketch of his leading geological canons, he distinctly refers to the more intensive energy with which physical causes must have acted in primordial times; and considers that these disruptions of the earth's crust, from the disturbances communicated to the incumbent waters, must have been attended with diluvial action on the largest scale. The *maximæ secutæ inundationes*, thereby occasioned, had produced their natural effects, when the period of repose succeeded—the *quiescentibus causis, atque acquilibratis, consistentior emergeret rerum status*, as he so beautifully describes one out of many recurring stages of paroxysm and repose during the Course of Creation.

Whatever views may be adopted on this momentous question, I shall conclude by observing that it is not necessary, in support of the one here advocated, to assume that the secondary causes which have produced the geological phenomena referred to, were different in kind from those in operation at the present day. But it is asserted that such physical causes must have been immensely increased, in the degree and intensity of their action, by the very different condition of the planet, and the circumstances under which, in consequence, they began to operate. As to the *millionade doctrine*, if I may so term it, there are in every view the greatest difficulties in the way of its adoption,—errors of calculation somewhere to be corrected, inconsistencies to be reconciled, conditions of organic life gratuitously assumed and to be rectified. It matters not, indeed, whether we take the organic or the inorganic structures of the several periods as the gauge of their probable duration—the living tribes that existed throughout such periods, and whose relative ages we can approximate to—or the dead rock in which the remains are interred, and in the accumulation and arrangement of which so many extraordinary agencies have been demonstratively concerned. The laws of nature, in the one case, are nearly uniform; species as well as individuals have their limited terms of existence; and experience establishes the fact, that the living tribes of the modern epoch have, in several instances, become extinct within a comparatively short period of time. The operations of nature, in the other case, are subject to vast diversity, great and sudden changes, and apparently limited by no ascertained maximum of development. And thus combined, so far as our present state of knowledge extends, the inference is warrantable, that in the geological register the error may be one—of MILLIONS of years' reckoning!

## CHAPTER VI.

### THE MOSAIC RECORD—ACCOUNT OF CREATION.

The conclusion attempted to be established by the preceding mode of reasoning, is not of the kind, nor will it be so satisfactory as, many desiderate. The sacred chronology, according to the common interpretation, remains as it was; and no harmony can thus be established betwixt it and the deductions of geology. Bring down the epochs to thousands instead of millions of years, and still the DAYS of Scripture are not explained. The historical and the scientific accounts of the course of creation are just where they were, the one based on the word of its Author, the other resting on rash or doubtful interpretations of the phenomena of nature. Leave us, says the geologist, to grope our own way: mystical as our records are, we disturb no established truth, and imagination delights to lose itself in the far-distant past. Let not, says the divine, the speculations of a new science—a science of yesterday—be mixed up with more important matters of religion: we are within the sacred precincts of revelation, and our oracles give forth no dubious meanings—no isoteric doctrines for the initiated only.

The marvels of geology certainly are, in every view that can be taken of them, deeply interesting to the mind. The volume of creation, read in the light of its discoveries, is traced back through pages which have been long hid from day; and these now make known to us a story of life and death, of activities and enjoyments, of catastrophes and revolutions, which surpass in wonder the inventions of the mere romance writer, or all that regulated genius can pour "from pictured urn" of her most fascinating lore. But be the time occupied in the elaboration of these records what it may, the records themselves have an actual being, and a language of intelligence indelibly impressed upon them. They are genuine, authentic documents of their author. They may be misinterpreted. Inferences may be deduced from them for which there is no warrant; constructions put upon passages which they will not legitimately bear; or the true key of the volume, in its great leading truths, may not as yet have been found. Still the work is of God, wholly and entirely the writing of his own hand.

Revelation is also His work; and, claiming to be from the same authority as the other, rests its pretensions to be received as an authentic document upon the ground of creation. It gives details, and enters into explanations of the nature and origin of creation; and it declares that the same Divine Being who made the heavens and the earth, has also recorded their history and revealed his will to man. It is by no mere casualty, therefore, or as a matter of indifference, that the Bible commences its narrative by an account of creation. That account is there as the foundation of one of its own claims to belief, testifying to its credibility that it is of God; that He placed it there, not as a skillful writer would do his preface, but because of the fact, that the invisible things of his nature are to be seen and understood by the things which are made.—What is thus declared upon the subject of creation, is likewise liable to misinterpretation. It may not be read aright. But of the account itself there can be no question,—that it is given as a real, as it ever must be regarded a true one, of the Divine operations.

In order, therefore, to arrive at any just conclusions respecting the comparison to be instituted betwixt the geological and the revealed account of creation, we shall first inquire into the kind, as well as amount, of information contained in the Mosaic record. The rendering of the term "day" will then fall to be considered in relation to the order of events indicated in both accounts.

I. The narrative proceeds with a fullness and minuteness of detail, which clearly show a purpose in the writer. Did Moses actually mean to trace the whole of creation in its primordial course and outline? Assuming that he did, the phraseology is pointed and admirably suited to its subject. Admitted into the presence-chamber of the Creator, he sees the instruments with which he works, the rapidity with which he executes, the subserviency of all being to his will, the arrangement and disposition of all things at his pleasure. Knowing, as we now do from the highest authority, *what* was the work of creation, and *whence* it originated, the intelligent mind discerns also the suitableness of the description, and the Divine selection of words employed to record it. There is inspiration in the pencil, as well as omnipotence in the hand, which traced out the plan of creation, and brought it into existence. The Cause willed, and the effect immediately was,—IN THE BEGINNING GOD CREATED THE HEAVEN AND THE EARTH.

Here, betwixt God and his work there are no intermediate agencies,—no pause or rest in the act of coming into being. A material universe is designed, and the substance of it is instantly produced. The inspired historian proves that he was inspired, by the brevity of the history of the event, by the employment of words so perfectly adapted to the nature of the act. He proves farther, that we have here indicated the precise course of creation, and that he meant so to represent it—that the heavens and the earth are of one and the same act—that the physical universe, through all its dominions and remotest spheres, started at one and the same time into being. The sun, moon, and stars were now all formed, as well as our own planet. The stellar systems were everywhere arranged ; and the worlds of matter had their places all assigned them through infinite space. This part of the Divine actings must not be confounded with the farther evolution of creation as described in the work of the fourth day, which has reference manifestly to the division of time and the appointment of the seasons, through the revolution of the planetary worlds.

The condition of the earth as it first came from the hand of its framer is next alluded to. It was "without form and void," and involved in darkness ; that is, the arrangements necessary to constitute a habitable globe, were not completed. There was no diversity of surface—no division into hill and valley, into seas and rivers ; the air, the dry land, and the waters, had not yet assumed their respective places. Form was not yet stamped upon the matter of the globe. Consequently it was also VOID, or without inhabitants. Neither vegetables nor animals were there. They could not exist before these necessary adaptations for life were adjusted. Let the reader note this stage of the work. Marking the precise, definite phraseology of the inspired writer, let him seriously reflect whether he has here before him the first state of the new world, or the shapeless ruined aspect of one of its subsequent geological transformations? None of the elements, he will not fail to observe, have been described as yet existing in separation. The course of creation has not advanced so far; and, if it had done so, no geologist pretends to assert, that at the close of any one of his epochs, the laws of nature were abolished, and all things reverted to their pristine formless condition. With what propriety, then, may it be asked, can an opening be made in this part of the narrative wide enough to embrace, or to have intercalated into it, all the phases of an archaic earth under his numerous formations, and the vast cycles of time in which they had been evolving? The language employed admirably represents what we can well suppose the original physical state of the planet to have been; and that state accords better with the first than with the last, or any of the intermediate series of the geological changes. And the earth was without form and void; and darkness was upon the face of the deep: and the Spirit of God moved upon the face of the waters; and thus gave shape and outline to the planetary mass.

The light was thereupon produced. We are not told whence, nor out of what. Like all the matter of the universe, it started into being at the call of the Creator, suddenly, as its own brilliant flashing emanations over the darkness at this hour. Then came day and night; and this implies, that there came along with them the revolution of the globe and the commencement of motion in the astral universe. The production of a firmament or atmosphere is next alluded to, and in immediate connection with this part of the work, whereby a medium was provided for the diffusion of the light and the play of all that beauty and variety of coloring by which the earth was to be adorned. "And God said, Let there be light: and there was light; and God divided the light from the darkness. And God called the light day, and the darkness he called night. And God said, Let there be a firmament in the midst of the waters, and let it divide the waters from the waters."

Light, the subtilest and fleetest of all elements, has nearly eluded every effort of man to detect or analyze its essence. It travels swift as thought through infinite space. It spreads its ethereal force over every opposing obstacle. It gives brilliancy to the gem, form to the crystal, color to the flower, health to animal life, and is so indispensable to every existing condition of existing physical nature, that, were the mandate of its creation revoked, we know just as much of its principle as to see in its annihilation a relapse into that state of chaos when all things were without form and void. Not only the beauty of organic structure, but the molecular arrangement of the mineral mountain masses of the earth, would, in all probability, have been an impossible condition of matter without the existence and agency of light. And light, whether glowing in the solar disc, gleaming in remotest stars, or breaking and sparkling in the rain-drop, what revelation has science made of it beyond its properties of luster and activity ?— We trace its effects ; we discern its influence upon all bodies ; but when we would go deeper, and seek to know it essentially and in itself, we can only speak of it as the utterance of Him who said,— LET THERE BE LIGHT.

Nor has science made any attempt, at least no successful one, to account for the origin of the atmosphere. Its constituent elements are known. They are every day made the subject of direct experiment. The solution and ascent of water in the air is also a matter of daily visible occurrence. But by what process this great mass of impalpable fluid was brought together, enveloping the entire earth, and suspended as a curtain over our heads, no ingenuity or dexterity of man has been able to determine. There is no evidence by which to explain it upon the principles of natural law, slowly elaborating the materials, and piling them high in the starry vault. The atmosphere, indeed, must ever stand in the original formation, the result of the immediate creative act, brought together in all its volume and vast incredible capacity of receiving and holding in its grasp the gaseous residue of all earthly things. And what of its electricity, its magnetism, the aurora and its streaming meteors,—its thunder, lightning, clouds, and rain,—

all, shall we say, the instantaneous effect of the authoritative command? AND GOD SAID, LET THERE BE A FIRMAMENT IN THE MIDST OF THE WATERS!

We every day see the conversion of water into steam, and steam into air; and the air, like the ocean, receiving every substance into itself. But, nevertheless, it is not inferred that there is any augmentation to the volume of the atmosphere, any increase or essential change upon its original mass. Without the existence of this fluid, the earth would have been no suitable place for any of its living inhabitants, vegetable or animal. Therefore was it created; therefore does the account of its creation stand in the order in which we find it in the Mosaic narrative; and, therefore, from this very circumstance, are we not warranted to infer that we have before us a description of the actual genesis of things—that it is not a remodeling or transformation of the old, but the veritable course under which all creation was at first brought into being, form, and parts, that the inspired writer intends to record?

We cannot refuse, by parity of reasoning, to conclude the same as to the immediately succeeding act in the Divine operations. The arrangement of the surface of the earth was now to be effected; and, just as one portion of the waters was lifted and expanded into air, so, in consequence of a different proportion in the elements, and evolution of new principles, the seas were formed and gathered into the depressions occasioned by the raising up of the dry land, its consolidation into rocks and mountains. This is the starting point of geology. The science can get no deeper. It begins all its researches, and builds all its calculations, upon that crystalline crust which is termed primary, which is co-extensive with the superficial area of the globe, which is found in every region, and beneath which no explorations have anywhere been made. And wherefore not assume this as an immediate formation, as a direct preparatory arrangement, like the seas and atmosphere, for the life that was just to be provided with a habitation upon it? A beginning for organic bodies is demonstrable upon geological evidence. The lowest fossiliferous rocks have been reached, and everywhere they are found to maintain the same relative position. The inference, therefore, is legitimate, nay, probable, that the primary formations of geologists constituted the first dry land, as herein described; and that Time, calculated according to the operations of natural mechanical laws, can enter in no way into our speculations as to their origin. "And God said, Let the waters under the heaven be gathered together in one place, and let the dry land appear: and it was so."

The course of creation proceeds. "And God called the dry land earth, and the gathering together of the waters called he seas." The globe was thus divided into land and ocean. An atmosphere embraces the whole, tempering the heat and cold of the one, receiving the exhalations of the other, and both prepared for the ministrations required of them. The dry earth is represented as being first the seat of organic life. The new and bare surface is covered with herbage. The grasses, shrubs, and trees all start into being, prepared each for the diffusion and continuance of their kind, by yielding seed and fruit. And then commenced on the theater of our globe the successive evolution of the *principle of life,* subtile, active, prolific, in all the boundless prodigality of nature, and mysterious still as the essence and fount of all-creative Being.

At this part of the narrative it is generally supposed, according to the common reading, that there is a retrograde step, as it were, introduced. The day and night have been made to precede the creation of the sun and moon; and now to supply the deficiency we are told of the appointment of these luminaries in the heavens "to give light upon the earth." But three days and three nights have already revolved. Doubtless they have, but not without light, for light has been created; and not without a provision for the night, for the light has been divided from the darkness. The earth has been revolving upon its own axis; that occasioned the succession of day and night then as now. Another motion is communicated, whereby it revolves in its orbit and circles round the sun; that causes the variety of the seasons, and the divisions of the year. The luminous matter diffused through space, and equally shining upon all bodies, has been assembled into the great central orbs, to be the dispensers each of light and heat to their respective systems; and upon these arrangements being established, both days and nights, seasons and years, are all dependent upon, as they all arise from, the revolution of the planets round the central luminary. "And God said, Let there be lights in the firmament of the heaven, to divide the day from the night; and let them be for signs and for seasons, and for days and for years."

"And God *made* two great lights; he *made* the stars also." The original does not bear out the sense of there being in these instances an act of creation; neither does the English term itself always imply that meaning. Light-bearers, or the depositories of illumination, is the true rendering of the Hebrew. The Septuagint translators have used similar relative terms, and in our own language the expression "made" often signifies fashioned, formed, used, constrained. And so the phrase here refers not to the creation, but to the uses of bodies already described as being in existence, and created along with all matter in the beginning. But now they are invested with new properties, are arranged so as to perform new functions, and stand in relations each to each, at the bidding of Him who brought them into being. Next to the summoning of the universe into existence, this was the most stupendous act of Divine power, and we know as much of the one as of the other. Some of the properties of matter we are acquainted with. The laws of motion we can define in some measure, and calculate also their effects. But whence the one, and *how* the arbitrary appointment of the other, through all the infinite diversity of systems and spheres — precise, harmonious, and orderly—baffles all the ingenuity of science to determine. Mark, too, the order of the introduction of this new class of facts, just in the due course and regulation of nature. When life is mentioned, and the earth is clothed with verdure, the seasons begin their round, and the divinely-instructed historian acquaints us with the cause. "And God set them in the firmament of the heaven to give light upon the earth; and to rule over the day and over the night, and to divide the light from the darkness."

The waters are now replenished with their stores of animal life, and by the same act of creation the air receives its stock of winged tribes. Then follows, as the work of another distinct period of time, the introduction of the terrestrial races—the living creature after his kind—the cattle—and creeping thing—and beast of the earth after his kind. The description here is general. The orders, genera, and species are not named. Still the catalogue is large and amply descriptive. The various types of organic structure are alluded to, and each term or epithet of the quadruple list is elastic enough to embrace one and all the diversified families of the most methodical naturalist. "And God made the beast of the earth after his kind, and cattle after their kind, and every creeping thing that creepeth upon the earth, each after his kind."

Such is the account, the order, and course of creation, as set forth in the inspired record. The description of the various generative acts is simple, distinctive, and consonant with the energies of the Will by which they are performed. The whole narrative is one of many, within the compass of the sacred volume, in which a strict adherence to the letter leads to a sound interpretation. The wisdom of man will be confounded when it tries to fathom the methods and devices of the divine Artificer in originating his works. His safety will often be in distrusting his own understanding, in not magnifying overmuch the ingenuity of his own speculations, and in sometimes believing that even science will be exalted by approximating to, rather than by departing from, the literalities of Scripture.

II. Compare now the epochs of geology with the DAYS of Scripture, and there will be observed at least a remarkable coincidence between them. The fossiliferous systems of the one are nearly the same in number with the descriptive paragraphs in the other. The order in the creation of organized bodies, the progression of life upon the earth, are also wonderfully striking in the records of both. The lowest of our fossiliferous deposits contain the impressions of plants—these stand at the beginning of the Mosaic list. The same groups, and the whole of the next in succession, are characterized by the prevailing abundance of marine tribes — the waters, according to the sacred narrative, then received their command, and multiplied abundantly the moving creature that hath life. Vegetables and animals, still of *the waters,* continue to increase during the carboniferous era, when a new system succeeds, and in this the foot-prints of birds are distinctly traced — so it was in the same order of succession that the winged fowl is sent forth into the open firmament of heaven. The Lias and Oolite formations immediately follow, filled with monsters of the deep, saurians and flying lizards,—the text speaks of the "great whales" of the period, as distinguished among the productions of the waters. The Wealden Chalk, and Tertiaries are replete with all kinds of reptiles, mammals, and quadrupeds—the horse, urus, and other forms of cattle—and so, in like manner, the last in the Mosaic list, as the highest in the geological strata, are the types of every beast, cattle, and creeping thing.

Now, can this running parallel be accidental or intended? Did the writer of the one record know anything of the contents of the other? Does the course of creation, as detailed in the strata of the earth, follow as a necessary consequence from the nature of things? or as the arbitrary appointment of Him who made them? Would plants, fishes, reptiles, fowl, mammals, all emerge in this precise order of succession, by any known law of organic structure? Or could not the first and last, or any of the intermediate kinds, have been at once, and as adaptively, brought together in one and the same period of time? Was the writer of the Genesis acquainted with the rich exuberant flora of the carboniferous age? and was it meant as a true exposition of its history that there were as yet no beasts or quadrupeds upon the earth to enjoy it? And knowing of it, as well as of all the other superficial arrangements,—the upheaval of the crust, the rise of mountains, the alternate shifting of sea and land,—does he describe the progress of organic creation precisely as it occurred, and as the changes of the planet became ADAPTIVE?

The series of creative acts terminates in the introduction of Man upon the stage of terrestrial being. "And God said, Let us make man in our image, after our likeness; and let them have dominion over the fish of the sea, and over the fowl of the air, and over the cattle, and over all the earth, and over every creeping thing that creepeth upon the earth."

Here both narratives are completely at one as to man's place in the course as well as system of creation. No fragment of his race has been detected in any of the rocky strata of the earth. Every other organic thing, of every class, and order, and tribe, has its representative in one or other of the geological epochs.

Man stands apart and alone in the geology as in the history. No mere link in the chain of organic existence, not a being of mere earthy mold, but fashioned in the image of his Maker, and fitted to explore, to understand, and to exercise dominion over the works of his creation. How much, again, in all this last and highest evolution of creative might, is the conclusion confirmed, and arrived at from so many converging lines, that the sacred record was INTENDED to embody an actual account of the creation of our globe, in its various primordial arrangements as well as in all its consecutive events, until its majestic close in the human epoch? For, looking back and comparing the whole narrative with the facts of geology, is it not highly probable that we have in that account distinctly shadowed forth the progressive researches of the science, the great physical truths of creation, as symbolized in the rocks? The brilliant vista through millions of untold ages, and upon scenes supposed to be unnoticed and unrecorded, vanishes indeed at the admission of this principle of interpretation. But a more consistent view of the world's history—of the comparative longevity of its successive tribes—of the various changes and alterations which its surface has undergone—and a less violence far to the obvious import of the sacred text—form no unpleasing substitutes on which, amidst such lures to doubt, bewilderment, and error, faith and reason will equally incline to repose.

III. The conclusions which have been, or which may be, deduced from a comparative examination of geology and the Mosaic record, fall to be noticed.

1. In order to preserve the literal rendering of the six days of creation, it is maintained that the Mosaic record takes no account whatever of any of the geological formations described. After the intimation, "In the beginning God created the heaven and the earth: and the earth was without form and void; and darkness was upon the face of the deep"—the close of the EPOCHS, with all their complement of strata and fossils, was accomplished; and then, as descriptive of the era of man, with all his living cotemporaries, and the several days with the works therein

accomplished, the new order of events referred to in the text commences with the declaration, "and the Spirit of God moved upon the face of the waters." The discoveries of geology are thus all cast back upon unrecorded anterior periods, and with regard to which the sacred record is silent; while of the new series of events, in precisely the same order of succession and enlarged amount of normal organic being, there is a defined literal account. This may be regarded as the generally received interpretation among the leading geologists as well as of a large class of eminent divines. It was early and eagerly adopted by Dr. Chalmers. The proof of its soundness is made to hinge upon certain ingenious criticisms regarding the terms *bara, asah, yatzan,* which in the common version of the Hebrew text are translated *created, made, formed.* According to the new rendering, wherever any of these words occur in any of the verses *after* the second, they are to be restricted to the simple act of fashioning, arranging, and constructing new bodies out of pre-existing matter. Hence, all the initial and secondary actings noticed in the narrative are in this manner clearly distinguishable. It is farther argued, that all the secondary class of arrangements are distinctively pointed to, and separated from the primordial, by the formula of expression, "and God said," which is introduced at the commencement of each of the six days, but not prefixed to the initial creative act of all matter in the beginning.

Now, against this mode of argument it may be objected that much of it does not bear upon the question at issue. The discrepancy is one more of things than of words. It is the physical solution, rather than the critical, that is the important matter of inquiry; and this no mere verbal emendations of the text will altogether and consistently help out. Observe the character of the acts spoken of after the second verse and introduction of the expression, "and God said;"—the calling light into being, the separation of the darkness, the division of day and night, the formation of an atmosphere, the fixed position of the firmament above and the waters beneath, and the separation of the dry land. These are the acts of the first and second days. But what of them *before* this? These elements and their arrangement were all required, and must have all existed, during the epochs recorded in geology. That is admitted. The light needed no renewal after any geological transposition of the land and sea. The revolutions of the heavenly bodies would be equally unaffected, and days, seasons, and years would remain and proceed in the same order of succession. The firmament and atmosphere would continue to occupy their relative positions. And so, according to the *usus loquendi* and legitimate import of all the terms employed in the text, we are reading of things that were neither in being nor in operation *before*, but which now for the first time are represented as being summoned into existence. We are equally unprepared for the admission made by some of the friends of revelation, that Moses knew not the full amount and nature of the knowledge conveyed in his narrative, just as "he was not aware of the profound spiritual meaning of much of the ritual which he was employed to institute. It was an obscure text, which awaited the Divine commentary of the christian dispensation."* There is no analogy between the subjects. The law was confessedly a preparatory, incompleted dispensation. The order of creation as traced by Moses embraces substantively everything which creation contains—the elements, disposition, and collocation of its parts—and that he saw not through the whole of a future, unfulfilled plan, furnishes no good ground for the assumption that he was ignorant of or purposely passes over the history of millions of hears of the very subject on which he was inspired to write, and on which he was to build his whole system of theism and of grace. This mode of interpretation, beside, assumes a *hiatus* in the text for which there is no just warrant, either in the verbal structure of the narrative, or in the physical character and order of the events described. It has always appeared to us to proceed upon principles of explication which violate all the canons of a pure and severe criticism, which indulgently gives way to new and gratuitously assumed difficulties, and which would leave nothing in any writing except what the reader chooses to find in it.

2. The principle of interpreting *the days* in Genesis as periods of indefinite time, and within which the several geological *formations* were successively evolved. They who adopt this hypothesis

* The Pre-Adamite Earth.

can plausibly argue that the *order* of creative acts as revealed in the sacred record, harmonizes in a very remarkable manner with the course of creation as detailed in the researches of geology. Hereby a comparison can be distinctly instituted, and a parallelism observed betwixt the peculiar work of each day and the leading phenomena displayed in the earth's crust—from the first appearance of dry land, when organic bodies had not been as yet created, and the primary rocks in which none have been detected—up through the silurian, devonian, and carboniferous series, in all which plants and marine organisms only are found—and onward until we reach the tertiary strata, where, in succession, the revealed order of animal life is so remarkably coincident. The details of the science are not indeed to be all, and minutely, read in the narrative. But the main truths and the leading dogmata are there; and if any departure from the literal rendering of the text can be permitted, so as to fit in and adjust the geological phenomena, it may be justly contended that there is less of violence and straining by the substitution of periods for days, than by casting aside the whole genetic description as having no bearing whatever upon the primary cosmogony of the globe. Then the various events, it may be farther argued, as recorded in the text—the creation of light—the formation of a firmament—the division of day and night — the appointment of seasons and years — the gathering together of the waters, and the elevation of the dry land—are all so described and placed in such juxta-position as can only be applicable to primary creative acts, to things which were not before, and which now for the first time were brought into being and condition.

The abettor of this view and mode of reconciliation will likewise avail himself, in defense of its being an orthodox interpretation, of the latitude of meaning ascribed to the term "day," in the Scriptures themselves. Even in the second chapter of the Divine word, and applied to the very subject in question—the order of creation—he finds the term to be used in an indefinite sense: "These are the generations of the heavens and of the earth, when they were created in the DAY that the Lord God made the earth and the heavens, and EVERY PLANT of the field." The solemn announcement at the close of this world's drama will not fail also to be adverted to—"in the last days perilous times shall come"—wherein periods of longer or shorter duration are implied as existing in the midst of days. Frequently too there occur the expressions: the day of grace—the day of salvation—the day of the Lord—the day of trial—the day of redemption—terms all of unlimited import and not to be defined by the planetary diurnal calendar, but to be determined by the arrangements of a dispensation in which man is viewed as a moral accountable being, and not by any necessities in which his physical condition and the world he inhabits are concerned. Thus by adopting this hypothesis, which assumes the entire narrative as a consecutive description of the order of creation, every day as bearing the initiative of its own class of phenomena, the plan and quality of the Divine works as all delineated and shadowed out, the progressive succession of the whole organic and inorganic historically described, and the phenomena, and the terms descriptive of them, are asserted to be in their proper places, and in harmony each with each.

3. There is another mode of defending the text in consistency with the general facts of the science, by assuming that the course of creation indicated through the epochs was in all its characteristic features *reproduced*, and substantially represented in the cosmogonic period of the Mosaic account. We have noticed from time to time, in the different stages of our description, in what the analogies consisted. In the earliest, as well as in the last, organic fossil types, there is the most perfect identity with all the vegetable and animal forms described in the narrative. The order of their reappearance is likewise similar. Moses, it is here supposed, saw the casting of the same molds, the agency of the same hand, and the "day" to be successively the period for the reproduction of the work.

Read now consecutively the whole account, and observe how the Historian passes in review the entire series of the Divine acts, and runs over again the great master-keys of this harmonious system. He is present, so to speak, when, in the beginning, the matter of the heaven and the earth was created. He witnesses the arrangement of the parts, which before were without form and void. He hears the command,—LET THERE BE LIGHT. And now, as the mighty structure expands in vision before the eye of his mind, the firmament and the waters and the dry land separating and drawing off to their respective places, he introduces a record of the period within which the several operations were effected. How long is that period? Just the division of time with which he was acquainted, and which he knew was amply sufficient for the completion of all the operations in question. The acts are successive. The will that performed them is omnipotent. Everything followed in its order and in the time that all creative power commanded it to be. Hence the days, with regard to all the initial acts, both of creation and arrangement, were literally of the duration assigned in the text. After the introduction of organic life on the third day, geology speaks definitively as to the successive order of the kinds and families of the structural forms created. But it gives no sign, and can give none, as to the portion of time required for their creation. It may have been an instant or a day,—a week or a period. The revealed account speaks positively upon the point; and shows how, at the bidding of the Divine will, the various elements—the water, the earth, the air—were replenished with their respective tribes in the old as in the new world, and under all the phases and epochs of their being.

The inspired narrative, it may be alleged, according to this view, is not only consistent with itself, but becomes a sublime illustrative introduction to the book of revelation. The matter of the heaven and the earth was the effect of a single command. The separation of its elements was the instantaneous effect of another.—Upon the creation of light, a division is given to time, and the morning and the evening hours were established. The arrangements of the second day followed, and were all completed in the period assigned. So with the remanent days and their respective included operations. The eye of the historian sees nothing intervening betwixt the cause and the effect; his mind is fixed upon the action, not the manner of its accomplishment; and knowing the whole to be the result of the same power and the arrangement of the same providence, he combines in one cycle or WEEK the entire series of events, one day of which unto the Eternal is as a thousand, and a thousand, but as one day. The work all accomplished, the immediately revolving period of time was established as the Sabbath of the Lord. Having made man in his own image, with knowledge to apprehend and adore the author of his being, the divine Architect RESTED; he ceased from any farther acts of creation; nothing of any material existence, nor of any living thing, has been added to his works since the completion of the six days, and so the rest has continued and will continue to the end of time—a Sabbath hallowed by the structure of the globe and the beneficence of the Creator.

These are some of the methods by which the geologist aims in bringing the conclusions of his science within the scope of the Mosaic record, and in freeing his speculations from all their incumbrances and responsibilities. There is still a great deal to be accomplished, even with all these approximations, toward a right and full and literal comparison with the sacred text. There is indeed no real conflict between the discoveries of geology and the declarations of the divine oracles; and, with so many doors of retreat from or avenues of approach into the inviting fields of its research, no friend of the truth need be afraid of an excursion through the most intricate depths of creation's works. Meanwhile, the metaphysicians have all been driven from the field, with all their untenable dogmas about the eternity of matter. Geologists repudiate the doctrine, and their science refutes it. But there is such a thing as others rashly rushing to conclusions, wherever they can see tendencies or leanings to countenance their impious materialism. In this direction, many think that geology, however falsely, wholly inclines. And even now it is better, infinitely better, to rest with unhesitating confidence in the received interpretation of Scripture than be borne away by sweeping generalizations, built most certainly somewhere upon loose conflicting elements of calculation. Countless millions of years are, we admit, as nothing in the records of eternity—of no account with the Everlasting of days. Nevertheless, if the time can be reduced, as unquestionably there are data for the reduction, the epochs and the days approximate all the closer; the speculations of the science are brought into better keeping with the dicta of revelation; farther discoveries will lead to farther adjustments; until what was done for the interests of the one by detecting the miscalculations of Hindoo astronomy, will again be effected for the other by scanning more intelligibly the geological horoscope.— And thus removing every ground of suspicion or offense, will serve to bring this interesting branch of knowledge from the outer court of the Gentiles to the innermost shrine of the TEMPLE OF TRUTH.

The father of the Inductive Philosophy thus expresses his views: "In the works of creation, we behold a twofold emanation of the Divine virtue; of which the one relates to its power, the other to its wisdom. The former is especially observed in the creating the material mass; the latter, in the disposing the beauty of its form. This being established, it is to be remarked, that there is nothing in the history of creation to invalidate the fact, that the mass and substance of heaven and earth was created, *confusa,* undistinguishable, in one moment of time; but that the six days were assigned for disposing and adjusting it."* This was emitted at a time when geology was in its nonage; the strata of the earth and their singular fossil contents were as yet unexplored;—still it is the oracular voice of one who had looked through the physical universe with the glance of science and of genius, and who knew and sought it only in relation to the Creator and his Word.

*1. De Augm. Scien. L. I.

# CONCLUSION.

## THE CREATOR.

THE magnificent work of creation, whose course we have been tracing in some of its primordial arrangements, in the geological phenomena of the earth's crust, and in its relations to the vast planetary system of which it is a member, is the result over all of design and intelligence. The changes wrought in the earth's structure and framework, from period to period, have not been brought about by merely mechanical changes of physical conditions. There are order and method in the inorganic, no less than in the organic forms, into which matter in any of the earth's revolutions has been cast. There is prospective contrivance each for each. The alterations made in the outward surface, whether of sea or land, have been always such as were best adapted to the habits and requirements of successive living tribes. And the whole amount of change, in both departments of nature, has ever been in such measure and degree as to show, from the beginning, a persistent principle of stability in the system, and a wise, all-controlling arm to be regulating and directing everything. The invisible things of God, from the creation of the world, are clearly seen; and we cannot, if we would, rid ourselves of the thought, that somewhere and beyond, there is, not a "primitive cause"* only, but a Divine Being, the master of the universe, potentially in and present through all things.

Aristotle concludes his treatise "De Mundo," with observing, that to treat of the world without saying anything of its Author would be impious, and he proceeds to show, on various grounds, the traces of an all-governing Deity. Newton concludes his great work, the "Principia," by some reflections on the nature of

*La Place.

the Supreme Cause, and infers from the structure of the visible world, "that it is governed by one almighty and all-wise Being, who rules the world, not as its soul, but as its Lord, exercising an absolute sovereignty over the universe, not as over his own body, but as over his work ; and acting in it according to his pleasure, without suffering anything from it." Speaking of the laws by which God governs the world, and giving his definition of the term LAW, Boyle says, "I look upon a law as a moral, not physical cause, as being, indeed, but a rational thing, according to which an intelligent and free agent is bound to regulate its actions. But inanimate bodies are utterly incapable of understanding what it is, or what it enjoins, or when they act conformably or unconformably to it : therefore, the actions of inanimate bodies, which cannot incite or moderate their own actions, are produced by real power, not by laws." "Hence," says Whewell, in his Bridgewater Treatise, "hence we infer that the intelligence by which the law is ordained, the power by which it is put in action, must be present at all times, and in all places where the effects of the law occur : that thus the knowledge and the agency of the Divine Being pervade every portion of the universe, producing all action and passion, all permanence and change. The laws of nature are the laws which He, in his wisdom, prescribes to his own acts ; his universal presence is the necessary condition of any course of events, his universal agency the only origin of any efficient force."

The researches of science, the deeper they go into the secrets of nature, issue in the surest and brightest disclosures of the Divine Architect of the universe. We are enabled, by the lights which are furnished by the various branches of ascertained knowledge, to read in some degree the mind and purpose of God in the creations of his hand. We see in many instances what is actually intended by certain arrangements and combinations,—why, and for what end, objects are constructed in a particular way, and how it is that trains of events are made to follow in one uniform order rather than in any other. The universe, we discover, is not only bound by laws permanent and unchanging : the laws themselves have an end to serve, a particular result to accomplish. Accumulations of matter are brought together with a definite precise view ; living substances are constructed with organs suited to their conditions of existence; relations of air, earth, and water, are established, which nicely answer the functions to be performed; and in ten thousands of cases are manifested the form, size, position, qualities of hardness, softness, and cohesion in the individual parts which can best secure their own special well-being along with the general conservation of the framework to which they are attached. How admirably, from age to age, do the organic as well as the inorganic structures of the geological narrative illustrate the truth of these remarks, where the manifestations of design are as numerous as the objects of creation, and as legible as if God had written their import by his own finger? The oldest, equally with the newest, book of nature, discloses the records of his will. We read them in the varied language traced and stereotyped upon their stony leaves. And in perusing the diversified contents of this wonderful volume, we cannot rise without the conviction that the being, attributes, and character of its Author, are brightly and indelibly impressed on every page.

The argument for the existence of a DESIGNING AGENT in the creation and arrangements of a material world, may be thus illustrated: A rude, unshapely piece of stone—say the "stone upon the heath"—does not at once impress the spectator with the conviction that it was made and placed where it is, by a designing intelligent being. But let it be chiseled into form, give it symmetry and proportion, and he immediately concludes that this is the result of skill and intention. Look at a piece of machinery—its framework of wood—its springs of iron—its wheels, beams and axles, composed of different metals, and arranged in different forms—and the inference is irresistible, that neither the forest, nor the quarry, nor the mine, yielded the materials in their present shape, nor combined among themselves to put them together.—Reason seeks for a different kind of agency, and experience tells that the mind and the hand of man have been there. We see water converted into steam, the steam brought into contact with a piece of metal, the vapor confined within an inclosure and acted upon by a condenser; and through means of this simple arrangement and the application of this natural power, duly regulated and sustained, we discern the triumph of mind over matter—the marvels which human industry and intelligence have been able to achieve. This combination of materials is not a thing of life.—Chance has produced none of these arrangements. The whole is the result of design, of aiming intention, of calculating intelligence. Examine the telescope, its apparatus of lenses, reflectors, and mirrors: look through that narrow tube as it is pointed in a clear starry night to the azure vault; and your shout of astonishment, when you first behold the increased magnitude of these orbs—their separation into systems and clusters—firmaments ascending in gradations of brilliancy, one above another—and the infinitely remote, studded and glowing with higher and higher galaxies—will partake of a mingled feeling of admiration at the immensity and grandeur of the universe—the wisdom and skill which combined to frame the instrument that brings within your ken, and enables you to gaze on, the glorious vision.

Now, in nature, we find the same indications of design, the same surprising combinations of skill, instruments framed with matchless wisdom and the most exquisite contrivance. Nay, all here, in every department of creation, leaves human ingenuity at an immeasurable distance. No statuary can rival that which is exhibited in the rocks, gems, and crystals of the earth. Machinery is transcendently surpassed, in the forms of every organic thing beneath or around, in minuteness, adaptation, and balancing of parts,—the steam-engine in energy and power—the ship by a more refined and skillful equipment of ropes, pulleys, and sails—and the telescope is not for a moment to be compared with the human eye in the beauty of its construction, the power of its movements, the amazing swiftness and variety of its glance.—But there is design and intelligence manifested in the works of man. They could not arrange themselves. They must have had an artificer. Draw near, look unto the works of creation, what cumulative evidence of their intelligent author, conclusive as the severest demonstrations of science. Man asks for a sign from heaven. Ten thousand intimations are given—millions, indeed, of miraculous contrivances meet him in every department of the universe.

This earth, however, is not an isolated body in the universe; it forms one of a system of worlds, and its geological history cannot be regarded as complete until we have viewed it in some of its more extended relations. The course of creation is traced in the planetary system, a series of masses of matter assuming one form, moving in one plane, following in one orbital path, revolving around a common center, enlightened and warmed by a common sun, and obedient, one and all, to the same great law of gravitation. The mighty problem of the universe has been solved upon the simple assumption, that a piece of our earth is like a piece of the other planets; that the properties of matter here are as the properties of matter above; and as the laws of motion and attraction below, so are they on high, and throughout infinite space. Astronomy thus derives all its achievements as a science from the earth, and the cause of the motions of the heavenly orbs is ascertained from experiments on the matter of the earth, which first led to the knowledge of regular dynamical laws. The field of astronomical research, in consequence, is not only the most wonderful, but it is also that in which our knowledge is the most accurate. Distant and infinitely remote as are the objects of the science, there is yet in no other department of natural philosophy results of investigation so completely satisfactory. With the precision of geometry, and the minute accuracy of numbers, the astronomer calculates the particular place of every one of the bodies of the solar system, at any particular hour and moment of the day. He determines the precise rate of their motions, and positions which they occupied in relation to the earth, in every past period of their history however remote, and even corrects the notations of former observers. He shows their relative distances, weights, dimensions, and influences upon one another; estimates the length of their days and years, eccentricities and perturbations; and describes the orbits in which they severally move, in their steady unwearied march through the heavens.—The undeniable effect of results like these, is to impress deeper upon the inquiring mind the conviction of foresight, method, and design in the vast system of which the earth is but a part; and as the earth gives lead to, and indicates some of the first lessons in, astronomy, so we derive in return a fuller knowledge of its various relations and past history than its own single geological tables can unfold.

When we proceed to speculate about the *manner* of Deity's actings, difficulties at once meet us in every quarter, partly from our utter incapacity to comprehend and partly from the imperfections of human language to express—even were our comprehension adequate to the task—the essential qualities of Deity himself. As the *anima mundi,* the ancients represented the Divine Being, as both the active and self-moving principle in nature, and likewise as passive, and acted upon by the external world. Newton, in order to express his idea of the Divine omnipresence, employed the term *sensorium,* as denoting the mode in which he was enabled to perceive whatever passed in space fully and intimately. And while nothing was farther from the mind of the great philosopher than the ascription of bodily organs to the Divinity, he had to defend himself from much bitter and vehement controversy in consequence. Equally liable to misrepresentation, and from the same cause—the imperfection of language—was the manner in which Newton spoke of the eternity or infinity of the Supreme Being, as if he regarded him as present in all parts of time and space by *diffusion:* whereas his notion simply was, that since He is necessarily and essentially present in all parts of space and duration, space and duration must also necessarily exist. Durat semper, et adest ubique, et existendo semper et ubique, durationem et spatium constituit,—is the tenet which he held.

No less difficult is it to express correctly the inference which we may legitimately deduce of the PERSONALITY of the Godhead from the works and course of creation. And yet the idea is immediately consequent upon the conviction of a Divine existence, and is inseparable from it. The conception of both is necessarily involved in the same process of thought. Wherever we trace the actings of mind or of intelligence, the impress of design or the operations of a discriminating, discerning cause, reference is at one and the same instant made to a distinct personal subsistence. Power, wisdom, and goodness, may, indeed, be regarded in one way as abstract qualities. We can reason about them, and hold them up to our contemplation, as something distinct or different from the bodies in which they reside. Hence all our speculations respecting the laws of nature, the primary and secondary qualities of matter, the relations of cause and effect, to which principle of abstraction in man the various sciences owe their origin. The inductive philosophy is entirely built upon it. The creations of poetry, the peopling of the streams, groves, and mountains, with the ideal impersonations of fancy, are derived from the same source; while, by lifting us above the dominion of mere sense and attention to our physical wants, our spiritual energies are thereby awakened, and the soul enabled by its own inner visions to hold communings with new worlds, and to anticipate a new life.

But the principle of abstraction does not stop here. It both separates and combines. While it deals with the inferior manifestations of ideal qualities, it unites and embodies into one—links the universe to its Creator — represents him as the cause of all causes, the source of all power, and the fountain of all life; out of whose boundless, illimitable essence is the efflux of all being and existence. The ancients erroneously clothed their conceptions of Godhead in human shape, and multiplied the number of divinities to accord to the varieties of human passion, making gods many, as there were principles of good or evil in their own hearts; but still their superstition had a reality and foundation in nature. Their mythology had its origin in a true, though corrupted, theism; and giving form and locality to their numerous divinities, they but obeyed the dictates of that sentiment of the inner man, which, in unison with the voice of all creation, proclaims the existence of a Being whose personal subsistence and personal superintendence we necessarily associate with the laws and management of nature. HE is there among his works, their Director as well as author.

The UNITY of the Divine Being follows, in like manner, from an extended observation of the course of creation. There is but one God, as there is but one system of nature—one universe where the same law which acts upon all terrestrial bodies pervades all space, rules over the planets, and guides systems of worlds in their courses. Our deepest researches into the structure of the earth show, that the same forces have been operative there, as are still traced in passing changes on the surface. Similar organic forms were from the earliest periods in being, endowed with similar instincts, performing the self-same functions in the economy of nature, with their living types of the present day. The air, the sea, the earth; plants, animals, and man, are under one scheme of providence. The seasons are uniformly successive. Year to year we see the same causes in operation. Time rolls on; changes, vast and progressive, have been effected in the moral as well as physical aspect of the world, while bodies remain essentially what they were before, the conditions of sentient existence unaltered, and man occupies the same high intellectual position in the great scale of being. The same government thus maintains over all; the parts shifting and changing, the whole stable and collectively advancing; bound together by one invisible chain, and moving in obedience to one great principle of destiny and superintending will. Hence, upon the presumption that the character of the works determines the character of their author, the intelligent power which presides over all this must necessarily be ONE. Since creation in its elements, arrangements, and means of general harmony, is constructed upon a plan, and since that plan manifests the most perfect order—deviations controlled within limits, and convulsions only contributive to its greater stability—the inference cannot be resisted, that the Creator is essentially one in his being, as he is undivided in his purposes and actings.

When we narrow the field of inquiry, and look to man alone, in his relation to the external world, and the character of his moral constitution, the conclusion becomes still more decided and apparent. Here we see that the last of created beings is not only the highest in the scale, but likewise in the most perfect and extensive unison with the general scheme of nature. He spreads himself over the whole face of creation, is capable of enduring all climes, of deriving sustenance from the products of all countries, conveniences and the means of improvement from the rocks of all ages. If we cannot demonstrate that this earth was made exclusively for man's use, we can still clearly show that he participates more largely in its various products than any of its other inhabitants, while it furnishes, not only to the individual, but to the race, generation after generation, the amplest field of mental and moral cultivation of which their natures are capable. The God of the outward world is also, and pre-eminently, the God of man's inner being. He who created the light, likewise formed the human body. The potter of the clay fashioned and quickened the immaterial spirit. The controller of universal nature reigns supreme in the dominion of the soul. The power that binds the planets in their orbits, gives law to the conscience, constraining it to acknowledge in its perception of truth and homage to virtue the reverence that is due to the One Righteous Governor over all.

Contemplated under this latter and most important aspect of our nature, we are brought, in fact, into immediate communication with the undivided Author of our being. The idea of many is excluded in the conviction that truth and duty are one and unalterable. The gravitating principle in matter is not more universal in its operation, nor more distinct in its constraining influence over all bodies, than is the principle of CONSCIENCE in referring the good and evil of all actions to the standard of rectitude and tribunal of a righteous judge. Tribes, the most remote from each other—the most debased in ignorance—the most polluted in guilt—agree in this common attribute of humanity. Mankind do not, indeed, acknowledge one and the same standard of morality, and in religious observances there is the utmost diversity of opinion and practice. But the sense of duty, the feeling of moral and religious obligation, is universally discriminative of the human family; the sentiment of right and wrong is engraven indelibly on all human hearts. And, amidst all the ignorance or misconceptions that may prevail as to the merit or demerit of particular actions, the moral principle points but to one foundation of truth—the One Supreme—the Lord of conscience as of creation.

The PERFECTIONS of the Supreme Being are, in like manner, as distinctly notified in the works of creation as the fact of the mere existence of a designing Creator. The immensity of the universe clearly demonstrates the *power* in which it originated, and by which all its movements are still sustained, guiding the infinite systems of celestial bodies and the geological revolutions of our own planet with the same ease that it watches over and upholds the minutest objects in existence. There is no exhausting nor wearing out of the energies of nature: the arm that reared, still directs the stupendous fabric; and as skill and contrivance are manifest in every part, the greatest simplicity combined with the most exquisite adjustments, the utmost regularity prevailing in every department, and no failure in the operations of a single law throughout the vastness of creation, the conviction of consummate *wisdom* and of infinite *omniscience* irresistibly strikes upon the mind. No less clear and convincing are the evidences of *goodness* in the system of creation which we have been contemplating. The works, formed by the Divine hand, and which now occupy the Divine care, are boundless in extent, and of infinite variety; and they appear, to the eye of the common observer, as well as to the searching intellect, all formed for use, all rich in beauty, all indicative of beneficence. There is not utility alone interwoven, but an inimitable loveliness painted on the face and stamped on every department of nature; while creatures innumerable, of various orders and of different structures, present themselves to our view, which, by their creation and preservation—by the powers they possess, and the enjoyments they attain—proclaim the liberality of their author to be boundless. Nay, the inanimate parts of nature bear testimony to the same truth; the sun warms and fertilizes the earth; the earth affords nourishment, and furnishes a convenient dwelling-place to the various living creatures that inhabit it; and thus dead matter, in all its arrangements and under all its past changes, by being framed in subserviency to the happiness of living and intelligent beings, clearly evinces the goodness of its Creator. But to Man, in addition, the inspiration of the Almighty has given understanding, and has constituted him supreme in this lower world. Whoever considers his nature and condition, the make of his body and the constitution of his mind, the provision that is furnished for the supply of his animal wants, the objects that are provided for the improvement of his intellectual faculties, and the scope that is afforded for the exercise of his moral affections, must acknowledge that, if the goodness of God be manifestly displayed in the other works of his hands, it shines with peculiar luster in the creation and preservation of man.

Thus, step by step, we rise to the loftiest conception which the human mind can embrace—the conception of a God—the personality, unity, and perfection of his being. How the conception of a Creator is formed, we cannot otherwise describe than by saying, that it springs up in the mind immediately upon the perception of an external world. It is not so much an exercise of reason, or elaborate effort of the understanding; but is rather a direct impression, traced at once upon the soul, as the image of Deity reflected from his works. All men possess it, for all men are so constituted, that they cannot look upon creation without the idea of a Creator accompanying and flowing from the act. The conception will be obscure, vague, and indistinct, according to the capacity, improvement, and general knowledge of the individual. But the conception is there, as necessarily as the effect follows the cause, the shadow the substance, the image the object which occasioned it. The heavens DECLARE the glory of God, the firmament SHOWS his handiwork, the earth bears the traces of his path. And just in the degree in which we study and examine his works—their uses and adaptations—their infinite variety, proportions, regularity, and magnitude — are our convictions of his existence deepened, our admiration of his being and attributes enhanced, our feeling of security under his rule strengthened, and our sense of obligation and responsibility increased and solemnized. Ignorance does not obliterate the sense of Deity; it confuses and multiplies the image of his existence: it leads to polytheism. Knowledge brightens the picture, and represents the Creator, as reflected in his works, EXCELLENT, GLORIOUS, AND INFINITELY PERFECT.

FINIS.

# GLOSSARY OF SCIENTIFIC TERMS.

ACCRETION. Increase of size or growth by the mechanical addition of new particles.

Aclinic Line. The magnetic equator.

Acotyledonous. Plants having no seed-lobes. Mosses and ferns belong to this division, and most of the coal plants are acotyledonous.

Actynolite. A green mineral found chiefly in primitive formations often crystallized in six sided prisms.

Aerolites. Stones which appear to have fallen from the higher parts of the atmosphere. They are sometimes called Meteorites.

Algæ. A division of plants including the common sea-weeds.

Aluminous. Containing alumina, or rather silicate of alumina, which is the base of pure clay. Thus, aluminous means *clayey*. The word is, however, sometimes used in the sense of containing *alum*, a sulphate of alumina and potash.

Ammonite. A fossil genus of many-chambered shells allied to the Nautilus, named from their resemblance to the horns on the statues of Jupiter Ammon.

Amorphous. Without regular form.

Amorphozoa. Animals without definite form—sponges.

Amygdaloid. Almond-shaped. Any rock is called by this name which contains rounded or elongated minerals imbedded in some simple mineral or base.

Amygdaloidal (in mineralogy). A conglomerate.

Analcime is found in granite and gneiss rock—generally in cubes of various colors. m

Ananchytes. A genus of fossil echini or sea-urchins—in the chalk, &c.

Anchylosis. (Gr., crooked), a joint is said to be anchylosed, when so diseased as to become, or when it becomes, stiff or immovable.

Annelidæ. (Annulus, a ring)—Lamarck's worm-shaped animals, as Serpula, vermilia, &c.

Anoplotherium. The name given to a characteristic genus of a group of extinct quadrupeds found fossil in the older Tertiary deposits, and nearly allied to the tapir and pig.

Anticlinal. Or *Anticlinal axis.* A saddle-shaped position of rocks, the result of disturbance.

Apiocrinite. Pear-shaped crinoidea —lily-shaped animals.

Aqueous. That which is dependent on water. Aqueous rocks are those produced by deposit from water.

Arborescent. Branching like a tree.

Arenaceous. Sandy.

Argentiferous. Containing silver.

Argillaceous. Clayey.

Articulata. A natural division of animals having their limbs articulated or jointed together, like the lobster.

Asaphus. An obscure genus of trilobites.

Asbestus. A fibrous mineral of which an incombustible cloth is sometimes made.

Asterolepis. (Gr., star scale). It is the largest fish yet found in the *Old Red Sandstone.*

Augite. (Gr., luster)—a mineral.

Basalt. An igneous rock, often columnar and supposed to be ancient volcanic lava It is the most common of the group called *Trap-rocks.*

Bed or Stratum. A layer of material the whole of which exhibits some common character.

BELEMNITE. A dart-shaped shell, probably the ancient representative of some of our cuttle-fish. The shell is conical and chambered.

BELLEROPHON. A small chambered-shell like the Nautilus.

BOTRYOIDAL (in Mineralogy). Clustered like a bunch of grapes.

BRACHIOPODA. A group of shell-bearing animals having two long spiral arms serving to assist in locomotion and for other purposes.

BREVIPENNATE. Short-winged.

CÆLACANTHUS. A fish of the Devonian formation.

CALAMITE. A fossil from the coal-measures resembling a gigantic reed.

CALAMUS. A fossil reed-like plant.

CALCAIRE GROSSIER. A coarse limestone of the Older Tertiary period, found in the Paris basin.

CALCAIRE SILICEUX. A compact silicious limestone sometimes replacing the calcaire grossier.

CALCAREOUS. Containing lime.

CAMBRIAN. Belonging to Wales. The "Cambrian system" in Geology, is a name suggested by Professor Sedgwick, to designate part of the Silurian series of North Wales.

CARAPACE. The upper shell of reptiles.

CARBONIFEROUS. Containing carbon.

CARNIVOROUS. Flesh-eating. The "Carnivora" in Zoology consist of a group of animals eminently carnivorous.

CAUDAL. Connected with the tail.

CEPHALOPODA. A group of animals of which the Nautilus and Cuttle-fish are examples, having the locomotive apparatus immediately over the head and stomach.

CEPHALASPIS (Buckler-head). A fish.

CESTRACION. A fish, a genus of an extinct family of sharks.

CETACEANS. The whale tribe.

CHALCEDONY. A silicious mineral, like Cornelian.

CHALYBEATE. Water holding iron in solution.

CHARA, CHARACIDÆ. An aquatic plant fossilized.

CHEIROLEPIS (Thorny scale). A fossil fish.

CHELONIA. Sea tortoise.

CHERT. A silicious mineral, resembling common flint, but of coarser texture.

CHŒROPOTAMUS. An extinct quadruped found in the Eocene of England.

CHEIRACANTHUS (thorny hand). A fish of the Old Red Sandstone.

CIRRHIPEDA (hair feet). Balanus—Coronula; Anatifa are of this family.

CLINOMETER. An instrument for measuring the dip and determining the strike of beds or strata.

COAL-MEASURES. The whole group of deposits, consisting chiefly of sands and shales, with which coal is usually found.

COCCOSTEUS. (Gr., berry on bone)—a Ganoid fish.

COLEOPTERA. Beetles whose wings are covered with a hard sheath.

COLUMNAR. Arranged in columns.

CONCHIFERA. One of the great divisions of Conchology.

CONCHOIDAL. Resembling a shell. Used in Mineralogy to designate a particular kind of fracture.

CONDYLE. A knob at the end of a bone, a joint.

CONFORMABLE. When the planes of bedding of two successive beds or strata are parallel to each other they are said to be *conformable;* when not parallel they are *unconformable.*

CONGENERS. Species belonging to the same genus.

CONGLOMERATE or PUDDINGSTONE. A rock made up of rounded water-worn fragments of rock or pebbles cemented together by another mineral substance.

CONIFERÆ. Trees that bear cones, as the pine.

COPROLITE. The fossil remains of excrement.

COSMICAL. Relating to the universe.

COSMOGONY. The word formerly applied to speculations concerning the earth's age and history.

COTYLEDONOUS. Plants whose seeds have but one lobe.

CRAG. The name given to certain Tertiary deposits in Norfolk and Suffolk.

CRETACEOUS. Belonging to the chalk.

CRINOID. Belonging to the encrinite family.

CROPPING OUT. The *out-crop* of a bed is its first appearance at the surface.

CRUSTACEANS. Belonging to the crab or lobster family, &c.

CRYPTOGAMOUS. Plants without apparent flowers.

CRYSTAL. The regular form in which a mineral is presented when that form can be described mathematically. A mineral is said to be *crystalline* when its atoms are arranged with reference to some definite form.

CTENACANTHUS. Belonging to the Placoids.

CTENOIDS. Fishes with comb-shaped scales.

CTENOPTYCHIUS. A fish of the chalk formation.

CULM. An impure kind of coal.

CUMBRIAN. Occurring in Cumberland. The "Cumbrian System" of Prof. Sedgwick is a part of the Silurian series of the Lake district of Cumberland and Westmoreland.

CYCADEÆ. Fossil plants of the coal-measures.

CYCLAS. A small bivalve shell recent and fossil.

CYCLOID. Marginated scales.

DEBRIS. The fragments of rocks removed by the action of weathering or by water.

DECORTICATED. Stripped of bark.

DEFLECTION. Deviation from a straight course.

DEGRADATION. The wearing away of rocks, generally effected by aqueous action.

DELIQUESCENT. Becoming fluid by the attraction of water from the atmosphere.

DELTA. The alluvial land formed by a river at its mouth, usually expanded in a fan shape like the fourth letter of the Greek alphabet ( $\Delta$ ), and thence called *Delta*.

DENUDATION. The act of laying bare rocks formerly covered up, the removal of the overlying masses being effected by water.

DERMAL. Belonging to the skin.

DETRITUS. Matter rubbed off by mechanical action from other rocks.

DIALLAGE. A mineral.

DIDELPHYS. A pouched animal, as the Opossum.

DINOSAURIA. Land lizards — only found fossil.

DIP (in Geology). The angle of inclination which the plane of a bed makes with the plane of the horizon.

DIPLOPTERUS, DIPLODUS, and DIPLOCANTHUS. Fishes of the Devonian or Old red sandstone.

DIPTERUS (having two wings). A fish of the Old red sandstone.

DODO. A large bird once found in the Isle of France, but now extinct.

DOLOMITE. Crystalline carbonate of lime and magnesia.

DYKE. A rock, generally crystalline, occupying a rent or fissure in some other and older rock. A dyke differs from a mineral vein chiefly in its greater magnitude and in the absence of ramifications.

DYNAMICS (Gr., power). Used in mechanics.

ECHINODERMATA. Having a skin like a hedgehog.

EFFLORESCENCE. The term used to describe the falling to powder of certain minerals on exposure.

EMBOUCHURE. The mouth of a great river.

ENALIOSAURIA, PLESIOSAURUS and PLIOSAURUS. Marine Saurians, as the Ichthyosaurus.

ENCRINITE. Stone lily.

ENDOGENOUS. Plants that increase from within, as lilies, grasses, and among trees, palms.

ENTOMOSTRACEA. One of Cuvier's sections of Crustaceans.

EOCENE. The name given by Sir C. Lyell to the lowest and oldest division of the Tertiary series of rocks.

EQUISETUM. A plant, fossil and recent.

ESCARPMENT. The steep face of a mountain chain or a ridge of high land.

EXOGENOUS. Plants which increase their wood by external additions or rings of growth.

EXUVIÆ. A name sometimes given to all fossil remains found in the earth's crust.

FAUNA. The whole group of animals peculiar to a country or natural region at some one period.

FELDSPAR. A hard silicious rock.

FERRUGINOUS. Irony, or containing iron.

FERN. (Lat., Felices), a class of cryptogamous plants.

FISSILE. Capable of being split asunder.

FLUSTRA. A parasitic zoophyte or polyparia, which covers sea-weeds and shells.

FÆCAL SEDIMENT. Dregs, excrement.

FORAMINIFERA. The name given to a group of many-chambered shells, generally microscopic, the chambers communicating by a small open orifice (*foramen*).

FOSSIL. A word originally applied to all substances dug out of the earth, including therefore all minerals, but now limited in its application to the remains of organic beings, whether vegetable or animal, buried beneath the surface.

FOSSILIFEROUS. Containing fossils or organic remains.

FRITH. A deep and comparatively narrow arm of the sea.

FRONDS. The leaf of a fern is called a frond.

FUCOID. That which resembles a *fucus*, or seaweed:—fossil remains of fuci are called fucoids.

FUSIFORM. Spindle-shaped.

GALENA. Sulphuret of lead.

GANOID. A group of fishes having enameled scales.

GASTEROPODA. A group of shell-bearing animals covered by one valve, and having a fleshy foot attached to the belly.

GAULT. A bluish clay underlying the Chalk and Upper green sand in England.

GAVIAL. A species of shark found in the Ganges.

GEODES (in mineralogy) a round hollow stone whose cavity is usually filled with crystals.

GLACIS. A gently sloping bank.

GLYPTOLEPIS. (Gr., carved scale.)

GLYPTOPOMUS. A Devonian fossil fish.

GNEISS. The name given to mixtures of quartz, feldspar, and mica, in which there is a laminated arrangement of the different ingredients.

GONIATITES. Chambered fossil shells.

GRANITE. A rock consisting generally of crystals of feldspar and mica imbedded in a quartzy base.

GRAMINÆ. Grasses.

GRAPTOLITES or SEA-PENS. Fossils of the lower Silurian system.

GRAUWACKE or GRAYWACKE. The name given by German geologists to some of the older fossiliferous rocks, and generally of a gray color, sandy composition, and fissile nature.

GRYPHIÆ. Fossil bivalve shells found in the Lias, &c.

HABITAT. The natural district to which a species of animals or vegetables is confined in its distribution.

HEXAHEDRAL. Having six equal sides.

HETEROCERCAL. Applied to the tail of a fish, means that the upper lobe extends farther than the under.

HETEROPODA. An order of univalve molluscs, whose feet form a kind of fin.

HOLOPTYCHIUS. A Ganoid fish of the coal-measures.

HORNBLENDE. An important mineral in the composition of some rocks.

HOMOCERCAL. Applied to fishes having equal lobed tails.

HORNSTONE. A variety of quartz found in volcanic districts.

HYALINE. Transparent like glass.

HYBODENTES. Fossil fish.

HYLÆOSAURUS. Fossil lizard of the Wealden.

HYPERSTHENE. A mineral.

HYPOGENE ROCKS. Rocks formed beneath others or which are assumed to have obtained their present aspect underneath the earth's surface.

ICHTHYODORULITE. The fossil spine of certain fishes resembling sharks.

ICHTHYOLITES. Fragments of the bones of fossil fishes.

ICHTHYOLOGY. The study and description of fishes.

ICHTHYOSAURUS. A marine reptile (fish-lizard), whose remains are very abundant in rocks of the Secondary period.

IGNEOUS ROCKS. Rocks, such as lava, trap, and some others which have been fused by volcanic heat.—

Granite and other porphyritic rocks are sometimes called crystalline.

IGNIGENOUS. Produced by fire.

IGUANODON. Extinct gigantic lizard.

IMBRICATED. Covered with scales overlapping each other like tiles on the roof of a house.

INOCERAMUS. A bivalve of the chalk formation.

INORGANIC. Not produced by vital action.

INVERTEBRATA. Animals not furnished with a back bone.

JUNCUS (in botany). A rush.

LACERTIANS. Lizards.

LACUSTRINE. Belonging to a lake.

LAGOON. A salt-water lake, or part of a sea nearly inclosed by a strip of land.

LAMINATED. Arranged in thin plates or *laminæ*.

LENTICULAR. Lens-shaped.

LEPIDOIDES. Extinct fish of the Oolite formation.

LLANDEILO FLAGS. A division of the lower silurian formation of Murchison.

LIAS. A provincial name now generally adopted to designate the calcareous clay or clayey limestone occurring between the Upper new red sandstone and the Oolite.

LIGNEOUS. Woody.

LIGNITE. Wood converted into an imperfect kind of coal.

LITHOLOGY (lithos, a stone; logos, a discourse). Description of stones.

LITTORAL. Belonging to the shore.

LOPHIODON. A fossil animal allied to the tapir.

LYCOPODIUM. A cryptogamous plant.

MACAUCO. A four-handed animal allied to the Ape family.

MAMMALIA. Animals that suckle their young.

MARL. A mixture of clay and lime.

MARSUPIAL. An animal having a pouch, as the kangaroo.

MASTODON. A gigantic extinct quadruped resembling the elephant.

MATRIX. The earthy or stony matter in which a mineral or fossil is imbedded.

MECHANICAL ROCKS. Rocks formed by deposition from water.

MEGALOSAURUS. A gigantic extinct lizard.

MEGALICHTHYS. Megas, great; ichthus, fish.

METAMORPHIC ROCKS. Rocks that have undergone change or metamorphosis since their original formation.

METATARSAL. The part of the foot between the ankle and toes.

METEOROLOGY. The science of the phenomena of the atmosphere.

MICA SLATE. Is the lowest stratified rock except gneiss—it is unfossiliferous.

MIOCENE. The middle of the three divisions of tertiary rocks, according to Sir C. Lyell.

MOLASSE. A provincial name for a sandstone associated with marl and conglomerates, found abundantly in the great valley of Switzerland. It belongs to the middle tertiary period.

MOLECULES. The ultimate particles or atoms of bodies.

MOLLUSCA. A division in Conchology.

MONOMYARIA. Bivalve shells having but one adductor muscle.

MORAINE. A Swiss term for the débris of rocks brought down into valleys by glaciers.

MYRICACIÆ. Plants of the Gale family.

MYTILUS. A marine shell, the mussel.

NEUROPTERIS. A fossil fern of the coal-measures.

NODULE. A rounded irregular-shaped mass.

NUCLEUS. The solid center, about which matter is often collected to form solids.

NUMMULITES. A group of foraminiferous shells, some of them of large size and very abundant, occurring in rocks chiefly of the oldest tertiary period.

OOLITE. A limestone composed of rounded particles, like the roe of a fish. The name *Oolitic* is applied to a considerable group of deposits in which this limestone occurs.

ORGANIC. Exhibiting organization, or the results of vital force. *Organic remains*, or *fossils*, are the remains of the animals and vegetables of a former state of existence found buried in rocks.

ORNITHIC. Relating to birds.

ORNITHORHYNCHUS. A singular animal, found in New Holland, called also the water-mole.

ORTHOCERA. A straight-chambered shell of the Silurian formation.

OSSEOUS. Bony: *Osseous breccia* is a conglomerate made up of bones cemented together by lime, and mixed with earthy matter.

OSTEOLEPIS (bone-scale). A fish of the Old red sandstone.

OSTEOLOGICAL. Relating to bones.

OUTCROP. The line at which a stratum first shows itself at the surface in inclined deposits.

OVIPAROUS. Egg-laying animals.

PACHYDERMATA. A group of animals so called from the thickness of their skin. The elephant and pig are well known examples.

PALÆONISCUS. A fossil fish of the Magnesian limestone of England.

PALÆONTOLOGY. The science which treats of fossil organic remains; it is the zoology and botany of the ancient conditions of the earth.

PALÆOTHERIUM. A genus of Pachydermata allied to the Tapir.

PECOPTERIS. A fern of the coal-measures.

PELAGIAN. Belonging to the sea.

PENTACRINITE. A stone lily with five-sided foot-stalk.

PETROLEUM. Mineral pitch.

PHÆNOGAMOUS, or PHANEROGAMIC PLANTS. Those in which the reproductive organs are apparent.

PHRYGANEA. A family of insects which breed in water.

PHYLLOLEPIS. Leaf-scale.

PHYSICAL. Literally *natural*, but used in scientific language in treating of the higher and wider views of various departments with reference to the whole external world, and not to mere human objects.

PHYTOLOGY. The department of Natural History which relates to plants. Botany.

PLACOID. A group of fishes, so called from the structure of their scales.

PLANORBIS. A fresh water univalve. Fossil and recent.

PLATYGNATHUS. (Greek; platus, wide, and gnathos, jaw or mouth.)

PLESIOSAURUS. An extinct genus of reptiles.

PLIOCENE, OLDER AND NEWER. The upper part of the Tertiary series, so called by Sir C. Lyell from the preponderance of recent shells in them.

PLUMBAGO (Black lead). The name commonly given to *graphite*, a form of carbon.

PLUTONIC ROCKS. Rocks supposed to be due to igneous action at great depths below the earth's surface, have been thus named by older geologists. The igneous action is not manifest in such rocks, but presumed, as in the case of granite.

POLYPARIA. A group of animals of which the *coral animal* is a well known example.

PORCELLIA. The papaw, a plant now called asimina.

PORPHYRY. Any rock having crystals imbedded in a base of other mineral composition. Thus granite is a porphyritic rock, having crystals of feldspar and mica imbedded in a quartz base.

PREDACEUS. Preying upon other animals.

PREHNITE. A mineral.

PRIMARY, or PRIMITIVE. This name is commonly applied to the rocks which underlie those that are manifestly of mechanical origin and contain fossils.

PRODUCTUS. A bivalve shell.

PTERICHTHYS. (Winged fish.) A fossil of the Old red sandstone.

PTERODACTYL. A remarkable genus of reptiles adapted for flight; its remains have been found in a fossil state throughout the Secondary rocks.

PTEROPODA. Marine animals having wing-like fins.

PUDDING STONE. The name often given to coarse conglomerates in which the fragments or pebbles are rounded.

PYRITES. A name given to the combinations of certain metals with sulphur.

QUA-QUA-VERSAL. The dip of beds in every direction from an elevated central point. The beds on the flanks of a volcanic cone dip in this way.

QUARTZ. The common form of silica; rock-crystal and flint are examples.

RACEME (in botany). When the florets are arranged along the sides of a general peduncle.

RADIATA. A division of the animal kingdom so called because the body is frequently presented in a radiated form like the common star-fish.

RETICULATED. A structure of crossed fibers, like a net, is said to be reticulated.

ROCK (in Geology). Any mass of mineral matter of considerable or indefinite extent and nearly uniform character, is called in geological language a rock, without regard to its hardness or compactness: thus, loose sand and clay, as well as sandstone and limestone, are spoken of under this name.

ROCK SALT. Common salt occurring in a crystalline state in rocks.

ROE-STONE. The name sometimes given to *Oolite.*

RUMINANTIA. An important group of quadrupeds including those which chew the cud, as the ox, deer, &c.

SACCHAROID. Having the texture of loaf sugar.

SALIFEROUS SYSTEM. The new red sandstone system, so called from the salt with which it is associated in parts of England.

SAURIAN (reptilian). Any animal of the lizard tribe, and many extinct reptiles only distantly allied to these.

SAUROIDS. Marine fishes resembling lizards.

SALMONOIDES. Resembling the salmon.

SCHIST. A name often used as synonymous with slate, but more commonly, and very conveniently, limited to those rocks which do not admit of indefinite splitting, like slate, but are only capable of a less perfect separation into layers or laminæ. Of this kind are gneiss, mica-schist, &c., often more or less crystalline.

SCIRPUS (in Botany). A rush.

SCORIÆ. The name given to volcanic ashes. The word means any kind of cinders, but its scientific use is thus limited.

SHALE. An indurated clay, less fissile than schist, but splitting with tolerable facility in plates parallel to each other, and to the original planes of bedding.

SHELL MARL. A deposit of clay, peat, and silt, mixed with shells, which collects at the bottom of fresh-water lakes.

SERPULA (in Conchology). A worm-like marine shell.

SERRATED. Having points like a saw.

SIGILLARIA. Fossil plants found in the coal-measures.

SILEX, SILICA. The name given by Mineralogists to a pure earth, more commonly spoken of as *flint,* and, when crystallized, called rock-crystal.

SILT. The name usually given to the muddy deposit found at the bottom of running streams.

SILURIAN. The name given by Sir R. Murchison to an important series of fossiliferous rocks well developed in, and first described from, a district in Wales and Shropshire formerly inhabited by the *Siluri,* a tribe of Ancient Britons.

SIPHUNCLE. A small tube passing through an orifice in the septum of a chambered shell.

SPHENOPTERIS. Fossil fern (leaf wedge-shaped).

SPHEROID. Having a shape nearly resembling that of a sphere or globe.

SPIRIFER. An extinct bivalve.

STALACTITE and STALAGMITE. Concretions of carbonate of lime and sometimes of other minerals, as quartz or even malachite, deposited by water dropping from the roof of a cavern or other vacant space.

STEATITE. Soapstone.

STIGMARIA. A coal fossil, an aquatic plant.

STRATIFICATION. The condition of rocks or accumulated minerals deposited in layers, beds, or *strata.*

STRIKE. The line of bearing of strata, or the direction of any horizontal line on a stratum.

SUPERPOSITION. An expression very commonly employed by Geologists to describe the order of arrangement when one bed or stratum reposes upon another.

SUPRA-CRETACEOUS. A term applied by Sir H. de la Bêche to rocks overlying the chalk. The term Tertiary is now universally adopted for this group.

SYENITE. The granite of the quarries of Syene in Egypt. It is usual to call by this name any combination of quartz, felsdpar, and hornblende.

SYNCLINAL AXIS. The line of depression between two anticlinal axes.

SYNCONDROSIS. Connection of bones by cartilage.

TEREBRATULA. A fossil shell.

TERTIARY STRATA. The series of sedimentary rocks overlying the chalk, or other representative of the Secondary period, and extending thence to the rocks of the Recent period.

TESTACEA. Molluscous or soft animals having a shelly covering.

THECODONT. A fossil saurian or marine lizard.

THERMAL. Hot. *Thermal Springs* are springs whose temperature is above the mean annual temperature of the place where they break out.

TETRAPTEROUS. Four-winged.

TIBIA. The principal bone of the leg.

TOAD-STONE. The name given by miners to beds of basalt, occurring in Derbyshire.

TRACHYTE. A feldspathic variety of lava.

TRAP. Crystalline rocks, composed chiefly of feldspar, augite and hornblende, combined in many ways, and exhibiting great varieties of aspect, are frequently called by this name.

TRIAS. The name given on the continent to the beds of the New red sandstone series.

TRILOBITE. A common fossil in the Dudley limestone, so named from the characteristic species having the body divided into three lobes. Trilobites are the remains of a remarkable extinct family of Crustaceans, of which the crab, lobster, &c., are modern representatives.

TRIONYX. A genus of tortoise, having three claws.

TUFACEOUS, TUFF. An Italian name for a variety of volcanic rock of earthy texture, and made up chiefly or entirely of fragments of volcanic ashes.

TURBINATED. Shells which have a spiral or screw-like structure are thus named.

UNCONFORMABLE SUPERPOSITION (in stratification). The condition of strata when one has been deposited horizontally upon the upturned edges of those immediately below.

UNIO. Fresh water bivalve.

VERTEBRATA, or Vertebrated Animals. A large and most important division of the animal kingdom, including all those animals provided with a back bone. Each separate bone of the back is called a *vertebra*.

VERTEX. The summit or upper part of a solid.

VITREOUS. Glassy. Used in Mineralogy to designate a peculiar luster.

VIVIPAROUS. Bearing young alive.

WARP. The deposit of muddy waters.

WEALDEN. The name given to an important fresh-water formation, occurring between the Cretaceous and Oolitic rocks, chiefly in the Wealds of Kent and Sussex.

WHIN-STONE. A provincial term ap plied to some trap rocks.

ZAMIA. A plant allied to the palm, plentiful east of the Cape of Good Hope.

ZEOLITE. A group of minerals which swell and boil up when exposed to the blow-pipe flame.

ZOOPHYTE. The term applied to some animals of low organization, which, during the greater part of their lives, are attached to some foreign substance, and are incapable of locomotion.

www.ingramcontent.com/pod-product-compliance
Lightning Source LLC
LaVergne TN
LVHW020124110826
845151LV00001B/264

* 9 7 8 1 4 2 5 5 4 1 2 3 1 *